Created and Directed by Hans Höfer

INSIGHT GUIDES
BALTIC STATES

Edited by Roger Williams

Photography by Lyle Lawson

Editorial Director: Brian Bell

HOUGHTON MIFFLIN COMPANY

APA PUBLICATIONS

BALTIC STATES

First Edition
© **1993 APA PUBLICATIONS (HK) LTD**
All Rights Reserved
Printed in Singapore by Höfer Press Pte. Ltd

Distributed in the United States by:
Houghton Mifflin Company
2 Park Street
Boston, Massachusetts 02108
ISBN: 0-395-65985-X

Distributed in Canada by:
Thomas Allen & Son
390 Steelcase Road East
Markham, Ontario L3R 1G2
ISBN: 0-395-65985-X

Distributed in the UK & Ireland by:
GeoCenter International UK Ltd
The Viables Center, Harrow Way
Basingstoke, Hampshire RG22 4BJ
ISBN: 9-62421-182-5

Worldwide distribution enquiries:
Höfer Communications Pte Ltd
38 Joo Koon Road
Singapore 2262
ISBN: 9-62421-182-5

ABOUT THIS BOOK

For most of the 20th century Estonia, Latvia and Lithuania have been faceless places in grey history books. So when light fell upon them as the former Soviet Union began to break up, one of the immediate questions was: what do these countries actually look like?

It was a search for the answer to this question that took this book's editor, **Roger Williams**, on an extended visit to the three Baltic states for London's *Sunday Times*. Williams, an experienced journalist who has edited Insight Guides to Great Britain and Catalonia, was pleased to have the opportunity to immerse himself further by editing the first comprehensive guide to the region. "They are fascinating countries, each one quite different, and it is an extraordinary time for anyone to visit them," he says. "Also, they lend themselves exceptionally well to Insight Guides' photojournalistic approach."

Summer tour

Viewing the countries with a professional photographer's eye was **Lyle Lawson**, a veteran of many Insight Guides, who spent a whole summer exploring the region and then returned to capture the first snows of winter.

"Many of my preconceived notions were shattered," she says. "On the one hand, there were open arms, wide smiles and hospitality so warm that it proved embarrassing because I knew how little everyone had. On the other hand, some people regarded me as an agent of the former Sovier rulers and turned away when I approached. I also fell victim to the ever-growing crime wave: the house where I was staying in Riga was robbed and my unexposed film was taken, as well as two jars of very precious instant coffee."

Williams began assembling his writing team by drafting two UK-based experts. The historian **Rowlinson Carter**, fresh from an epic journey through Eastern Europe for Insight Guides, provided the background perspective. **Lesley Chamberlain**, a former Reuters Moscow correspondent and author of two milestone books, *The Food of Russia* and *The Food of Eastern Europe*, flew out to sample the countries' food and culture. Her daughter, Elizabeth, came too and her autobiographical *In the Communist Mirror* recounts their previous adventures together.

An Insight regular, **Anne Roston**, who edited the guides to France and Provence, was rediscovered in Helsinki where she had been writing for the London *Times* and the *New York Times,* among other publications. "It was one of the few corners of the world that kept a steady eye on Estonia," she says. "Estonia is much less Nordic than its cousin across the Baltic, but many people understood my pidgin Finnish."

Four contributors were recruited in Tallinn. **Mihkel Tarm** is an American Estonian who runs the monthly *Tallinn City Paper* and works for Associated Press. He arrived after independence, and met and married his Estonian wife, Eve. "I had grown up knowing about Estonia," he says. "It was like coming back to Never Never land." His expertise has been tapped for a look at the future of the countries' economies. The managing editor, who oversees the paper's listings, turned out to be **Andrew Humphreys**, who had contributed to the Insight Guide to Cairo. He volunteered to provide the exhaustive Travel Tips for Estonia.

Lisa Trei is an American-Estonian jour-

Williams

Lawson

Carter

Chamberlain

Roston

nalist who began working on a book about the Baltics after independence. Her special concern has been pollution and her contribution is a chapter on The Environment.

Estonia also produces one of the most successful English language papers in the Baltics, the *Baltic Independent*. Its managing editor is **Edward Lucas**, a former Eastern Europe correspondent of London's *Independent* newspaper. Although he works in Tallinn, he commutes every week from his home in Vilnius. Having lived and worked the length and breadth of the three states, he welcomed the opportunity to analyse the Baltic character and write about Life Today.

Contributors in Latvia included the Canadian-Latvian **Kārlis Freibergs**, editor-in-chief of the other successful and respected English-language weekly, the *Baltic Observer*. He provided invaluable Travel Tips, with the help of colleagues **Alda Staprāns, Marika Bērziņa,** and **Marita Ozoliņa**.

Also in Riga is **Juris Lorencs** of the World Federation of Free Latvians and an expert on religious affairs, who writes on The Church and Religion. Not far away was **Valdis Muktupāvels** who is recognised as Latvia's leading authority on traditional musical instruments, which he plays and makes. His piece on The Singing Tree is added to the weight of information about folklore provided by **Anatol Lieven**. From 1990 Lieven worked as Baltics States correspondent for London's *Times*. On his father's side, he is descended from a Baltic German noble family in what is now Latvia, and his book, *The Baltic Experience*, is published by Yale University Press. For this guide, he also writes about Ethnic Diversity.

In Lithuania, we found two outstanding experts. **Matthias Lüfkens**, a correspondent for France's *Libération* and Britain's *Daily Telegraph,* also edits the city's bright and invaluable listings magazine, *Vilnius in Your Pocket*, which puts him in the ideal position to write on the capital and the country's second city, Kaunas. He provides the Travel Tips to both Lithuania and Kalìningrad, Russia's enclave that visitors from Europe may need to pass through en route to Lithuania.

For the rest of the country, we turned to **Professor Česlovlas Kudaba**, a lecturer in geography at Vilnius University who was also a deputy of the Supreme Council of Lithuania from 1990 to 1992. Another contributor from Vilnius is **Mykolas Mikalajūnas**, former director of the state encyclopedia publishers. He writes about one of the country's heroes, the athlete and transatlantic flyer Steponas Darius.

Local support

Mikalajūnas, his wife Jurate and their family provided Lyle Lawson with invaluable help in Lithuania, as did Leons and Ludmilla Alksnis and their daughter Christina in Riga. Maila Saar, Vivien Rennel and Silvi Blaumovitz at the Estonian Association of Travel Agents and Eriks Saks and Gundega Zeltinja of the Latvian Association of Travel Agents also went out of their way to help. Susan Maingay and the British Council in Riga were very supportive, and in London Terēza Svilāns and Imants Lieģis at the Latvian Embassy were good to have around.

The book was produced in Insight Guides' London editorial office, where **Jill Anderson** persuaded an Apple Macintosh to produce a bewildering variety of Baltics accents. The proof-reader was **Carole Mansur**.

Lucas

Lieven

Lüfkens

Kudaba

People & History

Features

Places

Maps

TRAVEL TIPS

**For detailed information
see page 369**

PEOPLE OF THE BALTICS

The people of the three Baltic nations are as different from each other as the Norwegians are from the Poles, or the Irish from the Dutch, but they share one characteristic: a quite remarkable tendency for self-absorption, accompanied by a constant need to discuss their plight. This is partly a consequence of being small countries but, more importantly, it is the result of a systematic, and partially successful, attempt by their eastern neighbour to exterminate them.

Repression did not have to have been much harsher for Estonians, Latvians and Lithuanians to have met the fate of the Ingrians, Kalmuks, Tuvans and other small nations who got in Stalin's way. As it is, the debasement of the language and national culture through Russification and sovietisation has been as pervasive and damaging in its way as the destruction of the natural and physical environments.

Soviet hangover: The people in all three countries suffer to some degree from a debilitating inferiority complex and self-pity – which they need to lose if they are to progress. This is the understandable legacy from the Soviets to all parts of its former empire and, in the struggle for survival in this new era of independence, it still may take many years for the true national characteristics to begin to shine through again.

Most noticeably the Soviet years have robbed them of their smiles, and they cannot understand why foreigners go around beaming. Queen Margrethe of Denmark was well advised when she made her first royal visit to the area bringing with her an exhibition of cartoons and caricatures of herself from the Danish press, which went on show in Vilnius. The message was clear: democracy means learning how to laugh at yourselves. (At the time there were fist-fights going on in the Lithuanian parliament.)

Of the three Baltic nations, it is the Lithuanians who are the most complex. A memory

Preceding pages: Latvian girl; behind the scenes at a parade in Rēzekne; mother and daughter, Lithuania; harvesting the rye; Vytautas Ciplijauskas, Lithuanian painter of the famous; children in the Old Town, Riga. <u>Left</u>, the Latvian look.

of the Grand Duchy which stretched from the Baltic to the Black Sea still has a profound influence. Sometimes the result is attractive: national self-confidence gives Lithuanians a zeal to succeed and regain their rightful place among what they consider to be Europe's "real" countries. In particular the desire not to be outstripped economically by Poland, their historical partner and sometime coloniser, is widespread and deep.

Its own imperial past can construct a ridiculous *folie de grandeur*. When a senior Lithuanian politician was told that the US president would be unable to meet him during a forthcoming visit to America and that he would have to make do with the vice-

important cultural and intellectual influence. Indeed, few Lithuanians could name the current prime ministers of major neighbours such as Poland, Sweden or Belorus. The idea, therefore, that economic or political self-interest should lead to a close engagement with countries such as these is regarded with amused indifference in the case of the first two, or, in the case of Poland, with suspicion and defensiveness.

Lithuanians tend to regard themselves as the natural leaders of the Baltic, and are happy to talk about (although seldom follow up) schemes for pan-Baltic co-operation. In spite of being interwoven with their northern neighbours through a similar language and

president instead, he had his staff inform the startled American embassy that he would settle for no one less than the Secretary of State. From any other country of just 3.8 million people, in desperate need of all kinds of diplomatic and economic support, such an insouciant attitude as this would have been simply unthinkable.

Most Lithuanians, however, would have regarded it as entirely natural that their own country should stand toe to toe with the most powerful nation in the world on a matter of dignity. Marquette Park, a suburb of Chicago, has the largest external Lithuanian community and America remains the most

history, outside of a handful of cultural contacts, Lithuanians treat their closest neighbours rather as Americans treat Canadians: benignly and with sweeping ignorance. (Canada has, in fact, been a major centre for exiled Latvians.) Contacts with next-door-but-one Estonia, despite the geographical and linguistic differences, seem warmer. "Neighbours never get on," say Lithuanians when asked about this.

Solid stock: Latvians are certainly not unfriendly but they may be the last to put themselves forward. Perhaps it is because they have been imbued with the German Protestant work ethic. They are reliable types, hard workers unruffled by flair. Of all the three countries they have been the least able to think up schemes for the West's start-up financial packages. "Have 10 jobs," they say, "but have 11 and you will be out of work." By which they mean work should not be dissipated. It is better to get on with the single task in front of you than to get greedy and take on too much.

Their forte is in administration, in clerical work, but really they don't much like town life at all, and are happiest living a more solitary life among their brown cows and sacred oaks. That is not to say they are without creativity: their poets and artists stand alongside those of their neighbours,

cities, which they never much wanted to work in anyway.

Not to be forgotten among the Latvians are the Livs, a handful of descendants of the original coastal tribe who speak a Finno-Ugric language like the Estonians. Latvians have a special respect for this almost extinct race and its mystical link with the past.

Language is a political tool as well as a social one and it has shaped the Estonians, who have a tendency to attribute national superiority to the Finno-Ugric bloodline. Sometimes they accuse foreigners of showing signs of "Indo-European" attitudes. These are, apparently, tribal-mindedness and a predisposition to quarrel, start wars and gener-

and Riga's contribution to art nouveau is among the greatest in all Europe.

Latvians tend to be honest, open and warm, and it is these characteristics which some say have been their downfall. All too often, their good nature has been taken advantage of: theirs was the most Russified of the three states, and they were the last to declare independence. And when it finally arrived, they found themselves in a debilitating minority, overwhelmed by Russians in Riga and Daugavpils and their three other major

Left, Estonian father and daughter. **Above**, floral tribute, Lithuania; Estonian island fisherman.

ally misbehave. Finno-Ugric peoples, on the other hand, are naturally solitary and therefore peaceable.

How the Finno-Ugric Attila the Hun fitted into this world view is not divulged. Equally incongruously, the next-door Finno-Ugric neighbours, the Finns, are regarded rather disparagingly, being nicknamed "moose". Of course, for many Estonians contact with Finns was limited for several decades to the boatloads of them who tipped up in Tallinn for the weekend intent on drinking themselves half to death (a pastime which is not unfamiliar to residents in all three states).

Estonians have had many years to brood

on the misfortune which has soured their history. Just as Lithuanians like to tell you that their country is the geographical centre of Europe, that their language is archaic and their folk art extraordinary, and just as Latvians will point out that in the pre-war years of their first independence they were one of Europe's great dairy exporters, so do Estonians relish any chance to explain that they were, before the war, more prosperous than Finland.

Estonia has its face set squarely towards Helsinki and Stockholm. Most young, economically active Estonians have visited one or both of these cities. Unlike Lithuanians or Latvians, whose emigrations are dispersed

in other hemispheres, one of the most active Estonian diasporas lies just across the Baltic Sea, in Sweden. Estonians are only too aware of the importance of their Scandinavian neighbours: indeed, many Estonians would be glad to shed their "Baltic" tag altogether. With their backs set firmly against Moscow, marriages between Russians and Estonians, unlike Latvians or Lithuanians, are extremely rare. When the Moscow correspondent of the London *Times* mentioned to a Russian in 1980 how much he liked Estonia, he was told: "Ah, now I can see you are anti-Soviet."

But it is not a rational attitude to geopolitics which distinguishes the Estonian national character, but rather its astonishing degree of reserve. Staying for more than a few days in Vilnius, a foreigner will find it impossible to avoid being invited into a Lithuanian household, stuffed with food, offered presents, taken on guided tours, introduced to family, friends and pets, and generally made to feel at home. In Latvia the visitor will find hospitality, too, though the atmosphere will be more relaxed and not quite so intense. Invited to a house, you will not escape without sampling some home produce, some of which may be pressed on you to take away.

Friends for life: In Estonia, on the other hand, a foreigner waiting for such an invitation risks dying of old age before it is proffered. Friendship, an Estonian may tell you, is for life and it would not be right for a new acquaintance to be invited into their home when they know that sooner or later he or she will go away. Though the idea that real friendship is like a precious cordial which should only be offered to one's nearest and dearest can be offensive and off-putting to foreigners, it must be said that Estonians are not truly selfish or unfriendly. Once the friendship is actually made, it is as solid and lasting as a steel rod.

The standard Estonian excuse for this behaviour is that most people's apartments are so cramped and run-down that they would feel ashamed to invite a foreign guest home. (This may be offered as a genuine excuse elsewhere.) More importantly, a natural tendency to reserve has been heightened – or distorted – by the imposition of an alien occupation. "Ugh! Just like a Russian," may be the response to an attempted hug. Displays of affection, eating garlic and wearing hats when it isn't winter are all regarded by Estonians with utmost disdain because, like hugging, they associate these things only with their least favourite neighbours.

Most Balts are nature-lovers but whereas young Lithuanians tend to go to the countryside in groups, make camp-fires, turn on music and have a party, and Latvian families will get together at home or head for a lake for a swim, Estonians crave peace, quiet and solitude. Their idea of a really good time is to go for a solitary walk.

Left, Riga teenager. **Right**, with the grandchildren on the allotment, just outside Vilnius.

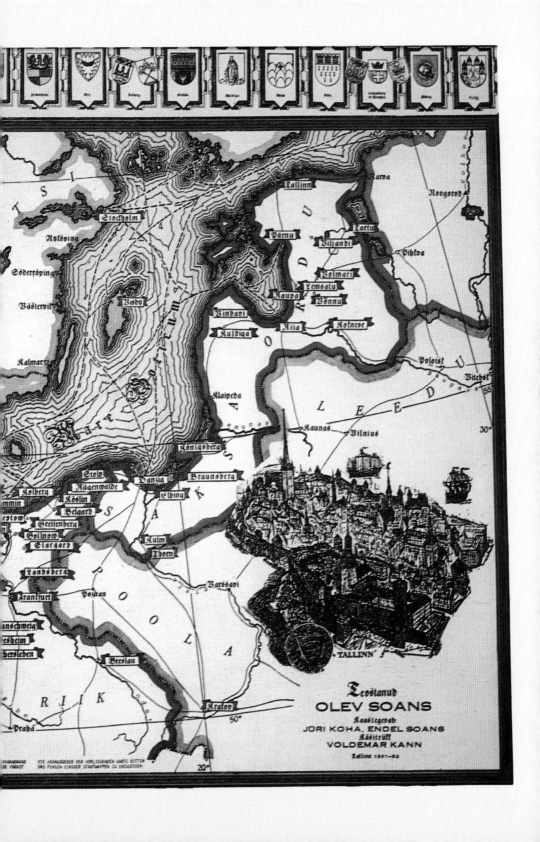

Eestimaa
OLEV SOANS
Koostegevad
JÜRI KOHA, ENDEL SOANS
Käsitrükk
VOLDEMAR KANN
Tallinn 1991–92

6000 BC: Finno-Ugric peoples from southeast Europe reach Estonia.

2500 BC: Indo-European culture arrives and merges with indigenous population in Latvia and Lithuania. Baltic tribes established: Kurs, Semigallians, Letgallians, Sels and Finno-Ugric Livs.

1000–1200 AD: Estonian tribes beat off Russian (Slav) attacks.

9th–10th centuries: Vikings on the coast utilise trade routes to Byzantium and the Caspian Sea via the River Daugava.

1009: The name Lithuania is written for the first time.

1201: German crusaders establish a bishopric in the Liv settlement at Riga under Albrecht of Bremen. It becomes the basis for the Baltic conquest.

1207: Livonia (Terra Mariana) recognised as part of the Holy Roman Empire, with Riga as its capital.

1219: Danes take Tallinn.

1230: Mindaugas unites Grand Duchy of Lithuania. For convenience he adopts Christianity and is crowned King of Lithuania (1252).

1236: Brief victory for Latvian and Lithuanian forces when they defeat crusaders at Saulė.

1237: German crusaders' Order of the Knights of the Sword becomes Livonian Order.

1280: Semigallian tribes fail in their attack on Riga and retreat to Lithuania.

1282: Riga joins Hanseatic League; Tallinn joins three years later.

1316: Under Duke Gediminas, founder of Vilnius and the Jogaila dynasty, the struggle against Teutonic Knights continues and Lithuanian expansion begins.

1343: Estonian rebellion on St George's night fails to bring lasting independence, but leads to Danes selling duchy of Estonia to the Teutonic Order.

1386: Lithuania and Poland united in marriage between Duke Jogaila and Queen Jadvyga. The countries remain united until 1795.

1410: Duke Vytautas and Jogaila defeat the Teutonic Order in the Battle of Tannenberg (Grünwald).

1520s: The Reformation establishes Lutheranism in Latvia and Estonia.

1558–83: Livonian Wars between Sweden and Russia result in Livonia being divided up (1562). Northern Estonia comes under Swedish rule; southern Estonia under Polish rule. Duchies under Polish suzerainty established in Kurzeme (Courland) and Pārdaugava in Latvia. German bishop of Piltene (Latvia) and Oesel (Saaremaa Island) sells land to Denmark.

1579: Vilnius University founded by the Jesuits.

1581–1621: Riga swears loyalty to Stephan Bathory, king of Poland and Lithuania, who introduces Counter-Reformation.

1600–29: Polish-Swedish War leaves Estonia and northern Latvia in Swedish hands; southern Latvia and Lithuania in Poland's.

1632: Tartu University founded.

1642–82: Flowering of Courland under Duke Jēkabs.

1694: St Peter's steeple, Riga, the tallest in the world, completed.

1700–21: Great Northern War between Charles XII of Sweden and Peter the Great results in Russian victory. Russia occupies Estonia and Latvia. It also produces the first poem to be written in Estonian, by Kasu Hans, about the destruction of Tartu by the Russians (1708).

1712: Martha Skavronska, a peasant from Latvia, marries Peter the Great and 12 years later is crowned Catherine, Empress of Russia.

1768: Rundāle Palace, Latvia, is completed.

1795: Lithuania becomes part of the Russian empire. Lithuania Minor (now Kalliningrad) falls to Germany.

1812: Napoleon marches through, on his way to Moscow, raising hopes of freedom from Russia.

1832: Vilnius University closed down by Russians following attempts to restore independence.

1860–85: The era of National Awakening. The abolition of serfdom combines with new educational opportunities and leads to a great literary and artistic movement.

1864: A 40-year ban on the printing of books in Lithuanian begins.

1869: First national singing festival held in Estonia.

1872: First strike organised by women workers in Narva.

1885: An era of intense Russification begins, following unsuccessful uprisings against Russia; local languages displaced.

1905: First socialist revolution demands independence. Manors burned, hundreds executed.

1914–18: War waged on three fronts: between Germans and white and red Russians.

Duchy. Poland, also newly independent, seizes Vilnius.

1923: Lithuania reclaims Klaipėda.

1934: Bloodless coup in Estonia. Parliament dismissed in Latvia.

1939: Hitler-Stalin Pact puts Estonia and Latvia under Soviet sphere of influence and Soviet soldiers arrive. Baltic Germans ordered back to Germany.

1940–41: Red Army terror. Thousands deported or shot.

1941–44: German occupation of Baltics.

Bolsheviks seize power in bloodless coup in Estonia, but unable to maintain control. Germany occupies Latvia, Lithuania.

1918: Republic of Estonia declared in Tallinn, Latvia in Riga. German army moves in and manors and power given back to German aristocracy. Germany loses war and Soviets move in. With some allied help, Soviets are fought back.

1920: Independence finally achieved, for the first time in Estonia and Latvia, and for Lithuania the first time since the Grand

Preceding pages: the Baltic and the Hansa ports. Above, crusader and bishop, Dundaga Castle.

Concentration camps set up. Extermination of Jews, especially in Vilnius. Russians and Germans fight over Baltic soil.

1944: Soviets reoccupy Baltics and turn them into Soviet republics. Stalinist era begins. Mass reprisals, deportation to Siberia.

1952: Armed resistance to Soviet occupation finally crushed.

1988: Opposition parties established.

1989: A 430-mile (688-km) human chain, from Tallinn to Vilnius, links up in protest.

1991: Soviet intervention results in 14 killed at TV tower, Vilnius; five outside the Ministry of the Interior, Riga. Republics finally restored to independence.

One of the most perplexing problems facing the Paris peace conference in 1919 was what to do about the Baltic provinces of tsarist Russia which the Bolsheviks, not without a fight, had consented to let go. Lithuania had once ruled the largest empire in Europe. It was somewhat overwhelmed by Poland before both were swallowed, almost but not quite whole, by Russia in the 18th century. Estonia and what was put forward to the peace conference as an independent state which called itself Latvia were, by any his-

ion with ties so close that they were virtually Russian provinces once again.

Ukraine and Belorus apart, nowhere did the Soviet mill grind finer than in Estonia, Latvia and Lithuania. They occupied a special place in Soviet strategy, an updated version of Peter the Great's "window to the West", which began with the founding of St Petersburg but envisaged expansion southward to maximise Russia's access to the Baltic, often referred to as the "Northern Mediterranean". Like its southern counter-

torical or political criteria, equally elusive.

Nevertheless, three independent states were internationally recognised under these names and lived a precarious existence while first the Bolsheviks and then Stalin made it plain that it was not a situation that could be countenanced forever. Their independence was sentenced to death by the Nazi-Soviet Pact just before World War II. The pact envisaged the Baltic states would be parcelled out between them, but of course it became academic with Hitler's invasion of Russia. The Red Army came back in force towards the end of the war, and the three states were incorporated into the Soviet Un-

part, it had a coastline over which the adjacent nations were ready to fight for every inch. Russia had initially been held to ransom by German Balts who controlled the Estonian and Latvian ports, and Peter the Great was determined that it would never happen again, a view with which the Soviet regime totally concurred. Lithuania was regarded in exactly the same light, and it was agents of the tsar, long before any thought of Soviet Man, who vowed to obliterate all signs of national Baltic identities.

The Russification of the Baltic provinces in the 19th century was so thorough that when the matter of their independence came up at the Paris peace conference one of the questions asked was sublimely naive: "Who are these people and whence did they come?" For three nations buried so deep in the history of others that their identities were long presumed to have been lost, they have surprisingly robust tales to tell.

They also have common bonds. With their backs to the Baltics, they have been hemmed in by the great powers of Sweden, Denmark, Germany and Russia who have not left them alone for 800 years. In fact, the peoples of the

nian, which has similarities with Hungarian, those words are *jumal*, *poeg* and *päev*. But it was a long time before the languages, with their extended alphabets and complicated word endings, were written down.

Baltic peoples also took longer than the rest of Europe to embrace Christianity, preferring their sacred oaks and thunderous gods. Some of the earliest Christian teaching came from Orthodox traders from the east. The trade routes were well established, up the River Daugava and down the Dnieper to

three countries come from two distinct groups, neither of them Slavic like the Russians or Teutonic like the Germans. In the north were the Finno-Ugric tribes of Estonia and the Livs of Latvia, of whom only a handful remain. Latvia was otherwise peopled by Letts who, like Lithuanians, were Indo-European Balts whose language has some similarities with Sanskrit. For instance, the words for "god", "day" and "son" in Lithuanian are *dievas*, *diena* and *sunus* and *devas*, *dina* and *sunu* in Sanskrit. In Esto-

Left, German crusader. **Above**, Catherine, the Baltic peasant empress, and Peter the Great.

the Black Sea. Amber was the singular commodity the Balts possessed, and others wanted it. This gem, made of fossilised pine resin, made its way to ancient Egypt and Greece.

First conquerors: Among those taking this trade route were the Vikings, and it was their leader, Vladimir I, who first united the Slavic Russians and made a capital on the Dnieper at Kiev. When the Scandinavians settled down on the Baltic coast, they did so in Estonia: *Taani Linn* (Tallinn) is Estonian for Danish town. By then the real conquering force of the Baltics was beginning to dig in. The German crusaders appeared in 1201 in Riga where they installed a bishopric for

Albrecht of Bremen. From there, they set down roots of a ruling class in all three countries that lasted into the 20th century.

This elite arrived in religious orders, which fought among themselves as much as they fought against those who opposed them. There were the ministerials of the archbishop, the burghers of the city and the Knights of the Sword who became Knights of the Livonian Order. The country of Livonia which they created put the different peoples of Latvia and Estonia under the same authority and established a healthy and lucrative environment for the merchants of the Hanseatic League, the German trading confederation which followed in their wake. Their archi-

1325 the Lithuanian ruler Gediminas allied himself to the Poles who had similar problems with the Teutonic Knights, added to which they wanted access to the sea, and at its height the Duchy was one of Europe's largest countries, stretching from the Baltic to the Black Sea. Gediminas's grandson married the Polish queen and the houses were united for the next 400 years.

Jesuit builders: Poland brought a strong Catholic influence and the Jesuits arrived to build their schools and fancy baroque churches, while the Reformation whipped through the Germanic northern Baltic lands in a trice, converting everyone overnight. In the brief period when half of Latvia became

tecture, of half-timbered *Fachwerk*, and store-houses with gables stepped as high as those beside Amsterdam's canals, spread from Klaipėda and Kaunas to Riga to Tallinn.

Lithuania, however, was not so easily brought to heel, and it frequently joined forces with the Kuronian and Semigallian Letts in clashes with the German knights. By the middle of the 13th century the Lithuanian tribes had been unified under Mindaugas who briefly adopted Christianity so the Pope, in 1252, could crown him king. When the German knights still gave him trouble, he reverted to his pagan beliefs, rolled up his sleeves and got stuck into them again. In

a Polish principality, everyone was Catholic again. The Balts had little say in this matter as in everything else. Compulsory church attendance made them indifferent as to how the service was conducted.

Every privilege was denied the local inhabitants. For centuries they could not build houses of stone, nor live within the city walls. Membership of the greater guilds was forbidden to them; even semi-skilled workers, such as millers and weavers, were brought in from abroad. The ruling society was impenetrable. In Estonia and Latvia the German descendants of the knights ruled; in Lithuania there was a rigid aristocracy of

Poles. It meant little that the state of Livonia was broken up by the Swedes in the mid-16th century when the ruling German Balts called upon them for help in pushing back the Russian empire which was rapidly expanding under Ivan the Terrible.

In spite of the violence wrought in its wars, first against Poland, then against Russia, the Swedish period is sometimes looked on as an enlightened one. But there was more talk than action. In Tallinn in 1601 Charles IX demanded peasant children be sent to school and learn a trade. "We further want them to be allowed, without hindrance, to have themselves put to use as they like, because to keep children as slaves is not done in Christendom

sold or exchanged for horses or dogs, and fugitives branded and even mutilated. Little became of her demands for change. In 1771 public auctions of serfs became illegal, but there are records of auctions for years afterwards, while in Lithuania a noble killing a serf could face a fine. The barons remained powerful, making laws and practising their *droit de seigneur*. Serfdom was not finally abolished until the middle of the 19th century.

In the 18th century the idea of nationhood had begun to be fomented by teachers such as J.G. Herder, but it wasn't until the 19th century and the Romantic movements, with towering poets and intellects such as Lithuania's Adam Mickiewicz, that the idea really

and has been discontinued there for many years." But his words fell on deaf ears.

And when Charles XI threatened to take away more than 80 percent of the domains occupied by the descendants of the Teutonic Knights, these German Balts called him a "peasant king" and turned to their other enemy for help. Russia was soon in charge and thereafter took control of Lithuania as well. In 1764 Catherine the Great visited Estonia and Latvia and found serfs still being

Left, a 19th-century Estonian fishing village. **Above**, anti-Soviet demonstrators in 1990; and the aftermath as Stalin is finally toppled.

started gaining ground. There was a lot of lost time to catch up on. The more enlightened German landlords did their best to make amends, starting schools and themselves learning the local languages perhaps for the first time.

Tartu University, near the Latvian border, was the intellectual powerhouse for the National Awakening in both Estonia and Latvia. But Lithuania suffered a setback with the closing of its university in 1832, followed by a ban on printing Lithuanian books. This was punishment for uprisings against the tsar. Paradoxically, throughout the Baltics there was as much Russification towards the end of the century as there was national fervour.

Discontent with the unenlightened tsars broke out into the Russian Revolution of 1905. It was a violent time that affected all the Baltic states, where many were delighted to torch the grand manors and other buildings of the ruling class. It was the start of a savage century. The two world wars were particularly fiercely fought. Although it was Russian against German, it was much like a civil war of brother against brother, and though many ended up in the uniform of one side or the other, neither was welcome.

Wars' wasteland: After the retreating Red Army had scorched its way homeward at the end of World War I, there was barely a breath left in the land. After World War II, only a few dozen people crawled from the rubble of major ports such as Klaipėda, Ventspils and Narva. In Vilnius, the Jerusalem of Lithuania, there was, as elsewhere, wholesale extermination of the Jews. The scars of both wars are still deep in the landscape, which is dotted with cemeteries and memorials.

The final injustice was the permanent imposition of Soviet rule and Stalinist terror. Anyone a visitor meets today in the Baltics is likely to have a relation who was sent to Siberia or was simply shot.

In between the barbarisms of war was an extraordinary flowering of three quite separate cultures, coming into their own as nation states. From 1918 to 1939 the land was all theirs for the first time for more than 700 years. The German Balts were sent home: first through land reforms, and in the end by Hitler who, under his pact with Stalin, ordered them out. There was great hardship to overcome, but the economies, based on agriculture, grew to match those in the West. Political life was exciting, if a little rocky.

It is this golden age that the people of the Baltic states looked back to for 50 years afterwards. It was a time to which they all wanted to return. Until the late 1980s it was hard to believe this distant ideal would become reality: but suddenly it was there. Renewed independence wasn't won without some bloodshed and there are continuing casualties in the peace. But the countries have opened their doors to a future over which they have control.

Right, Soviet tank outside the broadcasting centre in Vilnius, January 1991, when 14 were killed.

"It is easy to turn an aquarium into cold fish soup. It is more difficult to turn cold fish soup back into an aquarium."
—aide to Poland's president, Lech Walesa

Ask a Balt what real differences independence has made to their day-to-day lives and the most likely answer will be a sigh. Superficially, independence has transformed the three countries. Emblems of Soviet power such as statues of Lenin or the ubiquitous red propaganda boards have disappeared. Western goods, from bananas and beer to satellite televisions and contraceptives, are widely available. The national flags fly everywhere. Outspokenness brings no reprisals. Travel to the West is open to all. Private enterprise is flourishing. Embassies, not seen since the 1930s, dot the streets of the capitals.

Nevertheless, such conspicuous differences are not the important ones. Every sphere of life, from health care and hygiene to education, morals, family structure and the economy, is broken and contaminated by 50 years of the worst system of government yet devised in Europe.

For many locals, the problem begins with biology. "All the good ones died in the forest or left," is a local woman's typical complaint. In 1944, most of the brightest and best Estonians, Latvians and Lithuanians (of both sexes) did flee westwards. Of those who stayed behind, many more died in Siberia, or in the hopeless, bloody, resistance struggle of 1944–53. With the intelligentsia all but eliminated, the communists – as elsewhere – then constructed a system which methodically perverted the moral and intellectual basis of everyday life. For all but the very young or the very old, this is the only way of life they have ever known.

It is partly this which explains why the Baltic states are finding it so hard to struggle out of the Soviet bog. Repression and stagnation were worse, and continued for longer, than in the Soviet empire's other captive countries of Central Europe. In Poland, despite horrific sufferings in World War II and

Preceding pages: modern housing block, Latvia.
Right, pigs going to market in Estonia.

afterwards, there was by 1990 a tough-minded, thoughtful and well-rooted alternative political class to take over power from the communists. In Hungary, there was a thriving intelligentsia and a strong stream of liberal-minded reform communists developing their ideas throughout the late 1970s and '80s. Even in Prague, the dissidents and their friends kept alive the tradition of independent thought. In the Baltics, the brave, strong, intelligent, good and wise were thin on the ground when independent politics restarted in the summer of 1988, and there has been little time for a new generation to emerge.

So it is hardly surprising that the politics in all three countries still bears a strong resemblance to the paranoid, hypocritical nonsense of the Soviet era. Of course there are differences: instead of there being one huge political party, there are many, mostly with little in the way of a grass-roots base. The press is still polemical and unreliable, but at least there is a choice between different types of polemic and unreliability. The quickest way to deal with an opponent's argument is to call him a "KGB agent" (it used to be "bourgeois nationalist"). Corruption among politicians is notorious: if you meet one, ask what legal constraints govern his (it is unlikely to be her) business interests. The answer is simple: practically none. Just as in the

past politicians used their Communist Party privileges to enrich themselves, now they use the possibilities of the "free" (but in fact monopolistic) market.

Little of this comes out in public. Investigative reporting is almost unknown. Journalists, largely Soviet-trained, continue to recycle official communiques, or else pontificate dutifully in accordance with their paper's standpoint. Among the authorities, there is scarcely an inkling of the rights and duties of a free press, or the acceptable limits of state interference in radio or television.

Bribery and corruption: The rot continues downwards. The judicial system, largely filled with people who in the past had nothing more complicated to do than read out the verdicts approved by the Party, has exchanged one sort of corruption for another. Pity the poor (or, rather, foolish) businessman who resorts to law in search of justice. The size of the bribe, rather than the strength of the legal argument, will all too often decide the case. The police, too, still mostly staffed with people who trained in the Brezhnev era, are overstretched, underpaid, demoralised, increasingly corrupt, and usually useless.

The result is a crime wave, sometimes partly concealed, as the "Red Barons" of the former *nomenklatura* skim the cream of the newly privatising economy, and other times

all too visible, as burglars break open flimsy doors and carry off the goods of anyone they consider worth robbing. Car theft is epidemic. Street crime is increasing. And where are ordinary people to turn?

Certainly not to politicians. "Cleaning House" and similar slogans are popular among the first generation of pro-independence politicians but precious little attention has been paid, in any country, to the practical questions of running a post-communist state. In Lithuania, the ruling Sajudis coalition wasted the first year of independence on the easy and visible parts of regaining statehood. As autumn gave way to winter, unheated and with no sign of hot water, the voters' deci-

was little time or inclination during the struggle for independence to discuss what it would actually be like. Training judges, reforming the education systems, guaranteeing press freedom or public access to official information were marginal priorities at a time when regaining independent nationhood seemed as distant and unlikely as raising the *Titanic*. Now the ship has been raised, and sits barnacled, waterlogged and unseaworthy, while the exhausted, bickering crew face the dawning realisation that the hardest part of their task is yet to come.

Quite wrongly, perhaps, most Balts had a different idea about post-independence existence. It went like roughly like this: "We

sion to restore the former pro-independence communists was all too understandable.

Ask any politician what is being done to make his country more democratic, and you will receive at best a blank stare and most probably a lengthy lecture either (from the right) on the evils of communism or (on the left) the need for higher wages, lower prices, full employment and universal well-being.

The result is that the Baltic states are stuck. Busting the chains of annexation generated a wave of national unity and purpose, but there

Left, professional musicians busking in Riga. **Above**, former Soviet submarine pen, Liepāja.

will be like three Hong Kongs, funnelling Western expertise, goods and technology into the vast chaotic hinterland to the east, which we well understand, and bringing out, via our excellent ports, valuable raw materials for the West."

What this ignored was that the independence struggle had raised Western interest in the Baltic states to quite absurdly artificial levels. Politicians found their offices filled with journalists from the world's leading news organisations, and their in-trays stuffed with invitations to visit think-tanks, address parliaments, and pay visits. It did not last. When the Baltic states dropped out of the news, they dropped out of the minds of most Westerners. Lithuania alone received many millions of dollars of "free" publicity with its declaration of independence and defiant resistance to Soviet terror. Now the small countries must compete for business attention on their own merits alone.

This brings up the second mistaken assumption, which was to assume that the regaining of independence would somehow make the countries less sovietised and more attractive to the outside world. Almost nothing of the kind has happened: the physical, human, political and economic landscapes remain depressingly familiar.

A third problem is a remarkable unwill-

ingness to grasp the need for change. As most Baltic-based foreigners will testify, the most depressing aspect of the current difficulties is not the pervasive legacy of totalitarianism, but that so many Lithuanians, Latvians and Estonians sincerely believe that they already conduct their affairs to a reasonable standard of promptness and efficiency. When told that conditions are only a little better than the rest of the ex-Soviet Union, they react aggrieved, and then dismissive.

The effect on the pace of change is plain. Instead of using the Baltic as a bridge or gateway, West and East are dealing direct with each other, and the Baltic states, where

almost every step out of the Soviet-era bog is plagued by bureaucracy, corruption, incompetence and stubbornness, feature only as a view from an airliner's window.

It is important here to draw some distinctions. Estonia, as the Baltic state least isolated from the outside world (thanks to Finnish television programmes), and with the least undemocratic tradition pre-war, is further down the path of rebuilding a normal, civic society. In Lithuania, modernisation of society, economy and culture was already hindered by the extremes of national pride and patriotism ("This is Lithuania, we do things differently," one hears time and again when confronted with some irrational, Soviet-era method or problem). The return of the Democratic Labour Party added a dose of complacent nostalgia for the happier days of 1988–89 and was bound to break the hesitant steps to reform.

Poor housing: While the West holds back, or looks elsewhere, the Soviet system and infrastructure (but not the mentality) crumble by the day. The physical environment can be profoundly depressing. Dreary concrete tower blocks, mass-produced and badly-assembled, surround almost every town in the Baltic. The typical family lives there in cramped accommodation, increasingly-poorly served by public transport, a long way from the attractive historic city centres of the visitors' tours. People marry young in an attempt to leave home, but they often have to continue living in their parents' homes. In Latvia 20 percent of families and single people have been waiting for apartments or refurbishments for almost 20 years.

Communal apartments, where several families share a kitchen and bathroom and then each live in a single room, are common in Riga. Divorce rates are among the highest in the world. A telephone at home seems set to remain a luxury into the indefinite future. Low wages make even a brief trip to the West an enormous expense.

Even better-off Balts, supported perhaps by relatives abroad or a stint of illegal work in Scandinavia, cannot escape the pollution, disease and dirt of daily life. Food, whether in the state stores or markets, comes with little guarantee of freshness or hygienic production. A tomato may be the healthy produce of a back yard, or the pesticide and radioactivity-ridden survivor of a horrific ecological disaster area, hundreds of miles to the south. Milk may be straight from the cow, or brimming with bacteria. Meat, fish, mushrooms, eggs, dairy products, fruit and vegetables: all mean playing Russian roulette with one's health. For a visitor, the worst that is likely to happen is an upset stomach. For someone living entirely on a local diet, the results in life-expectancy and infant mortality figures are clear to see. For men life expectancy is 66.5 years, for women 75.7, that is 7.9 and 4.3 years fewer than for neighbouring Scandinavia. Infant mortality in Latvia is about 13 deaths per 1,000 live births. In Sweden it is 5.8, while in Russia it is a whopping 24.7.

that even this bleak estimate may have been understated. Barely a fifth of Baltic trade goes westwards, but the part headed east is now facing unimaginable disruption and difficulty. The near-collapse of Russia's banking system means that even willing customers find it hard to pay their Baltic suppliers, and there is limitless potential for fraud, delay and confusion.

Yet even if life seems unendurably depressing and harsh from a pampered Western point of view, it is surprising how resiliently most Balts face the future.

This stems partly from the underlying realisation that, however bad things may be in the Baltic, they are a great deal worse further

The education system, which ought to be the spearhead of the renewal, is still – even at university level – mostly staffed with badly-trained autocratic teachers, picked for their unthinking loyalty rather than any tendency they might have to encourage their pupils in independent thought.

If nothing else induces melancholy, reflecting on the short-term future of the Baltic economies is almost guaranteed to do so. In the summer of 1992 the IMF predicted drops in output of nearly one third. There are signs

east. Unlike in Russia, most Baltic families are only a generation, if that, removed from the land. As life becomes tougher, dangerous and unrewarding in the cities, there are signs of families moving back to the land. Subsistence farming may not be the face of the future, but it is at least a survival strategy for the present, and thus a blessing to be counted.

Secondly, compared to the horrors of war, occupation, deportation, Russification and stagnation, an immature political culture and the prospect of cold and hungry winters seems mild to many. "It's all over for me," is a depressing refrain. "But at least my children may have something like a good life."

Left, familiar concerns, Riga. <u>Above</u>, Virve and Vidrik Kivi's new B&B near Viljandi, Estonia.

At least since the 13th century, when the German and Scandinavian crusaders arrived to impose Christianity at the point of the sword, the territory of the present Baltic states has been one of mixed settlement. Over the intervening period, apart from the various native peoples who later came together to make up the Estonians, Latvians and Lithuanians, the area has also been settled by large numbers of Germans, Poles, Jews and Russians, and a smaller number of peoples, including West European merchant communities in the ports of Riga, Tallinn and Narva. Today, the question of relations between the Balts and the large Russian populations in the region is one of the key problems hanging over the future of the Baltic states.

Centre of Jewry: Jewish settlement began in the 14th century, when Jews were invited into Lithuania by the Grand Duke Vytautas. Precisely because the rulers of Lithuania, and later of Poland-Lithuania, were relatively tolerant towards the Jews, Lithuania became a great centre of world Jewry, and the "Litvaks" one of its most important branches. "Lithuania", as understood by the Jews, embraced the whole area of the former Grand Duchy, including Belorus and parts of the Ukraine. By the 18th century, its capital, Vilnius (in Yiddish, Vilna or Vilne) was known as "the Jerusalem of Lithuania", because of its large number of synagogues and its many *yeshivas*, or Hebrew schools.

Later in that century, Vilnius became a centre of Jewish Orthodox resistance to the Hasidic religious movement then sweeping eastern Europe. Gaon Street in the centre of the city's old town is named after the Gaon or "Genius" of Vilna, the rabbi who led the Orthodox, and whose prayer house stood on that street until it was demolished by the Nazis together with most of the rest of the ghetto. Nearby was the Great Synagogue (now a playground), which had the dimensions of a cathedral.

Preceding pages: Vilnius's synagogue. Left, the heart of the 1930s Polish ruler Marshal Pilsudski is buried in Vilnius. Above, priest at Kurämäe Orthodox nunnery, Estonia.

Before the holocaust, Jews made up 7.6 percent of the population of what is now Lithuania, and a much larger proportion of Kaunas (Kovno) and Vilnius. Many Lithuanian Jews had also moved to Latvia, and there was a small population of 5,000 or so in Estonia. The Nazis were to wipe out those populations almost completely, and today the few thousand that remain are being steadily diminished by emigration. The Lithuanian-Jewish writer Grigory Kanovitch has warned that if things go on as they are, "there

will soon be more Jewish organisations here than there are Jews".

Jewish emigration from the Baltics is encouraged by the memory of the holocaust, in which Baltic partisans and volunteers played a major part; indeed, the initial massacres in Lithuania were conducted entirely by Lithuanians without direct German involvement. This has cast a severe shadow over subsequent relations and, a year after independence, the allegation that the Lithuanian government was giving a blanket rehabilitation to former war criminals led to criticism in the Western press.

Baltic participation in the holocaust was

due partly to anti-Semitism (though there was no history of attack as there is in other parts of Europe), but more to the belief that Jews had played a major part in supporting the Soviet regime which was imposed on the Balts in 1940. This was indeed true, but what the Balts who make this charge forget is that the Jewish communists also turned on their Jewish opponents, and that in fact a higher proportion of Jews than Balts was deported to Siberia in 1940–41.

The lack of a serious dialogue between Lithuanians and Jews, of the sort which has occurred in Poland, means that the great majority even of Lithuanian intellectuals are unaware of this fact. However, all three

Lithuania. The Polonisation of Lithuania was helped by the Catholic church, the Polish nobility, and the fact that, as in all the Baltics until the 16th century, there was no written form of their language.

One cannot point to specific Polish monuments in Vilnius (Wilno, in Polish), because the whole of the old city is in effect a Polish monument, built by Polish architects, studded with Polish inscriptions and very similar to many baroque towns in Poland. Czesław Milosz, the Nobel prizewinning writer who lived there until 1941, described it as "narrow cobblestone streets and an orgy of the baroque: almost like a Jesuit city somewhere in the middle of Latin America". To this day,

Baltic governments have condemned the holocaust and Baltic participation in it, though they have not admitted its scope.

Poles' position: The official Polish presence in what is now Lithuania also began in the Middle Ages, with the marriage union of the Lithuanian Grand Duke Jogaila and the Polish princess Jadviga in 1386. However, for a century and more before that the Lithuanian Grand Dukes had ruled over large numbers of Slavic peoples, many of whom were ultimately to see themselves as Poles.

After the union, many Lithuanians, especially from the upper classes, also became Poles – a cause of enduring resentment in

Vilnius retains its character as a Catholic frontier outpost.

Until World War II, Lithuanians were a small minority in Vilnius, with Poles the largest community, followed by the Jews. Vilnius was the home city of a number of great Polish cultural figures like Milosz and Adam Mickiewicz. The latter's epic, *Pan Tadeusz*, begins with the famous invocation,

O Lithuania, my fatherland,
Thou art like health; what praise thou
shouldst command
Only that man finds who has lost thee
quite.
The passage also refers to the Gate of Dawn,

the chapel in Vilnius dedicated to Our Lady which is still a place of pilgrimage for Poles as well as Lithuanians. Worshippers from the two communities sometimes scuffle there as the Poles coming in for a Polish-language mass bump into Lithuanians coming from a Lithuanian-language one. The heart of Marshal Józef Piłsudski, the ruler of Poland between the wars and himself a Polish-Lithuanian nobleman, is buried in Vilnius's Rasu (Rossa) cemetery beside his mother.

In the 19th century, Lithuanian peasants participated in rebellions against Russian imperial rule together with their Polish-speaking landlords. By World War I, however, Lithuanian nationalists were distinguishing

Poland simply as a consequence of the Molotov-Ribbentrop Pact.

Today, many Lithuanians fear that the Poles want to recover Vilnius, but the Polish minority in Lithuania dropped by more than 50 percent after the Soviet reconquest in 1945, when almost all the Polish intelligentsia and upper classes emigrated to Poland (or were deported to Siberia). It still numbers more than 270,000. Tens of thousands of Poles also live in Latvia, the southern parts parts of which also used to be part of Poland; but whereas in Lithuania, fear of Lithuanian nationalism made many Poles support the Soviet communists during the independence struggle of recent years, in Latvia most Poles

themselves sharply from the Poles, whom they blamed for many of Lithuania's historical problems.

After both Lithuania and Poland achieved independence from Russia in 1918, the two countries clashed over Vilnius, until in 1921 it was seized by a Polish expeditionary force under General Lucijan Zeligowski. Newly independent Lithuania made the recovery of Vilnius the centrepoint of its foreign policy, and eventually it received the city back from Stalin in 1940, when he had won it from

Left, **Russian soldiers sightseeing at Trakai, Lithuania. Above, children in Narva, Estonia.**

were pro-independence. The Lithuanian nationalisation and land ownership laws have caused considerable tension between Poland and Lithuania. This in turn has caused difficulties on the Polish-Lithuanian frontier and severe hold-ups for goods going to and from the Baltic states.

The Catholic church, to which both peoples belong, may do something to bridge the gap between them. So far, this has not been the case, because of the close identification between the church in Lithuania and Lithuanian nationalism. However, with a Lithuanian émigré and former papal nuncio to Holland as Archbishop of Vilnius, and the

Pope himself a Pole, there are hopes that both sides will ultimately be able to overcome the narrow prejudices and fears which have been bequeathed by history.

Russians who remain: Lithuania's problem with the Poles appears minor, however, when compared to those of Estonia and Latvia with the local Russian-speakers, who make up 39 percent and about 48 percent of the respective populations. Small communities of Russians had lived in the area since the early Middle Ages, when some Baltic tribes paid tribute to Russian princes. After the conquest by Peter the Great, these were joined by Russian soldiers, merchants and officials. At the end of the 19th century a major influx

of Russian workers to the new industries began. This was interrupted by World War I and the Russian Revolution, which drove considerable numbers of white Russian refugees to the Baltic.

Before 1940, Riga was the greatest Russian émigré centre after Paris. When Stalin occupied the Baltic states in June 1940, these émigrés were naturally among the first to suffer from the secret police. Newspapers and cultural centres were closed and churches transferred to other purposes.

The reconquest of the Baltics by the Soviet Union in 1944–45 began a process of Russian immigration which drastically altered

the region's demography. Today, Tallinn is 50 percent Russian, Riga 67 percent (in 1939, it was 63 percent Latvian). The great majority of Russians now living in the Baltic are immigrants from the Soviet period or their descendants. The Latvian and Estonian parliaments have decided that these people have no automatic right to citizenship, and can only obtain it by a process of nationalisation modelled on rigid critieriä used by other European countries.

This has caused protests both from local Russians and from Moscow. It has been pointed out that Russians living in towns like Narva, where the population is 94 percent Russian, have few real possibilities of learning Estonian to the standard required, especially as most Estonian teachers do not want to live in Narva. However, most Russians are more seriously worried by the threat of economic and social discrimination, which the far more radical Baltic nationalists would like to introduce in an effort to persuade the Russians to leave.

The Baltic view of the Russians is coloured by the fact that most of the post-1945 immigrants were working-class (often ex-peasants), and they are sometimes held to have lowered the civic culture of the Baltic states. It is often said that they lack even Russian culture, but are pure examples of *Homo Sovieticus*. This is to some extent true; a majority of socially undesirable elements in Riga and Tallinn are Russian. However, Soviet rule has also had its terrible effect on the Balts themselves, who provide their own criminal element.

Most Balts hope that the withdrawal of the Russian army from the region will lead local Russians to forget dreams of restoring the Soviet Union, and to settle down as loyal citizens or residents of the Baltic States. How things will in fact turn out is unclear, but the Baltic Russians are engaged in their own search for an identity. A number of their spokesmen have said that this will be a different one from that of Russians in Russia, because they have been influenced and changed by the characters of their Baltic neighbours. If this is so, it will be a hopeful sign in what is bound in all circumstances to be an uneasy, and challenging, relationship.

Left, Orthodox cemetery, Mustvee, Estonia. Right, mosque of the community of Tatars, Lithuania.

Like Latvia's brown cows, the peoples of the republics like to have names and not numbers, and they have no wish to be part of the herd. The return to independence has brought with it a desire to go back to the pre-war idyll of the self-sufficient smallholder. Contentedly isolated and beholden to no one, people are digging into their new lands within sight of the woods and their spellbinding trees.

Many of the old Soviet collectives have now been broken up into smallholdings much as the land was redistributed during the First Independence when the Baltics became famous for their dairy products. But during nearly half a century under the "progressive" Soviet system, agricultural productivity increased overall by less than 2 percent. By putting the clock back, many believe the land will flow with milk and honey again.

A patch for all: Those without access to farmlands, particularly newcomers to the towns or the region, may have allotments, plots of 6,460 sq. ft (600 sq. metres), which were provided for company and factory workers under the Soviet regime. Densely planted with fruit trees, berry bushes, vegetables, herbs and flowers, they sprawl around the towns and cities. In spite of completely inadequate plumbing or other facilities, increasingly solid weekend shacks have been built on them over the years, and now that planning permission has slipped into the morass of largely unenforceable laws, two-storey brick-built houses are rapidly rising, their new roofs "topped out" with wreaths of oak leaves.

Whether farmhouses or summer houses, there is a great pride in making both the buildings and their contents by hand, by creatively using what materials are available (and there are precious few). There is a lot to be done. So many buildings in the country have been destroyed by revolution, war and neglect. So many were burned out by the end of World War I that the first of the popular open-air ethnographic museums was started to conserve a few specimens before they completely disappeared. Some of the old

Preceding pages: milkmaid, Lithuania. **Left,** gathering winter fuel in Alūksne, Latvia.

crafts, such as thatching and weaving, were already on the wane in the bleak years after that war. And after the next one came the Soviet occupation which sent landowners to Siberia and joined farms together in collectives, leaving more neglected buildings to fall into decay.

Restoration is already in hand, and new farms and country homes are being built as many people are buying land with nothing on it at all. Among the new smalholders' priorities is a sauna, built away from the main house because of the risk of fires. The hands of a farmer are ingrained with soil, with no hot running water to wash it away. Only the sauna, fired up at least once a week, has a

life. No one visits anyone, of either sex, without a small bunch as a present. Beside the flowers will be herbs, for pickling and spicing, for medicinal, cullinary and symbolic use. There will be dill and rue and caraway and sage. In the vegetable plots there will be tomatoes and small cucumbers that can be pickled with cherry and currant leaves. Dill is a vital culinary ingredient, especially in Latvia.

In Lithuania there will be plenty of *ruta*, or rue, which is not only the national flower and a girl's name, but also a symbol of virginity: a wreath of it is burned on a wedding night. There may be chickens and ducks and geese, and in the unfenced fields a tethered cow or

chance of getting rid of the dirt, while a swish of the birch twig stimulates the blood.

Also indispensable is the cellar where harvest produce can be kept through the winter. Sometimes the cellars are entered through doors in small mounds in the gardens, which look like bomb shelters. Even in a city the size of Riga, modern blocks of flats have cellars for residents to keep their country produce fresh. Homes often also have the wherewithal to smoke meat and fish.

Surrounding the farm buildings there will be beds of bright flowers, of roses, chrysanthemums, dahlias, fuschias, lilies and sweet peas. Flowers are an everyday part of Baltic

two – brown in Latvia, black-and-white "Dutch" in Estonia and Lithuania – which will be milked where they stand two and sometimes three times a day. A countryman's meal is incomplete without spoonfuls of their sweet or sour cream.

There is a theory that farm buildings are spread out, and not huddled in villages, for defensive purposes, because scattered communities are a more difficult target for a concentrated attack. But a basic Baltic character favours independence, and the further north you go, the more isolated they become. In the south, in Lithuania, smallholders and country people prefer the community of villages, and there the pull of the land, though still strong, does not embrace with such energy the ideal of daily rural toil encountered in Latvia and Estonia.

The changing year: Winters are long and dark. For up to four months of the year the ground is rock hard and snow keeps cattle and poultry indoors. Sledges make haulage easier and trees are felled and chopped into neat piles around the house. Holes are made in the lakes' thickly iced surfaces and fish, attracted by the light, can be scooped up by the bucketful. Illegal hunters follow beaver tracks in the snow. Wild animals seeking food may wander into the region from the icier heartlands of the great continent: there

When spring melts the snow, swamps rise and rivers often burst their banks. On the Teiči nature reserve near Madona in Latvia, Old Believers, without access to newspapers or televisions, are even more isolated as the waters rise around them. On the delta of the Nemunas in Lithuania, where some houses are built on stilts to escape the spring floods, and where the floors of some cattle barns can be raised by winches, there are often fatalities, usually drunks who fall from an unaccustomed boat.

As the earth warms, violets carpet the woodlands and bird cherry blossom creates a fresh white blanket on the trees, which lilac soon turns to blue. Sweet water is tapped

are bears in Estonia; wolves may move into Lithuania in hunting packs.

Elk, deer and wild boar, which live in nearly every forest, will be sought by licensed hunters, as will wild duck, capercaillie, black cock and hares as big as hounds (there are no wild rabbits). The stalkers are professional countrymen: hunting is not a great Baltic pastime. Dogs tethered up on the farms warn of attacks by foxes or hawks or by packs of eastern Usurian wild dogs which have been increasing in recent years.

Left, the plough is now back in private hands, Lithuania. **Above**, slaughtering a pig in Latvia.

from beneath the barks of birch trees, and sometimes from maples, and kept in the cellar to slake thirsts on hot summer days.

But it is only the arrival of the majestic storks that really means spring has returned. Each year they faithfully fly back to their nests perched high in treetops, on old chimneys or on cartwheels that farmers have put up on poles, for their presence is a guarantee of good fortune. They will repair and build up their nests and settle down for the summer, when they will high-step through the meadows feasting on frogs. Meanwhile, hidden from sight in the woods, the world's largest population of black storks settles in.

In summertime everyone who can leaves the towns and cities to stay in the country with relations and friends. Children break up from school at the beginning of June and are often sent to relations in the country for the whole of their three-month holiday; family bonds do not seem as close, on a daily basis, as they are in the West. Their mothers may join them; fathers come at weekends.

Sunday evenings see trains full of people returning from the country laden with buckets, baskets and bags. There is also a harvest to be had in the wild, of blueberries, cloudberries, whortleberries and tiny strawberries. In addition, every garden has red and black currants, and glass jars are filled with

jellies and jams. A visitor will be offered a plate of berries with perhaps a few vegetables, such as pods of fresh garden peas.

In the markets, sellers of a few jars of bright berries are joined by Azerbaijanis and Turkestanis who bring peaches and watermelons, looking out, it is said, for the fair local girls.

Vodka economy: Harvest time is hard work and requires all the hands it can get. Estonia and Latvia are reasonably mechanised, but horses and carts are still evident in most of Lithuania. Agricultural machinery is limited and out of date: straw is not automatically baled; hay is not bagged up for silage. Scythes

and pitchforks are as indispensable as they have always been. Under the Soviet system, a tractor driver was liable to be the local alcoholic: he was called on to plough and harvest the small plots people were allowed to keep, in return for which he was often paid in moonshine vodka. Many smallholders still use vodka as a currency. They make it from rye, or from just sugar and water with perhaps a few peas. It can ferment in milk churns which are kept in the sauna.

Barley and rye are the main crops, for beer and sourdough bread. There is sugarbeet, too, and a little maize. In this new age of nostalgia there is talk of planting the fields with flax again. It used to be a staple, for linen and rope, and in yesterday's summers its flowers turned the fields blue. Cannabis is also grown for hemp, and *kaņepu sviests* (cannabis butter) is a Latvian treat spread on rye bread.

Summer weather is unpredictable. It can be as hot as in southern Europe, and occasionally there are even mini-tornadoes. Harvests are unpredictable and nobody knows what will appear in the shops. This, coupled with a precarious economy, means that people view their smallholdings as an insurance against hunger and deprivation.

The summer comes to an end as the storks start to gather in the fields preparing for their migration south. At the beginning of September, amid parades, children go back to school and the speed limit on the roads is reduced for a few weeks to take account of their holiday-induced doziness. Those with apartments in the city will return to settle in with their produce for the winter.

But there are still a few autumn weekends left in the country, to go picking nuts and, the favourite of all, mushrooms. And there is one last berry to preserve, that of the rowan, after the first frost has made it sweet.

Then the woods and the flat fields fall under the grey skies of winter, and skiers and skaters wait hopefully for snow. It is then that the smallholder will reap the rewards of the summer's harvest. For, whatever happens to the economy, to unemployment, to the availability of petrol and other fuel, there will always be something in the cellar to keep the wolf – and the bear – from the door.

Left, when there's no mains water, Estonia. **Right**, milking a "Dutch" cow in Lithuania.

Baltic cooking today is straightforward fare not far removed from the country and barely affected by international diners' expectations. The plain, wholesome, unspicy dishes characteristic of all three of the states, but particularly Latvia and Estonia, demand little artistry, but homemade and home-grown, this food can be very good.

Take an hour or two to peruse the disused Zeppelin hangars which house Riga's massive – and massively crowded – market. Scores of indoor stalls tout fresh and fermented dairy products: vast slabs of soft white cheese, harder yellow cheese, bottles of sour cream, yoghurt and cultivated sour milk. In another hall, high-quality fresh pork gleams pink, and many varieties of sausage and ham wait to be sampled. Smoked fish sells at one end of the market, fresh fruit at the other.

In summer, baskets are piled high with early apples and pears – small irregular specimens that recognise no trading controls – and glass tumblers overspill with red and black berries and tiny yellow mirabelle plums. Notice too the nuts, the dried fruit, the umbrils of caraway seed drying on the branch, huge bunches of fresh, strong, flat-leaf parsley, pots of honey and barrels of sauerkraut lined up for tasting, and trays of fresh, homemade black, brown and white bread. These staple foods, brought in by private sellers from the nearby countryside, are the raw materials of Baltic cooking.

These ingredients reach the table hardly seasoned. In the vegetable hall you may smell dill and garlic – but for flavour Latvia mostly relies on fermented milk and smoked fish and cheese, and bacon, with a sprinkling here and there of caraway seed. Even blander is Estonian food, where fresh milk is the predominant flavour and onions are considered too strong. Lithuanian cooking, which has been partly influenced by the Orient, is the most pungent.

The hint of fire comes from Lithuania's complicated political past. From the 15th century exiled Crimean Tatars and refugees

from the Golden Horde flocked to this powerful state to coexist with Russians and Belorussians and Poles under the leadership of the Polish/Lithuanian noble class. The edible results today are a half-forgotten legacy of exoticism and luxury, recipes which dare to include black pepper and nutmeg and marjoram. The spices came from the East, the marjoram probably from Italy via Catholic Poland.

Nevertheless, you will find it hard to pick up their traces today, unless you eat in a

private home. In the first stage of privatisation ambitious restaurateurs can only think in bland international terms. All discerning visitors should pray for change in attitudes to public catering.

Bread baskets: Natural resources well used, good farming and careful husbandry determine the goodness of Baltic food. The cool, wet land hosts grains and berries, the dark forest sprouts moist tapestries of mushrooms, fish populate the rivers, lakes and sea, and pig and dairy farming flourish. There has always been enough to eat.

Excellent bread, especially rye bread, comes from this northern part of the world,

Preceding pages: meat stall, Riga central market. **Left,** Sunday lunch in Lithuania. **Above,** *cepelinai.*

where the hardiest of the cereal crops flourishes in cold, poor soil. Rye bread, with a strong rich taste, enhanced by molasses made from native-growing sugarbeet, and caraway seed, keeps well. Its sweet-sourness also seems ideally suited to the local beer, bland cheeses and pungent cured meat and fish. One type of pale rye loaf, which has a smooth, shiny, tan-coloured crust, is widely known as Riga bread and is best eaten when it is fresh and sweet. (Most bakers hang a two-pronged testing fork beside their self-service shelves.)

Other Baltic varieties include the plain dark rye bread featured in hotels, which should not be judged by the dryness and

locals who cry: "But where's the sausage to go with it, or the butter?" In the Baltics they still love their meats and fats as a sign of progress, but our Western diet has moved on – and back.

Porridge and potatoes: Porridge used to be a staple food, too. Porridges of cooked grain are now rarely seen in the towns except on special occasions. The ancient Latvian version, called *putra*, is made of barley, or of barley and potato mixed, and served with a ladle of bacon fat, smoked meat or fish, or milk products, as a main course. In Estonia you may find mixed grain porridges served with milk.

There is also a breakfast speciality, *kama*,

sourness it exudes when shaped like a shoe sole and left indefinitely exposed to the air. Among the white breads rank the robust and versatile French *baton*, not at all like its Gallic counterpart, and creamy-coloured sourdough loaves, usually homemade and worth seeking out for their extraordinary muscular texture.

These breads, which the Baltic states share with Germany and Poland and Russia, and Sweden and Finland, are top-class, especially now private producers are offering previously rare wholegrain varieties. More than one Western traveller has made a meal out of bread alone, to the consternation of the

made of ground toasted grains and raw oats mixed with yoghurt or milk, eaten with salt or honey. These gruels make good use of the region's barley, which doesn't have enough leaven for modern bread. Something like porridge is also made of mushy peas and then eaten with bacon fat. Grey field peas with fat bacon, in the German variety called Speck, is a local favourite in Latvia.

A Lithuanian asked to name a favourite dish would probably nominate something with potato. The Baltic Germans introduced this exotic tuber at the start of the 18th century, and the whole region fell for its charms, though none more than the Lithuanians. Today they eat boiled potatoes with everything from yoghurt to bacon fat, and like Poles and Jews they feast most happily on grated potato pancakes. The same grated potato goes to make a variety of filled rissoles, like *cepelinai*, so that no day passes without a helping of this potassium-rich foodstuff. Which leaves only yeast-leavened wheat dough as the remaining staple carbohydrate. This is the sort used to make genuine pasta bases in the West. On street corners in Tallinn you can buy slightly sweet white dough which tastes as if it has come fresh from your own oven.

In Latvia the array of savoury baking is enviable, with cheese- and meat-filled yeast-most as a dressing or garnish to the bread or pasta or porridge at the centre of their meal. For feasts celebrants reach not for the lean meat but the tastiest fat.

The most important meat is undoubtedly pork, followed in Lithuania by game. Pork includes salt pork and sausage and the black pudding (blood sausage) Estonians eat at Christmas. In the 15th century Lithuania had a world reputation for smoked wild boar. Domestic pig farming was later introduced by the Germans with exceptional results. So good was this industry that smoked lean pork from the Baltics, pink and wrinkled and juicy and tender, must have been the stuff of many a privileged Communist Party banquet and is

dough buns and yeast-dough horns filled with minced bacon. Meanwhile, if pizza makes you think of pasta, look no further than Lithuania, much influenced by Russian and Polish fondness for Slavic *tortellini*. It makes robust plain and filled pasta, cooked in boiling water, and still more pancakes out of wheat flour.

Fat feasts: One of the hallmarks of Baltic food is the non-prevalence of protein. Meat and fish, at least in Latvia and Estonia, are traditionally eaten in small quantities, al-

Left, cabbage seller in Ventspils; Latvian fish-monger. **Above**, Treecake for festive occasions.

still worth travelling for. It is certainly more inviting than the whole wedges of salted pork fat, dietary mainstay of the labouring male peasant a century ago, which still occur as a delicacy.

Neat fat? Most of us can hardly stomach it. On the other hand almost no traditional Baltic food is fried. The vegetables and carbohydrates are boiled, then the fat – whether bacon, or cheese, or butter – poured over. This constitutes a most distinctive aspect of Baltic food technology.

What about the fish, though, which is just as renowned as the pork table? Seek it out! Local fish preparations, such as smoked salt-water salmon, pickled herring, smoked sprats and smoked eel are amongst the best in the world and are a characteristic of the markets. In fact, smoking fish is so much part of the national heritage that the Latvian national poet Imants Ziedonis has since independence appeared on television to remind people of the best home-cure techniques. If you travel around the inland lake districts you will also encounter freshwater fish such as trout and pike.

In Estonia they make fresh fish soups with vegetables, thickened with flour and milk, while in Latvia and Lithuania fish may be cooked with bacon fat – a rare case of frying, with the added benefit of greatly masking the

at breakfast time in the larger restaurants: breakfasts are anyway a mix of a northern diet of cheese and meet as well as vegetables and cream.

The cold table could be supplemented with soup. In fact, this is also not a strong tradition, though there are old recipes in Lithuania for varieties of beetroot soup like the Russian/Ukrainian/Polish *borshch*, and for mushroom soup, and these are often on the menus of the self-service canteens. Typically Lithuanian beetroot soup has a sour-sweet base made with sorrel. If you see anyone picking leaves from waste ground in summer, the prize may well be wild sorrel, rich in iron and vitamin C.

smell of the fish. You will also find excellent Russian caviare on every hotel menu – while stocks last.

Of course, on commercial menus you will come across hot, fresh meat dishes more familiar to the visitor than anything mentioned so far. But one reason why meat cutlets, fried escalopes, meatballs, boiled and fried sausages are often mediocre is their foreign – mainly German – origin. Traditional Baltic cuisine was made up two-thirds by its cold table until early this century and, just as in Sweden and Russia, it is still the best way of showing off local produce.

The cold table seems to come into its own

Estonia's soups are much softer, made mainly with milk and vegetables, or with yoghurt and dill cucumber. A classic contains milk, dried peas and buckwheat grains. Something restrained and serene characterises all the food of Estonia, in line with the general culture of the people.

Special occasions: Christmas is celebrated with pork in Estonia, goose in Protestant Latvia and Lithuania, and fish and mushrooms in Catholic Lithuania. But the festival which gives star billing to the all-important Baltic dairy industry is midsummer. A special dense yellow country cheese, smoked and flavoured with caraway, is traditional for Jani in Latvia, and a similar spicier cheese is also eaten in Lithuania. You may sample both in the Riga market.

Salads are part of the cold table, and usually richly sauced, to be eaten with bread. One of the culinary highlights of a visit can be a bowl of tomatoes and cucumbers picked straight from a country garden, tossed with fresh dill and parsley and sour cream. It is a great pity, then, that in some restaurants and cafés this traditional dressing is supplanted by taste-obliterating bottled mayonnaise.

Sometimes strips of meat or cheese are used in the same way as raw vegetables to make composite salads for the cold table and these too tend to get bound up in sweet, fake

the sweetest tomatoes, ridge cucumbers, courgettes, beets, kohlrabi, potatoes, swede and turnips grow in profusion alongside peas and cabbages and rhubarb. Somewhere near the vegetable garden you will also find apples and plum trees and, in an ideal world, a beehive. A guest might enjoy an inspiring summer tea of tea of baked sour windfall apples sweetened with clear plum jam and macaroons. Nothing is wasted. This is both the spirit and the goodness of the kitchen garden.

The garden means work outside in spring and summer, and further labours indoors to pickle the cucumbers and bottle the fruit for winter. Meanwhile sturdy vegetables will be picked and stored to make carrot and bacon-

stuff from a bottle. They represent only a poor attempt at a quick urban cuisine adapted from the country.

Garden produce: The country garden is the thing, and it cannot be stressed enough what a vital and happy part it plays in Baltic food culture. One of the most charming and important poems in Lithuanian literature, rightly compared to Virgil's *Eclogues*, is called *The Seasons*, by an 18th-century clergyman, Kristjonas Donelaitis. In the kitchen garden, which became popular in Donelaitis's time,

flavoured cabbage pies. From beyond the garden, also for storing and preserving, are gathered nuts, wild berries and mushrooms. Black currants, bilberries, cranberries, red and white currants, and blackberries all go to make jams, and by tradition, a sour-sweet pudding, of juice thickened with potato flour, called in Latvian *kīsels*.

Sweet stewed rhubarb, stewed apples and stewed berries are popular in Estonia. Spoon food, so characteristic of old-fashioned rural diets, spans the gap more firmly established in modern eating between sweet and savoury, soup and pudding.

Under German influence, Latvia and Esto-

Left, homemade beer, Lithuania; wild mushrooms, Estonia. **Above**, picking berries in Latvia.

nia used to make a sweet bread soup out of leftovers. Since the bread was probably sour and black the resulting dish was closely related to the sour-sweet *kīsels* made with summer berries. Beer soups also belong to this curious category.

Cakes and ale: Cakes are more widespread nowadays than desserts. Look out for treecake and for honey cakes in Lithuania. Treecake is made by adding dough in layers to a rotating wooden pole in front of a hot fire. The result is a cake with many age lines, and what look like fungi clinging to its outer bark, where dollops of egg and lemon dough have been thrown on last. People order the required size by stipulating the number of eggs that should be used.

In cafés, which sell many varieties of shortbreads, shortcrust and flaky pastries, and eclairs, you can't help noticing that Latvians and Estonians have a German-style penchant for sweet whipped cream in or with their cakes and coffee.

Coffee is one dietary feature which marks off Russia from the Baltics: here coffee is more prevalent. Both tea and coffee are served without milk; sugar has to be requested and costs extra. Bottled beer is common, delicious and familiar, though far too scarce in modern establishments. In village and city street corners it is delivered in nozzles from tankers into bottles and jars.

The industrial soft drinks of recent origin, oversweet and tasteless, hardly relieve the thirst. Mineral water is normally good, although some is full of unpalatable salts, which can fail to slake thirsts in Riga where the tap water should not be drunk.

Herbal *eau-de-vie*, Riga Black Balsam, a dark brew tasting like a mixture of treacle and Campari, sweet Lithuanian liqueurs, Russian vodka and "Soviet" sparkling wine complete the modern bar line-up. You may also find good wines from Georgia, Hungary and Romania for local currency.

Soviet life did nothing for the quality of food and service in restaurants. A few pseudo-Western restaurants and hotdog stalls make it easier for tourists to manage today while the Baltic states rediscover a more gracious identity. Best is to picnic or eat in a private home, though the old hotels can work wonders if you're simply hungry.

Right, time for a party in Riga.

Throughout the Baltics churches and monasteries are opening their doors for business again. Property has been denationalised, religious schools are starting up, tracts are being published and the media is open to preachers. In the streets there are saffron-robed Krishnas and smart-suited evangelists from Sweden, Germany and the United States. Money from the Vatican, from northern Europe's Lutherans and from America's varied sects is pouring in, to refurbish the fabric and educate the eager congregations.

The Baltics, ever at the mercy of changing spheres of influence, have amassed a collection of churches with an extraordinary variety of styles. Their history has also left the countries with some two dozen differing beliefs and created such a tolerance towards other people and their religions that there are Lutherans who regularly attend Catholic Mass and Catholics who sing in Orthodox choirs. In Tallinn Methodists and Seventh Day Adventists share the same church.

Orthodox beginning: With the help of Greek Orthodox Russian merchants, the first teachings of Christ were in the 11th and 12th centuries but Christianity did not arrive in full force until the early 13th century when the German crusaders subjugated Estonia and Latvia. This belated start meant that the early European ecclesiastic style, Romanesque, was on the wane. Only St George's in Riga and the remains of Ikškile church on an island on the River Daugava give a glimmer of that expiring style. Church architecture in the Baltics really begins with Gothic.

In Estonia the earliest stone churches, built of limestone and dating from the end of the 13th century, are on the islands. These were simple Gothic buildings without towers, and were used for protection. On Saaremaa the churches at Kaarma and Valjala have interesting murals and the one at Karja has beautiful sculptures.

Lithuania converted to Christianity nearly two centuries after its Baltic neighbours, in 1387. Although nothing remains of Vilnius's

first church, it must have echoed the red-brick building of the castle. When St Anne's and the Bernardine monastery were built in the 15th century, its bricks, like those of the cathedral in Kaunas, would not have looked as out of place as they do today.

The Reformation took hold almost immediately after Martin Luther published his thesis in 1520 and its first centres were Tallinn and Riga, where sacred paintings began to be destroyed. There is a good painterly tradition in Baltic churches, on

collection chairs, priedieus, pews, galleries, altars, tryptichs, tablets and doors. Many churches had decorated walls and ceilings which were painted over during the Reformation, and afterwards. These were mostly done by Balts, and only the "easel" paintings produced by foreigners.

In Tallinn, the late 15th-century Baltic painter Bernt Notke, who produced the High Altar of Aarhus cathedral, Denmark, and Lübeck cathedral's great cross, was responsible for the folding altar at the Holy Ghost Church (1483), which has more paintings than any other in the Baltics. He also produced the macabre Dance of Death painting now in the the Niguliste church museum. In the middle of the 16th century the newly formed Duchy of Courland sought to secure its power base by ordering the building of 70 new Lutheran churches.

Catholics sought refuge in the Polish territories of southern and eastern Latvia and Lithuania where the Jesuits began to build their sumptuous churches. Their special style, which has completely shaped Vilnius through most of its 40 churches, is a rich 17th-century baroque created by Italians. The first, begun in 1604, was dedicated to the city's patron saint, Casimir. Among the finest is the Sts Peter and Paul church, supposedly built on the pagan temple to the goddess Milde. Its

church all trustworthy bishops were eliminated and it was impossible to ordain new priests. Today the world's largest Old Believers congregation, numbering some 20,000, is in the gold-domed Grebenschikova temple in the Moscow district of Riga. The church's walls are lined with stunning icons depicting only the saints' faces, and services are led by someone from the congregation, elected teachers (*nastavniki*) of the church.

Class distinctions: Though they tend not to last as long, there are still a number of wooden churches throughout the three countries, mostly in Lithuania. The oldest date from the middle of the 18th century. The ethnographic museum near Riga has a typical example. Its

Italian sculptors adorned it with more than 2,000 white stucco figures, many of them quite beautiful. The churches, often with a facade of two towers, are in an almost Spanish South American style. In Latagale it produced St Peter's in Daugavpils and the huge, isolated church at Aglona which attracts pilgrims from all over eastern Europe on the Feast of the Assumption.

Catholics were not the only refugees. A split in the Russian church in the 17th century brought an influx of Old Believers to the Baltics and elsewhere. They belong to the *bezpopovci* (without ministers) faction: during Russia's great repressions against the

figurative carvings and round log walls were all hewn with nothing more refined than an axe. It has a special fancy seat for the local German landlord and the front pews were more elaborately made for German workers. The native peasants were obliged to sit at the back – and were put in the stocks if they failed to attend services.

Because the Lutheran churches in Estonia and Latvia served the interests of the overlords, the Herrnhuters, or United Brethren Church, gained many followers during the 18th and 19th centuries. Services were conducted in farmers' houses or specially-built prayer halls and it became known as "the people's church", with an emphasis on education and religious enlightenment.

The United Brethren's activities diminished during the middle of the 19th century as pressure was put on them by both the Lutheran church and the tsar who won some conversions to Orthodoxy after promising support for the farmers' interests against the German land barons. After Poland failed to gain independence in the 1863 uprising, the tsarist government also fell heavily on Old Believers, whom it looked on as renegades, and Catholics, whom it hought were a threat to the empire. A huge building programme brought a crop of onion-domed churches including the Othodox cathedrals of the Holy

even became involved in the old pagan religions, a romantic revival which was wound up in the independence movements. After World War I and the break with Russia the countries formed independent Evangelical Lutheran churches, while all the Catholic churches came under the direct subordination of the Pope.

Jewish populations were well established in the Baltic region, which was one of the world's largest Yiddish language centres. Vilnius, the "Jerusalem" of Lithuania, had 98 synagogues, and there were synagogues in nearly every town in the countryside where a large proportion of the shops and small businesses were Jewish-run. Almost the en-

Theophany of Our Lord in Riga (1844) and the Alexander Nevski in Tallinn (1900). Many can be seen, abandoned, throughout the countryside today. There are still a few dozen Orthodox congregations who conduct their services in Latvian and Estonian.

Towards the end of the 19th century the first Baptist churches appeared in Estonia and Latvia, and around the turn of the century Seventh Day Adventists and other Protestant sects arrived. At that time people changed their convictions quite freely and

Left, Krishnas on the streets of Vilnius. **Above**, Judrenai Catholic church, Lithuania.

tire population was deported or killed during the Nazi occupation: more than 200,000 died in Vilnius; Estonia was the only country Hitler triumphantly declared *Judenfrei*. Though some of the synagogue buildings around the countries remain, it is hard to identify them. One or two synagogues have re-opened in the capitals to serve the 30,000 or so who have not yet left on their hoped-for emigration, and the one in Riga has been beautifully restored.

The church underground: During the Soviet years, all church properties and holdings were nationalised and many churches became concert halls or museums. St Casimir's in Vilnius was turned into a Museum of Atheism, and Riga's Orthodox cathedral became a planetarium and café. The state continually interfered with the works of the church and those who attended it: their careers were in jeopardy, and their children would be banned from higher education.

Even though the Soviet rule was harsh, local authorities in the Baltics were more lenient and liberal compared with the Soviet heartland. There were many more working churches in Riga than in Leningrad, which had nearly three times the population. Because it was easier to register a church and educate children in the Baltics, many Baptists, Adventists, Pentecostals and other be-

lievers emigrated from Russia, the Ukraine and elsewhere.

The Roman Catholic Seminary in Riga educated all new priests from the entire Soviet Union, except for Lithuania. Other institutions survived, such as the only Orthodox nunnery in the Soviet Union, at Kuremäe in Estonia. The church battled on, and many priests, evangelists and activists were imprisoned for their work. Estonia lost more than two-thirds of its clergy in the first Soviet years. The Catholics, along with the smaller Protestant churches (Baptist, Adventist and Pentecostal), were most successful in organising their opposition and keeping in touch.

A group of Catholic priests regularly published the underground *Chronicles of the Lithuanian Catholic Church*, which informed the world about repression and human rights violations. The people, too, remained resilient. The Hill of Crosses, just north of Šiauliai on the Kaunas-Riga highway, is not as tall as it once was. This bizarre manifestation was bulldozed by the Soviets three times, and each time the crosses would return.

Changing congregations: Today the Baltics are still centres of religion. The Commonwealth of Independent States has its bishop's chair for the German Evangelical Lutheran church in Riga. Vilnius is re-establishing itself as one of Catholicism's citadels in Europe. People are returning to the church but things have changed. The Lutheran and other Protestant congregations have fallen in the intervening years, and many country churches have only a handful of worshippers. By contrast, the Catholic church, through its diligence, organisation and might, has held its flock. In Latvia, where there are nearly twice as many Lutheran as Catholic churches, the number of baptisms is now about the same, around 10,000 a year.

Everywhere there are still signs of the religious mix. In Trakai is the church of the Karaites, a surviving Jewish sect of Tatars who arrived in the 14th century at the behest of Grand Duke Vytautas. There are Muslims and Mormons, Uniats and *dievertu*, pagan Latvians whose churches are holy places around sacred oaks.

Not all the ecclesiastic splendours of the Baltics are on the beaten track. The splendid Pažaislis monastery must be sought out near Kaunas. One of Riga's architectural secrets is hidden behind the Academy of Sciences: the Church of Jesus, the Lutheran bishop's seat, is a beautiful wooden octagonal building, in the empire style, from 1822. The largest wooden church in the country, it is 90 ft (27 metres) wide and has eight ionic columns supporting elliptical domes. And when you have seen everything in Estonia, acquire a Russian visa and visit Pechora in the Plesavas region, which both countries claim. A great fortress wall encircles this powerful 15th-century monastery, an abiding symbol of the church's struggles and endurance.

Left, Mother Superior, Kuremäe. **Right**, Lutheran confirmation in Šilutė, Lithuania.

Folklore is at the very heart of Baltic culture. Indeed, until the 19th century, folklore in effect *was* Baltic culture, because German and Polish rule from the Middle Ages on had meant that no real literary culture in the Baltic languages had been able to evolve. In the 19th and 20th centuries, the Baltic scholars and writers who developed the new Baltic literatures and cultural identities did so above all on the basis of peasant folklore.

Fortunately this folklore was of immense richness, especially in the field of music. Songs appear to have played an important part in the worship of the ancient Baltic gods, and ever since have been at the heart of the Balts' sense of themselves. Almost every Baltic village has its own choir, many of them of a professional standard. State and public occasions often begin with folksongs. As a Latvian *daina*, or folksong, has it:

I was born singing, I grew up singing,
I lived my life singing.
My soul went singing
Into the garden of God's sons.

A visit to some sort of folk-performance is recommended for any visitor. Fortunately, apart from the major festivals, performances of one sort or another go on all year round. From the beginning, folklore and the Baltic national movements were mixed up together. The first Estonian and Latvian national song festivals, held in 1869 and 1873 respectively, were also political events of the first importance, symbolising the reawakening and unity of the new nations. The independent republics between 1920 and 1940 turned them into great official symbolic events.

The Singing Revolution: Under Soviet rule, these festivals were among the very few ways in which national feeling could be legally displayed, although several of the more patriotic songs were banned. After Mikhail Gorbachev came to power, these songs were restored, and the various folklore festivals became key symbols of the national independence movements in a process which has been dubbed, especially in Estonia, the

Preceding pages: a senior citizens' singsong in Lithuania. **Left,** folk-art painting, Lithuania. **Right,** Saaremaa wedding socks.

"Singing Revolution". It was at the "Baltica" festival in 1987 that the old national flags of the former republics were publicly displayed together for the first time under Soviet rule – that is, without those responsible being promptly arrested.

The national song festivals are astonishing affairs, with the choirs numbered in thousands and the audiences in tens or even hundreds of thousands – a large proportion of the population. The air of such an occasion, almost a feast of racial harmony, can

become oppressive, but a charming element of informality is added by the tradition that, after every song, girls run on to the stage to give flowers to their favourite conductors.

Folklore was also the key to rediscovering, or reinventing, the beliefs and society of the pagan Balts which existed before the Christian conquest. These seem to have been based on the idea that the world was itself created partly through song and story-telling:

"Once upon a time, the Lord God walked
through the world, telling stories and
curses, asking riddles..."

In our time, scholars like the great French-Lithuanian semiologist, Algirdas Julien

Greimas, have used surviving folktales to try to establish the nature of the ancient gods and their worship: Perkūnas or Pērkons, god of thunder, akin to the Slavic Perun and the Scandinavian Thor; Laima and Māra, goddesses of luck (good and bad, because Laima, like some Indian goddesses, also brings the plague); Aušra (the Dawn), and many lesser gods and goddesses, some of them figures in their own right, others merely aspects of the main divinities.

The 14th-century priest Peter of Dusburg wrote that the Balts of his time "worship all of creation... sun, moon, stars, thunder, birds, even four-legged creatures down to the toad. They have their sacred forests, fields and

waters, in which they do not dare to cut wood, or work, or fish."

Until the 18th century, Catholic priests in Lithuania were still cutting down sacred oaks in an effort to stop their worship, and until the 20th century, some of the ancient spirits lived on in folk tales about forest spirits such as the leprechaun-like *Kaukai*, the *Aitvarai* (who can lead people to hidden treasure) and the *Barzdukai*, a form of bearded gnome. The *Kaukai* were originally neutral spirits who could be won over with gifts. Later, however, they came to be identified with the Christian devil. The Devils Museum in Kaunas, unique in the world, contains a magnificent collection of portrayals of the Devil by Lithuanian folk-artists. Unfortunately, this is also to some extent a museum of historical anti-semitism, since most of the devils are obviously meant to be Jewish.

Midsummer frolics: By the 18th century, awareness of the old Baltic religions as such had disappeared or become completely mixed up with Christian beliefs. Thus the great pagan festival of Midsummer Night was renamed St John's Eve, but it has retained many of the old pagan legends and customs, especially those connected with fertility. One of these is that on that particular night and only then, a flowering fern appears, and if a boy and a girl together find it, it will bring their heart's desire. Of course, ferns don't actually flower, but the tradition is a good excuse for young couples to go off together into the forest at night.

For many centuries, Christian priests and ministers did their best to stamp out much of Baltic folklore, precisely because it embodies so much paganism. The earliest records of Latvian folksongs are provided in evidence for 17th-century witch-trials, and it has been suggested that "witches" at this period were in fact the linear descendants of the old pagan priests and sorcerers.

In the 1920s and '30s, efforts were made by some people to resurrect the old pagan religions. In Latvia, this took the form of the *dievturība* movement, which continues to this day. Because in the 1930s the movement was closely associated with Latvian fascism, it was savagely persecuted under Soviet rule. Its ideology today remains intensely nationalist. "We have always believed that Latvia should be only for the Latvians," one of its leaders has said. "God is a Latvian – or at least, our god is."

Its theology maintains the existence of a single godhead who takes different forms. This, however, is a modern construct which is only very partially derived from the real, but almost forgotten, ancient pagan religion. The Dievturi number only a few hundred, but their past sufferings and the purity of their folksinging gives them a prestige.

A certain holistic, pagan-influenced mysticism, a willingness to see divinity in all the works of nature, has however been very characteristic of all three Baltic cultures up to our own time. This is true both of those authors who hark back directly to the ancient traditions, and those, like the Estonian poet Jaan Kaplinski, who render them into wider, universal terms – in his case, neo-Buddhist.

The new attitude to folk-traditions in Europe dates back to the later 18th century and the rise of Romanticism. Baltic folklore played a part in this cultural shift, because a key figure in it was the German philosopher Johann Gottfried Herder, who was profoundly moved by Latvian folksongs and stories when a Protestant minister and teacher in Riga in the 1760s. His influence led to later generations of research by Baltic German scholars and, in the mid-19th century, their work was taken over by the first generations of the native Baltic intelligentsia.

dreds of thousands of examples. These give clues to an ancient tradition: for example, beer-mugs were decorated with "male" symbols, such as suns and horses.

Lithuania has a particularly rich tradition of folk-carving, which is summed up in the intricately carved wooden crosses to be found outside many villages. Covered with ancient symbols, they resemble the pagan totem poles which they probably originally were. The carved crosses on the famous Hill of Crosses at Šiauliai is an apotheosis of Catholic piety and of Lithuanian nationalism, but also of ancient pagan symbolism. Another sight to watch out for in the Lithuanian countryside is Rupintojelis ("The Thinker"), a mournful

Their first task was the recording and codification. In Latvia, this process is connected above all with the name of Krišjānis Barons, who assembled the *dainas*, or Latvian folksongs. The 217,996 items form one of the largest collections of oral folklore in the world. After the formation of the independent states after 1918, the governments and universities also set out to collect folk-art.

The Estonian National Museum in Tartu (now returned after being confiscated for 46 years by the Soviet Air Force) houses hun-

figure, now presented as Christ, but much older than Christianity. Removed under Soviet rule, these are now being restored.

However, the task of recovering the meaning of such figures, and the ancient Baltic tradition in general, is an intensely difficult one, both because of the long burial by Christianity, and the effects of modernisation, especially the brutal modernisation which took place under Soviet rule. One of the reasons why many Estonians wish to recover the area of Petseri, or Pečory, captured by Estonia from Russia in 1920 and transferred back by Stalin in 1944, is that the small Setu minority who live there, because of their

Left, festive crown, Lithuania. <u>Above</u>, Latvian sashes; a wedding knot tied by Lāčplēsis's belt.

greater backwardness, preserve folk traditions which have been lost in Estonia itself.

The first major guide to Estonian folk stories (as opposed to folksongs, which had been published in various collections from Herder on) was *Old Estonian Fairy-Tales*, compiled by Friedrich Kreutzwald and first published in 1866. It is still vastly popular in Estonia, and is held to have contributed to the creation of an Estonian prose-style independent of the German models which it had previously imitated.

In 1861, Kreutzwald published the "national epic" *Kalevipoeg* ("Son of Kalev"), a reworking in verse of stories about a giant hero; the work was explicitly intended to

and several other works. Under the first Latvian republic, the Order of Lāčplēsis was the highest state award, and this is to be restored. Kangars, the traitor in the epic, has become a generic name for traitors, while Laimdota, Lāčplēsis's beloved, has given her name to boutiques and hairdressers, and Spīdola, the witch, to ships and yachts.

Pumpurs also gave the ancient Latvians a pantheon of pagan gods, like the classical Olympus – quite unhistorical, but another passport to European respectability in his time. It is to this period that there dates the contemporary habit of giving children "traditional" pagan names, like Laima or Vytautas (after the Lithuanian medieval Grand Duke).

help build up a national spirit, and prove to a sceptical world that the Estonian folk-tradition was capable of an epic, then held to be the highest literary form. As with the Finnish *Kalevala*, debate has raged ever since.

Invented gods: The *Kalevipoeg* is still taught in every Estonian school, but otherwise its influence has progressively diminished. This has been far less the case with the Latvian national epic, *Lāčplēsis* ("The Bear-Slayer"), by Andrējs Pumpurs, in which another mythical hero is made a leader of the medieval Latvian resistance against the German invaders. *Lāčplēsis* has since become the theme of a verse play by Jānis Rainis, a rock-opera,

Today, this rich folkloric tradition is threatened from two directions: the first is by Western mass culture, especially influential in countries as poor as the Baltic states have become under Soviet rule. On the other side, there is also a danger that the over-use of folklore on official occasions, in schools and so on, may eventually drain it of the joyous spontaneity which so far has kept Baltic folklore alive and part of Baltic life, and not – as so often in the West – either a museum-piece or an artificially revived hobby.

Above, song festival in Tallinn, an exuberant nationalistic and inspirational event.

THE SINGING TREE

Most traditional musical instruments are common throughout the Baltics and Eastern Europe: the goat-horn, whistle, flute, reed, violin, squeeze-box and zither. Other instruments belong to particular regions: the bagpipe in Estonia and Latvia's Protestant part, the hammer dulcimer in Lithuania and Latvia's Catholic part, and the *hiukannel* or bowed harp in the Estonian islands. But one instrument unique to the Baltic lands is a kind of board zither with between five and 12 iron or natural fibre strings. Its history can be traced with some certainty back at least 3,000 years and its Baltic names have supposedly originated from the proto-Baltic word *kantles,* meaning "the singing tree": *kantele* in Finnish, *kannel* in Estonian, *kandla* in Livonian, *kokles* in Latvian and *kankles* in Lithuanian.

This is supposed to be the instrument of the gods and, according to folk beliefs, the tree for its wood must be cut when someone has died but isn't yet buried. In a fairy-tale a youth helps an old man who turns out to be a god and he rewards the good-hearted lad with this particular instrument.

Thus the Apollonic, heavenly aura and the fine, deeply touching tone quality have made *kokles* a symbol of national music for Estonians, Latvians and Lithuanians. Unfortunately the playing of the original instrument has almost died out. In the beginning of the 20th century *kokles* developed into a zither of 25 to 33 strings, like a harp. "Modernisation" during the Soviet time resulted in a soprano, alto, tenor and bass *kokles* family. Folksong arrangements and compositions of questionable musical quality were played and presented as the national music.

A folklore revival in the 1970s and 1980s restored an interest in traditional instruments. Many of them, such as the bagpipe, jew's-harp, whistle, flute, reed, horn, clappers and rattles, are made by enthusiasts and played informally. They are used by both solo performers and folklore groups and it is now hard to imagine a celebration of calendar customs, folk-dance parties or folklore festivals without them.

The most important festivals are the summer and winter solstice celebrations and there are large gatherings at such festivals as the "Baltica", which involves all three Baltic republics and sometimes includes Scandinavian countries, too. More local but no less exciting are "Skamba,

skamba kankliai" in Lithuania, and the children's and young people's folklore festival, "Pulka eimu, pulka teku", in Latvia. There are also a number of festivals which are associated with individual towns and villages.

In Lithuania visitors should try to listen to *sutartines* which is endless sonoric meditation, both vocal and instrumental. For a while it seemed this unique ancient polyphony style had become extinct, but recently it has been revived by folklore groups. The instrumental version of *sutartines* is played on *kankles*, pan-pipes, trumpets or horns.

Primitive musical instruments are usually made by the players themselves. The more sophisticated ones such as the *kannel/kokles/kankles,* bag-

pipes, flutes, violins, accordions and zithers are made by just a few skilled masters. Being in great demand, these instruments are not easy to obtain, though they can be found at fairs and folk-crafts festivals where there is also a good variety of bird, devil and animal-shaped clay whistles, usually played by children.

The most popular musical instruments in the Baltics are the accordion and, of course, the guitar, which are played at family celebrations and informal parties. Catholic and Lutheran churches mostly have organs with distinctive characteristics. The organ of Riga Dom is recognised world-wide, while those in the rural areas can have their own unique charm. ∎

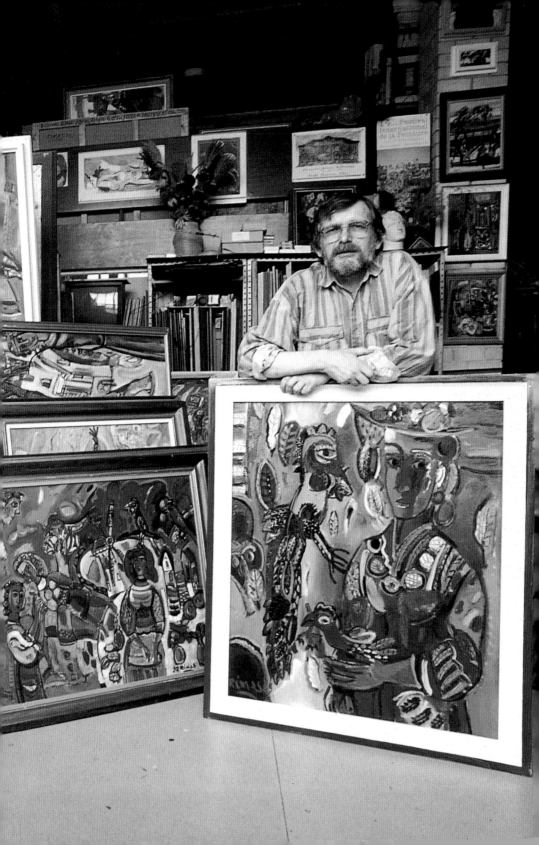

Unhappy the land that needs heroes, said the radical German poet Bertolt Brecht. Yet the Baltic states could hardly have survived 50 years of political and cultural subjugation without consolation from folklore and literature. Heroes from old legends embodying the national fate, and painting, poetry and music generally, offered freedom and a refuge to those who felt the Soviet occupation had snatched away their homeland.

"Internal emigration" happened almost regardless of formal education. Theatres, opera and ballet were packed – and packed with half-hidden national significance, which the censors either ignored or missed. Writers for decades exploited communist subsidy to keep national pride and independent thought alive. They fostered the climate for independence which in the 1980s popular culture – rock music – finally brought to the surface. Banned under communism, it united classical composers, politicians and people in a mass gesture of defiance, thus earning itself a unique place in Baltic history.

Today, the bubble has burst. Without a patron state, the cultural world is struggling financially, as it is in all the former Soviet empire. Suddenly creative artists are no longer waged and need to finance themselves by selling their talents and wares: and this is no time at all to be trying to interest the Baltic public in high-priced quality merchandise. Painters, given choice studio flats in the Soviet system, have had to look elsewhere for work. Music publishers have gone to the wall. For writers, an irony is that although they can now at last freely write and publish what they want in their own language, they enjoy only a fraction of the market the Russian language used to offer. There is not much money to fund opera and ballet.

The quality of work is also suffering. Right up until independence, there was a reactive energy to be tapped: a well of rage and sadness that could charge talent with creativity and power. Painters and sculptures could deal in allegories, playwrights and song-

writers could pit their imaginations against the censors; filmmakers were not short of documentary material and song-writers were inspired by the challenge of pulling the wool over the censors' eyes.

In the absence of an alternative political structure, intellectuals and artists have been looked to for leadership. Baltic writers, painters, musicians, sculptors, composers and philosophers have long been prime movers in public life. Raimond Pauls, one of Latvia's better known pianists and composer of many

pop hits, was made first minister of culture. Musicology was no bar to Vytautas Landsbergis becoming president of Lithuania, nor was being a novelist anything but a plus when Lennart Meri ran (successfully) for the Estonian presidency. In fact, the achievements are often viewed together: a musician or artist's popularity frequently depends on their perceived current standing in the national political debate.

Roots of literature: By their comprehensive involvement, intellectuals and creative artists have nurtured the idea of independent nationhood since it first emerged in the early 19th century when the three languages began

Preceding pages: Rimas-Zigmas Bičiūnas, Vilnius painter. Left, Kati Ivaste, Tallinn ballerina. Above, Māra Zalīte, Latvian poet.

to be written down. The freedom to write, and to express a national sentiment, arrived in a burst of romantic novels and epic verses from which the modern culture took off.

Latvian Andrējs Pumpurs told in *Lāčplēsis* the tale of the bear-slayer drowned in the River Daugava, who when he regains life, will ensure the eternal freedom of his people. Friedrich Kreuzwald fathered the national Estonian epic, the *Kalevipoeg*. A tsarist ban on their printed languages fettered mid-century development but a Lithuanian priest named Maironis wrote landmark lyrics, *Pavarasario balsai* (*Voices of Spring*, 1885), expressing national striving and romantic sentiment. His involvement was of symbolic

1838 Richard Wagner managed the German Opera and Drama theatre. Since Russian laws closed Vilnius University from 1832 to 1905, many culturally active Lithuanians also lived in Riga.

Tartu, on Estonian soil, educated Balts of all origins. Students of the 1850s included Latvia's Krišjānis Barons, who first collected the Latvian folk songs call *dainas*, and his friend Krišjānis Valdemārs and Juris Alunāņš, who founded Latvian theatre. Much Latvian effort went into overcoming perceived German colonial condescension. Budding Estonian culture was less adversarial. Many Germans teaching and studying in enlightened Tartu shared Estonian fascina-

significance, for it was generally priests and doctors who established the Baltic written cultures, first in German, later in Estonian, Latvian and Lithuanian.

The Baltic peoples could boast early of high-quality European centres of learning and a fertile intellectual ambience. In Lithuania the Jesuits created Vilnius University in 1579, and in 1632 the Swedes commanded a university in Tartu. Riga, meanwhile, acquired cosmopolitan cultural importance. The East-Prussian-born Johann Gottfried Herder (1744–1803), the translator and author of the idea of nationality, was a popular young preacher at the Dom cathedral. From 1837 to

tion with the native language and themes. But for young Estonians the birth of their nation was above all romantic. As Kristjan Jaak Peterson (1801–1822), a poet and Tartu graduate living in Riga, declared:

Why should not my country's tongue
Soaring through the gale of song,
Rising to the heights of heaven,
Find its own eternity?

Peterson's question has remained relevant to the present day.

Literature led the emerging 19th-century arts with the novel of social realism. The Lithuanians Jonas Biliūnas, writing under his own name, and the famous assumed names of Julija Žemaitė, Juozas Vaižgantas and Antanas Vienuolis all described peasant life. In Estonia the novelist Eduard Vilde and the playwright August Kitzberg exercised a similar function while the two brothers Kaudzīte wrote the first Latvian novel, *The Times of the Land Surveyors* (1879).

Exiled genius: Then suddenly from Latvia emerged a world-class genius, Jānis Rainis (1865–1929). A complex, multi-talented figure, lyrical poet, dramatist, translator (of *Faust*), political activist and cultural founding father, Rainis wrote his best plays in Switzerland, where he fled after his involvement in the 1905 Revolution. His 15-year refugee fate set a sad precedent for future

romantic poet and early feminist, is almost equally revered. Both are remembered in a museum in their Jūrmala home.

To Latvian literature, always close to the folk tradition and rustic life, the terse, philosopical *daina* gave a lyrical, inward quality. The dramas of Rūdolfs Blaumanis (1863–1908), also a master short-story writer, set a high artistic and psychological standard. Blaumanis's folk comedy *The Days of the Tailor in Silmaāi* (1902) is still staged outdoors every midsummer. Affected by his German education, Jānis Poruks (1871–1911) introduced introspection, melancholy and dreams to Latvian poetry and prose. Kārlis Skalbe (1879–1945), called a Latvian Hans

Baltic literature. His play *Fire and Night* (1905) is a dramatic statement of the Latvian spirit. *The Sons of Jacob* (1919) deals with Rainis's own conflict between art and politics. Jānis Tilbergs's portrait of Rainis in the Riga art gallery conveys his authority as a national elder, and also the personal loneliness, expressed in his poetry. Modern Latvian literature still rotates around this giant figure, while his wife Aspazija (1868–1943), a

Left, Jaan Kross, Estonia's premier novelist. **Above**, Monika Biciuniene, Lithuanian painter, with portrait of Vytautas Ciplijauskas; Egilis Straume, saxophonist, at Riga Academy of Music.

Christian Andersen for his allegorical tales, is also an exquisite poet and short-story teller. Other poets include the symbolist Fricis Barda, Anna Brigadere (1861–1933), and Aleksandrs Čaks (1901–50), whose modern Imagist style burst forth with Latvia's 1918 independence and brushed the realities of urban life in Riga with lyrical excitement.

Lithuanian literature did not develop such early power and variety, which may account for its greater openness to European currents. The literary group Four Winds, formed by Kazys Binkis (1893–1932), was devoted to Futurism; others imitated German Expressionism. Vincas Krėvė-Mickievičius (1882–

1954) was, however, a great prose writer and dramatist whose work continued in exile. Krėvė, having briefly become Foreign Minister, fled in 1940. He left unfinished his epic masterpiece *The Sons of Heaven and Earth*.

The Young Estonia or Noor-Esti movement,, devoted to raising Estonian literary standards to a European level, flourished from 1905 to the middle of World War I. The prosaist and traveller Friedebert Tuglas (1886–1971) brought the world to Estonian readers through his romantic exotic stories, and conveyed the problematic existence of the artist. A. H. Tammsaare (1878–1940), author of the huge novel *Truth and Justice*, and influenced by Dostoevsky, Knut Hamsun

and Bernard Shaw, has been called the greatest Estonian prose writer this century. A more radical experimental literary group, Siuru, nurtured the spirits of poets Jaan Oks (1884–1918) and Marie Under (1883–1977). Under, who spent the Soviet period in exile, is still Estonia's most highly regarded poet.

Romance and mysticism: Foreign influences and rural, national life stimulated Baltic visual arts and music. National Romanticism, a style acquired in the 1900s in St Petersburg, replaced old-fashioned academic painting and influenced architecture, taking over from European art nouveau. When that dreamy style became exhausted, the new schools of

national painting properly began. The Baltic national romantic style incorporates folk heroes and legends and recalls world-class painters from Munch to Beardsley, Klimt to Boecklin and Bakst. In this vein, over Latvia's Rudolfs Perle (1875–1917) and Estonia's Nikolai Triik (1884–1940), towers the Lithuanian mystical painter and musician Mikalojus Konstantinas Čiurlionis (1875–1911), a Baltic William Blake.

In thin, richly-coloured oils Čiurlionis created symbolic landscapes suggesting a mystical universe, with motifs such as the wise serpent from Lithuanian folklore. He conceived many of his memorable paintings as linked musical movements or as cycles of life and death, day and night. They are extraordinary pantheistic, poetic distillations of human life. Čiurlionis's own nature was rich and varied. He travelled widely, wrote for newspapers, and almost single-handedly founded the national cultural life before dying aged 36. His pictures can be seen and his music heard at his own museum in Kaunas.

After Čiurlionis Lithuanian painting, in the hands of the Kaunas-based *Ars* Group, grew into a satisfyingly complex art of landscape and portraiture, abreast of European developments, and using a rich, dark palette. Emerald green, dark pink, mauve and a touch of yellow evolved into national colours, and a persistent motif was the inclusion of folkloric wooden figures and toys.

The first Estonian art exhibition was held in Tartu in 1906, out of which emerged Triik and the Expressionist Konrad Magi (1878–1925). Magi co-founded the Pallas art school in Tartu, which produced the thoroughly individual painter, best-known for his graphics, Eduard Wiiralt (1898–1954).

But any Baltic visitor interested in painting must return to Latvia where professional painting became established when Vilhelms Purvītis (1872–1945), Jānis Rozentāls (1866–1917) and Jānis Valters (1869–1932) joined European Impressionist, Fauve and German Expressionist tendencies to their own distinctive approach to landscape and portraiture. Their influence extended to Lithuania and their talents, combined with those of the next generation they inspired, make a visit to Riga Art Gallery memorable.

Purvītis, founder of the Riga Art Academy, captured the Latvian landscape but most of his work was burned in Jelgava during the war. Valters, who studied in Germany, painted landscapes coloured by subjective mood and represented in stark Fauve colours. Rozentāls's work, now Renoirish, now Impressionist, now in the vein of Purvītis depicting Latvian nature, climaxes in his portraiture. Generally the Latvian portrait tradition is outstanding. Rozentāls's rendering of his mother, and the painting by Voldemārs Zeltiņš (1879–1905) of opera singer Pavils Gruzdna, using Purvītis's pale Latvian colours, lead into the later highly-coloured avant-garde movement. Artists such as Oto Skulme, Leo Svemp and Jānis Tīdemanis bring this rich period to life.

The fine arts of the pre-war Baltic nations

composition, *In the Forest*. The symphonic work suggests to a modern ear Bruckner, Mahler and Sibelius, but Čiurlionis was a distinct genius. Later he reworked many folk-songs, wrote choral pieces, and organised national musical life in Vilnius.

From the First National Awakening all the Baltic cultures developed strong traditions in choral singing. The first operas were written on national themes in the early 20th century, establishing opera as a popular but conservative genre. Baltic symphonic music otherwise evolved from the St Petersburg conservatoire, echoing to the memory of Tchaikovsky and Rimsky-Korsakov. Outstanding were Latvia's Emil Darziņš, par-

differ markedly in colour and mood. Rationalism and abstractionism were always present in Estonia, where the 1923 Estonian Artists Group was strongly drawn to Cubism and Bauhaus and art deco, whereas Latvia took a more determined emotional path.

Notable music: Čiurlionis is a founder of modern Lithuanian culture also through his music. An intensely active year at the Leipzig Conservatoire produced works still recorded today, including the String Quartet in C minor and the first Lithuanian symphonic

Left, altar painting, Dundaga, by **Jānis Rošentāls**.
Above, *Vietys preliudas* by M. K. **Čiurlionis**.

ticularly his *Melancholy Waltz*, influenced by Tchaikovsky and Sibelius, and Estonia's Artur Kapp who wrote symphonies and oratorios. Germany also initiated such figures as Latvia's Emils Mangeles into western romanticism. Latvians consider Alfreds Kalninc a musical father-figure for his varied work, both romantic and choral. His son Jānis also became a composer, later well-known in Canada as John Kalniņš.

In all the arts Scandinavian influence between the wars was very strong. An equally strong sense of alienation was felt from the Russian soul – the so-called "asiatic principle". Among the other arts which flourished were ballet, in the Russian tradition. In the applied sphere, the Baltic states notably excelled in graphic art and in book publishing and illustration.

The aesthetic spirit: In architecture the distinct characters of nations are most visible. The Lithuanian spirit includes a hankering after lost grandeur, and some Lithuanians would love their Central European capital, with its baroque and neoclassical buildings, to be known as the Athens of the North. The rational Estonians combine their functional buildings with a fairy-tale German Old Town and a skyline outstanding in its aesthetic balance and beauty. Perhaps they have most successfully fitted their national artistic spirit

vincialism. The Latvians Anšlāvs Eglītis, Zenta Maurina and Mārtiņš Zīverts, the Lithuanians Antanas Vaiculaitis and Krėvė and Estonia's Marie Under continued the best pre-war literary traditions of theatre, prose and poetry abroad. But many writers died in the war, or shortly after. A literature of suffering and displacement, recounting the mass deportation of artists and intellectuals to Siberia, emerged only in the 1980s, though in 1946 *The Forest of Gods* recounted the experience of Lithuanian intellectuals in a German camp with irony and humour. The Estonian Jaan Kross (born 1920), imprisoned by the Nazis, spent nine years in Russian camps and his novels and short stories

into the modern world. The bourgeois quality of Riga is much more perplexing, diluted by closeness to countryside and modern poverty, and heightened by the creative arts and the density and mixture of population.

All the Baltic cultures reach out to the larger world through theatre, frequently devoting half their repertoire to world classics, with many adaptations also from prose. A strong tradition of open-air performances, with real animals on stage, persists in Latvia alongside rather wordy poetic theatre.

After the war alien ideology and unwanted exile cramped development of arts which were just emerging from an inevitable pro-

are a fine account of his country's history.

Stalin's Socialist Realism might have destroyed the Baltic arts but they showed lurking independence by managing mostly to avoid the official prescription. Latvia's talented Andres Upits and Vilis Lacis turned controversial Soviet apologists, as did the much-appreciated Lithuanian woman poet Salomeja Neris.

Soviet avant-garde: A new creative generation emerged in the 1960s, during the Khrushchev thaw, ready to exploit the easier position of the arts on the fringe of a centralised empire. The Baltics became the home of the Soviet avant-garde, with productions of

Becket and Ionesco, and in the mid-1980s open publication of George Orwell's *Nineteen Eighty-Four*. This relatively liberal climate pre-empted dissident activity. It also produced notable opera singers and ballet dancers, in particular Mikhail Baryshnikov and Boris Godonov from Riga, and a proliferation of bold, immensely popular poetry against the official tide.

Music managed to experiment with atonality and minimalism. Communist Poland, where Baltic composers were allowed to travel, was a rich source of ideas and a window on the West. The coincidence of modern ideas with folksong atonality was carefully exploited. Estonian music has since

world-class producers, represented today by Jonas Vaitkus and Josas Nekrosius. Poet Paul-Eerik Rummo's *Cinderella Game* is the best of a flourishing absurdist and fringe Estonian theatre tradition. Estonia is also well-known for its cartoons. Adolfs Šapiro and Pēteris Petersons are active, cosmopolitan figures in Latvian theatre.

Popular present-day writers include the Latvian poet and children's writer Imants Ziedonis and the prosaist Zigmund Skuins, and Lithuania's Juozas Aputis, much suppressed by the Soviets. The novels of Lithuanians Vytautas Bubnys and Vytautas Martinkus, otherwise in quite different styles, show the continuing attraction of folk themes.

flourished, in the person of émigré composer Arvo Part. The Latvian conductor Mariss Jansons, and from Lithuania choral composer Velio Tormis and modernist Osvaldas Balakauskas, also enjoy world renown.

The later Soviet period brought more abstractionism into painting, from Jonas Svazas and Dalia Kosciunaite in Lithuania, to Mari Tabaka in Latvia. Estonia's Mari Kurismaa sought a refuge from absurd, punitive Soviet reality in ideal geometric poise.

Lithuanian theatre, meanwhile, generated

Estonia's Jaan Kross and the poet Jaan Kaplinski have both acquired an international following.

Post-occupation, rediscovering the arts of the 1920s and '30s, suppressed in the Soviet period, has been disappointing: the sleeping beauty has nevertheless aged. Some writers say the need to repair the human psyche is as acute as the desire to mend history. They also want to make the Baltic cultures better known, through or despite their little-known languages. But economic problems loom and the languages are a barrier. Meanwhile, Western mass electronic and pulp book culture knocks at the door.

Left, Pēteris Plakidis, Latvian composer. **Above**, Leonids Vigners, Latvian conductor.

After the Soviet Union fell apart, Estonians, Latvians and Lithuanians found themselves, for the first time in 50 years, longing for the future. It promised the best that democratic capitalism had to offer: vibrant economies, higher standards of living and responsive government. But these things don't happen overnight and the immediate future hasn't been nearly as good as advertised.

Baltic observers now believe that the dramatic social and economic changes will come in perhaps five or 10 years. Then, say the most optimistic, the Baltic states could be flourishing little Hong Kongs, dynamic and wealthy. The biggest hope, expressed regularly by Balts even before independence, was that the three countries could become economic bridges between the former Soviet Union and the West.

Already an estimated 85 percent of all trade west of the Ural mountains runs through the Baltics. And of six ice-free ports used by Russia to export its rich supply of raw materials, four are in the Baltic states: Kleipėda in Lithuania and Liepāja, Ventspils and Riga in Latvia. Tallinn in Estonia can be kept open by ice-breakers if necessary in winter months. At Latvia's main port, just outside the capital, Riga, the harbour cranes are busier than at any time in their history. The upturn has been caused by increased shipments of coal to the West from the resource-rich CIS states. Ironically, this boom has been fuelled by the economic troubles faced by coal mines elsewhere in Europe. As high-cost coal output decreases, producers such as Germany and the United Kingdom are ordering cheaper coal from the East, which means that more coal than ever before is being channelled through Baltic ports.

Maurice Cartwright, a British entrepreneur who founded a joint venture with a Kazak coal mining company, has been using Riga's port since March 1991. He says that his firm, called Kazmin International, is shipping as much as 20,000 tons of coal from Kazakstan through Riga every month. He is bullish on the prospects for trade through the

Preceding pages: sea traffic, Tallinn. **Left,** combine harvester, Latvia. **Right,** Tallinn's port.

Latvian port, though it has limited capacity, handling only 700 tons of cargo an hour, compared with a main port like Rotterdam, which can handle 16,000 tons an hour. And though port authority bureaucracy is still maddening, Cartwright says it is not nearly as bad as bureaucracy he has dealt with elsewhere in the former Soviet Union.

If trade ever booms, as many Western experts predict, Estonia is in a position to benefit, too. It has the most technologically advanced port, Tallinn New Port, which was

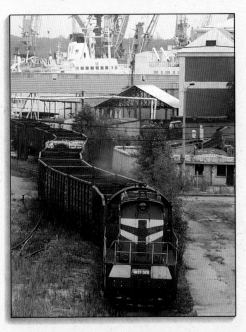

completed with Soviet funds a few years before it became obvious the empire was going to disintegrate It has a depth of 60 ft (18 metres).

Baltic highway: To fulfil the role of an East-West bridge, the Baltic states are also counting on a proposed highway system that will run from Tallinn, through Riga and Kaunas, to Warsaw. The road already exists, but it is being widened and resurfaced to meet international standards. It is hoped that the highway, dubbed "Via Baltica", will serve as the cheapest way for cargo to be transported from Scandinavia and St Petersburg to Central and Eastern Europe. Attracted by the economic potential of the inter-Baltic highway, Western companies, the majority of them from Scandinavia, have been building and renovating a whole variety of service stations, stores, hotels and restaurants along the road.

In 1990 the Finnish oil conglomerate Neste began to pump in millions of dollars, building sleek, Western-style service stations in all three capitals. The Swedish company Ake Larson Byggare AB has also built service stations in Tallinn for the Norwegian oil company Statoil and has the largest petrol station in the Baltic states outside Tallinn.

The Swedish telecommunications company Eriksson has also invested huge sums

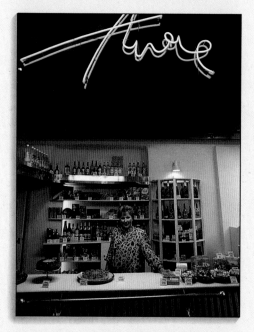

of money in a mobile telephone system for the Baltic states. Scandinavians have been involved in a number of hotel joint ventures and German and Austrian companies are also looking at Lithuania's tourist potential, particularly in the resorts and backwaters of its unspoilt coast.

The "Baltic bridge" concept doesn't stop with trade and inter-state commerce. Balts also see their countries, like Hong Kong and Taiwan, as financial and business bases for international investors who have an eye on lucrative former Soviet markets. The distinctly European capitals, Tallinn, Riga and Vilnius, should be more comfortable bases

for businessmen than, say, Moscow, Kiev or Tashkent and, if the banking systems improve, the capitals would offer launching points into the East.

The giant cereal-maker Kellogg has apparently been convinced already. It is building a processing plant near Riga and will initially sell its Latvian-made cereals in Latvia. For Kellogg, Latvia is a means to break into the much bigger, potentially far more lucrative Russian market. McDonald's, already established in the world's busiest restaurant in Moscow, is setting up a base in the Baltics, in Riga, where it plans three restaurants, plus a fourth in Tallinn, costing $3 million and employing 300 people.

Sympathetic observers here argue that Estonians, Latvians and Lithuanians will serve as ideal mediators for Westerners trying to crack Russian markets. "Balts understand Russians," say the Baltophiles, "and because they are Europeans themselves, they understand the West."

Foot in the door: John Battle, an American investor, has already taken the words to heart. His US-based company has invested hundreds of thousands of dollars in the Baltic States. Its most ambitious project is an office complex for Western businessmen in Tallinn's picturesque old town, despite some objections from local Estonians who fear that Western investors might overrun the country and buy all the best property. Battle admits that bureaucratic obstacles occasionally drive him crazy, but he chides other businessmen for waiting too long to strike at the opportunities here. "Now is the time for Western companies to get their foot in the door and prepare for the future," he says. "In the long run the Baltics will be profitable places to do business."

But there hasn't yet been a full-scale rush to invest. Western businessmen are intrigued about doing business in the Baltic states, but they remain wary about the overall economic situation and about the possibility of political instability.

"They didn't believe that new national currencies could work," said one American analyst. "They also don't believe that they can trust Baltic partners. There have been so many stories about people getting burned, businessmen here just don't have enough credibility."

Many international investors also say that

the Baltic market, with only 7 million people, isn't worth the effort. If they want to reach the Russian market, many wonder why they shouldn't just skip the Baltic bridge and go straight to Russia.

Most big-name companies are still just sniffing around or are making token investments. Car-makers such as General Motors, Honda and Mercedes, for instance, have opened dealerships in the Baltic states, but they have not considered building factories.

Despite the boast that they can do business with Russia and prosper by it, down deep the Balts don't trust their big eastern neighbour, while Russia, in turn, alleges that Baltic governments are practising discrimination.

lackadaisical attitudes to work and rampant incompetence constitute the greatest obstacle to economic success, not the lack of money, equipment or knowhow. The biggest question is whether Balts can grow out of the debilitating character flaws which developed during the Soviet era. Can they regain the dynamic and hard-working reputation they built up during the years of independence before World War II?

American investor John Battle believes that it will take one-and-a-half generations before typical Soviet attitudes are washed out of Baltic characters. "That's quite a long time," he said. "But on the other hand, it will take three time longer before characters

It has threatened to impose trade blockades if Russian-speakers aren't given full citizenship rights. There is an outside chance that they will be locked in disputes in the future, but, for the time being, a weak Russia has too much to lose to think about threatening the Baltic states.

Most Balts, however, understand that current hardships have little to do with outside enemies. They realise that what they have to battle against is themselves. As any locally-based businessman understands too well,

Left, Anre, a bright new restaurant in Riga.
Above, Vilnius's famed Stikliai restaurant.

change in Russia and in the rest of the former Soviet Union."

Balts encourage the comparison with the rest of the Soviet Union because they know that it makes them look so much better. They frequently point to their past as evidence that their futures are brighter than, say, Russia's. They take pains to explain that as independent, pro-free-market states in the 1920s and 1930s standards of living came close to Western European levels. Estonia's and Latvia's approached Sweden's and Denmark's, and surpassed Finland's.

"We did it before, we can do it again," is a common sentiment. "Unlike the Russians," say the Balts confidently, "we haven't forgotten how to work hard."

Unfortunately, the Balts have forgotten more than they like to admit. As more and more realise, economic conditions today are very different. In the 1920s and 1930s, Europeans needed more butter, milk and cheese and gladly imported it from the agrarian Baltics. Today, with dairy surpluses spilling out of warehouses throughout Europe, these products are needed like a hole in the head. The expected increase in agricultural production will ensure that Balts can always feed themselves, but they can forget exports.

Wood products: Economists here say that textiles and wood products, such as furniture

ful of Baltic mediators very rich. According to one press report in Estonia, middlemen who make deals between local suppliers and foreign buyers are making a profit of up to $400,000 a year. But the foreign demand is also driving up the price of trees beyond the reach of local furniture factories.

There is an existing electronics industry – the world's first miniature camera was made at VEF in Riga – and somewhat overconfident Balts have suggested that, like some poorer Asian countries, they could mass produce high-tech goods for export. The confidence that they can do anything the West can do probably comes from the tendency, even among Western analysts, to

and handicrafts, are the Baltics' best export prospects. The quality in these areas is indistinguishable from Western-made goods, according to Western experts, and they can compete right away with the West.

With few natural resources, the backbone of the export trade since independence has been trees, cut from the rich forest that spreads across all three Baltic states. Sweden and Finland have been buying them up, usually in the form of pulp, which is used to make paper, and Sweden is showing particular interest in local birch, from which superhigh quality paper is made. A boom in the export of wood resources has made a hand-

overrate Baltic economic potential. It is certainly true that the Baltics are, economically speaking, 10 times better off compared to the rest of the former Soviet Union. But the more important fact is that they are also 10 times worse off compared to the rest of the Western world. They don't come close in workmanship, infrastructure, banking, services, plumbing. There has been insufficient training in job skills. For years the Soviets imported Polish workers to renovate the old cities. Now embassies find they have had to bring in builders as well as materials to refurbish their residences.

"We will have a stable democracy and a

growth economy after only 15 years," predicts Trivimi Velliste, the Estonian Foreign Minister. "Only then, will you be able to start talking about prosperous, Western-looking nations."

Inevitable crash: Before then, there will be plummeting GNPs and sky-rocketing unemployment. The IMF predicted in early 1992 that GNP would fall by at least 20 percent within a few years, a result primarily of the cut-off of raw materials from Russia and the collapse of Eastern markets.

Hundreds of rusting Soviet-style monster factories as well as smaller businesses will be forced to close down. Some economists predict a corresponding rate of unemploy-

money, which has to be paid back at 7.6 percent interest, will be used to buy such essential imports as heating oil, agricultural chemicals and medical supplies.

Even before world financial institutions arrived on the scene to give them a hand, the three countries had gone a long way toward laying the foundation for free-markets. All three have passed wide-ranging legislation on corporate law, foreign investment, taxation and more. Estonia was also the first former Soviet republic to introduce its own national currency. Latvia and Lithuania soon followed on.

As for privatisation, the process has been fastest and most radical in Lithuania, which

ment at 30 percent or more. A large wandering mass of disaffected workers could also lead to political instability. The hope is that the inevitable economic crash will be more organised, more civilised. The creation of economic opportunities for all sectors of society would give people enough faith to persevere through the hard times.

In an effort to try to smooth out the road to free markets, the World Bank and the IMF have provided loans to the three Baltic states, the largest amount going to Lithuania. The

<u>Left</u>, brewery at Utena, which makes Lithuania's premier beer. <u>Above</u>, timber for export, Pärnu.

has otherwise been generally regarded as the economic slow-poke of the region. The government began selling off apartments and enterprises to private citizens in late 1991. Progress towards privatisation in Estonia and Lativa has been much slower, with parliaments locked in dispute over how exactly to proceed. Estonia's centre-right government has pledged to cut taxes, raise business confidence and, in general, speed up anything that looks like a free-market reform. It has also pledged to sweep out ex-bureaucrat flunkies from all ministries and government departments. In contrast, the Lithuanians threw out their more radical government in favour of reformed communist politicians. A government made up of leaders who aren't as gung-ho about capitalism could mean that Lithuania will take smaller, less drastic economic steps.

Although all three states have said they are interested in letting foreigners participate in the purchase of state property during the privatisation period, all three have also expressed the fear that foreigners will buy up everything in sight. "The Soviets came here and took everything," explained one Lithuanian analyst. "Now there is the fear that Westerners are going to come and take everything, too."

Asset-strippers: A main concern of many observers in all three countries is that former bureaucrats and members of flourishing organised crime will sabotage the future by ripping off all the most valuable state assets. "It will come to the day when all you can do is get shares in a waste treatment plant and maybe keep the lousy apartment you're living in," said Jüri Estam, a journalist in Tallinn. "That's all that will be left of the privatisation process."

The rise of the post-Soviet rich has not been accompanied by the rise of a stabilising middle class. Nor is it likely to happen soon. More likely will be a sharp increase in the very rich upper class and a corresponding increase in the numbers of poor.

But it is not all gloom and doom. The signs of change for the better are ever more evident in the Baltic capitals where new shops, restaurants and services start up every day. Western goods, though still too expensive for most Balts, are on shelves everywhere. Kiosks and stalls are continually being put up. Stores seem to be getting cleaner all the time and many have been renovating and expanding. Service in state-owned stores seems to be improving as managements start to feel the heat of competition and employees begin to worry about the prospect of being out of a job.

Even local restaurants, notorious for their barbarian standards of service during the Soviet era, are begining to understand the once-alien notion of the customer as king. Doors are less frequently locked and the retired KGB goons who used to yell at you at restaurant entrances are being replaced by more human attendants.

Western restaurateurs have also been moving in to fill a void of top-class eating establishments. Chen Dong, a Belgian-Chinese businessman, opened the Baltic's first Chinese restaurant in Vilnius. Called the Golden Dragon, the restaurant is located on the premises of an old engineering company that fell on hard times. A meal for the equivalent of around $10, served by waitresses in kimonos, consists of everything from sweet-and-sour pork to fried bananas and green tea.

In Tallinn Old Town, the Indian restaurant Maharaja is probably one of the classiest between the Baltic Sea and Vladivostok. Although the English and Estonian partners have been at loggerheads on questions of business, they still manage to achieve near world-class food and service. But, at close to $100 a head, you pay for what you get. In Vilnius the German-run Idabasar, near the Gates of Dawn, established a good reputation the moment it opened at the end of 1992.

But most of the changes up to now have not touched the average Balt. If the craziness of shortages and long queues has ended, prices have gone through the roof. Most people are struggling harder than ever to make ends meet, spending at least half their money a month on such basics as milk, bread and butter. And though unemployment still stands below 10 percent in all three countries, everybody knows that for the first time in their lives their jobs are at risk.

Although the Baltic states long abandoned the notion that the West will bail them out economically, they still believe that moving closer to the West, especially Europe, is the ultimate goal. Politicians say they would like to join the European Community as quickly as possible, preferably before the year 2000, and the Eurocrats in Brussels talk about "when" the countries join, and not "if". But unless Europe lowers its economic standards or unless an economic miracle happens in the Baltics, Estonia, Latvia and Lithuania are likely to remain closer to the Third World for at least 10 years.

Whether the outside world has faith in them or not, most Balts will say that, deep down, they are convinced that they will eventually prosper, that the future will work. And even if they inherit a hard future, it has to be better than the inheritance of the past.

Right, Beati, Riga's first private boutique, in the Old Town, sells locally made clothes.

In the spring of 1992, an elk was spotted standing in the waters of the River Daugava in the centre of Riga, too frightened to budge. Framed by the city skyline and the yawning bridges that connect this industrial capital of nearly a million people, the elk made an appearance on national television before scientists captured it and released it in one of Latvia's many forests. No one knows how such a shy animal ended up in the heart of the Baltic states' largest city, but it apparently felt quite at ease in the Daugava's waters which are so polluted that human swimmers have come out in infections and skin rashes.

Throughout the three countries there is a clash between poorly planned urbanisation and a countryside left to run wild after half a century of communism. One of the problems for visitors now is that much of the resultant pollution is impossible immediately to see or gauge. Six months after the elk went to town, Karl Gustav XVI of Sweden visited the Sloka paper mill nearby on the River Lielupe. The mill pours its hazardous waste into the Daugava and twice protesters have had it closed down. On inspection, the king declared that it did not seem as bad as he had been led to believe.

Coastal hazards: The Lielupe and the Daugava rivers empty themselves in the middle of Riga Bay beside Jūrmala. This has long been regarded as the Baltic Riviera, a high spot on more than 1,000 miles of white sandy coast that stretches from Narva on the Russian border in Estonia to just beyond Nida at the Lithuanian border with Kaliningrad. On a fine day it is often hard to imagine that the Baltic Sea's tempting blue acres, breaking in long, lazy curves over spotless white beaches, are not as pure as driven snow. But into this sea flows the cess and chemical waste of conurbations both within and beyond the Baltic states.

The Sloka mill reopened because the country needed newsprint, but it has since been mooted that it is not the main source of pollution of the coast. A study team whose

Preceding pages: polluting power plant near Narva, Estonia. Left, elk goes for a paddle in the Daugava, Riga. Above, nesting white storks.

work was published in *Ecocide in the USSR* blamed the pre-war sewer system in Riga as well as in Jūrmala where 14 million annual man-days of holidaymaking and 219 coal-fired hot-water systems had taken their toll. (Tap water in Riga should not be drunk.)

There are other water-borne hazards, too. The eastern end of this Riviera, around the mouth of the Daugava, is a good place to look for amber. Children, thinking they are in luck, have picked up small lumps of phosphorus and literally burned their fingers.

The beaches at Jūrmala have, from time to time, been officially closed. But the visitor has otherwise no way of knowing if the water is clean. There can be a warning sign of a ribbon of green algae along the water's edge but there is no hard and fast rule. Dedicated conservationists would not put a toe in a drop of Baltic water; locals dive in to its potentially most hazardous spots. One answer is that you are probably quite safe away from the towns, in particular industrial centres such as Klaipėda, Ventspils, Riga, Pärnu, Haapsalu, Tallinn and Narva.

Local people are not oblivious to the problems, but they have had to live with them.

Families around Kuršių Lagoon in Lithuania continue to catch and eat lead-contaminated bream, perch, roach and eel because during the Soviet period nobody told them not to, and now they cannot afford to eat anything else. The Nemunas, which brings mercury, phenols, DDT, HCH and phosphorus compounds into the lagoon and Klaipėda's port, is the country's most polluted river. There is, however, no sign of dead fish being constantly washed up on the riverbanks or sea shore, and fish is regularly caught and sold in the markets and eaten at home and in hotels.

Marine life has also suffered as a direct result of Soviet fishing policies. The natural balance has been destroyed by overfishing

The climate is one thing that cannot be blamed on the Soviet occupation. In fact, the years of occupation actually benefited parts of the countryside through its incompetence and wilful neglect. Most dramatically, an obsession with secrecy protected the whole coast from development, and for nearly two generations much of it remained out sight.

For the first time in nearly 50 years people are discovering beautiful beaches, from the Estonian islands to the dune-backed Neringa Spit in Lithuania, all formerly heavily patrolled by the Soviet army. The Kolka peninsula in northwest Latvia, once the preserve of armed, KGB-trained border guards, has a degree of protection simply because of its

and during the 1980s spawning fish in the entire Baltic fell by more than 50 percent. In the past 20 years concentrations of nitrate from improperly treated waste water have trebled and quadrupled during winter months. This has increased organic material on the sea bottom, which has reduced oxygen levels and led to a decline in salinity. Stocks of whitefish and smelt have dropped and cod reproduction has been seriously affected.

Sea life has also suffered from climatic changes. Mild winters have left the coast free of ice, depriving seals of their natural breeding grounds. A number have died when they have been forced to breed ashore.

poor roads. In its centre is the 27,000-acre (15,000-hectare) Slītere State Reserve where ornithologists from Western Europe come to see the spring migration of buzzards.

The reserve's director, Elmārs Peterhofs, is concerned about its future now that the Soviets have gone. "I have seen what tourists have done to the Finnish islands," he says. "We must stand very firmly against such developments. This territory is only interesting as long as it stays the way it is." Even when fires swept through 7,400 acres (3,000 hectares) of the reserve's dry forest and peat bog in the summer of 1992, he was not pessimistic. "The fire was unique for Western Europe. This territory has not been influenced by man for more than 100 years. We can see how the natural ecosystem responds."

Throughout the Baltic states, naturalists say that Soviet mismanagement has actually saved large tracts of beaches, woodland and wildlife, sustaining habitats that have disappeared forever elsewhere in Europe. Each of the three countries has a long list of natural parks and special areas set aside as being of particular scientific interest, from plants and animals to geological sites. Under the Soviets it was relatively easy to designate territory because the state owned everything. And, although not all areas of special interest have avoided damage and pollution, some 25,000 birds are, for example, reckoned to live in soggy forests the Soviet administrators tried to drain but actually made wetter.

Furthermore, unlike the rest of Europe, the percentage of rural land has increased since 1940. In Latvia more than two-thirds of the population lived in the countryside. By the end of the Soviet era, Stalin's mass deportations, emigrations to the West, collectivisation and immigration of Russian labour to work in Soviet factories had shrunk rural populations to less than one-third. Dozens of ruined stone farmhouses can be seen in southern Estonia. In Lithuania 10 percent of the rural population migrated to rural areas every decade from 1950 to 1980.

"The socialists were too lazy to spoil nature," says Valts Vilnitis of the Latvian Environmental Protection Committee. "During the First Independence period 29 percent of the country was forested. Now it's 42 percent. That kind of increase is unique in Europe. Agricultural lands also decreased. It was simply bad management."

Wildlife inhabitants: These habitats have benefited all manner of animals and birds. The coastal wetlands are breeding grounds for ducks, waders, terns and swans, the uplands are scavenged by birds of prey, corncrakes chatter in summer meadows and white storks nest everywhere. City streets are pecked over by the ubiquitous hooded crow. In the woods are the elk and the deer, martyn, lynx, boar. And the abundant rivers and lakes support beavers and otters.

The World Wide Fund for Nature reports

that in Latvia alone there are 400 wolves, 4,000 otters, 50,000 beavers, 400 lynx, 70,000 roe deer and 30,000 boar. Among the 208 bird species to breed or pass through is the world's largest colony of black storks, but these are shy birds, hiding in the forests. The best chance a visitor has of seeing wildlife is in the Gauja National Park north of Riga, where there are boars, deer, and even bison. Lahemaa National Park east of Tallinn is home to brown bears, lynx, cranes and mink.

Sometimes this wildlife profusion becomes a nuisance. On the Estonian island of Saaremaa, people have purloined 2-ft (60-cm) high metal sheets from an old air base and erected them around potato crops to keep out

wild boar, or "forest pigs" as they call them.

The reserves have always provided local licensed hunters with seasonal game, from duck and capercaillie to deer and boar. Now trophy-hunting is on the increase, culling the animals and bringing in much-needed foreign revenue. High on the list are the shy elk, favoured by Germans who also go to Lithuania to hunt wolves. Organised trips bring hunters from as far away as the United States to bag any of these animals as well as lynx and, occasionally, brown bear.

Unofficial hunting does of course go on, and this may now be on the increase as more guns are brought in. Former Soviet army

Left, cement plant in Venta, Lithuania. **Above**, the Ignalina atomic power plant.

weaponry can be bought with reasonable ease in the big markets in the Baltic capitals. At risk, too, are the habitats, now that land may be properly cultivated by the newly returned private farmers. International organisations have already become involved in conservation projects. The World Wide Fund is, for example, working with Latvia to protect the country's previously untouched natural habitats, and 15 percent of the land is to be set aside for this purpose.

There is also concern about the insufficient legislation controlling privatisation of land, which may be used in ways that can cause serious damage to important habitats. IUCN, the World Conservation Union, is

Decades of mining have created sharp-tipped slag heaps more than 300 ft (100 metres) high. These black mountains contain toxic heavy metals and organic compounds with large amounts of phenols that are washed by the rain into the sea.

The oil shale burned to produce electricity leaves ash that is mixed with water and pumped to the top of flat sedimentation basins where the alkaline liquid forms bright blue lakes before it evaporates. More than 150 million tons of grey ash have accumulated in these giant, barren fields that stretch for miles. Experts say that if the petrified ash is ever used, it will take more energy to grind it down than was originally generated in

working with each of the states to find ways of dealing with the problem which will help both the land and the people.

Fuel crises: Forests are already threatened by a burgeoning black market for timber exports, and, with fuel crises, they will increasingly be looked to for heating homes during the long, dark days of winter. Wood and peat currently account for about 4 percent of energy needs.

Energy is a crucial question, and the search for it has been a major contributor to the pollution of the Baltic states to date. Undoubtedly the most evil is the oil shale industry in Estonia up near the Russian border.

burning the oil shale. Revelations about such industrial vandalism began to come out in the mid-1980s and they helped to galvanise the movement towards independence. It was then that the Soviets' plans to build a large hydro-electric power station on the Daugava were first revealed by Dainis Ivans, a Latvian journalist.

He concluded that the project, which would flood historic villages on a pretty stretch of the river above Daugavpils and turn the river into a series of lakes, would not actually result in enough water to keep a power station working. Ivans and a colleague wrote a critical article, which led to public opposition and, a year later, the cancellation of the plan. Ivans was subsequently elected chairman of the Latvian Popular Front, the first organised opposition to the Communist Party, and after independence he became a member of parliament.

Chernobyl also stirred fear in the Baltic states, not only because the 1986 explosion caused fallout across the three countries, but also because a plant of exactly the same faulty design was under construction in Ignalina, Lithuania. No geographic survey or seismic studies had been carried out before it was built. Two reactors are now up and running, but plans for a construction of another two at the same site were halted follow-

country's ground-water supplies. In 1987, as Gorbachev's *perestroika* gained momentum, public pressure to halt the mining increased. *Ei Ole Üksi Ükski Maa* ("No Land Stands Alone") became the rallying cry for the Estonian nation. Moscow finally called a halt to further mining in the region.

Now that many of the protesters are in power they find their hands tied by lack of money. Exploitation of oil shale in Estonia continues. Its thermal power stations produce 52 percent of the country's output, and the country's total output is twice the amount that it needs. It imports gas and oil (27 percent) for heat. The oil shale supplies will run out in the next century and, in spite of

ing demonstrations organised in 1988 by the Lithuanian Greens and the pro-independence Sąjudis movement. "The protest about the environment was a kind of protest against the government," says Rapolas Liuzinas from Lithuania's Environmental Protection Department. "It made people realise they are hosts in their own land and shouldn't accept the dictates of others."

In Estonia there were protests against a phosphate mining enterprise in the north, which would have polluted a large part of the

Left, hunters on Hiiumaa island, Estonia. Above, brown bear, still living in parts of the Baltics.

Chernobyl, nuclear alternatives are considered. "Sooner or later we will have to come to that," says a former industry minister, "but opinion has to be created."

In Latvia, Ivans concedes: "I don't like nuclear energy but other kinds of energy are too dirty." The country is completely dependent on outside energy supplies and much of its electricity comes from its two Baltic neighbours.

Like Estonia, Lithuania has no natural fuel resources and produces twice as much energy as it consumes, both at the Ignalina nuclear station and at a thermo-electric power plant in Elektrėnai near Vilnius. Lithuanian officials don't plan to close down Ignalina but, with the help of Swedish experts, they are trying to increase the reactors' safety.

In the meantime, little has been done to promote heat and light conservation at home. Windows are often badly fitted, buildings poorly insulated, and the anonymous concrete blocks of flats erected in every town have no modern thermostat control. Through central planning, the government can regulate the heat in the blocks of flats but on previous occasions when fuel crises have prompted governments to lower their temperatures, the occupants have simply turned on their hot-water taps and steamed up their homes. Even when winters are mild, light is

necessary for all but four hours of the day.

From air and water: The environment ministries in each of the countries say that waste water treatment in many towns is obsolete and in need of repair. Feasibility studies have been carried out, but money remains the obstacle for renovation. Riga is particularly bad, and people have been boiling their water there since an outbreak of hepatitis A in 1989. Most rural areas get their drinking water from wells where run-off from agriculture may pollute ground-water supplies. The Lithuanian Ministry of the Environment reports that about 40 percent of all well water is unsuitable for drinking because it contains large amounts of organic substances, oil products, ammonia, pesticides and detergents.

In the countryside, lichen grows abundantly in most of the damp woods – a sign of relatively clean air. Estonia, however, poisons not only its own atmosphere, but Finland's too. Oil-shale-fired thermal power plants near the Russian border emit hundreds of thousands of tons of sulphur dioxide and nitrogen oxide compound annually. Prevailing winds carry it to Finland where it kills forests. "Estonia, with its temperate climate, and Estonians, with their modest temperament, cannot boast many world records," states a report published by the government for the 1992 Earth Summit in Rio de Janiero. "However, there is no doubt that we hold at least one first in the whole world: production of sulphur dioxide per capita." In 1988 it was 308 lb (140 kg) per person. East Germany ranked second with 275 lb (125 kg).

Elsewhere, Soviet-built industry still sends its foul breath into the air. In cities and industrial areas, metallurgical, chemical, fertiliser, oil shale, cement, cellulose and paper companies are some of the worst offenders. Transboundary pollution also causes headaches and finger-pointing. In 1990 the River Daugava was poisoned with an organic cyanide spill from a polymer factory in Belorus, while Lithuania's cement plant in Akmenė and an oil refinery and power station in Mažeikaiai send air pollution to Latvia. Lithuania itself suffers from Polish industrial pollutants and waste from Kaliningrad that feeds into the River Nemunas.

Since independence, pollution in some areas has dropped off as industrial output has slowed, mainly through a catastrophic shortage of raw materials traditionally supplied by the former Soviet Union. There is also growing co-operation among all the counties around the Baltic Sea. Several have contributed money and expertise for dealing with pollution and hazardous waste.

But water and air pollution continue to affect everyone's lives. "We don't know what we are eating or drinking," says Valdis Segliņš of the Latvian Environmental Protection Committee. "Everything depends on living standards and where people live For most people it is not a matter of choice."

Left, marsh plants thrive in the large boggy areas. Right, pristine beaches on Latvia's coast.

...UVA

LATVIJA

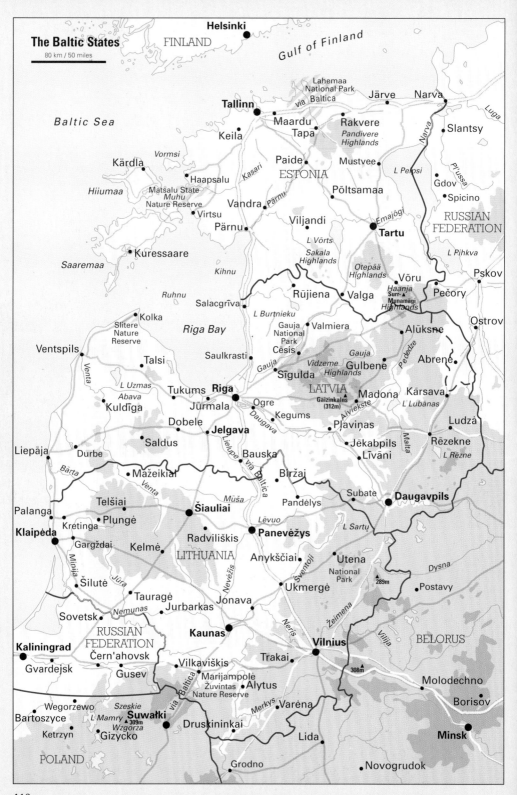

The Baltic States

80 km / 50 miles

FINLAND

Helsinki

Gulf of Finland

Baltic Sea

Lahemaa
National Park
via Baltica

Järve

Narva

Luga

Tallinn

Maardu

Tapa

Rakvere

Slantsy

Keila

Pandivere
Highlands

Vormsi

Paide

Mustvee

L Peipsi

Kärdla

Haapsalu

Kasari

ESTONIA

Gdov

Pärnu

Põltsamaa

Spicino

Hiiumaa

Matsalu State
Muhu
Nature Reserve

Vandra

Virtsu

RUSSIAN
FEDERATION

Pärnu

Viljandi

Emajõgi

Tartu

L Pihkva

L Võrts

Kuressaare

Sakala
Highlands

Otepää
Highlands

Võru

Pskov

Saaremaa

Kihnu

Haanja
Surr ▲
Munamägi
Highlands

Pečory

Ruhnu

Salacgrīva

Rūjiena

Valga

Ostrov

L Burtnieku

Gauja
National
Park

Valmiera

Alūksne

Kolka

Riga Bay

Cēsis

Gauja

Abrene

Slitere
Nature
Reserve

Ventspils

Saulkrasti

Vidzeme
Highlands

Gulbene

Madona

Kārsava

Talsi

Gauja

Sīgulda

Pededze

L Uzmas

Venta

Tukums

Riga

LATVIA

L Lubānas

Abava

Jūrmala

Ogre

Gaizinkalns
(312m)

Alviekste

Ludzà

Kuldīga

Dobele

Kegums

Plaviņas

Malta

Rēzekne

Saldus

Jelgava

Daugava

Jēkabpils

L Rēzne

Liepāja

Durbe

Bauska

Līvāni

Bārta

Lielupe

via Baltica

Biržai

Subate

Daugavpils

Mažeikiai

Venta

Pandėlys

Telšiai

Mūša

Šiauliai

Lēvuo

L Sartų

Palanga

Plungė

Radviliškis

Panevėžys

Dysna

Kretinga

Gargždai

Kelmė

LITHUANIA

Utena
National
Park

▲ 289m

Postavy

Klaipėda

Anykščiai

Minija

Nevėžis

Šventoji

Žeimena

Vilija

Šilutė

Tauragė

Jonava

Ukmergė

Jūra

Jurbarkas

Nemunas

Sovetsk

Kaunas

Neris

Vilnius

BELORUS

RUSSIAN
FEDERATION

Trakai

308m

Kaliningrad

Čern'ahovsk

Vilkaviškis

Molodechno

Gvardejsk

Gusev

Marijampolė

Žuvintas
Nature Reserve

Alytus

Merkys

Varėna

Borisov

Wegorzewo

Szeskie

Suwałki

Druskininkai

Bartoszyce

L Mamry

▲ 309m
Wzgorza

Lida

Minsk

Ketrzyn

Gizycko

Grodno

Novogrudok

POLAND

The three Baltic states, each about the same size, sit side by side on the eastern edge of the Baltic Sea between Poland and the Gulf of Finland. Tallinn, the northernmost capital, is on roughly the same latitude as Scotland's Orkney islands and southern Alaska. This means summer days lengthen into white nights and winter days are grey and short. A point in Lithuania marks the centre of Europe, between the Atlantic and the Urals.

Although they have linguistic, cultural, and historic differences, the three countries share a similar landscape and coastline. The overwhelming image is one of quiet roads and flat lands, rising in rolling hills towards the east, of myriad small rivers and lakes and of forests of the tallest pines. Scattered through them all are ancient hill forts and occasional boulders, "presents from Scandinavia" left by retreating glaciers often imbued with magical qualities.

It is essentially a rural landscape, with vast tracts of unfenced arable and pastureland inherited from the collective system. A few manors, often neoclassical, from the former occupying Russians, Swedes, Germans and Poles remain. And in the cities it is the legacy of these conquerors that prevails, particularly the Hansa merchants who for centuries monopolised trade in the Baltic Sea.

The "Amber Coast" is a wonder of endless white pristine beaches backed by dunes and pine forests stretching for hundreds of miles. Its rest homes and cure houses, spas and safe swimming beaches have made its resorts popular for millions of Balts, Russians, Belorussians and Poles for more than a century, though post-independence has seen the numbers of holidaymakers fall radically.

The Soviet legacy is a mixture of tedious satellite suburbs, and conserved city centres unmolested by high-rise buildings. The traditional domestic architecture, of two- and three-storey houses built of solid wooden planks is still evident, though many country farms have fallen into disuse, and thatch and wood-shingle roofs have mostly been replaced by corrugated iron. A national pride did survive the Soviet years, and there are many small museums throughout the three countries, devoted to bee-keeping, folklore, poets, and other local heroes.

Travel through the three countries by public transport is slow but not difficult. The roads are generally in good repair and wonderfully empty, and the Via Baltica drives through them all, from Warsaw to St Petersburg. Together the three countries are the same size as Washington State, and a little larger than England and Wales. A visit to one country can easily include a day or two in part of another.

Preceding pages: commemoration of a celebratory meeting of Estonia, Lithuania and Latvia during the First Independence in 1934.

The most northerly of the three countries, Eesti Vabariik, the Republic of Estonia, is the smallest, least densely populated and the most Westernised. It was the first independent Soviet state to have its own currency and for many years television sets had been directing people's attention towards Finland and the West.

The fact that Estonian is a Finno-Ugric language, and the country's conquerors have been Danes and Swedes, has made Estonians feel more a part of Finland than of neighbouring Latvia, with whom they have shared much of their history. Finns, for their part, have long taken advantage of Estonia's relative cheapness, and have taken the ferry over from Helsinki to Tallinn, where a lot of their money is spent on booze.

Tallinn, the capital of Estonia, is the prettiest city in the Baltics, a medieval enclave set on a hillock above its port. Within the remaining old walls and towers, beneath frugal Protestant church spires, are winding cobbled lanes leading to the old square. The city was a showcase in the 1980 Moscow Olympics when, just to the east of it, by Pirita Beach, a new port was built to stage the sailing events in the Games. Sailing around the country's islands is a pleasure waiting to be rediscovered.

Estonia has a second city in Tartu, in the south, a distinguished university town that brims with student life. On the Russian borders around Narva there is a high population of Russians working in the shale-oil industry, the basis of the country's wealth and a worry for its environment. Much of the Russian border is otherwise taken up by Lake Peipsi, the fourth largest lake in Europe.

Nearly 40 percent of the country is forested, with pine, spruce and junipers, and brown bears and beavers are among its inhabitants. Nearly half of the land is made up of marshes and there are around 1,500 lakes. There are also around 1,500 islands. The largest, off the west coast, are Hiiumaa and Saaremaa, rural backwaters where the earliest stone churches in the Baltics are to be found. It is hard to imagine a quieter place in all Europe.

Preceding pages: summer country garden in Saska, near Lake Peipsi; Palmsa manor, Lahemaa National Park; Uus Street, Tallinn Old Town. **Left**, Estonia's national dress.

Estonia

32 km / 20 miles

FINLAND

Baltic Sea

Naissaar

Tallinn

Väike-Pakri
Suur-Pakri
Paldiski

Keila

Keila

Osmussaar

Rummu

Vormsi

Risti

Rap

Palivere

Kõpu

Kärdla

Rohukülla
Heltermaa

Taebla

Märjamaa

Haapsalu

Vigala

Suuremõisa
Käina

Hiiumaa

Kassari

Matsalu State

Kasari

Jarvaka

Matsalu Bay

Vana-Vigala

Emmaste

Muhu

Nature Reserve

Lihula

Saaremaa

Orissaare

Koguva

Pärnu-Jaagupi

Too

Panga
Leisi
Angla

Virtsu

Vatla

Kalli

Karja

Mustjala

Valjala

Kihelkonna
Viki

Karrma

Sindi

Karla

Püha

Pärnu

Paik

Kuressaare

Pärnu Bay

Abruka

Kihnu

Sääre

Ikla

Ainaži

Ruhnu

Staicel

Salacgrīva

Mazirbe

Kolka

Via Baltica

Ventspils

Dundaga

Roja

Riga Bay

Limbaži

Valdemārpils

Nogale

Mērsrags

Gulf of Finland

Prangli

Loksa · Võsu

Lahemaa
National Park   via Baltica

Maardu

Kuusalu · Haljala   Kunda

Jägala

Kehre

Rakvere   Kiviõli   Järve

Aegviidu   Kadrina · Vinni   Püssi

Pirita   Tapa   Pandivere

Kose   Aravete   Tamsalu   Väike-Maarja

Ardu   Järva-Jaani   Highlands   Passvere   Iisaku

Kuimetsa   Koeru   Rakke

ehtna   Paide   ESTONIA   Mustvee

Türi   Järva-Jaani

Särevere   Imavere   Jõgeva   L Peipsi

Vohma   Põltsamaa   Palamuse   Kallaste

Vändra

Kolgi-Jaani   Tabivere

Viljandi   Viiratsi   Emajõgi   Tartu

Kõpu   L Võrts   Puhja   Ihaste

Elva   Nõa   Ühnurme

Sakala Highlands   Rõngu

Abja-Paluoja   Saverna   Räpina

Karksi Nuia   Otepää   Põlva

Tõrva   Otepää Highlands   Kanepi

Rūjiena   Väimela

Mazsalaca   Naukšēni   Antsla   Haanja   Võru

Aloja   Valga/Valka   Rõuge   Surr-Munamägi   Vastseliina   Pečory

Seda   Highlands   Misso   Izborsk

Strenči   Mustjõgi · Mõniste

Valmiera   Ape   Lavry   Palkino

Liepa   L Alūksnes

Gauja   Smiltene   Alūksne

raupe   Rauna   LATVIA

National Park

Narva Bay

Narva-Jõesuu   Luga   Ivangorod

Narva   L Narva

Slantsy

Vasknarva

Kauski

Gdov

RUSSIAN

Spicino

FEDERATION

Znamenka

Piirisaar

Pl'ussa

L Pihkva

Pskov

Velikaja

Pededze

129

In the days when visitors to Estonia often arrived by sea, the first glimpse of Tallinn, the capital, made a lasting impression. It was of ancient ruins and quaint houses with steeply peaked roofs, more Mediterranean than Baltic. In summer, it might have been the South of France, with 19th-century Russians making an annual summer pilgrimage from St Petersburg. "I have seen delicate creatures," wrote an English visitor in 1841, "who at first were lifted from the carriage to the bathing-house, restored day by day, and in a fortnight's time bathing with a zest that seemed to renew all their energies."

In the evenings, "a band of military music plays, and restaurants offer ices, chocolate, etc, and you parade about and your friends join you, and you sit down and the gnats sting you; and if you don't like this, you may adjourn to the *salle de danse* close by, where the limbs so late floating listlessly on the waves now twirl round in the hurrying waltz."

Estonia had been a Russian province since 1721, and while the lot of the Estonian peasant had been pathetic throughout – and all ethnic Estonians were peasants – tsarist rule became increasingly repressive in the latter half of the 19th century. There were no more foreign tourists, Russians excepted, and as far as most foreigners were concerned, Estonia ceased to exist.

Surprising new state: A declaration of Estonian independence after World War I caught the world at large by surprise. Russia, torn apart by revolution, was unable to do much about it. The authors of travel guides rushed in to appraise the reincarnated nation. "The broad visage of the Estonian," wrote one, as if reporting on a newly arrived specimen at a zoo, "has slanting eyes, low forehead, high cheekbones and projecting lower jaw." His conclusion was that Estonian origins were "not of Europe".

Estonian independence lasted only until World War II. It then disappeared under the even heavier hand of communist Russia and was presumed lost for all time. Rather suddenly in 1988, extraordinary reports were

received in the West of a "Singing Revolution". Tens of thousands apparently spent that summer giving throaty voice to all the old Estonian songs and defiantly waving the long-hidden national flag. Within two years, although not without moments of nail-biting uncertainty, Estonia was independent again.

For all the ravages of a Soviet economic policy which had aimed at turning Estonia into an annex of heavy industry, much of the character which delighted visitors of 150 years ago had survived. Russians were still

visiting in droves, but for the "Old European" atmosphere and the food rather than the beaches and swimming, which were prime casualties of environmental vandalism. As for the re-emergent Estonians, they seemed to have borne the burden of the previous half-century with commendable fortitude.

The "non-European" physical features are a reflection of Finno-Ugric ancestry. Because of the similarities between the Estonian and Finnish languages, Estonians had been able to follow Finnish television during the Soviet era. Its terms of reference did not flatter the Soviet system.

Estonia's frontiers have been chopped and

Left, 15th-century soldier. **Right**, Konstantin Päts, the country's leader during the First Independence.

changed over the centuries. Their present configuration makes Estonia a country of some 17,000 sq. miles (44,000 sq. km), small enough to be covered by a day's driving in any direction, with a population of one-and-a-half million of whom about 75 percent are ethnic Estonians. The balance are predominantly Russians, most of them relatively recent arrivals sent in to man the industries which represented Estonia's role in the Soviet economic scheme of things. A few living in the eastern part of the country are the descendants of 17th-century Old Believers, a sect which fled from Russia to escape, among other things, the tax which Peter the Great imposed on the beards they traditionally

first to arrive, and there were others who followed after them, so it may be worth going back to the beginning.

Hardy beginnings: The future Finns and Estonians were among the first tribes to drift across Europe from Asia. Leaving the lower slopes of the Urals, they followed the river courses, subsisting mainly on fish and clothing themselves in animal skins. They had already reached the Baltic coast when mentioned by Tacitus in the 1st century AD. "Strangely beastlike and squalidly poor, neither arms nor homes have they. Their food is herbs, their clothings skin, their bed the earth. They trust wholly to their arrows, which, for want of iron, are pointed with

wore. A smaller minority apart from those mentioned above are the diluted remnants of Estonia's most influential settlers, Germans.

They came in two guises. The first were 13th-century Teutonic Knights who arrived ostensibly as bearers of Christianity but also with an urgent need to find somewhere to live, having recently fallen on hard times in the Holy Land. They were followed by German craftsmen and merchants who formed the burgher class which ultimately monopolised the towns and cities. To an unusual degree, Estonians have squirmed in a back seat while others have written their history. These 13th-century Germans were not the

bone… Heedless of men, heedless of gods, they have attained that hardest of results, the not needing so much as a wish."

There seems to have been some pushing and shoving among new arrivals on the Baltic shores, especially when large numbers of Slavs turned up, but eventually the future Finns, Estonians, Latvians and Lithuanians took up positions in more or less the pattern that pertains today.

The first conquerors were the Danes under Valdemar II who arrived with what should have been an invincible armada of 1,000 ships. The Estonians resisted the invasion so fiercely that the Danes were in danger of being routed. They were rescued, so the story goes, by a red banner with a white cross floating down from heaven – the first sighting of the future Danish flag. Their spirits up, they took possession of Tallinn.

Some years earlier, in 1200, around 500 heavily-armed German knights had landed farther south in the Gulf of Riga with a commission to spread the Word of God. They did so more efficiently than the Danes, who were recent converts themselves, could manage in Estonia.

In the end, the Danes asked the Teutonic Knights to lend a hand against these truculently unreceptive pagans. The knights tackled the task with customary efficiency and

rest, which is to say the Estonians, were serfs. This system survived every political and religious change for six centuries. In 1347, the Danish monarchy was desperate for cash. Tallinn, or Reval as it came to be known, was sold to the efficient and prosperous knights.

A large part of the commercial success of Reval and Narva, Estonia's two ports, was a virtual monopoly on trade to and from Russia. When Ivan III seized Narva and made it a Russian port it so alarmed the Baltic Germans that they sought the protection of Sweden. Under Gustavus Adolphus, Sweden was energetically bent on expanding their Baltic holdings, but there was no desire to tamper

declared, in 1227, that the task had been accomplished.

The knights transformed an economy which had previously rested on primitive agriculture and products of the forest into perhaps the best farming and most enlightened commerce of the Middle Ages. They built castles and founded towns everywhere, filling them with craftsmen and merchants recruited from Germany. Their social system was simple: Germans occupied the positions of noble, burgher and merchant; the

Left, the Danes take Tallinn, 1219. **Above**, the capital as it looked in 1615.

unnecessarily with a German infrastructure which worked so profitably. Later Swedish kings, particularly Charles XI, did interfere by taking over German-owned estates and either giving them to Swedes or, increasingly, keeping them for themselves. The dispossessed and disgruntled who had previously turned to Sweden for protection against Russia, decided they now needed protection against Sweden. With perfect impartiality, they turned to Russia. Peter the Great readily agreed to help.

The outcome was the titanic struggle between Peter and the equally legendary Charles XII of Sweden. A Russian force 35,000 strong made for Narva, then held by a much smaller Swedish garrison in the castle. Charles, who was not yet 20, hurried to its aid. He arrived with 8,000 men and, in the middle of a snow storm, plunged straight into battle. The Russians were cut to pieces, losing every piece of artillery Peter possessed. Charles's advisers urged him to press on to Moscow. "There is no glory in winning victories over the Muscovites," he said breezily, "they can be beaten at any time."

While Charles went off in pursuit of other enemies, Peter laid the foundations of Petersburg and planned a second attack on Narva. He entrusted the command to a Scot named Ogilvie who not only succeeded in

plague. The Great Northern War between Peter and Charles was far from over, however, and in the course of fighting that swept across Europe the Baltic states were utterly devastated, the horror compounded by plague. By the Peace of Nystad in 1721, Sweden finally ceded its Baltic possessions and Estonia, for one, prepared for its first taste of Russian rule.

Like the Swedes, Peter was not inclined to upset the way the German hierarchy ran Estonia, and the Estonians continued, according to one commentator, "to live and die like beasts, happy if they could subsist on dusky bread and water". Nothing much had changed by the middle of the 19th century.

overwhelming the garrison but decided, apparently off his own bat, to take no prisoners, military or civilian. The most frightful massacre was going on when Peter showed up. He is said to have stopped the proceedings by cutting down some of the crazed attackers with his own sword. Moreover, he said, there was a perfectly good use for able-bodied Swedish prisoners: the conditions at the Petersburg building site were so bad that the work force was dropping like flies.

With Narva under his belt, Peter turned to Reval and its Swedish garrison. The defenders put up a marvellous fight but ultimately they succumbed to thirst and an outbreak of

"Beyond his strict adherence to his church," it was reported of the Estonian peasant, "we can find but little interesting in his character; nor indeed is it fair to look for any, excepting perhaps that of a servile obedience or cunning evasion, among a people so long oppressed... Provided he can have a pipe in his mouth, and lie sleeping at the bottom of his cart, while his patient wife drives the willing little rough horse... he cares little about an empty stomach. Offer him wages for his labour, and he will tell you, with the dullest bumpkin look, that if he works more he must eat more."

The same source, a Lady Eastlake, moved

in privileged circles during her stay, but she kept her eyes open and provides a wonderful insight into conditions. So paranoid was the ruling Tsar Nicholas I about revolutionaries – the revolutions of 1848 were just around the corner – that police surveillance everywhere was oppressive. If nothing else, though, it kept crime figures low. Over a whole year, she reported, there had been only 87 misdemeanours among Reval's 300,000 population, "and five of these consist merely in travelling without a passport".

Most illuminating of all, perhaps, are Lady Eastlake's observations about the cloud that hung over young men in the form of military service in the Russian army. The conscripts

and with not a rouble in his pocket – to seek his daily bread by his own exertions for the remainder of his life, or to be chargeable to his parish, who by this time have forgotten that he ever existed, and certainly wish he had never returned."

Impossible choices: The last years of the 19th century saw the emergence of the Young Estonians, a sign of awakening nationalism. The social order as they saw it was still dominated by the German heirarchy, but being anti-German did not make them pro-Russian, and certainly not Russian royalists. They were simply against the status quo, and for people in that mood Marxism was a very reasonable answer. The savage oppression

were chosen by ballot, No. 1 being the unlucky number. "From the moment that the peasant of the Baltic provinces draws the fatal lot No. 1, he knows that he is a Russian, and, worse than that, a Russian soldier, and not only himself, but every son from that hour born to him; for, like the executioner's office in Germany, a soldier's life is hereditary… If wars and climate and sickness and hardship spare him, he returns after four-and-twenty years of service – his language scarce remembered, his religion changed,

of the St Petersburg uprising in 1905 destroyed any sympathy for the tsar.

For most Estonians, World War I presented an impossible choice between Germany and Russia when, in truth, they would rather have been fighting against both. Nevertheless, tens of thousands found themselves in tsarist uniform, their plea to form their own units under their own officers falling on deaf ears. The Russian Revolution in 1917 simplified the choice, the more so when it was announced that an Estonian national army was to be formed. About 170,000 volunteers immediately joined up, while a not inconsiderable number of Estoni-

Left, Fat Margaret on fire, 1917. **Above**, a 19th-century view of conscription into Russia's army.

ans preferred to join the supposedly internationalist ranks of the Bolsheviks. From their various places of exile, members of a provisional Estonian government sent up a cry for independence.

Fierce battles were fought over Tallinn between local Bolsheviks backed by Red Guards against nationalist irregulars who included schoolboys and the Tallinn fire brigade. The tide at first went in favour of the Bolsheviks. By the end of 1918, they held Narva and Tartu, and Russian comrades had advanced to within 20 miles of Tallinn. It amounted to civil war and it was fought with the savagery associated with one.

The tide eventually turned, although not not inclined to accept the new government. There was an attempted putsch in 1924 which resulted in street fighting in Tallinn. Numerous other disturbances were countered by increasingly authoritarian measures. In the end these amounted to dictatorship and the sad conclusion among Estonia's friends was that the country was not quite ripe for parliamentary democracy.

Regained rights: Prior to the war, more than half of Estonia had belonged to 200 German-Balt families. An Agrarian Reform Law passed after independence took over all baronial and feudal estates, together with those belonging to the church and the former Russian Crown lands, and redistributed them as

without considerable clandestine help given to the nationalists by the British Navy. The details are veiled to this day, but it seems to have involved using captured Russian destroyers and raids by torpedo boats which penetrated the naval defences with which Peter the Great had ringed the Russian Baltic ports. The final battle was at Narva, and resulted in the nationalist coalition driving some 18,000 Bolsheviks across the Russian border. One year later, with the Bolsheviks still engaged in heavy fighting elsewhere, Russia renounced its sovereignty over Estonia "voluntarily and for ever".

Communists elsewhere in Estonia were 30,000 new farms. The lot of the previously hapless peasant was further improved by the right to engage in trade.

Estonia was still struggling to find its feet when any gains were put in jeopardy by the secret protocol of the 1939 Nazi-Soviet Pact. Stalin and Hitler agreed between them that the Soviet Union would annex Estonia together with Finland and Latvia, and Germany could help itself to Lithuania, although this was later amended to give Lithuania to Russia as well. A blatantly rigged election set the stage for an outright annexation on 6 August 1940, and almost immediately 60,000 Estonians went missing. They had been forcibly conscripted into the Soviet army, deported to labour camps or executed.

The collapse of the Nazi-Soviet Pact naturally changed everything. German forces invaded in July 1941, meeting determined resistance in Estonia where large numbers of Soviet troops were cut off. Estonia had only about 1,000 Jewish families, nothing like the numbers of Latvia and Lithuania, but even so 90 percent of these were murdered as Germany set about incorporating the country in the Third Reich. By the end of the war, however, some 70,000 Estonians had fled to the West, so one way or another the population dropped from its pre-war level of 1.13 million to no more than 850,000 at the end. The educated classes did not wait to find out what would happen when the German forces in Tallinn surrendered to the Red Army on 22 September 1944.

Tens of thousands of those who did not flee were consigned to Soviet labour camps, and into the vacuum thus created were introduced comparable numbers of Russians with the dual purpose of manning heavy industry and completing the Russification programme begun by the tsars. There was little Estonians could do except to turn their television aerials towards Finland to see how their Finno-Ugric cousins were getting along.

At home, Soviet policies continued unabated so that during the 1980s the proportion of Russians and other Soviet implants living in the country rose to 40 percent. With virtually the whole of the country's industry under Moscow's remote control, no thought was given to the ecological impact of belching industrial works which in some instances were erected in the middle of established residential areas.

With their stars firmly attached to Moscow's wagon, Estonia's loyal Communist Party members were totally opposed to any sign of a nationalist revival in Estonia. The long-term implications of *glasnost* and *perestroika* were not lost on them, and they took no comfort at all from the 2,000 demonstrators who screwed up enough nerve to mourn the anniversary of the Nazi-Soviet Pact in Tallinn's Hirvepark. In this respect, the party hard-liners and the large Russian minority were as one.

While members of the Estonian Heritage Society went about discreetly restoring national monuments, the radical-chic banner of environmental concern brought the independence movement to life. The first scent of the potential came with the cancellation of plans for increased open-pit phosphorus mining in the northeast. This was followed by demands for economic self-management and then, most extraordinarily, came the "Singing Revolution".

The extent to which the Estonian establishment fell into line with the new mood was revealed when the Estonian Supreme Soviet defied the USSR Supreme Soviet in endorsing the legitimacy of a declaration of

sovereignty. When the independence movement properly got under way, there were tense moments as the world waited to see whether there would be a repetition of Czechoslovakia in 1968. In the event, the dissolution of the Soviet Union happened so quickly and on so many fronts that Estonia moved gratefully to the side-lines.

The Russian connection, which had begun with Peter the Great's victory over Charles XII of Sweden, was finally ended when Estonia was offered – and politely declined – membership of the Commonwealth of Independent States, the hastily contrived successor to the USSR.

Tallinn is a curious city, where the cosmopolitan brushes shoulders with the medieval and a general sophistication is veiled by a rundown air. Only 53 miles (85 km) across the Gulf of Finland from Helsinki and midway between St Petersburg and Stockholm, the city holds a blessed maritime position that has made it a little bit too interesting over the centuries to other nations. Resulting layers of cross-cultural history have given the city its special flavour.

Estonians were the first to build a stronghold here, in the 10th century, but they were overcome by the powerful seafaring Danes in 1219 and, in 1285, the city, which came to be called Reval right up until the beginning of the 20th century, was enlisted into the Hanseatic League. The Estonians, nonetheless, persisted and eventually, in 1346, the Danes sold the prosperous but troublesome town to the Teutonic Knights. A year later it was bought by the Livonian Order. Meanwhile, Tallinn's merchants grew fat, guilds burgeoned and the old part of town was expanded and refined.

In 1561 Tallinn was seized by the Swedes, and all-important trade between Russia and the West was broken off. This did little for urban development, and the economic depression was further burdened by plague. The Swedes remained in control until the end of the Great Northern War in 1710 when the Russians took over and turned Tallinn into a garrison town. Under Russian rule for the next two centuries, Tallinn also began to be industrialised and the city spread outwards rapidly from the medieval centre.

In 1918, after nearly a millennium, the Estonians managed to get their capital back, but in 1940 it was annexed by the Soviet Union. The Soviets added their own touches: large, uniform suburbs and a huge migration of Russian nationals. In 1990 the Estonians re-

Preceding pages: Tallinn's skyline. **Left**, a light dusting of snow on the city walls.

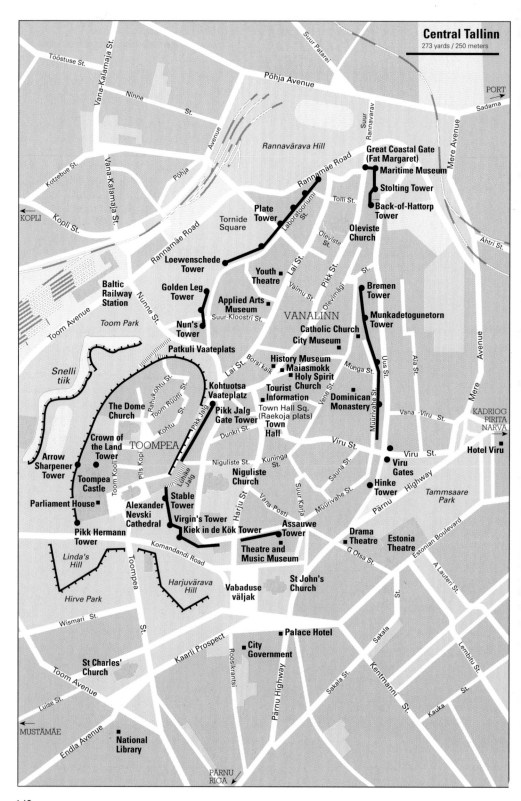

Central Tallinn

273 yards / 250 meters

Tööstuse St.

Vana-Kalamaja St.

Ninne St.

Põhja Avenue

Suur Patarei

PORT

Sadama

Kotzebue St.

Vana-Kalamaja St.

Põhja Avenue

Rannavärava Hill

Suur Rannavärav

Mere Avenue

KOPLI

Kopli St.

Rannamäe Road

Great Coastal Gate
(Fat Margaret)

Maritime Museum

Stolting Tower

Ahtri St.

Baltic
Railway
Station

Tornide
Square

Plate
Tower

Laboratooriumi St.

Tolli St.

Back-of-Hattorp
Tower

Oleviste St.

Oleviste
Church

Loewenschede
Tower

Rannamäe Road

Youth
Theatre

Lai St.

Pikk St.

Bremen
Tower

Toom Avenue

Nunne St.

Golden Leg
Tower

Applied Arts
Museum

Vaimu St.

VANALINN

Olevimägi St.

Munkadetogunetorn
Tower

Toom Park

Nun's
Tower

Suur-Kloostri St.

Catholic Church

City Museum

Snelli
tiik

Patkuli Vaateplats

Lai St.

Borsi kaik

History Museum

Maiasmokk

Holy Spirit
Church

Munga St.

Uus St.

Aia St.

Mere Avenue

The Dome
Church

Rahukohtu St.

Toom Rüütli St.

Kohtuotsa
Vaateplatz

Tourist
Information

Town Hall Sq.
(Raekoja plats)

Dominican
Monastery

Müürivahe St.

Vana-Viru St.

KADRIOG
PIRITA
NARVA

Crown of
the Land
Tower

Kohtu St.

Pikk Jalg

Pikk Jalg
Gate Tower

Vene St.

Town
Hall

Viru St.

Viru St.

Hotel Viru

TOOMPEA

Dunkri St.

Arrow
Sharpener
Tower

Toom Kooli St.

Niguliste St.

Kuninga St.

Sauna St.

Viru
Gates

Toompea
Castle

Toom Kooli

Niguliste
Church

Harju St.

Vana-Posti

Müürivahe St.

Hinke
Tower

Pärnu Highway

Tammsaare
Park

Parliament House

Pikk Hermann
Tower

Alexander
Nevski
Cathedral

Stable
Tower

Virgin's Tower

Kiek in de Kök Tower

Linke Jalg

Suur-Karja

Assauwe
Tower

Drama
Theatre

G Otsa St.

Estonia
Theatre

Estonian Boulevard

A Lauteri St.

Komandandi Road

Theatre and
Music Museum

Linda's
Hill

Toompea

Harjuvärava
Hill

Vabaduse
väljak

St John's
Church

Hirve Park

Wismari St.

Luise St.

Kaarli Prospect

Roosikrantsi

Palace Hotel

City
Government

Pärnu Highway

Sakala St.

Sakala

Kentmanni St.

Lembitu St.

Kauka St.

St Charles'
Church

Toom Avenue

MUSTÄMÄE

Endla Avenue

National
Library

PÄRNU
RIGA

claimed their city which, architecturally, can never be called simply "Estonian".

Giant's tombstone: The first place to visit is the Old Town, perched on a low hill by the shore. Held distinct from the rest of the city by old fortification walls, this is one of the purest medieval old towns in all of northern Europe.

The upper town, or **Toompea**, site of the original Estonian settlement, crowns the hill at 157 ft (48 metres) above sea level. The lower town spills out over an inclined horseshoe below. As they developed, they each acquired distinct personalities: the ecclesiastical and feudal powers lived above, the merchants and guild members below.

You must pay to bring a car into the Old Town and its beauty is far too detailed to be appreciated in passing. So, to tour it, put on a good pair of walking shoes – although all the local women manage to wear them, high heels are devils on its worn cobbled streets – and head for the central Viru Gates.

These gates (14th to 16th centuries) used to join directly with the old town walls, which can be seen to the north along Müürivahe Street. Walk a little way down this street and you will see a low brown door on your left. Dipping through it will take you into a narrow passageway posted with old stone grave-markers. They come from the 13th-century **Dominican monastery**, which is behind the wall now on your right.

The monastery was once a huge maze of churches and dormitories – paid for mostly by the monks' brewery – but a fire in 1531 destroyed almost all of it and the **monastery church**, reached by coming out the other end of the passage-way into a small courtyard, is now a cinema warehouse. To see any of the former interior, you must head down Vene Street and into another courtyard. There, behind a nearly hidden brown door beside Tallinn's **Catholic church**, is the small **Monastery Museum**.

Vene Street was named for the many Russian merchants that once lived on it and a little further down is the yellow **Nicholas the Miraclemaker Orthodox Church** (1822–27). The **City Museum** lies across the street, at No. 17, in a 14th-century merchant's home. The house was worked on up until the 17th century and still has an early portal and windows; inside is a carved ornamental stairway. The collection centres on objects from bourgeois households in the 19th century.

Snaking around Olevimägi Street will bring you to the **Olaviste church**, first documented in 1267 and now run by Baptists. Its original steeple was 460 ft (140 metres) high, which made the building supposedly one of the tallest in the world and it doubled as a lighthouse. But in 1820 the church was devasted by fire and a smaller 394 ft (120 metres) tower was added.

The church was named for the Norwegian King Olaf, considered a holy man, but legend has given it another origin. As the story goes, when the church was almost finished no one would consent to build its steeple because of a curse that whoever did would fall to his death. Finally, a young foreigner named Olev agreed. Sure enough, no sooner had he finished the work than he fell

Fat Margaret, home of the Military Museum.

and, as the curse had promised, a snake and a frog crawled from his mouth.

St Olaf's is on Pikk Street, the main street of the lower town, connecting the upper town with the harbour. Its furthest end is marked by the 15th-century **Great Coastal Gate** and 16th-century **Fat Margaret's Tower**, which supposedly won its name from a huge cannon kept there during the 17th century. It now houses Tallinn's **Maritime Museum**.

Attached to the Great Coastal Gate are the **Stolting Tower** and the **Back-of-Hattorpe Tower**, just two of the many towers from the early fortifications still standing along this part of the old town. In Laboratooriumi Street are seven more. Outside them, where the moats once were, sprawl handsome municipal parks.

Just a couple blocks down from St Olaf's towards the gate are three attached and nearly identical yellow houses, at Pikk 71, that locals call the **Three Sisters**. These are mirrored by three narrow houses also from the 15th century, at Lai 38–42, dubbed the **Three Brothers**. Lai runs parallel to Pikk and was the lower town's second main street; while Pikk housed the merchants, Lai was the craftsmen's address.

These streets are crowded with fascinating medieval houses. Much has been left untouched – in fact, few of these houses even have modern heating systems or running hot water – and in every corner is another architectural treasure left over from the times when individuals took care to put personal stamps on the buildings they lived and worked in.

The most famous guild building on Pikk Street, at No. 26, is the yellow **House of the Brotherhood of the Blackheads**. (The odd name of this organisation of unmarried merchants came from their African patron saint, St Mauritius.) Dating from the 15th and 16th centuries, the building's Renaissance facade is completed by carved stone plates of the Brotherhood's coat of arms on either side of the portico. It is now used for concerts and banquets and holds a youth club.

More former guild houses stand at

Pikk 18 and 20, and at No. 25 is the **Peeping Tom Building**. It took its name from a bachelor pharmacist who lived here and, supposedly, used to peep in on the daughters of the family across the way. His stone face spies out from top left of the facade.

The **Great Guild House** (1407–17), at Pikk 17, has been converted into the excellent **History Museum**. Beginning in the back hall, its exhibition traces the history of Estonia, from its origins, and the museum labels – in English, Estonian and Russian – go well beyond just names and dates. The building, which once covered the entire block, is also remarkable. The twin-naved main hall has high-vaulted ceilings and is completely original.

The Dragon Gallery, across the street at Pikk 18, is proof that life didn't stop altogether for the Old Town after the Middle Ages. It was built in 1911 with stone dragons and half-naked Egyptian women carved all over its facade; the merchant owner had been in the east. Its downstairs is a contemporary art gallery.

Next door to it is one of the oldest and most favourite cafés in Tallinn, the **Maiasmokk (Sweet Tooth) Kohvik**.

People used to walk in the middle of the street in the Old Town, with traffic moving on their either side, and every house had a fine portal with stone benches and steps leading down on to the street. Most of these were removed in the 17th century when pavements were introduced.

At 23 Lai Street, however, is a 15th-century house that still has its front step; the left side is original and the right side a recent duplicate, with the emblem of the **Youth Drama Theatre** that now owns the building on it. The beam coming from its centre was used to hoist goods to the upper floors.

In keeping with its craftsmen history, Lai Street still houses many types of art organisations and museums. One that is easy to miss but very pleasant is the **Applied Art Museum** at No. 17, tucked away in an old granary. Beautiful and airy inside, it displays Estonian craftwork from the 1920s to the 1990s.

Up and down hill in the Old Town.

The Borsi Kaik passage leads back to Pikk Street, facing out on Puhuvaimu, or **Holy Spirit church**, first mentioned in 1316. On its facade hangs the oldest street clock (1680) in Tallinn, and its intimate interior is rich with Gothic to classical fittings. Most valuable is the doubled-winged wooden altar made by Bernt Notke of Lübeck in 1483. The north balcony is decorated with paintings depicting the life of Jesus.

The Church of the Holy Spirit is squeezed in just before the entrance to Saiakang, or White Bread Passage, so-called because it was once lined with bakeries. Although only a few paces long, a crowd of old shops and cafés still manages to squeeze into this narrow alley and it is always one of the busiest places in Tallinn. The smallest building in town, just 4 ft 3 inches (1.3 metres) wide, used to stand at No. 3 and house an entire family.

This passage leads out on to the spacious and cobbled **Town Hall Square**. Now a busy thoroughfare of restaurants and shops, with a small blue train and horse-drawn carriages for summer tourists, it goes back in time every June for the week-long "Days of the Old City" festival. Outdoor gatherings are also often still held here, but it used to be the absolute centre of activity in the lower town. A weigh house functioned in one corner for many centuries but was destroyed in the war.

The sturdy and monumental **Town Hall** (Raekoja) still stands to its south side, erected between the 14th and early 15th centuries as both a fortification and a storehouse. The weathervane on its church-like steeple – topped by an image of Old Thomas, the town mascot – is baroque, but the rest of the building is unflinchingly Gothic. The stern interior is closed to the public. There is a small **City Council Museum** with historical exhibitions in the basement.

The **Town Council Apothecary**, at 11 Raekoja near the mouth of White Bread Passage, is another Town Hall Square landmark. This pharmacy was first documented in 1422 but is believed to have existed even before then; it has

Town Hall Square, an unhurried hub.

been closed several times for restoration but is proclaimed the longest continually functioning apothecary in Europe. It was run by the same family for 350 years. In 1583, a Hungarian named Johann Burchart began as a salesman in the apothecary and eventually managed to lease it. After 106 years, his family bought it, and it was from then on handed down from eldest son to eldest son. Some of them also became famous as doctors; in 1725 one was summoned to Peter the Great's deathbed. (The tsar died before he arrived.) The Burchart coat of arms is carved above the front entrance.

The **House of Tourism** curves on to the Town Hall Square at 3 Vanaturu Kael, with colourful reliefs of the apostles peering down from its facade. The originals are on display inside, along with a permanent exhibition of purchasable graphic art. Continuing down past it would take you on to busy Viru Street with its many little shops and back to the Viru Gates.

Harju Street on the opposite corner of the square leads to the **Niguliste church**, built on a monumental scale by merchants in the lower town to vie with the church on Toompea. The first written record of it dates from 1316, but it had to be rebuilt in the 15th century after it was gutted by fire.

Niguliste's several buildings were devastated by World War II and only the church itself has been restored. It is still impressive but has been turned into a museum with the result that though it looks like a church, the interior feels anything but sacred. However, some of its treasures that have survived are well worth seeing. The wooden altarpiece, for example, was made by Hermen Rode of Lübeck in 1482 and there is a fragment from the *Danse Macabre* canvas by Notke. One creepy gravestone to a Dr Johannes Ballivi in 1520 is carved with a skeleton.

Lühike Jalg, or "Short Leg", behind Niguliste climbs straight up on to Toompea, the upper town. This is where the Estonians first settled and where the Danes built their 13th-century castle,

Left, carving in the old Town Hall. **Right**, the Holy Spirit church pulpit.

which became known as "the Small Fortress". The rest of Toompea, home to the feudal lords and the Tallinn bishop, was called "the Big Fortress".

Toompea Castle was constantly bombarded over the centuries and was mined in 1944 but, amazingly, much of it still stands. The castle was separated from the town by a 65-ft (20-metre) stone wall and a deep moat, and the western and northern stretches of this wall are intact. The highest of its four towers – the 150-ft (46-metre) **Pikk Hermann Tower** – has survived, as well as the **Crown of the Land Tower** and **Arrow Sharpener Tower**.

The castle itself, however, has been greatly made over and is now fronted by the elaborate pink **Parliament House** (1870) with lofty gardens on its south side. To see it in its original limestone form, head down Komandandi Road past Linda's Hill. This hill was the starting point for the **Baltic Chain of Freedom**, which stretched nearly unbroken from here to Vilnius in Lithuania in August 1989. It is crowned with the sad **Statue of Linda**, the widow of Estonia's legendary hero Kalev.

Across the windy castle square is the mustard-yellow **Alexander Nevski Cathedral** (1894–1900), built in the style of Moscow churches of the 17th century. It is not a local favourite and the writer Tuglas Friedeberg once declared: "It looks like a samovar and should be blown up." You cannot ignore it even with your eyes closed, however, for it is topped with 11 bells, including the largest (15 tons) in all of Estonia. The interior is a zig-zag of red-olive-and-white tile.

The **Neitsitorn**, or Virgin's Tower, which was bombed in 1944 but restored and turned into a café and wine cellar, is behind the Alexander Nevski. Just below it is the **Kiek in de Kök tower**, built in the 15th century to hold gunpowder. The small round holes in its stalwart facade were made to mount guns. It is now used as a **Historical Museum** and a photographers' gallery. From the top floor is a marvellous view of the city.

Heading further up from the Castle

Parliamentary building, Upper Town.

148

Square, along the steeply winding Pikk Jalg Street, will bring you to the melancholic, dark-grey **Dome church**. It was first mentioned in 1223 and it has remained a strict and noble embodiment of the Gothic style, except for a baroque tower added in the 18th century.

Many people were buried over the centuries within the church, and their gravestones and burial vaults now command its interior. Most were military leaders and noblemen – such as the Swedish Commander-in-Chief Pontus de la Gardie and his wife, the daughter of Swedish King Johann III – with Scandinavians on the left side of the altar and Germans on the right. A few, however, were common folk: in the southwest corner, marked by a big boot, is the epitaph of seven shoemakers.

Before leaving Toompea, head towards Rahukohtu Street and turn into the yard of the house at No. 3. From here, on Patkuli Vaateplats, the view is spectacular, looking out over both Tallinn and Kopli bays. Squeeze down the narrow Linnus Street to Kohtuotsa

The Old Town: café life on Pikk Jalg.

Vaateplats for another gorgeous view – this time over the Old Town. The steep and smooth-stoned Pikk Jalg (or Long Leg) Street nearby will bring you back into the lower town.

Seaside parks: The Old Town is the tourists' favourite in Tallinn, but on weekends the locals wander in the parks on the east side of Tallinn Bay reached through the Kesklinn, or city centre.

Kadriorg Park was laid out between 1718 and 1725 by the Italian architect Niccolo Michetti under the orders of Peter the Great who named it in honour of his wife, Catherine. It is a woody untailored sort of park, planted with lime, oak, ash, birch and chestnut trees and punctuated by open fields.

One trim garden, nonetheless, stands in its oldest, southern end, with a monument to Estonia's literary giant Friedrich Kreutzwald (1803–82) and a large duck pond. Peter's peach-and-white **Kadriorg Palace** is a bit further in and until recently housed the National Gallery. In front of it is a splendid royal garden and pool. Behind the palace is another

Sailing And The Sea

Arthur Ransome bought a boat in Tallinn in 1919. "Reval was built as a fortress on a rock," he wrote, "and from the rock one looks out over a wide bay, with the green wooded island of Nargon on one side of it, a long promontory on the other, and far out beyond the bay a horizon of open sea. I do not believe that a man can look out from that rock and ever be wholly happy until he has got a boat of his own. I could not."

Ransome, English journalist and author of popular children's books, played chess with Lenin and helped to negotiate independence for Estonia. He had a boat designed for him in Tallinn and built in Riga and he spent many months sailing the eastern Baltic, with his wife Evgenia, a former secretary to Trotsky, writing up the experience in *Racundra's First Cruise*.

Sailing around the three countries' waters remains a pleasure, and the coast's many islands give it added spice. The silver grey waters of the Baltic, lacking any discernible

tides, are a gulf of the Atlantic, connected to the North Sea by narrow channels. Fed by rivers such as the Narva, Daugava and Nemunas, the sea has a low salt content and at 163,000 sq. miles (422,000 sq. km) it is the largest area of brackish water in the world. It is also a very shallow sea, with an average depth of 197 ft (60 metres), and it freezes over easily. In 1658 and 1809, it was completely covered with ice.

There are sailing clubs in each of the countries and regattas are a part of the summer scene. In Riga, where boats are still built, there was an annual pre-war race which took yachtsmen from the city castle around the island of Ruhnu in the middle of Riga Bay, which involved one night at sea.

But the smartest club is the Olympic Sports Centre at Pirita just outside Tallinn, built for the 1980 Moscow Games. Optimistic dinghies bob in its calm waters and larger yachts pull in from all parts of the sea. There are few proper marinas on the coast, but island havens, working ports, such as Liepāja in Latvia, or some of the fishing villages on Lithuania's Neringa Spit, are prime targets for development and outside companies are already showing an interest. Larger harbours will have more to offer with the disappearance of the Soviet Fleet.

The hazards of sailing the Baltic waters include half-hidden rocks and promontories: 1,578 miles (2,540 km) of Estonia's 2,350-mile (3,780-km) coast belongs to its 1,500 islands. A particular danger is the strait between the country's west coast and the islands of Hiiumaa and Saaremaa, and on the landward side of the smaller islands of Vormsi and Muhu.

The principal 40-mile (64-km) Muhu Vain channel dodges one way and another between marker buoys, and many vessels have failed to make it from one end to the other. The 30-mile (48-km) long Irbenskiy Strait, between Saaremaa and Latvia, is also navigated with care, round the 7-mile (11-km) shoal that spills down from the island. A hazard of going aground is that there is no tide to lift vessels free.

But the shallow waters make bathing both warm and safe. It is not surprising that the coast, with its spas and sanatoriums, has for more than a century been a popular resort, not just for Balts, but for everyone from here halfway to the Black Sea. ■

Dinghies at the Pirita Olympic port.

baroque-style building in peach: the Estonian Presidium identifiable from the Mercedes-Benz limousines lined up in its car park.

Not far from here is the popular **Song Festival Stage** (1960). The startlingly enormous amphitheatre looks like the yawning mouth of a great white shark and it can hold 32,000 singers. The grounds, built for 150,000, were stuffed with more than a quarter of a million for an historic rally of the "Singing Revolution" in 1989.

Kadriorg Park is separated from the water by a wide highway. On its other side lies a seaside walk, where hooded crows hop and strollers, come rain or snow. A small amusement park for children stands at its start and a little further down the road the beautiful **Russalka Memorial** (1902). It was erected in memory of the 170 Russian sailors who drowned just off Tallinn harbour on the iron-clad *Russalka* ("Mermaid") in 1893. The granite foundation represents a ship crashing against underwater reefs and the base rises as a sharp cliff. Posed

on top is a bronze angel, cross in hand, facing the sea.

The **Maarjamägi Memorial Complex** (1960) is down the road, back on the inland side of the highway. Distinctly Soviet in its austere monumental lines and not very popular locally, it is nevertheless surprisingly affecting. It is divided into five sections: an obelisk dedicated to the 1917 revolution; two human-sized palms with a (no-longer) eternal flame; a "wounded seagulls" archway representing the resilience of the revolution; a headstone for the Tallinn divisions of the Great Patriotic War in 1944–45; and a grave to a World War II sailor named Yvgeny Nikolov, martyred at the hands of the Nazis.

The highway, here called Pirita Tee, leads on to the **Olympic Yachting Centre**, which was created for the sailing events of the 1980 Olympic Games in Moscow but is still much used by local yachts. **Pirita Beach** stretches along the harbour north of here, though swimming from it is not recommended.

Pirita convent (1407–36) lies over

Below left, blowing hot in the cold. Right, Peeping Tom, Pikk Street.

the bridge and across the highway. It was built for the Swedish-based St Bridget's order of nuns and in its time was one of the two largest buildings in Tallinn (the Dominican monastery was the other). The nuns lived on its north side and the priests and their assistants on the south; behind the vestry was a parlatory with a central partition containing a number of holes through which they could communicate.

The convent was destroyed in 1577 during the Livonian War but the 115-ft (35-metre) high western facade with its arched portal of flagstones is still quite beautiful and the shell of the rest of the main church is also intact. The gravestones strewn over its front yard come from several centuries, for peasants continued to live on the site for a considerable time after its destruction.

One graveyard that simply must be seen is Tallinn's **Forest Cemetery**, situated at Kloostrimetsa, down the road from Pirita. The Baltic peoples are fond of their cemeteries and some people say this is the most beautiful place in all of

Tallinn; surely, it is one of the most beautiful cemeteries in the world. It looks almost like a national park, with graves running up and down small hills under a deep forest of fir trees.

The writer Eduard Vilde was, in 1933, the first to be buried here and most of Estonia's favourite stars have since been buried here, including Georg Ots, Lydia Koidula and Konstantin Päts. Rising just to the right of the main gates is the so-called "hill of celebrities".

On the opposite, western side of Tallinn and in easy reach of the city is an **Open-Air Museum**. Situated at Roc al Mara on the Kakumäe Peninsula, it was opened in 1964 and has more than 60 buildings brought here from all over the country, showing how life has typically been lived in rural Estonia. The museum also serves as a suitable venue for folk-music and dancing.

Suburban reality: Really to understand Tallinn, of course, you must venture off into one of the residential neighbourhoods. Not far from the Forest Cemetery is **Lasnamäe**, an enormous concrete sea of nearly identical buildings with virtually no landscaping, which was the source of great controversy during the Soviet years. Begun in the late 1970s, it was nicknamed the "suburb of Leningrad" because the housing authorities repeatedly installed new immigrants from Russia in them no matter how long locals had been on the waiting-list. It is now more than 70 percent Russian and is commemorated in a song about a young person "with empty eyes" who comes to live here.

The **Kose District** behind Lasnamäe is its virtual opposite. Almost all the homes here are one-family, and there are gardens everywhere. Other pretty neighbourhoods of this kind are **Nõmme** and **Merivälja**. The latter is where most ambassadors and newly rich types live. Conversely, **Mustamäe** and **Väike-Õismäe** are the other "Russian" districts, built during Soviet times with few parks and unstraying structure. The worst part of town is **Kopli**, near the former Soviet military base where people live in barrack-style housing, and the crime rate is high.

Left, fancy gutter, Tallinn. **Right**, St Bridget's convent, Pirita.

NARVA AND THE EAST

The skyline of the most Russian of Estonia's cities is dominated by the Russian and Estonian fortresses which face each other across the border provided by the River Narva. Estonia's second largest city, **Narva**, is the hub of the country's industry, a position reinforced by the building programme undertaken during the Soviet occupation. The city of 100,000 is also closer geographically to Russia's second city, St Petersburg (85 miles/137 km), than to its own capital, Tallinn (131 miles/210 km). With a population that is 98 percent ethnic Russian (few came voluntarily), the questions of citizenship and property ownership will be acute political issues in the coming years.

Narva's name may come from a Baltic/Finnish word, *narvaine,* meaning "the threshold". And indeed Narva has been the focus of attention of great or emerging powers since its earliest days. The city was first mentioned in 1240 when it was listed in census records by the Danes who built Fort Narva (once called Herrmannstadt) which they sold to the Teutonic Order in 1347. In 1492, the year Columbus sailed to the New World and the Russians finally repelled the Mongols, Tsar Ivan III built a fort at Ivangorod on "his" side of the river.

The Teutonic Knights responded by enlarging theirs to overlook Ivan's. The tsar swiftly tried to outdo the knights but, in the rush, the engineers forgot to include a church. The story goes that the furious tsar gave the engineers just another 24 hours to construct a church or risk death, which they did.

In 1558, after the Russians had taken Narva, the Teutonic Knights asked the Swedes for assistance. By the late 1600s, Sweden had appropriated all German properties so the knights turned to their old enemy, the Russians, for help. Peter the Great obliged.

The result was the Northern War which began near Narva in 1700. When the Peace Treaty of Nystad was signed in 1721, the city was once again under Russian control where it remained and flourished for two centuries.

By the late 19th century Narva was an industrial giant and major seaport, rivalling Tallinn. Its largest company, Kreenholm Textile Manufacturing, employed more than 10,000 people in its factories where Estonia's first strike was organised in 1872.

During the first republic Narva remained part of Estonia, but was affected by economic depression during the 1920s and 1930s. On 17 August 1941 the Germans arrived and when, in July 1944, they were finally driven out, 98 percent of the city had been destroyed.

After the war, the Russians set about rebuilding Narva. Two hydroelectric plants were built on the river with a third, powered by oil, situated about 5 miles (8 km) west of the town. Together they produce most of the energy for northeastern Estonia and a region of Russia extending into St Petersburg.

The new and the old: The city has not changed any of the old Russian street names and it has the last remaining

statue of **Lenin** in the Baltics standing at the edge of a small park on **Leningrad Boulevard** just beyond the roundabout. On the back side of the same park are two adjoining buildings which date from the Swedish period and once formed part of the old city walls and main gate. The rest of the charming **Old Town** lies between here and the river.

The **Friendship Bridge** is the main crossing between Russia and Estonia, and most foreign visitors will need a visa to make the 5-minute walk across it to see Ivangorod. On the Narva side, all sightseeing, except for the impressive **1872 Kreenholm Strike Memorial**, is north of the fort and easily explored on foot. The memorial is inside the factory on Lenini Prospekt; permission to see it is needed from the supervisor's office.

Inside the multi-storied **Fort Narva** a permanent exhibition of local history fills several rooms. Of particular interest are the photographs showing how Narva looked before it was destroyed during World War II by Russian and German bombing. Other parts are given over to touring exhibits; there is a small concert hall, and the surrounding countryside is on display through the small windows on the top floor of **Pik Herrmann** (Long Herman) tower.

The walls around the fort are walkable and photographers should note that in the late afternoon the southwest corner bastion offers superb views of both forts. The more adventurous may want to walk along the river's edge to the beach and then up the bluff for pictures of both forts separated by the river.

The **Old Town Hall**, built by the Swedes, was one of the few buildings left standing after World War II. It is located on Komsoli Street, two blocks behind the river and is now a school for artistically talented children. An elaborately beamed period ceiling can be seen in the foyer.

Bastions once circled the city, but many were destroyed during World War II leaving only those along the river. A pleasant, tree-shaded stroll along them leads to the **Narva Art Centre** on Kumunarov Street. Once a palace built **The Swedish Town Hall in Narva.**

158

for Peter the Great, it is an exhibition centre, and under its director, Karina Taudre, it gives classes on art awareness to children from the age of five. It shows local artists' work and has a permanent collection from the Lavrezov family which includes historical portraits of local gentry and 18th and 19th-century Russian genre paintings.

The 9-mile (15-km) drive north along the river to **Narva-Jöesuu** on the coast is a dull and flat one. At intervals are monuments commemorating the many regional battles dating back to the Northern War, and brides still leave their bouquets as a tribute to fallen heroes.

Peter the Great visited the town when it was originally called Hungerburg and gave it its present name. Narva-Jöesuu was a popular 19th-century spa town which attracted many Russian artists and writers among its visitors, but today the intrusive factory chimneys make the beach uninspiring. The town is, however, still filled with turn-of-the-century **gingerbread houses**, and one of the most colourful is just off Ranna Street. The **Orthodox Church**, created from rough-hewn logs, is a gem.

To the west, near **Meriküla**, look for the **Shiskin Tree**, festooned with bright ribbons. Couples come here on their wedding day to make a wish, then tie a ribbon on to as high a branch as possible. The higher the ribbon, the better the chance that the wish will be granted. If the couple wish to start a family soon, then a pink or blue ribbon is also added.

West to Tallinn: Leaving Narva, the M11 courses through industrial suburbs until beyond **Sillamäe**. Just to the south of Sillamäe, however, is the farming community of **Sinimäe**, clustered around the only wooded hill in the area, which has seen innumerable battles since Viking days. During the Northern War, Swedish troops used it as a defensive position; in 1918 the Estonian Nationalists defeated the communists here, and in World War II over 45,000 Russian and 15,000 Germans were casualties on these gentle slopes.

Another Northern War battle site is at **Toila** on the coast between Sillamäe

and **Johvi**. There is a large **regional park** here containing over 200 different plants, nature walks and a beach of round pebbles. The park is on the former property of a German baron who had a manor house built in 1899. Estonia's first president used it as a holiday retreat but it was destroyed in 1943. The **River Saiut** flows through the park and in 1700 Charles XII of Sweden stood on its high western bank, facing his Russian counterpart on the other side.

Between **Johvi** and **Kohtla-Järve** rolling countryside begins, and several **windmills** dot the skyline, all that remain of the hundreds which once covered the landscape. The large mounds which are visible from the road are slag heaps left from shale-oil exploration early this century. Today, underground fires are common and large sinkholes may appear without warning.

The **cliffs** which run for about 18 miles (30 km) between **Martsa** and **Aa** form part of a limestone-based plateau and are best reached via the road to Ontika. Rising 182 ft (56 metres) above

the sea, the views from them are terrific.

Purtsee Castle at Purtsee to the west of Kohtla-Järve is easily missed as it stands several hundred yards from the M11 in the middle of several other buildings. The recently restored red-roofed building dates from the Swedish period when the town was a freeport. Although partially destroyed during the Northern War, people continued to live in it until 1938. The keeper of the keys lives in a nearby farmhouse and will show visitors around.

Kunda, 9 miles (15 km) off the main road on the P18 and beautifully situated on the coast, is marred by a fine coating of white dust from the enormous local cement plant. Recently bought by a Finnish/Estonian/American consortium, the new owners are trying to reduce the air pollutants, which are carried as far as southern Finland.

Midway between Narva and Tallinn is **Rakvere**, the country's seventh largest city. The **castle**, which acts as a beacon, was built in 1253 on the site of a wooden one which was destroyed dur-

The castle at Rakvere.

ing the Livonian War. There are also the ruins of a **Franciscan monastery** from 1515 and several charming streets of late 19th-century buildings

Green lung: After the industry of the east, **Lahemaa National Park** comes as a breath of fresh air, and locals point to the coincidence of Soviet bigwigs living in the area when it was created in 1971. Until 1989 permits were required to visit the park which covers 162,500 acres (65,000 hectares) of land, water and off-shore islands between Rakvere and Tallinn. Now it is open to everyone.

More than 75 percent of the park is woodland and the population is less than 20 per square kilometre. There are remains of ancient settlements, freshwater lakes, a few farms and four manor houses (restored or in the process of). Sheltered bays dip between craggy promontories which thrust into the Gulf of Finland. It is an important wildlife area with deer and elk, and during the migration season, bird-watchers look for special species such as the black stork. Plant life abounds and among the 850 documented varieties is the rare arctic bramble.

Vösu and **Loksa** are the park's two main towns; Loksa is much larger, with a cargo port, little ambience and a mainly Russian population. From either, it is easy to make trips around the park.

Palmse, south of Vösu, is the most famous of Lahemaa's manor houses. In 1286, a group of nuns from the Cistercian Order of St Michael in Tallinn were given the land by King Erik Montvert of Denmark. One of their first projects was to build a pond for their fish farm, and the one they created is still in use today. In 1673, the estate was bought by the Vaan der Pahlen family who built the current manor house in 1785. The Estonian government confiscated it in 1923; during World War II it was a German command centre, and it was destroyed by the Russians in 1944. Renovation lasted between 1972 and 1985, and today the estate is a perfect period piece, filled with Empire furniture.

The **lake** at the rear of the house is inhabited by a family of extremely nasty

Lahemaa National Park.

swans. A **summer house** and a **winter garden** add to the beauty of the grounds. In the orchard are over 30 varieties of fruit trees, many dating from the end of the 19th century.

The nearby church of **Illumäe** was built by and contains the grave of the most illustrious member of the Vaan der Pahlen family, Carl Magnus. He fought against Napoleon Bonaparte, allowed the peasants who worked the farm to use his last name, and in 1823 opened the first school for local children. In front of the church is a **memorial** to those killed during the 20th-century's wars and those who perished in the Gulag.

Vergi, on the coast but east of Võsu, was home to a large Soviet naval base and the last of its occupiers left in 1992; the white building at the tip of the peninsula is a customs house. Beyond Vergi is **Altja**, a living museum of thatched-roof, weatherbeaten houses. The nearby headland is dotted with picturesque sheds for storing fishing gear.

Sagadi, to the south, is another restored German manor house. Built in 1765, it became a school during Estonia's First Independence. Restoration work was finished in 1986, and although its original elegance remains outside, inside houses a **Museum of Forestry** and a mixed bag of furnishings.

On the western side of the park, the manor of **Kolga**, now the administrative centre for a large collective, remains unrestored. (Plans were drawn up for its makeover, but a lack of funds has caused an indefinite postponement.) The graceful 18th-century building is a cliché of a crumbling pile with falling plaster, exposed beams, peeling wallpaper and a cracked exterior. The owners have turned one of the old stable blocks into a small, very basic **hostel**, and if enthusiasm were the basis for a rating, would be given 10 out of 10.

Käsmu, the peninsula on the west side of Võsu's bay, has some of the cleanest waters between Tallinn and St Petersburg. The impressive wooden houses were built by smugglers who made illegal vodka and sold it in Finland during the early days of this cen-

Left, unrestored Kolga manor. Right, restored Sagadi manor.

tury. The town was once a major ship-building town with an apprentice programme which attracted young men from the entire Baltic region.

Off-shore, towards the end of Käsmu's peninsula, is **Hell Island**, and beyond it is **Mohni Island**, an uninhabited nature reserve. The coastline is noted for the boulders which dot the shallow waters, and many of the largest have been given names. Nearby are large piles of stones and it is customary to add to them: if you put yours on without the others falling, your wish will come true.

At **Viitna**, south of Palmse on the M11, the 17th-century **coaching inn** has been restored and turned into a restaurant for hungry travellers. Tallinn is about an hour's drive from here; the M11 is a dual carriageway for most of the way and forms part of the new Via Baltica linking Tallinn, Riga and Vilnius.

South to Tartu: Just east of **Jõhvi**, look for signs to **Vasknarva**. Travelling south via this old Livonian fortress town on Lake Peipsi is not the most direct route into southern Estonia, but it is the more interesting, and adds less than 25 miles (40 km) to the 115-mile (185-km) journey to Tartu.

Approaching **Kuramäe**, the green domes of the cathedral of Pühtitsa (Estonian for "holy place") convent beckon through a forest of oak and pine. This is the only **Eastern Orthodox nunnery** in the Baltic States, built on a site which has been sacred since the 16th century when a peasant saw a vision of the Virgin Mary on the top of a hill. An icon was found beneath an ancient oak tree near the same spot, and the icon of the Assumption of the Mother of God is still the convent's most prized possession, surrounded by precious gems and mounted on a pillar to the right of the cathedral altar.

The first nun was sent to Pühtitsa in 1888 to establish a convent, and the complex of buildings, circled by a high granite wall, was designed by Mikail Preobrazhensky, a professor at the St Petersburg Academy of Arts.

The five-domed, three-aisle **Cathedral of the Assumption,** which will

Communal dining hall, Kuramäe nunnery.

accommodate up to 1,200 worshippers, was finished in 1910. There are five other churches in the complex, including a small one outside the main walls which is used for funeral services. The **Church of St Sergius of Radonezh** is located at the apex of the **Holy Mount** where the first miracle occurred, and is a five-minute walk along a lime-tree shaded path from the convent's central area. Built in 1895, the church is dedicated to the patron of the Order, Prince Sergi Shakhovsky, and it contains his family sepulchre.

Under post-war Soviet occupation buildings were allowed to deteriorate and by 1961 it appeared the convent could close. A change in Moscow's attitude toward religion and a new bishop in Tallinn began the convent's physical rejuvenation.

Today there are over 100 nuns in residence, ranging in age from 18 to 80-plus. Some 60 acres (24 hectares) of the 187-acre (75-hectare) property is farmed. Cash is raised from the sale of icons and other religious items made by the nuns. These, plus tapes and records of the convent's choir, can be bought at the small information centre.

Tours are offered between 9am and 5pm. Women are requested to wear skirts that come below the knee; men long trousers, and both sexes must have their upper arms covered. Divine Services are held at 6pm daily and 9am on Sunday. Anyone may attend but, unless of the Orthodox faith, you are asked to remain in the back of the church and refrain from walking around, talking and/or taking photographs.

Nothing about the small cluster of houses which comprise **Vasknarva** (Estonian for "waterfall") reflects its great past when it was the guardian of the river route into Narva at the northern end of **Lake Peipsi**, Europe's fourth largest lake which forms a large part of Estonia's eastern border. The town was founded at the beginning of the 12th century as a way-station on the trade route linking the principalities of Novorod and Peskov with Tartu and Tallinn. However, after the decisive Russian victory in the Northern War, the need for a stronghold waned, and Vasknarva began its slide into obscurity. All that remains of the old **Livonian fortress** is part of two walls.

Fishing has long been the mainstay of the village, but with Estonian independence its geography has once again made it part of a trade route. However, instead of the north-south commercial axis, the small boats do thriving business transporting contraband Western goods eastward.

The road along the top of Lake Peipsi goes through forests of tall conifers and beside white beaches of bleached oyster shells. There are occasional fishing villages strung along the water's edge, their clapboard houses painted a variety of colours, each fronted by banks of vibrant flowers and backed by greenhouses which are used to extend the short growing season.

Mustvee, 40 miles (65 km) north of Tartu, is Lake Peipsi's largest town. It has two Orthodox churches, a fish processing plant and several out-of-place modern apartment blocks.

Left, gathering shells, Lake Peipsi. Right, fishermen at Vasknarva.

TARTU AND THE SOUTH

People often call southern Estonia, probing into the shelf of northern Latvia and western Russia, the "real" Estonia. This is where the percentage of non-Estonians in some towns falls into the single-figures, the dialect is deep Finno-Ugric, and the locals have kept up a tradition of hospitality and generosity.

The region is split roughly between the undulating Sakala, Otepää and Haanja highlands. Each has its own "metropolitan" focus – respectively, Viljandi, Otepää, and Võru – but these cities have a rural feel. For the most part, industry is secondary or subordinate to agriculture.

Brains of Estonia: The largest city in the southern half of Estonia, with 115,500 residents, is **Tartu**, to the east and 116 miles (187 km) south of Tallinn. Just as many say the south is the "real" Estonia, many call Tartu the "real" capital.

At the very least, Tartu is the intellectual capital. Founded in 1632, **Tartu University** was also a powerhouse for Latvian intellectuals during their National Awakening. It has endured as the main seat of higher education in the humanities and currently has 8,000 students. It is also endowed with non-esoteric institutions: an agricultural and a medical school.

Tartu was first noted in 1030 as a stronghold built by Grand Duke Yaroslav of Kiev. The city has been razed on several occasions since – by Estonians in 1061, Germans in 1224, the Northern War in 1708 and fire in 1775 – and most buildings in the Old Town date from the 18th century.

The city has developed in a north-south fashion along the Emajõgi River, with most of the main university buildings sprinkled on the northern end where the Old Town lies. This district is immediately distinguishable by the wide cobbled Raekoja Plats (**Town Hall Square**) in its centre, anchored by a pinkish neoclassical Town Hall (1798) at its head. The grey clock-tower surging from the middle of its roof was added in the 19th century to help the students be on time for classes.

Running along the northern side of the square is an unbroken row of pastel-coloured buildings greatly responsible for Tartu's reputation as the neoclassical prima donna of Estonia. The most noticeable of them is **Barclay House** (1793) at No. 18. Erected on a wooden foundation in marshland that later dried up, it leans pronouncedly to the left. Inside is the **Pildigalerii**, whose permanent collection centres on the Pallas Higher Art School that existed in Tartu from 1919 to 1940.

The **University Building** lies just a couple of blocks away, at 18 Ulikooli Street, a stately oasis in the cramped and crumbling side streets of the Old Town. Pale yellow with six white columns, the University Building is the most impressive neoclassical structure in Estonia. Completed in 1809, it was designed by the architect Johann Krause.

Further down Jaani Street is the 14th-century brick Gothic **St John's church**. It has been closed for restoration for

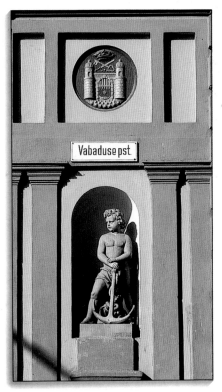

years, but hundreds of tiny terracotta sculptures can be seen on its exterior. The 15 faces above its pointed portal represent the Last Judgment.

Across the street is a green building (1640–90) that was one of the first sites of the original Swedish-run university. Restored in 1766 and again in the end of the 19th century, it is now the **Tartu Police Station**. Locals call it "the most expensive hotel in town". In 1944, 192 Tartu citizens were rounded up by the communists and murdered in the yard.

The neoclassical rule is further broken on the south side of Town Hall Square. First along Vabaduse Street is the grim brown **market hall** (1937), heavy inside with the smell of smoked sausage. The **bus station** stands on the next block, and then the **outdoor market**, devoted half to foodstuffs and half to dry goods: in fact, anything you can't find easily in stores. Across the road from each is its more recent counterpart: the Tartu Department Store on Riia Street, the bus terminal and the Central Supermarket.

Ritual heights: The **Vanemuine Theatre** (1977), at 6 Vanemuise, and adjacent **University Library** (1980), at 1 W. Struwe Street, are the final modern touches. Both are white and functional, but the library is distinguished by the students perpetually gathered on its wide cement plaza for a quick smoke.

It is a short walk from here to **Toome Hill**, the park that dominates the Old Town. The **People's Monument** (1807) stands opposite the west entrance. It was designed by Krause to commemorate the gravesite on which the university building was erected. Turn up from here under the grey **Kuradisild** (1913) or Devil's Bridge – named for a Professor Mannteuffel from Germany who, in the late 19th century, introduced Estonia to the use of rubber gloves in surgical operations but whose name translated to "devil" – and you will find yourself between the **University Internal Hospital** (1808) and the **University Maternity Hospital** (1838). Straight ahead is the pink **Angel's Bridge**, also named as a result of a linguistic confu-

House in the Soup District.

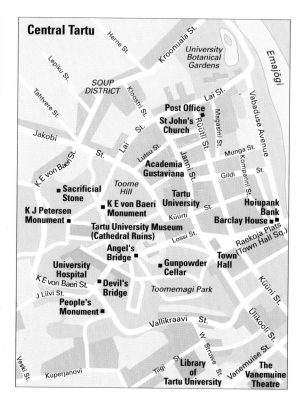

Central Tartu

- Herne St.
- Lepiku St.
- Kroonuaia St.
- University Botanical Gardens
- Emajõgi
- SOUP DISTRICT
- Tahtvere St.
- Kloostri St.
- Lai St.
- Vabaduse Avenue
- Jakobi
- Post Office
- St John's Church
- Riiütli St.
- Magasini St.
- K E von Baeri St.
- St.
- Lai St.
- Lutsu St.
- Munga St.
- Kompanni St.
- Academia Gustaviana
- Janni St.
- Gildi St.
- Toome Hill
- Sacrificial Stone
- K E von Baeri Monument
- Tartu University
- Hoiupank Bank
- K J Petersen Monument
- Küürti St.
- Barclay House
- Tartu University Museum (Cathedral Ruins)
- Lossi St.
- Raekoja Plats (Town Hall Sq.)
- Angel's Bridge
- University Hospital
- K E von Baeri St.
- Devil's Bridge
- Gunpowder Cellar
- Town Hall
- J Liivi St.
- Toomemagi Park
- Küüni St.
- People's Monument
- Vallikraavi St.
- Ülikooli St.
- Veski St.
- Kuperjanovi
- Tiigi St.
- W. Struwe St.
- Library of Tartu University
- Vanemuise St.
- The Vanemuine Theatre

sion: Toomemagi Park was laid out in English style and the locals confused the words English and angel.

Toomemagi is strewn with statues of people connected with Tartu University. In spring biology students traditionally wash the pensive head of Karl Ernst von Baer – a professor linked to Darwin – with champagne and put a tie around him. The monument to the writer Kristjan Jaak Peterson – the first Estonian national to enter the university – is shown erect with a stick in his hand because he is said to have walked the more than 155 miles (250 km) from Riga to Tartu.

The "Romantic Corner" of the park lies to the left from the statue of Baer. It consists of a stone mound called the **Hill of Kissing** to the top of which bridegrooms must carry their new wives, a low **Bridge of Sighing** with a well-worn stone bench, and **Sacrificial Stone** where the lovelorn can leave a prayer to the ancient gods. Sacred stones are found all over Estonia; people used to wait for a Thursday full moon then gather about

them to pray, leaving (non-bloody) sacrifices. Tartu students have continued this ritual by ceremonially burning their notebooks here at midnight on the Thursday before their exams.

The monumental ruins of the **Cathedral church**, for whom the hill is named, loom above this part of the park. Begun in the 13th century, this was once the largest brick-Gothic church in the Baltic countries, but the main body was destroyed in the Livonian War. The broken wings of 10 flying buttresses give an idea of its former grandeur.

The huge choir on the church's eastern end was completely restored in the early 1800s under the direction of Krause. For a time it served as the university library, but it now contains the **Tartu University Museum**. On each floor are exhibitions of the history of the university, from its opening in 1632 in honour of the Swedish King Gustavus Adolphus. A lovely white baroque hall on the second floor is a public concert room with walls lined by cases of antique biological species. On the south-

The ruined cathedral.

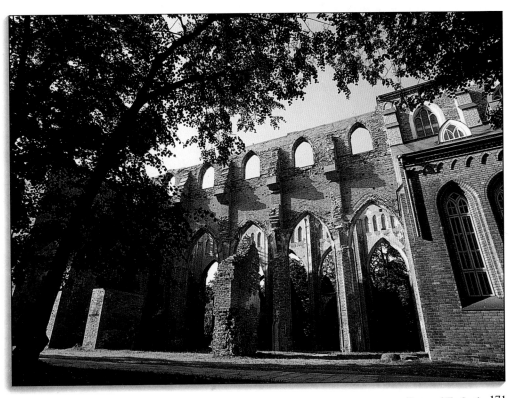

east edge of the park is the Gunpowder Cellar or **Pussirohukelder Restoran** (1778), now a vaulted-ceiling restaurant built troglodyte-fashion into the side of Toome Hill. From its "roof" is a nice view over the city.

Neighbourhoods with flavour: Tartu is split into different districts, each with its own name. Lai Street divides the Old Town from **Suppilinn**, or Soup Town, which got its name because its streets are called after soup ingredients such as Bean and Potato. The industrial area where the Hotel Taru stands is the **Ropka District**, and the attractive **Karlova District** has cut-corner wooden houses built during the Estonian Republic as boarding houses. The area of stately homes behind Toomemagi Park, where mostly university professors live, is the **Tähtvere District.**

Some of the most curious buildings in Tartu are ordinary houses created in these districts over the past two centuries. The weathered house at 65 Marta Street, beside the wooded park in which the dilapidated **Karlova manor** stands,

for example, is a marvel of wood and stone edging work.

At 27 Riia, **St Paul's church** (1919) was designed by the Finnish architect Eliel Saarinen. Created in red brick with a square tower, it looks a bit like a fire station. One wing has been made over into Tartu's **Sports Museum**.

Westward: The small city of **Viljandi**, 48 miles (77km) to the west on the P57, clings to the slopes of a primeval valley plumbed by **Lake Viljandi**. Now the capital of the **Sakala upland**, with 23,000 inhabitants, the site has been settled since AD 1000, but the Old Town is tiny; one small grid between Tallinna and Tartu streets and the **Castle Park**. Its appeal depends on its handsome lakeside setting and the ruined castle that is perched on a series of hills above the water.

A good place to start a tour of the town is the **Viljandi Local History Museum** (1779–80) at 12 Kindral Laidoneri Square, in the Old Town. This square used to be the market place and its central fountain covers what was the **Dancers in Viljandi.**

town well. The museum is installed downstairs in Viljandi's third oldest building and contains a model of the former castle. It also contains an abundance of painstakingly decorated old objects of daily use, such as tankards and horse yokes. There are also regular exhibitions of continuing local handicraft and artwork.

Two houses down, at No. 8, is the **Cultural College**. Viljandi has contributed substantially to Estonia's cultural history, and the town now has three well-known choirs: the Koit Merited Mixed Choir, the Sakala Male Choir and the Eha Female Choir. A professional drama company is housed in one of the town's few contemporary buildings, the **Ugala Theatre** (1981), beside the Valuoja River.

First a grand hotel, the building of the Cultural College was occupied during World War II by the Nazis, who called it "the hospital". It is presumed to have been a site of human experimentation. At dawn, a truck would cart corpses away. The 18th-century **Town Hall** stands one block away from here on Linnu Street.

The entrance to the Castle Park is just down Lossi Street, over a long wooden footbridge. Begun in 1223, the **Order Fortress of Viljandi** is presumed to have been the largest fortress in the Baltics, designed to stretch over three adjacent hills, with its only entrance on the first hill, occupied by servants. The second fold, once split between servants and horses, is now an airy field edged with bits of old wall. A dog show is held here every summer and, in June, a midsummer bonfire. If you climb (carefully) up on the stone by the edge, you will get a great breezy view over a long and narrow lake. The third hill supported the castle, the church and the prison. This final section has more ruins than the other two and they stand out starkly against the sky.

A bright red-and-white **suspension bridge** now leads from this end of the castle grounds into the rest of the park. Built in 1879, the bridge was brought to the town from Riga in 1931 by a Ger-

The view from Big Egg, near Võru.

man count whose favourite daughter, the story goes, had stubbornly persisted in using it for racing her horse across.

The 15th-century church of the former Franciscan monastery, **St John's**, has its own small wooden footbridge, at the head of Castle Park just off Pikk Street. It is used primarily for concerts. The town's main Lutheran church, **St Paul's** (1863–66), lies outside the park across Vaksali Road, closer to the centre of town. Red brick with stone inlay, it has an industrial-age Gothic veneer.

By the lake's shore Viljandi has a different feel: sportier, happier, younger. At one end are tennis courts and a town stadium, and there is also an **athlete's hotel** and a **waterside restaurant**. Boats and pedalos can be rented from the pier beside the restaurant. **Viljandi Lake** is supposedly not polluted, but it is advisable to row out to the centre if you want to jump in because the floor is so muddy.

Winter resort: Estonia's entire southern region is dotted with pretty lakes, many of which are swimmable (though it is always good to check with a local).

The largest, at 105 sq. miles (270 sq. km), is **Vorts Lake**. It is, however, at its deepest only 20 ft (6 metres).

The lakes of **Otepää** in the **Otepää Highlands** help make this cosy town not just one of Estonia's most popular winter resorts but a gracious rest spot in summer. Otepää is only a short drive southwest from Tartu, but in peacefulness it could be a million miles away. Its population doubles in winter to around 5,000. About 30 of the town's residents are non-Estonian.

A local sausage factory serves the community with a shop on its premises and the largest single employer is the Otepää Truck Repair Garage. Resort facilities include an unpretentious ski jump, cross-country ski paths, a scattering of downhill slopes, a public beach, and a few hotels and bed & breakfasts. The biggest event is a 37-mile (60-km) cross-country marathon that draws about 12,000 skiers every February.

The town and its surroundings have been designated a "protected area". Building above three storeys is forbidden, salt cannot be used against ice on the roads, and motorboating on Otepää's lakes and hunting and camping in its woods are prohibited.

The town clusters up against these woods, and the centre has a pleasantly closed-in feeling, accentuated by a skinny triangular central park. The **Tourist Information Centre** is lodged here, at 9 Lipuväljak, and the **Otepää Theatre**, home to an amateur theatre company and most town gatherings.

The oldest building in town is **Otepää church**, a hill and dale away. Opened in 1608, it was built by Estonian peasants so that they wouldn't have to attend the church (no longer extant) of the German population. The folklorist Jakob Hurt was its first Estonian pastor, from 1872 to 1880. The current steeple was added in 1860 and is 168 ft (51.5 metres) high.

When the Estonian Students Co-operative was forbidden from consecrating their flag in Tartu in 1884, they defiantly brought it to the Otepää church. Stone reliefs on the front doors that depicted this momentous nationalistic event were destroyed by the Soviets, but

A miller takes a break.

the locals replaced them with bronze casts in 1990. The **Monument to the 54** in front of the church, dedicated to the soldiers from Otepää who died in the War of Independence, was also blown up by the Soviets – once in the 1950s, and again in the early 1980s – but each time it was stubbornly replaced by the people of Otepää.

Linnamägi, former site of a 10th to 11th-century wooden stronghold and a bishop's 13th-century stone castle, is a small tree-covered hill a short walk south from the church past a municipal garden. The first level of the hill is marked with a large stone monument dated 1116, the year when Otepää was first recorded. Locals use this spot for their midsummer celebrations. The excavated ruins of the castle stand on the shelf above. The expansive vista from here makes it easy to imagine why ancient warriors fought for it.

Dryad magic: In ancient times Estonians gathered under oaks whenever they had to make important decisions. The most famous oak – the one that deco-

rates the two-krone bank note – is a couple of miles outside the centre of Otepää centre. Standing wide and noble between a cow pasture and vegetable patch and Püha Lake, the **Pühajärv Oak** is 65 ft (20 metres) tall. Five people linking arms can reach around it and it is believed to be the biggest and oldest in the country. Its popular name is "the Sojatamm", or War Tree, because of its part in independence history. In 1841, a local German landlord tried to force the Estonian peasants on his land to use heavier equipment than they felt their horses could draw. They refused, which resulted in a battle beneath the oak. The peasants lost, but their act became a legend of Estonian solidarity.

Neitsijärv, or Virgin's Lake, which you pass on the way from the town to the War Tree, derives its name from the Middle Ages when brides had to spend their first married night in the bed of the Pühajärv landlord. One beautiful young girl left her wedding for the manor and never appeared. In the morning, they found her bridal dress beside this lake –

Neighbours, Mehikoorma, Lake Peipsi.

where she had drowned herself. The largest lake in the area is **Lake Püha**. It is alluring, but swimmers should be wary of hidden springs. Nearly every summer someone drowns in it, cramped by unexpected ice-cold water. The public beach at the end is safe: there is a lifeguard here all summer, and pedalos and boats can be rented.

The Soviet dissidents Andrei Sakarov and Alexander Solzhenitsyn both used to spend quiet weeks by Lake Püha and, if you ask, locals will show you where the prime minister of Estonia under the Soviets kept his holiday home. (He alone was allowed to use a motorboat here.) His house is now a guest house owned by Tartu University.

English paean: About 13 miles (20 km) south from here is **Sangaste manor** (1874–81) built for Count Friedrich Georg Magnus von Berg as a small-scale copy of Windsor Castle. It is a particularly inorganic-looking orange-brick mansion set back amid acres of agricultural plains. The manor was seized in the 1930s and most of the family fled to Finland. Sangaste has passed through many hands since, even housing hay and a tractor in its octagonal, multi-vaulted ballroom after World War II. In the 1970s, it was used as a Young Pioneers' Camp. It is these days a hotel and a conference centre.

Wide pastureland separates Sangaste from **Valga**, the southernmost city in Estonia, straddling the border so narrowly that part of it actually lies in Latvia. Many non-Estonians live here, and unlike other southern towns it is not in the hills and it is industrially developed with a huge animal feed factory and wine distillery.

If you edge down along the border for a while you will plunge into one of Estonia's largest forests. The **Mõniste Outdoor Museum** lies this way, in which is re-created a 19th-century southern Estonian farmhouse.

About 30 miles (50 km) due east, and due south of Võru, is the peaceful hamlet of **Rõuge**. The picture of southern harmony, Rõuge curls in around seven clear lakes. One, called **Rõuge Suur-**

Vastseliina castle.

järv, or Rõuge's Big Lake, is the deepest in Estonia (125 ft/38 metres). Rõuge church (1730) is a little jewel with a smooth white exterior and red-roofed bell-tower. Its organ was built by the famous Kriisa Brother organ-makers who came from the area. Behind the church lies the **Valley of Nightingales** which attracts hundreds of these tuneful birds in spring.

Further east is the centre of the **Haanja Highland**. Haanja is slightly higher than the Otepää and Sakala uplands and its forests are deeper, but it has also been widely tamed by potato fields and pastureland. Its climax is **Suur-Munamägi**, or Big Egg Hill: the highest peak in Estonia, reaching 1,044 ft (318 metres) above sea level. A 115-ft (35-metre) observation tower has been added to its summit, and the result is a view that truly is heavenly. On the clearest days, you can see all the way to Russia and Latvia.

It may also be possible to glimpse the ruins of **Vastseliina Castle**. To reach it, head east towards the "new" Vastseliina

village, whose cultural centre is in an 18th-century manor house.·

The "old" village, called Vahtseliina, was built in the 14th century around the castle, but not much is left of either. The red-and-beige-brick castle has been reduced to two towers and one section of wall, lost in an overgrown section of field. The 19th-century Vahtseliina **coach stop**, where a tsar once stayed, has been turned into a restaurant.

The folds of Haanja were created during the Ice Age, and the landscape is smooth and eternal. Gentle pasture are edged by lone farmhouses and tiny lakes appear then fade.

The **A S Etas Ski Area**, 7 miles (12 km) south of Võru, has only one small car-park and ski lodge, at the crest of a sudden bowl, 230 ft (70 metres) high and 4 miles (7 km) long, that falls into a tree-lined valley floating in mist. The lift equipment is being updated and there is no equipment for making artificial snow. But you can also cross-country ski or sled, and the surrounding woods are filled with game. You may well

encounter a deer bounding gracefully across the road.

The most popular place for fishing in the area is **Verijärv**, or Blood Lake, a bit closer to Võru and filled with perch and pike. Large and picturesque, at the base of another steep forested bowl, it got its name because a servant supposedly once drove a cruel lord of the manor into its waters.

Võru, the urban centre for the Haanja highlands, is sprawled out around the biggest lake in the town, **Tamulajarv**. Along with agriculture, Võru depends on furniture-making and dairy production and the population is about 19,000 (about 90 percent Estonian).

The town was officially established in 1784, and the small yellow Orthodox church and the also yellow St Katarina church were built soon after.

The most famous 18th-century structure in Võru, however, is the **Friedrich Reinhold Kreutzwald Museum** (1793), on 31 Kreutzwald Street, where the Estonian writer and doctor lived for most of his life. Kreutzwald was born in

the Rakvere region in 1803 and studied in Tartu from 1826 to 1833. But he spent the next 44 years practising medicine in Võru where he compiled *Kalevipoeg*, the Estonian national epic.

The museum is divided between three houses. The first is where the small home of Kreutzwald's Estonian mother stood; she couldn't live in the same house as Kreutzwald's wife, Maria, who was from a wealthy German family in Tartu. This house has an exhibition of his life and many publications.

His own home has been kept as much as possible as it was when he lived there and it includes portraits of the family, who, ironically, spoke only German at home. Maria couldn't understand why her husband bothered with Estonian. On the walls of the low building at the back of the yard are interpretations of the *Kalevipoeg* from a panorama of artists, including some of Estonia's best-known, such as Erik Haamer, Juri Arrak and Kritjan Raud.

Kreutzwald Park runs towards the lake down Katariina Street to a statue of Kreutzwald. Võru's **Regional Museum** stands at the start of the park.

The drive from Võru back up to Tartu on the P64 gradually becomes less and less hilly but the forests remain. Tucked into one that has been protected by the state as a "gene bank", just beyond Põlva on the right, is the **Kiidjarve Mill**. Constructed in 1914, it is unexpectedly fine, with careful brick trimming on orangish brick. It is the largest functioning watermill in Europe.

The **Karilatsi Outdoor Museum** lies on the other side of the Tartu road just beyond Kiidjarve. One section displays farm equipment in sheds that look very shaky. The other has an old schoolhouse still set for lessons, a windmill you can enter and an overgrown garden that was designed to be a map of the region.

Just outside Tartu is a better maintained outdoor museum of agricultural history, the **Ülenurme Museum**. Fittingly, the surrounding landscape is anchored by far-flung farms and many are under construction. It is a sign that the south is ploughing on, refusing to be shaken by the vagaries of the north.

Left, Võru house of the writer Kreutzwald. **Right**, the town's oral traditions.

PARNU AND
THE WEST COAST

The spas of Estonia's western shore used to be favoured by Russian tsars, and even under the Soviets Russians flocked here for their summer holidays. But years of neglect have left many of the prettiest resort buildings crumbling, and almost all the beaches are now either officially closed or should be, due to pollution.

Fortunately, most of Estonia's coastal towns nurtured cultures of their own over the centuries, reaching back to feudal times. The hardest hit town has, naturally, been the most developed resort. **Pärnu**, 80 miles (130 km) due south of Tallinn on the M12, lived for its long sandy beach and four sanatoriums. As Russian tourists have dropped off in number, it has begun to take on the hollow feeling, especially by the water, of a forlorn dinosaur.

Still, Pärnu remains one of the few places outside Tallinn where people know how to deal with a tourist. Not that this means it is the most gracious. Although with a population of 54,200 it isn't quite a metropolis, Pärnu has some less pleasant big-city elements such as hard-eyed men in cheap jackets hanging around bus and taxi stops waiting for vulnerable holidaymakers. But the service community is pleasant and generally sympathetic to tourists' needs.

And holidaymakers still have reason to come. The long beachfront and numerous parks continue to be restorative places to stroll, and the **Old Town** is ripe with structural curiosities. Younger Estonians particularly like Pärnu; every July there is a large jazz festival, and all summer the bar and cafés are hopping.

The city proper, first noted in 1251, is divided by the Pärnu River. Rather confusingly, the Old Town lies on the south bank within what the locals refer to as the "new" city. The "old" city, north of the river, is where the newer buildings are. The reason for this is linked to Pärnu's complex history. During the 14th century, the area where the Old Town stands was occupied by a castle

and fortification. But when the Swedes took power in 1617, they began to build across the river instead. The castle fell into decay and was finally destroyed during the Northern War. This made the section on the north bank the oldest part of the city when, in subsequent centuries, development began to spill back over to the former castle area. This "old city" was, however, flattened during the last war, putting the area with the oldest *buildings*, or the "old town", *back* on the south side of the river.

Touring Pärnu's Old Town is far less complicated. For one thing, it isn't very large. Visiting would take only a couple of hours – if so many of the most eye-catching buildings didn't also contain ear-catching bars and cafés.

Puhavaimo Street, running through just about the Old Town's centre, is one example. First on the block is a delicate yellow building (1670), fronted by a proud balcony that bears four small lions' heads. Squeezed in next to it is an odd red and mustard-coloured house (1877) that mixes everything from corinthian

columns to a flowery grey trim. It in turn more or less melds directly into a green baroque structure (1674) trimmed with courtly white and crowned with an old street lamp. Its cellar is also a popular rock hang-out, the **Crown Mary Bar**.

Generally, however, the Old Town isn't so very old; most buildings date from the 19th century. But it does have two intact 18th-century churches, which are perhaps most remarkable for their physical proximity but absolute disparity. **Ekaterina's** (1765–68) is a weird Orthodox conglomeration of knobs and ledges, with green roofing and unevenly soaring spires. The interior is almost lunatic in its iconicity; silver icons like shields crowd the white walls. Meanwhile, the faded-white Lutheran church, **St Elisabeth's** (1747), at 22 Nikolai a few blocks away, is the ultimate in smooth austerity.

There are also two remnants of the original 14th-century fortifications. One is the peach-coloured "**Red Tower**", saved during the Swedish time to house prisoners. Tucked down a small alley off Hommiku Street, it is easy to miss but the exhibition of excavated objects – such as the only remaining stones from the castle and cannonballs from the 15th and 16th centuries – in its downstairs level is worth seeing. There is also a sketch of how the town used to look in the 15th century. Upstairs is a shop for so-called "local art".

The other piece left of the ancient walls is the **Tallinn Gate**. Sky-blue with tall green doors, it doubles as a bar; **Baar Tallinn Varav** has been carved into the earthworks above it.

Passing through the gate, you suddenly find yourself on a long, tree-lined walk beside a finger of the Pärnu River curled in to create a duck-filled pond. This is the beginning of the lush parks that surround the sanatoriums in an awesome hush.

The sanatoriums still offer a wide variety of treatments. Most frequented the **Mud Baths**, housed in a neoclassical building (1926) at the end of Supeluse Street. But it might be good to think twice about sampling them yourself –

Left, Pärnu Town Hall. Right, starting school.

the mud comes from Haapsalu on the far side of the Matsalu Nature Reserve to the north. Most of the sanatoriums there have been shut.

The mauve **Beach Salon**, next door at 22 Mere Avenue, functions as a cultural centre with a bandstand behind it. Its front pavilion, facing the beach, is an elaborate maze of ornamental wicker arches and fountains.

These two buildings stand by the northwest edge of the **Pärnu Beach**, beginning with the **Women's Beach** where only women and small children are allowed so they can sunbathe nude in peace. You can walk for miles from here south along the tree-lined promenade that parallels the beach, eventually leaving the sanatorium area but continuing past former beach pavilions in octagonal and crescent shapes, dog-walkers, tennis courts and soccer fields, and finally fields of dank, waving reed.

The Old Town has its own walks. Most famous is the triangular **Lydia Koidula Park**. The poetess Koidula (1843–86) was born in a village outside Pärnu but lived from the age of seven in the city until, at 20, she moved with her family to Tartu. At 30, she married a Latvian doctor in Kronstadt. She died there 12 years later of breast cancer.

Many consider Koidula's collection of verse, *The Nightingale of Emajogi,* to be the foremost work of Estonia's period of National Awakening, and the pen-name Koidula, given to her by a fellow artist, means literally "singer of the dawn". Her real maiden name was Jannsen, and the modest wooden schoolhouse where her family lived is on Jannseni Street. The house itself is now the **Lydia Koidula Museum**, but for those who don't speak Estonian it is a bit dry since the contents are mostly cases of her poetry, books and writings.

The **Pärnu Museum**, on the other hand, is surprisingly rewarding. Located in a dim, Soviet-style building, its appearance is dreary but, after a first room of flea-bitten taxidermal examples of local fauna, the artifacts become much more interesting. Archaeological finds are from 8000 BC and include a 13th-

Mud-bath house and sanatorium, Pärnu.

century woman's costume, a 16th-century Gothic chalice and embossed-leather Bible, and 19th-century furniture.

North into Läänemaa: The P74 northwest from Pärnu leads to the small town of **Lihula** which has a huge, Soviet-built **cultural centre**, orange-plaster-and-stone **Orthodox church**, and point-spired, cream-and-red **Lutheran church**. From Lihula, the P38 heads directly north into the **Matsalu State Nature Reserve**. Matsalu Bay has a blend of habitats including reed-beds, water-meadows, hay-meadows and coastal pastures, and it was already noted for its birdlife fauna back in 1870. Among the species found here today are the avocet, the sandwich tern, the mute swan, the greylag goose and the bittern. There are also some white-tailed eagles. Ruffs perform their special mating dance in its waters every spring.

The reserve itself was formed from 98,000 acres (39,700 hectares) of the bay area in 1957. It can be visited by car or, since water covers some 65,000 acres (26,300 hectares) of this same area, by boat. Either way, it's best to notify the reserve office ahead of time.

Matsalu Bay lies in the southern part of the coastal district of **Läänemaa**. One of the flattest sections of the already rather flat Estonia, it is also low in arable land but the overall tenor is certainly pastoral. The quietude is a bit misleading: this is the one area of the Baltics that has seismic activity.

The main town is **Haapsalu** with close to 15,000 inhabitants. The large military base and fishery established here under the Soviets led to an influx of 30 percent Russians. Although the entire district has been under either Russian or Soviet control since 1710 (except for the 20 years of the republic), the locals identify strictly with the Swedes, who ruled over them for 129 years from 1581.

Still, it was under the Russians that Haapsalu became a spa of great repute and it was to satisfy Russian demands that many of its fanciest buildings were constructed. Of course, it was also under the Russians – and then the Soviets

Tori house farm.

– that these ornate structures were allowed slowly to fall apart and for Haapsalu's highly touted curative mud to become too polluted to recommend.

The town originally centred around the **Haapsalu Episcopal Castle**, which was begun in 1279. Little of the castle itself remains, but its Romano-Gothic **cathedral** is one of only three functioning cathedrals in Estonia.

One-naved and towerless, Haapsalu cathedral was built to double as a fortress, and its immense facade still looks stubbornly impenetrable. Inside, the tall white walls and high vaulted ceiling are almost bare.

In a side chapel is a baptismal font from 1634, with Adam, Eve and the snake etched into its bowl; a vivid reminder of original sin to be washed away. Against its wall leans a sad wooden sculpture of a woman holding a child; a memorial to the people from Läänemaa deported to Siberia. The box beneath it, marked "1949–1989", contains Siberian ground.

Directly above this memorial is the **window of the white lady**, focus of Haapsalu's favourite local legend. As the story goes, a monk from the castle cloister fell in love with a sweet village girl and managed to bring her into the castle disguised as a boy. But when she began to sing in the choir, their perfidy was discovered. As punishment, she was built into the walls and he was thrown into the cellar.

Every August, at the time of the full moon, the poor girl returns, and nary is the villager who hasn't seen her white reflection in the aforementioned window. She is not shy; she will appear before even a large crowd, and during this time, in fact, Haapsalu holds a "White Lady Festival" of varied cultural events that climaxes with the audience walking around en masse to the southwest side of the cathedral where this window stands. Locals absolutely promise the white lady will appear – as long as it doesn't rain. The only thing that scares her away is clouds.

Directly in front of the castle entrance is the large square that was the town

Farmyard life.

market and just to the left (or west) is the space that served as the Swedish market. It now encloses a very pleasant **café**. On the square's east side is the salmon-coloured **Town Museum**, within what used to be the Town Hall. Many of the artifacts inside come from the castle and there are exhibitions about the region's old farms and Haapsalu's days as a summer resort.

You can see the ghosts of Haapsalu's spa days by walking down to the "**African Beach**", so called because there used to be, along with little bathing houses, statues of wild animals set in the water. Although the water isn't swimable any more, locals are still fond of strolling its seaside **promenade**. The former **Casino**, built at the turn of the century, is now a shell of chipped, green-painted wood and lacy cut-out porticos, but concerts are still held in the bandstand beside it.

The statues to have survived include a sundial and a set of steps by the artist R. Haavamagi, who was born in Haapsalu, and the **Tchaikovsky Bench**.

Tchaikovsky used to favour Haapsalu for his holidays and even used a motif from a traditional Estonian song in his *6th Symphony*. The bench – decorated with the composer's likeness and some notes from the *6th* – stands where he came every evening to watch the sunset.

Continuing further down Sadama Road from this point will bring you to the **Haapsalu Yacht Club**, perhaps the only watery aspect of the town that is currently thriving. The 1991 World Ice Yachting Championships were held in the bay here, and since its official opening to the public in the summer of 1992 the club has received yachts from all over the Baltic.

Town activity has moved away from the castle and beach down the lengthy **Posti Street**. But wandering the quaint back streets or the curious and creepy overgrown **Old Town Graveyard** – which lies on Posti Street opposite the very comfortable **Haapsalu Hotel** – is better for understanding the appeal that Haapsalu has held for artists.

Ilon Wikland, for example, illustrator

Flowers for teacher as autumn term begins.

of the Pippi Longstocking books, was born in Haapsalu and, although she fled with her family to Sweden at 14, has used the town and the small house on Ruutli Street beside the Adventist church where her father was minister in many drawings. Some original works hang in the **Pippi Boarding House**.

The town has also been rich in handicraft artists, and the "Haapsalu Shawl", created of such fine wool that it can be drawn through a ring, is known throughout Estonia. A couple of shops specialise in local crafts, most notably the **Amadeus Shop** at 7 Jaama Street beside the **town market**. At the end of this street is the once splendorous **railway station**, built in 1905 to receive Tsar Nicholas II on his summer holiday.

Heading out of town back towards Tallinn will take you past the home of Ants Laikmaa, an influential early 20th-century Estonian painter. Laikmaa was also eccentric, and the home he designed for himself, now the **Ants Laikmaa Museum**, is an odd amalgam of red-and-white piping with a steep moss-covered roof that has to be seen.

A small sign points towards a bumpy road leading through the woods. The house stands at its very end, in a large yard pecked by chickens. Begun in 1923, it was changed in design so many times that it never was finished during Laikmaa's lifetime.

Laikmaa was immensely popular in Haapsalu, but it was probably useful he had such a private area for his daily life. Known for using carriages long after the advent of the car, his handsome moustaches, and appearing in costume when the mood struck him, the artist was the host of many unusual house parties. To get an idea, note the two small caricatures, signed "E.B" and hanging upstairs, of him and his crowd.

From here Tallinn is about an hour's drive northeast. If you feel that you have not yet truly experienced the sea, head west. At **Rohuküla**, about 5 miles (8 km) west, you can catch a ferry to the islands of **Vormsi** or **Hiiumaa** where the water is cleaner and there have been no attempts to turn them into resorts.

Gone fishing, Haapsalu.

THE ISLANDS

Most of the 1500 or so islands off the coast of Estonia are mere hiccups, but two are so sizeable that island acreage ultimately accounts for some 10 percent of Estonia's total land territory. These larger islands, **Saaremaa** and **Hiiumaa**, are perhaps the most unspoiled and winsome corners of the country.

Ironically, their state of naturalness is due partly to the Soviet occupation. Clustered off the western shore, these islands were (rightly) considered likely points of escape to the West as well as strategic security posts. They were therefore kept for the most part incommunicado from the rest of the Union. Meanwhile, since they clearly were impractical for any industrial projects, military personnel were virtually the only people to be brought in.

The islanders have continued to require most arrivals from the mainland to present visitor cards, even after independence. They say that this is the reason their islands have remained so peaceful and crime-free – which they certainly are. In the 13th century the islands were divided between the Oesel-Wiek (Saare-Laane) bishopric and the Livonian Order. Three centuries later, Saaremaa (Oesel) reverted to Denmark while Sweden took Hiiumaa. In 1645, Saaremaa also was assigned to the Swedes and from then on they were destined to share Estonia's fate.

Somehow, the islanders stubbornly retained a distinct way of life. They also began to stockpile impressive monuments left behind by the parade of conquering egos. The 13th-century churches and 18th-century manor houses that now decorate their shores are for the most part in poor repair – but they also are as blissfully free from disfiguring reconstruction and commercialisation as the islands themselves.

Across the sea: To reach Saaremaa, the largest of all the Estonian islands, it is necessary first to cross Muhu, where the ferry from Virtsu on the mainland docks. Estonia's third largest island, Muhu is

only 78 sq. miles (201 sq. km) and, along with about 500 smaller islands, belongs to the greater Saaremaa County. It hasn't developed any tourist trade of its own, and its accommodation is strictly for year-round and summer residents. But it does have at least one sight worth stopping to see.

The area around the **Koguva Outdoor Museum** is presumed to have been settled back in the late Iron Age, but this still-inhabited fishing village was first documented in 1532. Of the 105 buildings standing, parts of three date from the early and mid-18th century, making it the oldest preserved conglomerate of peasant architecture on the islands.

Koguva is not far from the **causeway** that leads to Saaremaa. It is a beautiful highway, and terribly romantic. The water on either side is filled by a beckoning green carpet of swaying reeds. In spring, it changes to white as thousands of swans come here to mate.

Saaremaa is, at 1,030 sq. miles (2,668 sq. km), spacious but still a quiet and unassuming place. Much of its land has

been cultivated, and the simple island roads are laced by field after field of livestock grazing and wheat, interrupted only by patches of thick forest. Industry is at a minimum, and those inhabitants who aren't at work on the land tend to be connected to the sea.

There is only one town of real consequence, **Kuressaare** on the south side of the island, where 17,000 of Saaremaa County's 41,000 inhabitants live. Kuressaare is said to have been particularly popular with party officials during the Soviet regime (explaining perhaps how the town received the funds for the renovation of its centre), and it certainly is very handsome. Indeed, if it weren't so unselfconscious – and low on tourists – it would be a classic tourist trap.

Most of the buildings in the centre are gems of late 18th and early 19th-century neoclassicism, with pretty wooden houses and gardens mixed in beside them. Side streets reveal an ancient hand-pump for water or a freshly painted home with a paint-can tied proudly to its wooden gate. On Kaevu Street, an old **windmill** has been transformed into the posh **Veski bar and restaurant.**

Activity focuses around the triangular plaza where Tallinna Street turns into Lossi Street. At this juncture are the **market**, the **administrative halls** and, after 9pm, the main spot for local youths to see and be seen. The yellow **Town Hall** (1654–70) lies along the hypotenuse of this triangle, its entrance protected by stone lions. To its left, an 18th-century fire station of burnt-brown wood has a new lease on life as a **tourist information centre**.

Opposite it is the **Weigh House** (1663), with a stepped gable. Now a dingy food store, it encloses one side of the tiny **Market Square** where you may find displayed, in addition to jars of gooseberries in season and packets of foreign cigarettes, distinctively patterned, hand-made woollen sweaters and mittens for sale.

Sometimes there will also be a table or two piled high with slippery black mounds of the expensive Saaremaa specialty, eel. Some claim that it was

Kuressaare, capital of Saaremaa.

this and the locally brewed beer, considered by many to be the finest in Estonia, that made Kuressaare so popular with Soviet party officials.

A second, smaller triangle, fashioned into a piazza, lies a few steps down Lossi Street. This has the **County Seat** and a **Monument for the Fallen in the War of Liberation**. This is actually the third such monument erected here; twice the Soviets tore it down and three times the town re-erected it.

Continuing down Lossi from here will take you past the **Apostolic Orthodox St Nicholas church** (1790). Its fancy front gate tied with large silver-painted bows is unmistakable and its white exterior is topped with rounded green spires. The interior echoes this colour scheme, and treads between neo-classical and Byzantine styles.

Kuressaare's main tourist attraction and, indeed, its original *raison d'être* is at the end of the street. The **Kuressaare Episcopal Castle** was built as the bishop of Oesel-Wiek's foothold on Saaremaa, and the earliest record of its existence

dates back to 1384. It is the only entirely preserved medieval stone castle in all of the Baltic nations.

Ringed by a large and beautiful public **park**, a moat and imposing bastions erected during the mid-17th century, the castle is in the unyielding, geometric, late-Gothic style, made of white-grey dolomite quarried in Saaremaa. Each corner is crowned by a tower with an orange turret and at the heart of the castle is a tiny, symmetrical courtyard.

From the courtyard, stone steps lead down to basement rooms coated with soot and up to a narrow, vaulted cloister. The former refectory lies on the west, and to the north are the severe former living quarters of the bishop. Ten elaborate wooden epitaphs from the 17th century represent coats of arms of noblemen in Saaremaa and their individual preoccupations. One has oars, another tools, a third stags and arrows.

Climbing the towers is worthwhile but requires fortitude; the watch-tower in the southeast corner of the convent building is connected by a drawbridge

Koguva Farm Village in Muhu.

suspended 30 ft (9 metres) above the ground, and the defence tower is combed with stone stairways.

Some upper rooms have been devoted to exhibition halls of modern Estonian art, and a few contain the **Saaremaa Regional Museum**. This rich collection traces the inhabitants of Saaremaa from the 4th millennium BC and has the oldest preserved wooden sculpture in Estonia – "Seated Madonna with the Infant" (1280–90). The labelling is in Estonian and Russian, but there are lengthy plaques in English.

From the castle, it is a pleasant walk down to the small **harbour** and the broken-down wooden building that during the Estonian republic served as the local **yacht club**. Twenty years ago, this was a favourite place for bathing. Swimmers now must head south of the town to the **Mandjala-Jarve beach**.

Island road trip: Other spots to visit in Kuressaare include the still-functioning **Sanatorium**, specialising in baths of curative sea mud since 1876 – although the smell of the mud is so evil it is hard to imagine anyone's health could be improved by soaking in it – and the **Kingiseppa** and **Linnakodaniku museums**, exhibiting early 20th-century objects from the island. But be sure to leave time to tour the rest of the island.

Travelling to **Kihelkonna** in the west, and following the coast up to **Leisi** in the north, then back south to Kuressaare will take you past many of Saaremaa's interesting sites. First stop is the **Mihkli Farm Museum**, close by the town of Viki. Although small, this open-air museum exactly preserves a farm typical to western Saaremaa. The main dwelling house (1834) stands with most of the other buildings in a circle enclosing a yard and a quaint little flower garden. Most of the roofs are covered with reed, and the walls are of dolomite or wood. Original objects from the farmstead include household equipment cut with the Mihkli family emblem.

Turning at Kihelkonna north towards **Mustjala**, you will first catch a glimpse of the pointed red bell-tower of the medieval **Kihelkonna church** and then

Island fishermen.

the centuries-old, weathered-grey **Pidula watermill**. From here it is a short drive to the **Panga Scarp**.

This limestone scarp is one of the highest points on the island and one of the loveliest. The water below is almost olive green but so clear you can easily make out the thousands of pebbles that line the sea floor. In the distance, the horizon stretches blue and seemingly endlessly, except for the tiny shadow of Hiiumaa Island. In summer the sound of crickets fills the quiet.

Unsurprisingly, this magical place has played a central role in island superstitions. In pre-Christian times, locals would throw one baby boy, born the winter before, off the cliff into the water every spring; an offering to the Sea God with the prayer that he send back a lot of fish. In later times, they flung a ram. Island brides have continued the tradition of scarp pitching to this day. On the eve of their wedding they often write their maiden name on a piece of paper, put it into a bottle and toss it off the cliff.

Turning east from here takes you to

Leisi, an attractive rural town, from where you will turn south. A few miles down the road are the **Angla windmills**. In the mid-19th century, there were about 800 windmills on Saaremaa. Only a small proportion have survived, but at Angla there are still five left, sticking up suddenly on a slight swell amid wind-swept wheat fields.

Nestled innocently behind a moss-covered stone wall on a sloping lawn across from fields of cattle a mile (2km) from here is one of Saaremaa's greatest treasures: the 14th-century **Karja church**. Saaremaa is rife with some of the earliest churches in the Baltics but none other has as marvellous stone sculptures still intact.

These sculptures hold 1001 nights-worth of tales to tell. A relief on the first left buttress upon entering, for example, depicts village life. A woman listens to another with a pig on her back, meaning gossip, while the man beside her has a rose behind his ear, the symbol of silence. This is on the northern and thus colder side of the church, the side where

Kaarma church.

the women sat because they were considered to be stronger. St Katherine of Alexandria, to whom the church is dedicated, is carved into the northern arch before the altar. This 14th-century beauty, the legend goes, was wooed by King Maxentius of Egypt, although he was already married. She refused him and, enraged, he had her arrested and torn to pieces. The sculpture shows her with Maxentius's wife on her left clinging to her skirt, St Peter on her right and the evil king crushed beneath her feet.

Directly opposite is St Nicholas, the protector of seamen and on his left are three village girls who were too poor to marry until he became their benefactor.

Painted on to the ceiling above the altar is an interesting table of Christian and pagan marks: the Star of Bethlehem and the symbol of Unity, both drawn with endless lines; the three-legged symbol of the sun; the "leg" devil; and two pentagons, symbols of gloom, which locals gleefully point out was also a symbol for the Soviet Union.

The church still holds services two Sundays a month. At other times, except Mondays and Tuesdays, an old woman caretaker will unlock the doors with a big metal key and let you in.

If you head south again, turning right at the **Liiva-Putla** fork, you will reach the tiny hamlet of **Kaarma**, site of another medieval church. **Kaarma church** was begun in the latter half of the 13th century but it was rearranged over subsequent centuries and is strikingly large. Its artifacts are more mixed than those of Karja. The christening stone, for example, dates from the 13th century, the wooden "Joseph" supporting the pulpit is from around 1450, and the elaborate Renaissance pulpit itself is marked 1645. Current restoration has exposed fragments of early mural painting.

Other 13th and 14th-century churches in the area worth visiting include **Valjala church** and **Puha church** situated east of Kuressaare. The latter most clearly shows how these churches were built not just to be religious centres but also strongholds.

If you turn left at the Liiva-Putla fork,

Left, crab fisherman.

Right, windmill keeper.

you reach a much older landmark. The **Kaali meteoric craters** are not beautiful. The largest one, behind the Kaali Elementary School, is referred to as **Lake Kaali** and it looks like a big opaque green puddle. But it is remarkable to think that the bowl surrounding it was carved out by part of a 1,000-ton meteor that hit the earth here at least 2,800 years ago. Eight smaller craters, made from other chips of the meteor, dot the woods surrounding it.

A wilder cousin: For spots of natural beauty, **Hiiumaa Island** is perhaps more rewarding. At 382 sq. miles (989 sq. km), it is Estonia's second largest island but only has 11,000 inhabitants, 4,000 of them in the capital of **Kärdla** on the north coast. There is virtually no settlement in its heart where there is a peat moor (peat bogs growing directly on sand) and swamp – and almost all agriculture focuses on the southern and western edge. Some yet to be cultivated areas in the south belong to another natural oddity, "wooded meadows", and the rest of the island is overwhelmed by pines and junipers. There are so few cars on the road that inhabitants typically drive on either the left or right according to whim, and many don't even bother about licences. Less than 5 percent of the population is non-Estonian; during the Soviet regime, it was the only area in Estonia without a single Russian-language school.

Fishing is the most important industry, although until the late 1980s barbed-wire was wrapped along the shore from Kärdla in the north to **Emmaste** in the far south and the coast is notoriously treacherous to approach because of the shallow waters of endless shoals and rocks. This means also that you have to walk out quite a way over pebbles simply to get your stomach wet. But unlike the coastal waters of most of Estonia, these are clean enough to swim in, and invitingly so.

The eastern harbour of **Heltermaa** has been slightly dug out, and it is to here that the ferry from the mainland, at **Rohuküla** by Haapsalu, arrives. Just inland is the historical hamlet of **Suure-**

Family home, Saaremaa.

móisa. Hiiumaa once had about 25 stately 16th to 19th-century manor houses, but most by now have either been destroyed or have irreparably deteriorated. The **Suuremóisa manor** is one exception. Built by a Swedish family called Stenbock in 1772, then bought in 1790 by O.R.L. v. Ungern-Sternberg – for decades Hiiumaa's richest and most powerful landowner – this manor still has its main building, stable master's home and stables, several outbuildings and cellars, and expansive front and back lawns. Inside the main building are 64 rooms, some with original painted ceilings and ceramic fireplaces. The bottom floor is currently used for aerobics classes and the local "cinema", and the top floor for an agricultural school. Under the trees on the right side at the back, stone grave-markers are for the baron's pair of much-feared black guard dogs and two for his son's.

Just down the road is **Puha church**. First built of wood in the mid-13th century, then replaced with stone in 1770, its tall white bell-tower, topped by a hexagonal brown roof, has been extended three times since then. Turned by the Soviets into a cellar, the church resumed offering services on Christmas Eve 1990.

On its south side stands a squat white chapel containing the tomb of Ebba Margarethe Grafin Stenbock, Suuremóisa manor's first owner. On its north side, strewn amid alders, are a tumble of other old graves. Around the northeast corner is a log inset in the church wall; this is the spot through which the priest used to hand out bread to the poor and to strangers.

At **Hagaste** – 3 pebbly miles (5 km) down the road – island authorities have assembled a traditional Hiiumaa farmstead. The yard is surrounded by the slanting basketweave (*korendusaed*) fence particular to both Hiiumaa and Saaremaa, and a small windmill (1925) stands in its foreground. The resident caretaker will demonstrate how it works. His home is an old storage-hut, built during the Swedish days and roofed with stones. There is also an apiary, an

Farmer's daughter, Hiiumaa.

old sauna and a *paargu*, an outdoor kitchen to be used in summer that looks like a teepee built of stout tree branches.

Back up the coast in the main town of Kärdla, **the Rannapaargu Café**, in front of the grassy **Kärdla Beach**, has been named for this same special sort of kitchen. To reach the café, you must walk down Lubjaahju Street past yet another Hiiumaa peculiarity, the giant swing. Found in villages all over the island, giant swings are the traditional meeting places for young people, and they are especially busy on Midsummer's Eve.

Some of Hiiumaa's most interesting structures are the lighthouses that twinkle along the shore. The most remarkable is the **Kõpu Lighthouse**, halfway out along the thickly forested **Kõpu peninsula**, on the windswept western wing of the island. This soaring four-cornered and red-crested white lighthouse looks something like a cross between a space rocket and a pyramid. But, first lit in 1531, it is considered to be the third oldest continuously operat-

ing lighthouse in the world. Climbing the old stairway to its top is perilous to the forehead but the view makes every step worthwhile. Way below, the world spreads into a sea of dark-green pine and endless water.

One of the few patches of cultivated land is at nearby **Ulendi Village**, a modest collection of steep-roofed, wooden houses, farm plots and weatherbeaten outbuildings. The sheep pasture immediately on the right upon entering the settlement contains a **burial site** used as early as 4000 BC.

Artists' retreat: Understandably, many of Estonia's best-known artists and writers keep summer retreats on Hiiumaa, and conductor Eri Klas, for example, has his on Kõpu. But the most popular spot for summer cottages is **Kassari**, just southwest of Heltermaa.

Kassari is one of the between 200 and 400 (depending on the level of the water) islands that cling to the coast of Hiiumaa. But it arcs so close to the shore by the town of **Kaina** that it has been incorporated into the larger island with

Hiiumaa's east coast.

two short bridges. The bay between them, **Kainu Bay**, used to be rich in curative sea mud but is now too polluted. Nevertheless, birds like it, including golden eagles and other rare species. You may even see an eagle or two flying over the road. These birds, in turn – along with the island breezes and the sea – are behind the richness of flora all over Hiiumaa. In fact, the island boasts all in all about 975 different species of plant, some of them, such as the orchids, also quite rare.

Kassari, however, is richest in junipers, whose berries and bark might be called the island staple. Still used variously – the wood for butter knives that keep butter from turning rancid; the branches for sauna switches to perk up the kidney; the berries for a vodka spice, a source of vitamin C and other medicinal purposes – this scraggy dark bush has even been wrangled into furniture.

Junipers crowd the pebbly projection of **Saaretirp** with special determination. This mile-long promontory is a favourite place to picnic or ponder for

all the Kassari residents. Like many beauty spots, Saaretirp has several local legends. Leiger, the island hero and a very big man, is said to have built it one summer as a bridge for Suur Toll (Saaremaa's hero and also a giant) to come to eat apples with him the following autumn. Accordingly, it stretches out south towards Saaremaa, ever narrowing as more and more land slips under the sea. At the end of the headland nothing remains but a needlish point and a large heap of stones: if you find a pebble with a hole in it, make a wish and place it on the pile, and your wish should come true.

Kassari's sheltered position makes the water warm, and beside it the apples crop early. The last owner of the former **Kassari manor house**, Baron Edvard Stackelberg, had an especially large apple orchard, though neither it nor his home still remains. But the small servants' house directly opposite where it stood is in good shape and houses the **Hiiumaa Koduloomuuseum** of local culture containing a huge light reflector from the 19th-century Tahkuna lighthouse, maps of island history and traditional fishing tools.

Down one more pebble-laden lane is the **Kassari chapel**, the only stone chapel still extant in Estonia with a roof of thatched reed. Carefully restored in 1990, it has been kept without electricity and is illuminated by a simple central candlabra and candles burned into the end of each old blue pew. The walls are decorated only with ancient oak-leaf wreaths, taken from funerals in the surrounding graveyard.

A graveyard spills around the church, darkened by shivering trees. Baron Stackelberg's is next to a swineherd's, curiously, to show that in front of God all people are equal.

One final church to note on Hiiumaa just inland from Kassari is the **Kaina Kirik**, built between 1492 and 1515. Although heavily bombed during World War II, it is still a very affecting spot with wind rushing through the limestone shell and over the old tombs set directly into its floor. Every summer a song festival is held here.

The main highway of the Baltics has been the 640-mile (1,030-km) River Daugava. "Its banks are silver and its bed is gold," said Ivan the Terrible, who failed to get his hands on it. Others were more successful, starting with the German crusaders who arrived in Riga, near the river's estuary, which they made their base for the conquest of the Baltic peoples. Today, Riga is the most exciting city in the Baltics. It is rich with the architecture of the Hansa merchants, with their gabled homes and store-houses dating back to the 15th century. In the expanded 19th-century city are exquisite art nouveau buildings, many designed by Mikhail Eisenstein, the father of Sergei Eisenstein, who was also born here.

With a population of a million, Riga seems too large for its own country, which has a total population of 2½ million. It is an industrial city and the whole country has been greatly Russified through industrialisation. Russians are in the majority in its five largest towns, and Riga's seaside, Jūrmala, the "Baltic Riviera", attracted a large number of retired Soviet officers.

A secondary highway is the River Gauja, which is the centre of a fine national park. To the east are the more remote blue-lake lands of Latgale, which fell into Catholic hands under Polish rule. To the west is Kurzeme, the former territory of the Lutheran Duchy of Courland, where tall pines became masts in Duke Jēkabs's ship-yards at Ventspils. Too big for a duke, too small for a king, he built an empire with toeholds in the Caribbean and in Africa. War has left very little sign he was here.

One building belonging to a Courland duke which has survived is Rundāle palace, the most spectacular piece of civic architecture in the Baltics. It was built by Rastrelli, architect of the Winter Palace in Leningrad, for Johannes Ernst Birons, a lover of the empress Anna Ivanovna, and he was briefly regent of Russia himself.

But the soul of Latvia and the Latvians lies in the countryside among its magic oaks and ancient hill forts. To find it, visitors should head for Lāčplēsis on the banks of the Daugava, where they can see the hero's magic belt, woven with symbols, that can foretell the future of the whole nation.

Preceding pages: Eisenstein facade, Elisabetes Street, Riga; birch forest; Jūrmala beach. **Left**, sweet peas and gypsophila, Riga market.

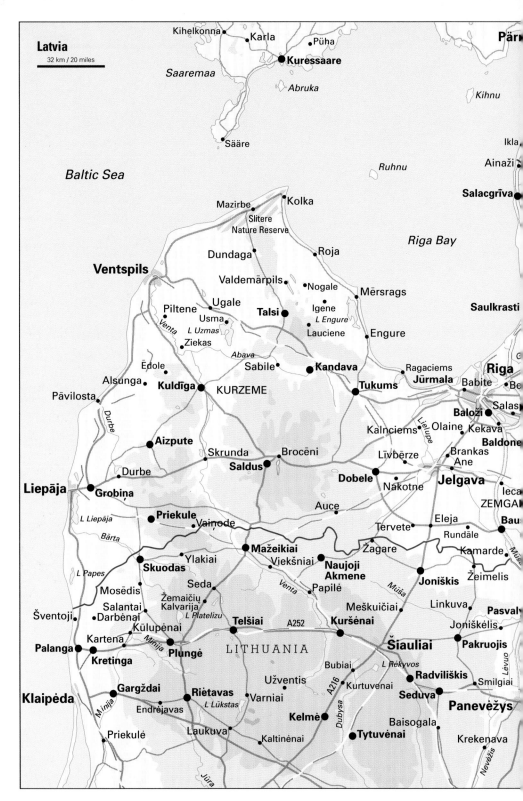

Latvia

32 km / 20 miles

Baltic Sea

Saaremaa

Kihelkonna
Karla
Pühä
Kuressaare
Abruka
Kihnu
Sääre
Ikla
Ainaži
Ruhnu
Salacgrīva

Mazirbe
Kolka
Slitere
Nature Reserve
Roja
Riga Bay
Dundaga
Valdemārpils
Nogale
Mērsrags
Saulkrasti

Ventspils
Piltene
Ugale
Usma
L Uzmas
Talsi
Igene
L Engure
Lauciene
Engure
Ziekas
Abava
Ēdole
Sabile
Kandava
Ragaciems
Riga
Alsunga
Kuldīga
KURZEME
Tukums
Jūrmala
Babite
Be
Pāvilosta
Durbe
Baloži
Salas
Kalnciems
Olaine
Kekava
Baldone
Aizpute
Skrunda
Broceni
Līvbērze
Brankas
Ane
Durbe
Saldus
Dobele
Nākotne
Jelgava
Liepāja
Grobiņa
Auce
Ieca
ZEMGAI
L Liepāja
Priekule
Vaiņode
Tērvete
Eleja
Bau
Bārta
Rundāle
L Papes
Mažeikiai
Žagare
Kamarde
Ylakiai
Viekšniai
Naujoji Akmene
Joniškis
Žeimelis
Skuodas
Seda
Papilė
Mosēdis
Žemaičių
Kalvarija
L Platelizu
Venta
Meškuičiai
Linkuva
Pasval
Šventoji
Salantai
Darbėnai
Telšiai
A252
Kuršėnai
Joniškelis
Kartena
Kūlupėnai
Minija
Šiauliai
Pakruojis
Palanga
Plungė
LITHUANIA
Radviliškis
Kretinga
Bubiai
L Rėkyvos
Smilgiai
Užventis
Seduva
Kurtuvėnai
Gargždai
Riėtavas
Varniai
A216
Panevėžys
Klaipėda
Endrėjavas
L Lūkstas
Kelmė
Baisogala
Priekulė
Laukuva
Kaltinėnai
Tytuvėnai
Krekenava

Pär

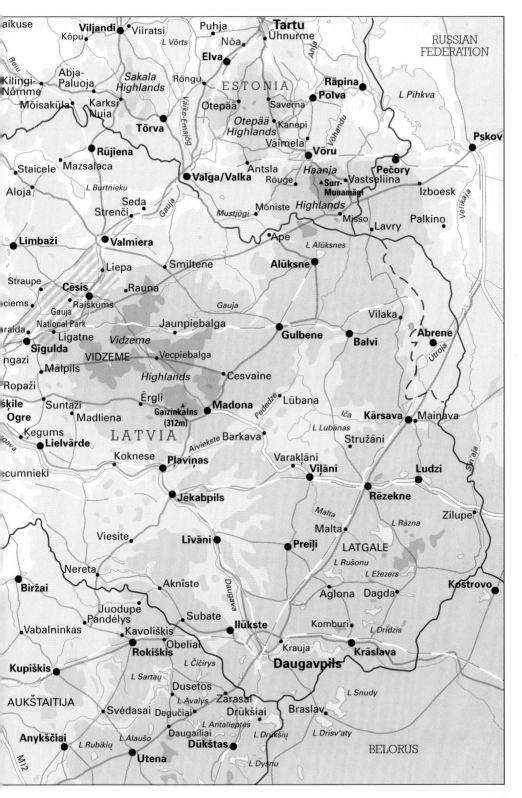

aikuse
Viljandi •Viiratsi
Kōpu• *L Vōrts*
Puhja
Tartu
Ūhnurme

RUSSIAN
FEDERATION

Nōa
Elva
Nōmme
Kilingi-
Abja-
Paluoja
Sakala
Highlands
Rōngu•
ESTONIA
Rāpina
Polva
L Pihkva

Mōisakūla•
Karksi
Nuia
Otepāā
Otepāā
Highlands
Kanepi
Saverna
•Staicele
Mazsalaca
Tōrva
Vaimela
Vōru
Pskov

Rūjiena
Antsla
Haanja
Rōuge•
▲Surr-
Munamāgi
Vastseliina
Pečory

•Staicele
Mazsalaca
Valga/Valka
Izboesk
Aloja•
L Burtnieku
Seda
Strenči•
Mustjōgi
Mōniste
Highlands
Misso
Lavry
Palkino

Limbaži
Valmiera
•Ape
L Alūksnes
Straupe
•Liepa
•Smiltene
Alūksne•
ciems•
Cēsis
•Rauna
Gauja
Vilaka•
Abrene
Gauja•
•Raiskums
Jaunpiebalga
Gulbene
Balvi
raida•
National Park
•Ligatne
Vidzeme
Vecpiebalga
Sigulda
VIDZEME
Highlands
Cesvaine
Utroja
ngazi•
•Mālpils
Ērgli
Ropaži•
Suntaži
Madliena
Gaizinkalns
(312m)▲
Madona
Lūbana
Pededze
Iča
Kārsava
•Mainava
škile
Ogre
LATVIA
Barkava•
L Lubānas
•Kegums
Lielvārde
Aiviekste
Varaklāni•
Stružāni•
Sh'aja
cumnieki•
Koknese
Plaviņas
Viļāni
Ludzi
Jēkabpils
Rēzekne
Malta
Zilupe•
Viesite•
Līvāni
Malta•
L Rāzna
Preiļi
LATGALE
Nereta•
L Rušonu
L Ežezers
Biržai
•Aknīste
Daugava
Aglona•
Dagda•
Kostrovo
Juodupe
Pandēlys
Subate
•Vabalninkas
•Kavoliškis
Ilūkste
Komburi•
L Dridzis
Obeliai•
Krauja•
Krāslava
Rokiškis
L Čičirys
Kupiškis
Daugavpils
L Sartau
Dusetos
L Snudy
AUKŠTAITIJA
•Svēdasai Degučiai
Zarasai
Drūkšiai
Braslav•
L Avalys
Anykščiai
L Rubikių
L Alaušo
Daugailiai
Dūkštas•
L Drūkšių
L Drisv'aty
L Antalieptės
BELORUS
Utena
L Dysnu

When Latvian independence was self-proclaimed in 1918, the country had to be assembled like a jigsaw puzzle out of territory inhabited by Lett-speakers. This amounted to the southern half of what had previously been Livonia together with Latgale and the Duchy of Courland. To complicate matters, the city of Riga, Latvia's capital, had hitherto been for all practical purposes an independent city-state with an overwhelmingly alien population. It was a German city from the day the crusaders landed, and it had remained a predominantly German city through all the vagaries of Polish, Swedish and Russian rule. At the outbreak of World War I, the non-Latvian element was as high as 90 percent.

The Latvians managed to restore themselves to a majority of something like 75 percent over the country as a whole between the world wars, but independence was then snuffed out by Soviet annexation. The combined effect of mass deportations and Russian immigration inexorably reversed the trend, so that by 1989 the Latvians were reduced to the barest majority of 51.8 percent. Against the backdrop of massive impending change in Eastern Europe and the Soviet Union, Latvians knew they were in a private race against time. It had been the Kremlin's intention all along to obliterate the 1918 frontiers so that Latvia, like Estonia and Lithuania, was in effect an unbroken extension of Russia itself. The struggle which ensued was a replay of events leading up to World War I, the reincarnation of the land of the Lett-speakers.

Beginnings: Curious events had led to the arrival of the German crusaders in 1200. Almost 1,000 years after Christianity had been adopted as the official religion in Armenia and then Rome, it had still not reached the eastern shores of the Baltic, and there was rather a rush among the Pope and various Christian princes to make up for lost time.

To this end, a number of missionary monks were despatched, the area around the

mouth of the River Daugava falling to a certain Meinhard of Bremen. He arrived in 1180 and persuaded Latvians to be baptised in the river in such satisfactory numbers that he was made a bishop. The real test came when he informed his converts that the price of salvation was the payment of a tithe. They not only abandoned the faith en masse but put the good bishop in fear of his life. He implored Pope Clement III to send help.

The Pope had other problems. The crusade in the Holy Land had gone disastrously

wrong and large numbers of crusaders, expelled from their strongholds, were homeless. Among these were the Knights of the Sword under Bishop Albrecht von Buxhoerden and they were dispatched to the Daugava where they went about their business with Teutonic efficiency. "All the places and roads were red with blood," wrote a chronicler of the Knights of the Sword.

Almost at once, Riga had a defensive wall, a fortress and at least one church. By 1211, Bishop Albrecht was ready to start a cathedral. Word was sent to the Pope that the Daugava mission had been accomplished and that a contingent of knights was being

Left, the Reformation arrives in Riga, as shown by a stained-glass window in the Dom. **Right**, a 12th-century knight of the Livonian Order.

sent north – to Estonia – where the Danes were experiencing similar difficulties with truculent pagans.

The Knights of the Sword were in due course amalgamated with other orders; these came to be known collectively as the Teutonic Order. Having discharged their divine duties, they tackled the secular task of creating a city-state for themselves with immense zeal. They imported fellow Germans not merely to build the city and port but also to organise agriculture. The Latvians were excluded from the process except as labourers.

The military power of the Teutonic Order was eclipsed in the 15th century but by then the German economic and land-owning oli-

garchy was thoroughly entrenched in Latvia. It was safe as long as Russia was kept out of contention by the Mongol empire. With the demise of the latter, however, an alarming threat materialised in the person of Ivan the Terrible. The only recourse was to seek the protection of Poland-Lithuania, and then there was a price to be paid. Lutheranism had made inroads in Latvia under the German influence and Poland was uncompromisingly Catholic. The Jesuits were to be given a licence to bring Latvians back into the fold.

The way the Jesuits went about their task revived memories of the Teutonic Order, and this was coupled with a rigid Polish

feudal order harder on the peasants than anything previously experienced. The country was sharply divided on the desirability of Polish protection. Riga profited enormously by being elevated to the role of Poland's principal port, so the merchants had no complaints. The landed gentry and the peasants, however, were paying the price and increasingly desperate for protection against the protectors. Protestant Sweden seemed the most likely candidate. The resulting Swedish-Polish war saw the Swedes repulsed but left Latvia a wreck. It was followed by the bitter winter of 1601 in which 40,000 peasants died from hunger and cold.

Gustavus Adolphus tried again 20 years later and this time a Poland much weakened by events elsewhere succumbed. The Swedes rebuilt Riga castle, added barracks outside the Swedish Gate and built castles on the River Daugava. Poland remained in charge of Latgale in the east and, in the south and west, the Duchy of Courland and Semigallia. In 1561 this small slice of Latvia had belonged to Gotthard Kettlers, the last Grand Master of the Teutonic Order, who had submitted to Poland, and had been granted a degree of independence. Its importance grew under Duke Jēkabs, who became a prince of the Holy Roman Empire.

A duke's empire: Though Protestant, the Kettlers had been friends of the English Stuart kings and Jēkabs (James) had been named after his godfather, James I. He had been a great shipbuilder, and at Ventspils he built an impressive navy, turning out 24 men-of-war for France and 62 for Britain. With unbounded ambition he acquired territory for the duchy in the Gambia and Tobago and he devoted much of his long rule to attempting to colonise them.

The duchy brought a degree of stability to the south of the country. In the north there had been few tears when the Jesuits were sent packing by the Swedes. The barons, however, were horrified when their estates were expropriated and given to the Swedish aristocracy. Hoping to be third time lucky, they looked for a more sympathetic protector: their choice was Russia.

The Great Northern War of Sweden versus Russia was a titanic struggle which swept across the entire breadth of Europe. In and around Latvia, the Swedish crown sought to finance the war by itself taking 80 percent of the estates, dispossessing both the Swedish barons, who had only just been given them, as well as the remaining Germans. These lands were squeezed for all they were worth and reached the point where they were providing the Swedish crown with more revenue than all other sources put together. Latvia then produced in the person of Johan Reinhold von Patkul someone who proposed to take matters into his own hands.

Patkul, a German land-owner, sent word to Charles XII that the Teutonic Knights had conquered Latvia and converted it to Christianity long before he or his ancestors came on the scene. The descendants of those knights, among whom he numbered himself,

find that the Swedish ambassador had just negotiated a new 30-year peace treaty with Peter the Great. His fears were allayed when he noticed that Peter did not seal the agreement with a kiss on the Cross. Peter had got wind of Patkul's proposal and thought it was excellent, but he wanted to modify the division of the spoils. Russia would take Estonia, Augustus could have the rest of Livonia, and Denmark could help itself to what was left, including Sweden itself.

Augustus launched the scheme in 1700 with an invasion that got as far as Riga before it was halted. Peter was called on for help, but his forces were tied down at Narva in Estonia. In the event, the Russians suffered a

had an inexpungable right to rule. Charles's reply to this tirade was to sentence Patkul to death. He specified that both his head and right hand should be cut off.

With this sentence hanging over him, Patkul approached Augustus II, the odious Elector of Saxony, who prevailed upon him to include Russia in his scheme in return for a promise that there would be none of the "usual barbarities" in the event of an invasion of Latvia. Patkul was taken aback, on arriving in Moscow in September 1699, to

shock defeat at Narva and the victorious Charles turned his attention on Augustus. The Elector of Saxony was in no position to resist, and the terms of his surrender included handing over the wretched Patkul. The earlier death sentence still stood, but Charles specified an amendment. Patkul would still have to lose his head but he could keep his right hand. Instead, the beheading was to be preceded by breaking on the wheel.

Sweden was not destined to hold on to Latvia or its neighbours for much longer. Peter the Great's ultimate victory in his duel with Charles XII opened the way to realising his dream of Russian control of the Eastern

Left, Jēkabs Kettlers, the famous Duke of Courland. **Above**, Riga in the 6th century.

Baltic. By then he had another, purely personal, interest in the region. Some years earlier, he had been struck by a voluptuous woman who had turned up at court on the arm of first one and then another of his ministers, the second being his crony Prince Menshikov. She was a waitress, the daughter of a Lithuanian slave, who had been employed by a Protestant pastor in Latvia before marrying a Swedish army officer. The marriage had fallen by the wayside and Martha, as her name was, was pursuing other interests among the Russian nobility.

Menshikov loyally relinquished the lovely Martha and she became Peter's mistress. On embracing the Orthodox faith, she

tiered system. The result was that the Lett language and everything that went with it was pushed farther and farther into rural backwaters. As these conditions applied for all of seven centuries, it is amazing that there was anything left to rescue in 1918.

Catherine I died after a reign of only two years, but the Latvian connection with the Russian crown was renewed when Peter's niece Anna acceded. While Catherine was undoubtedly fast, Anna was downright debauched. More to the point, she was the dowager Duchess of Courland, and she brought German Balts from Jelgava, Riga and elsewhere to the Russian court en masse. Jelgava, then called Mitau, was the capital of

changed her name to Catherine and after eight years of companionship he married her. Peter changed the law to allow him personally to crown her Empress in 1724.

On Peter's death, Catherine was proclaimed empress in her own right. The accession to the Russian throne of a Latvian peasant was all the more extraordinary because there was practically no social or economic mobility in Latvia: they weren't even allowed to own property in their own capital. Martha's change of name and religion is an indication of the way in which ambitious Latvians had to leave behind the indigenous culture in order to break out of a rigidly-

Courland. Anna's father-in-law was Duke Jēkabs's son, and he had introduced French opera and ballet into its social milieu. Anna granted the first Russian constitution in Jelgava in 1731, but it was her chamberlain and lover, Johannes Ernst Birons, who has left the greatest mark. An opportunist and a scoundrel, he became the Duke of Courland after Anna's husband died and was a power behind the throne. He managed to find enough money to bring in Bartolomeo Rastrelli, architect of St Petersburg's Winter Palace, to build him the sumptuous palace at Rundāle. He was also responsible for sending some 20,000 to Siberia. When Anna died he became Regent of Russia, but was eventually himself sent to Siberia for a brief term of banishment.

The German Balts in Russia's courts used their influence to restore the port of Riga after the depredations of the Russo-Swedish wars but ignored a countryside no less devastated and, moreover, stricken by plague. It was said that, Riga apart, Latvia was ruled by wolves for a century afterwards.

Neglect and ghastly conditions led in 1802 to a peasant uprising led by "Poor Conrad" who, reflecting the revolutionary mood in France, was called "the Lettish Bonaparte". The revolt was put down ruthlessly and Poor Conrad died an excruciating death. There

the symbol of German domination. The Russian Orthodox church hastened to exploit anti-Lutheran feelings. The Orthodox catechism was translated into Lettish and given away free in large numbers. German landowners retaliated by refusing to make any more land available for Orthodox churches. German-Russian rivalry took on a life of its own, and the role of the German Balts sparked a furious row between Tsar Alexander III and Bismarck. Lutheran pastors were locked up or sent to Siberia, and as many as 30,000 of their flock were formally advised that they were henceforth Orthodox.

The Latvian peasant derived some benefits as the region was drawn into the Rus-

was a repetition in 1840, with the peasants directing their fury at the Lutheran church.

Four centuries after the demise of the Teutonic Order, the Latvian establishment was still dominated by German aristocrats and burghers. The country had subsequently been ruled by Poland, Sweden and Russia, but the old German system had somehow endured in spite of the efforts, particularly by Sweden, to dislodge it. To rebellious 19th-century peasants, the Lutheran church was

Left, the 1905 Revolution breaks out in Latvia.
Above, Valdemārs (second left) and other key figures of Latvia's National Awakening.

sian economic sphere to counteract German influence. The Russian railways were extended to the Baltic coast, and Riga handled a large share of Russia's trade. At the same time there was a remarkable sprouting of literary activity in Lett. The rich Germans held on to their positions, but the lower rungs had to make room for Latvians. All of this increased Latvian political awareness, but satisfaction at overcoming the old German obstacles did not necessarily make organisations like the Young Letts pro-Russian. Political sympathies on the workshop floor in Riga were more inclined towards Karl Marx.

The Baltic Revolution of 1905, which

coincided with the St Petersburg uprising, was aimed with equal venom at everything German and Russian. Order was restored in Riga only by the intervention of the Imperial Guard. The tsar then had no qualms about letting the outraged German barons take their revenge, and when they had done so he rewarded them with concessions, like permission to re-open five German public schools. One way or another, then, the German element clung on with its customary tenacity and at the onset of World War I, the population of Riga was still at least 50 percent Baltic-German.

The wounds of the rebellion had not yet healed when World War I broke out. The

country was at first occupied by a defensive Russian army. In 1915, and not without Russian misgivings, the Letts were permitted to raise a national army. When the Russians were withdrawn in confusion after the Bolshevik revolution, the Latvians put up a spirited defence of Riga against the advancing Germans at the cost of some 32,000 casualties. When the Germans took Riga, it was not the prize they were hoping for. The port was inactive, the machinery having been stripped and shipped to Russia.

A secret national organisation bent on Latvian independence was formed within the first months of German occupation and was in contact with refugees in Russia and exiles who had fled after the 1905 rebellion. Events took a curious turn in April 1918 when the tottering German emperor, of all people, was offered the Baltic crown. Moreover, he accepted. The Latvian nationalists' argument was that some kind of autonomy would be possible as part of the German empire, whereas no Russian party would countenance any degree of independence.

The Allied victory in November 1918 made things easier. A state council simply proclaimed independence and offered citizenship to all residents apart from Bolsheviks and German Unionists. The fly in the ointment was that 45,000 German troops still occupied Riga and there were as many again scattered about the rest of the country. When they withdrew, the Bolsheviks stormed in and there was no organised force to stop them. They declared Latvia a Soviet republic. The situation was rescued by Estonia which drove the Bolsheviks off its soil and then crossed the border to help the Latvians do likewise.

Independent Latvia was in a sorry state. The population was a third below pre-war levels, industrial output was virtually nil, and many childen had never been to school. A land reform programme expropriated the German baronial estates and redistributed them in parcels to Latvian peasants.

The Bolsheviks professed an end to tsarist imperialism, but in reality they were as determined as Peter the Great had ever been to hold on to the Baltic coast. To make matters worse, Latvia almost went to war with its erstwhile ally Estonia over title to the border town of Valka.

Hanging by a thread, independent Latvia nevertheless went ahead. Agrarian reform was supplemented by a take-over of industry and commerce, or what was left of them. The Lett language was of course given official status, and there was a general revival of Latvian culture. Perhaps the most significant statistics were the changing population ratios. By 1939, Latvians were in a commanding majority, as high as 75 percent.

Steady if unspectacular progress came to a jarring halt in 1939. The Bolshevik undertaking to respect the independence of the Baltic states "voluntarily and for ever" was torn up by the Nazi-Soviet Pact of 1939. A Soviet invasion was followed by annexation, although not one that was ever recognised by the Western powers. The Nazi-Soviet Pact was short-lived, and in June 1941 the German army drove out the Soviet forces. Latvia, together with Estonia and Lithuania, was made part of Hitler's Ostland, a welcome development as far as many of the ethnic German population were concerned. The consequences for Latvia's 100,000 Jews were horrific: 90 percent were murdered.

Riga was reconquered by the Soviet Army on 8 August 1944, and with that the NKVD set about restoring order in its customary manner. An estimated 320,000 people out of a population of just 2 million were deported to the east; most never returned. Active guerrilla resistance to the Soviet regime continued until as late as 1951, but very little news of it leaked out.

More executions and deportations followed in the purge of so-called bourgeoisie nationalists in 1949–53, and all the time Russians were surging in ostensibly to man the industrial machinery of the Five-Year Plans. Khrushchev purged 2,000 influential locals who raised their voices in protest, replacing them either with Russians or so-called Latovichi, Russians who purported to be Latvians on the strength of a few years' residence in the country.

Notorious Latovichi like Arvids Pelse and Augusts Voss enforced Russification policies with a severity which matched if it did not exceed anything attempted by the tsars. Even such mundane activities as folk-singing were driven underground. Signs of a quiet and gentle revival surfaced in the 1980s. It began with the unobtrusive restoration of derelict churches, and then the odd historical monument here and there. Poets and folk groups performed discreetly.

The catalyst which brought protest out into the open was the Green Movement. Environmental concern then served as cover for the formation of nationalist pressure groups, and before long the underground press was addressing such taboo subjects as the activities of the secret police and human rights. The breakthrough occurred in 1986 when public protest managed to stop the construction of a hydro-electric scheme on the River Daugava.

Left, the Black Brotherhood building, a casualty of World War II. **Above**, Latvian soldiers.

With this victory in hand, and a softer line on public protest emanating from Moscow, the resistance movement began to talk of national sovereignty within a Soviet Federation. The National Independence Movement of Latvia (NIML), however, founded in June 1988 largely by victims of earlier purges, was more radical in its aims. They maintained that the illegal annexation of 1940 invalidated the Soviet regime and all its works. A 1989 census which revealed that Latvians were on the brink of becoming a minority in their own country – they represented just 51.8 percent of the population – lent an air of urgency to the campaign. For their part, the Russian minority rallied in

opposition under the colours of an organisation called Interfront.

The Soviet Union eventually collapsed so quickly and so passively that it is easy to forget how bravely Latvians stuck their heads above the parapet with escalating demands for "total political and economic independence" and, specifically, a free market economy and a multi-party political system. Nor will Latvia forget the five killed by Soviets at the Ministry of the Interior in January 1991.

Elections gave the nationalists a two-thirds majority. and the country was renamed the "Republic of Latvia".

RIGA

Riga is the largest and most exciting city in the Baltic states. With a population of around a million, it seems too big for the country it occupies: just over twice that number live in the whole of Latvia. It is also the least ethnic of all the Baltic capitals, for the Russification of this cosmopolitan city was swift after the war, and by the time of the recent independence a full 70 percent was Russian.

It lies 5 miles (8 km) from the great sagging dip of Riga Bay and for some 3,000 years its warm waters have provided both a gateway and an outlet for the continental heartlands by way of the River Daugava on which Riga stands. Like Tallinn in Estonia, its skyline is an impressive collection of towers and spires that the 20th century has so far failed to obscure.

Its former prosperity can be seen in its churches, its guild halls and in one of the largest collections of Jugenstil buildings in Europe. In the 1970s the city was earmarked for restoration and Polish craftsmen have spent nearly two decades among its decay: there is still an incalculable amount to be done. A final blessing for Riga's citizens is Jūrmala, the sandy beach at the mouth of the Daugava, favoured by generations of holidaymakers from all over the former Soviet empire.

The Old Town: Riga is not a difficult town to get around and nearly everything of merit or note can be reached on foot. The dead-straight main street, Brīvības iela (Freedom Street), heads down to the riverfront past the former Intourist high-rise hotel, the **Latvija**, around the monument to freedom, and dives into the car-free streets of the old city where it is renamed Kaļķu Street.

Continue down Kaļķu Street past the Hotel de Rome, the smart, German-run establishment on the edge of the Old Town. The third turning on the left, with

Preceding pages: Riga's "skyline" outside the railway station. **Left,** St Peter's shadow falls beside St John's.

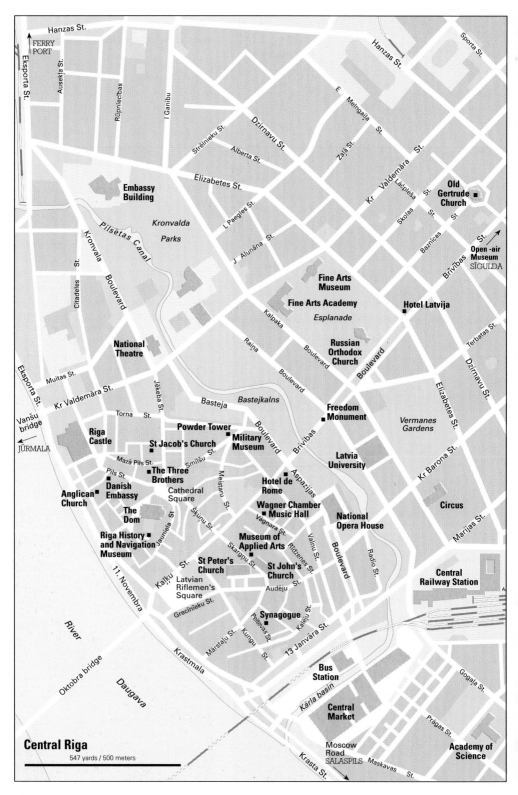

Central Riga

547 yards / 500 meters

FERRY PORT

Hanzas St.

Eksporta St.

Auseklu St.

Rūpniecības

I Ganību

Strēlnieku St.

Dzirnavu St.

Alberta St.

Elizabetes St.

E Melngaiļa St.

Hanzas St.

Sporta St.

Zaļā St.

Kr Valdemāra St.

Lāčplēša St.

Skolas St.

Baznīcas St.

Brīvības St.

Old Gertrude Church

Open-air Museum
SĪGULDA

Embassy Building

Kronvalda Parks

Kronvalda Boulevard

Pilsētas Canal

St.

Citadeles

L Paegles St.

J Alunāna St.

Kalpaka

Fine Arts Museum

Fine Arts Academy

Esplanade

Russian Orthodox Church

Hotel Latvija

Tērbatas St.

National Theatre

Muitas St.

Eksporta St.

Kr Valdemāra St.

Torna St.

Jēkeba St.

Raiņa

Basteja

Bastejkalns

Boulevard

Boulevard

Freedom Monument

Vermanes Gardens

Elizabetes St.

Dzirnavu St.

Vanšu bridge

JŪRMALA

Riga Castle

Powder Tower

St Jacob's Church

Military Museum

Smilšu St.

Mazā Pils St.

Pils St.

The Three Brothers

Danish Embassy

Anglican Church

The Dom

Cathedral Square

Mazā Pils St.

Meistaru St.

Jauniela

Šķūņu St.

Skārņu St.

Hotel de Rome

Wagner Chamber Music Hall

Vagnara St.

Aspazijas

Brīvības

Latvia University

National Opera House

Circus

Kr Barona St.

Mariijas St.

Riga History and Navigation Museum

Museum of Applied Arts

St Peter's Church

Latvian Riflemen's Square

Kaļķu St.

Grecīnieku St.

St John's Church

Audēju St.

Rīdzenes St.

Vaļņu St.

Boulevard

Radio St.

Central Railway Station

11. Novembra

Synagogue

Peldavas St.

Mārstaļu St.

Kungu St.

13 Janvāra St.

Kalēju St.

Bus Station

Kārļa basin

Central Market

Gogaļa St.

Prāgas St.

River

Daugava

Oktobra bridge

Krastmala

Moscow Road
SALASPILS

Krasta St.

Maskavas St.

Academy of Science

226

the hard-currency Jever restaurant on the corner, is Skārņu Street which leads to the **Church of St Peter**, Riga's patron saint. This ancient building with an elegant steeple, is a good place for a tour of the town to begin. A lift glides heavenwards to a viewing platform 236 ft (72 metres) up in the 380-ft (122-metre) steeple, which has been resurrected since its destruction during World War II.

The first church here, made of wood, was built by the city's tradesmen and craftsmen in 1209. Two centuries later it was rebuilt in stone. In 1709, 15 years after the steeple was completed, the city fell to the Russians and Peter the Great took a special delight in climbing to the top of the tower, then the tallest wooden structure in Europe. In fact, when it was struck by lightning in 1721, he personally helped to put out the fire.

Peter was very pleased with his prize, the warm-water port Russia had so long craved, and the city he looked down on is not difficult to imagine today. This was a Hansa port like many between Holland and St Petersburg, with red-brick fortifications, and multi-storeyed merchant- and store-houses rising in gables of high steps and violins curves.

Pride of place among them was the **Blackhead Brotherhood building**, opposite the **Town Hall**, which Dutch builders renovated in 1617. Founded in the 13th century, the brotherhood organised the city's social life and it became a meeting place for bachelor merchants arriving from abroad. One of their three patron saints was Saint Mauritius, who was black and gave the brotherhood its name.

Until World War II these venerated old buildings stood in what is now the **Latvian Riflemen's Square** between St Peter's church and the river where the city's medieval port used to be. This square commemorates, with an ugly statue and a museum, the heroics of the local unit which was chosen as Lenin's personal guard. In this land of dramatically changing fortunes, the Riflemen remain heroes today.

In the corner of the square, at 18 Grēcinieku Street, is the half-timbered **Mentzendorff House** which offers a

good idea of what life was like in a prosperous German's home in the 17th–18th centuries, though the building itself dates back 300 years. Among its former owners was Andreas Helm, head of the Small Guild, and Rheinhold Schlevgt, master of the Order of the Blackheads who set up a pharmacist's on the premises. Its interior, restored between 1982 and 1991, has *trompe l'oeil* wall decoration and painted ceilings inspired by Watteau. The rooms have been furnished with period pieces from the Museum of the History of Riga and Navigation.

For nearly 100 years before Peter I's arrival, the city had been in possession of the Swedes, who had rebuilt its **Castle**, the flag-topped citadel to the north just by Vanšu bridge. Riga had been the largest city in their empire, bigger even than Stockholm. But after they had been driven out in a nine-month siege by Peter's Russian army, the city was in no great shape, and two-thirds of the population had died. Among them were many Latvians who were barred from living

Snow scene from the top of the Latvija Hotel.

within the city walls, where they could not own property. Since the arrival of the German crusaders and the construction of the city in stone, they had been relegated to the lands beyond the city walls, and to Pārdaugava on the river's far bank, where they lived in buildings that had to be built out of wood. Each time the city was threatened, as it had been by the Russians, they had to burn their property and accept the protection of the city walls.

The eighth and last time this happened was in 1812 when an eagle-eyed watchman on St Peter's belfry spotted a distant cloud of dust heralding the French invasion. Four churches, 705 houses, 35 public buildings, and hundreds of acres of vegetable plots were torched before it became clear the dust was caused by a herd of cows. Napoleon crossed Latvia via a different route.

Facing St Peter's on the north side are two other important churches. **St George's** now houses the **Museum of Applied Arts** and it should be visited if only to see the building's interior where soft outer shoes are provided to glide over the fine wooden floors. This was the original church in the city, founded by the crusading Bishop Albrecht of Bremen in 1204 as a chapel for the Sword-Bearer's Order. It stood beside the castle complex which launched the first crusades against the Baltic people. Rebuilt after a rebellion in 1297, it was the first stone building in the city and it remains the only example of Romanesque. It has not been used as a church since the Reformation when it was turned into a storehouse.

Next to it the redbricked **St John's** is distinguished by a steeply stepped Gothic pediment. The church started life in 1234 as the chapel of a Dominican abbey. In 1330 it was enlarged and its buttresses became the dividing walls of the new side altars. It was taken from the Dominicans during the Reformation and in 1582 a divine service in Latvian was held here for the first time. On the south wall, facing St Peter's, is a grille covering a cross-shaped window behind which two monks were cemented

Left, Milda. **Right**, the Dom, St Peter's and the English church.

228

up during the building of the church and for the rest of their lives they were fed through the small gap. Behind St John's is Jāņa sēta, a small square abutting part of the old red-brick city wall, whose upkeep was the responsibility of the city's guilds.

Rīdzenes Street, running parallel, marks the former small river of Rīdziņa which ran into the Daugava, and it was around here that the earliest Liv and Latgalian fishing and trading settlements were established.

As you wander round the streets and lanes of this area, where some of the remaining two dozen ancient store-houses are still being restored, look out for the **house of John Rheuttern** at 2/4 Mārstaļu Street, where exhibitions are often held. It was built by this rich German merchant in 1685, during the Swedish occupation, and beneath the roof is a frieze showing the Swedish lion devouring the Russian bear. At No. 21 is another baroque mansion which was built in 1696 for Rheuttern's son-in-law, a burgher named Dannestern.

Mentzendorff House Museum.

Both have fine portals by the local stone-mason Hans Schmiesel, who was responsible for the handsome if rather out of place portal on St Peter's church. Just past it on the left is Peitavas Street where a **Jewish synagogue** has been beautifully restored both inside and out. It should not be passed by without taking the opportunity to look in.

To the north, off Kaļķu Street, is Vāgnera Street which has both the sumptuous **Wagner Chamber Music Hall** where recitals are regularly held in its elegant surroundings, and, at No. 13, a pharmacist's which is the only rococo building in the city.

Cathedral and citadel: The "newer" part of the Old Town lies on the north side of Kaļķu Street, which goes down to the river and crosses it at Oktobra bridge. Immediately evident is the yellow art nouveau **House of Cats**, with splended black cats on its turrets and, opposite, the **Great and Small Guild Halls**. The House of Cats is supposed to have been built by a Latvian aggrieved that his nationality disqualified him from mem-

FEARLESS FILM-MAKER

There was a tangible anxiety in Latvia after Juris Podnieks was reported missing on 23 June 1992. Everyone was concerned for the man who had so many times risked his life for the films, which so eloquently explained their life and times. He was a man of creative talent and complete dedication whose charisma, courtesy and kindness touched everybody he met.

The police were called out, divers were sent to Lake Zvigzde just west of Kuldīga in Kurzeme where he had last been seen. Psychics and mystics tried to divine where he might be. It was eight days before his body was brought up from the lake. It was hard to believe that this heroic 41-year-old film-maker had died in a silly scuba diving accident, after he had so often tempted a much more dramatic fate.

Podnieks was born in Riga, a city with a film tradition that goes back to Sergei Eisenstein, who was born here in 1898. He trained at the Moscow Film School before being apprenticed at the Riga Film Studios

in 1968. In 1982 he made his first major documentary about the last surviving members of Latvia's famous Riflemen who had been Lenin's guard.

On the eve of *glasnost*, he was in the right place to explain to the West what it was like to be living in different parts of the Soviet Union. *Is It Easy To Be Young?*, made in 1987, included interviews with disillusioned veterans from the Afghanistan war. It was the first time people had queued to see a documentary at the cinema. It received awards and accolades abroad.

The following year the nuclear power station at Chernobyl erupted and Podnieks was the only cameraman to capture it from the air and from the ground. "The world had to know," he said simply when asked why he had taken such risks. He used the footage in his film about life in the Soviet Union called *Hello, Do You Hear Us?*, which won the the 1989 Prix d'Italia.

His news footage was regularly used in the West and his documentaries continued to mirror the changes taking place in Latvia and the Baltics, and also to hurry them on. On 13 January 1991, he was in Vilnius in neighbouring Lithuania when Soviet soldiers shot and beat unarmed civilians, killing 14. His images were on news programmes around the world. A week later the Soviet special police turned their attention on Riga. On 20 January Soviet black berets began an assault on the Interior Ministry and shots whistled around Bastejkalns Park, the tranquil haven between the Freedom Monument and the Art Museum.

Podnieks was immediately in the thick of it, with his teenage son and cameramen Gvido Zvaigzne and Andris Slapiņš. The pink, smooth-topped stones in the park are memorials to the five men killed that night including both cameramen. Slapiņš, a friend as well as a colleague, insisted Podnieks pick up his blood-stained camera and record his dying words. "Keep filming…" he said.

Podnieks used this footage and Slapiņš' last words became famous in *Homeland*, a hymn to Latvia which included a moving record of the 1990 Song Festival. Slapiņš left an unfinished film of his own, *The Baltic Saga*, about the 20th-century killing fields of Kurzeme and, among other projects, Podnieks was engaged in finishing the work when he died. ■

Podnieks: a sympathetic eye in a dangerous world.

bership of the Big Guild, and he topped its two towers with black cats with their backsides pointing at the Guild building. A court case ensued, the cats were turned round and the Latvian was admitted to the Guild.

Traditionally only Germans were allowed to belong to the Great Guild of St John's, a merchants' guild founded in 1384. The building was last redesigned in 1866 by the city architect J. D. Felsko and today it is the home of the Philharmonic Orchestra. The Small Guild of St Mary's was for artisans and was started in the mid-14th century. Both functioned until the 1860s but they were not finally dissolved until the 1930s.

All streets here lead to the **cathedral square**, the cobbled focal point of the old city, where buskers provide constant entertainment for the pavement cafés. The square was in fact only created in 1936 when Karlis Ulmanis, the first and last prime minister under the first independence, had a number of buildings demolished so people could gather to hear him speak on the balcony

Popular pavement café in Cathedral Square.

of the bank building on the corner, which is now leased to Radio Latvia.

St Mary's Cathedral, the Dom, is a magnificent red-brick structure, with a gable like a Hanseatic merchant's house and a bulbous dome of northern Gothic solemnity. Steps lead down to the north door because in the city's constant rebuilding, the ground level has actually risen over the years. If you take Jauniela Street down to the left of the cathedral and go behind the Pūt vējiņi restaurant (must book, the cabinet eat here: better to try Pie Kristapa in Bockslaff's art nouveau building opposite). Here the arches in the back of the cloisters show how much the land level has risen.

The cathedral was begun by Bishop Albrecht just after St George's, in 1211, and he is buried in the crypt. The plaques, tombs and headstones decorating the interior show just how German the city remained, no matter who owned it. The most impressive part of the building is the **6,768-pipe organ** and if there is a concert, it should not be missed (the booking-office is in a building opposite

the main door). Choral works can be particularly hair-tingling.

The **cloister gardens** have recently been undergoing refurbishment, but the adjoining building of the former monastery houses the **Museum of the History of Riga and Navigation**. This is an eclectic collecion of historical items and memorabilia, and doesn't have too much to do with the sea. Its scope is very wide and it is the best museum in the city, showing the wealth of its merchants. It was the first public museum in the Baltics when it opened in 1773 and it was based on the collection of Nicolaus von Himsel, a medical practitioner who died nine years earlier at the age of 35.

Pils iela (Castle Street) leads off the Dom square in front of a large, elegant, green art nouveau building with ruched curtains that give it something of the air of a boudoir. This was the city's original **stock exchange** and today it is just one of several.

In the corner of Anglikāņu Street off Castle Street is a smart brown Renaissance-style building, which belongs to the **Danish Embassy**. It was originally built as the British Club for expatriates, merchants and sundry travellers (Napoleon called Riga "a suburb of London"), and every brick and detail of the Anglican church behind it was brought here from Britain, including a shipload of earth to provide the foundations. Wives and other women were allowed in the club once a year.

Pils Street arrives at the **castle** or citadel the Swedes designed in 1652. The first castle was built here in 1330 by the Livonian Order who later decamped to Cēsis. In 1481, in one of many internecine wars within the city, it was razed by the townspeople, but the Livonian Order returned to besiege the town 34 years later and it was rebuilt. Today it houses three museums: **History of Latvia**, **History of Literature and Art**, **and Foreign Art**. None is a must. In front of the castle overlooking the river is a well-appointed café, which sometimes has *sashliks* on a barbecue.

Opposite the castle, Mazā Pils Street dives into the narrow lanes of the Old

Left, merchants' store-houses in the Old Town. Right, Swedish Gate.

Town again. The most attractive group of buildings here, and perhaps in the whole of the city, are the three buildings known as **The Three Brothers**. These are the oldest residences in the city, merchants' homes of almost doll's house proportions dating from the 15th century. They have been colourfully restored, and they show how the families would live on the lower floors while leaving the upper areas for storage. Two have now been amalgamated internally into an art gallery and give an opportunity to snoop around.

Nearby is the red-brick **St Jacob's**, the principal Catholic church. Its 240-ft (73-metre) thin green spire, topped by a gold cockerel, is one of the three sky-pricking steeples that shape the city's skyline. In 1522 it became the first church in Latvia to hold a Lutheran service, but 60 years later, when the Polish king Stephen Bathory took the city for a brief spell, it was handed to the Catholics who have kept faith here ever since. In front of it is the peach-coloured **residence of the archbishop** and on the

north side is the **parliament building** on Jēkaba Street which was blockaded against Soviet attack in 1991.

Jēkaba Street leads directly to the grey **Swedish Gate**. Built in 1698, this is the only gate left in the city walls and through it the condemned were led to their fate. The executioner lived in the apartment over the gate; he would place a red rose on his window-ledge on any morning he had to perform.

The street on the far side of the gate is lined by the steel grey barracks erected for the occupying Swedes. Turn right up Torna Street past the old houses built against the city wall. Some of the red-brick wall has been restored and a café is proposed in the battlements. At the end of the street is Pulvertornis, the **Gunpowder Tower**, the last of 18 city towers to remain. Its fat round red-brick walls and concave, conical roof, topping 85 ft (26 metres), are reminiscent of Lübeck, Queen of the Hansa. Russian cannonballs are stuck in its walls and a **Museum of Warfare** fills its insides.

The Sand Road, Smilšu Street, leads

The lofty naves of St Peter's.

CITY OF ART NOUVEAU

rt nouveau, the architectural style which brings such an unexpectedly decadent air to Riga's streets, celebrated the triumph of the bourgeoisie at the turn of the century. From Edinburgh to Brussels, Vienna to St Petersburg, and in highly-developed Riga more than in any Russian city, the new urban middle classes found prosperity. The first self-consciously modern architecture sprang to the task of designing residential blocks, academies, schools, department stores, libraries, banks, restaurants and factories. The boulevard city which grew up in the 1900s is about 40 percent art nouveau – what the French call *style moderne*, and the Germans *Jugendstil*.

Riga hosted a mixture of new, ahistorical, often decorative approaches to building. The residential houses in Alberta Street, built by civil engineer Mikhail Osipovich Eisenstein, father of the great Russian filmmaker, are saturated in finishing details. Inside the entrance hall to 2a Alberta Street the exterior decoration evolves into a tur-

quoise hall of columns, embroidered with leaves and curves.

Eisenstein's "decoratively eclectic art nouveau", a staggering synthesis of rationality and ornament, is shared by other contemporary Riga architects including the Baltic Germans Friedrich Scheffel, Heinrich Scheel and Reinhold Schmaeling. All studied in St Petersburg, where art nouveau flourished. The entrance hall to Scheel and Sheffel's residential block with shops at 8 Smilšu Street shows a characteristic affinity with the Arts and Crafts Movement. That thread takes the curious visitor back to one of Riga's most important architects, the Baltic German Wilhelm Bockslaff. Bockslaff built the graceful, turreted, brick Stock Exchange (1905), since 1919 the Latvian Art Academy, on Kalpaka Boulevard. The pastel-painted assembly hall, its ceiling embroidered after William Morris, is a treasury of stained glass, and the whole building is a fine monument to art nouveau's eclecticism.

The houses, shops and banks on Brīvības Street and in nearby Gertūdes and A. Čaka streets employ the perpendicular to express the solidity and the excitement of town life. Architects of this so-called rational art nouveau from the mid-1900s include Latvians Jānis Alksnis, Eižens Laube and Paul Mandelstamm and Konstantia Pēkšēns.

Mandelstamm, Laube, Pēkšēns and Aleksandrs Vanags, though in touch with St Petersburg tendencies, all graduated from the Riga Polytechnical Institute, which encouraged them to develop a more specific modern Latvian style from 1905 to 1911. A general heaviness, in some cases as if the building had been poured out of a mould, in others as if it were a test-run for many different building materials, including stucco, wood, stone, brick and plaster, characterises this national romanticism. It incorporated stylised ethnographic ornaments and the natural materials used in an urban setting, together with tapered window recesses and steep roofs, suggested a continued link with rural life.

The individual features of scores of un-modified, unmodernised buildings make a walk round Riga a joy, particularly in winter when no foliage obscures one of architecture's happiest testaments to high-spirited urban living. ∎

Sumptuous facade in Elisabetes Street.

past the tower back to the cathedral. This was the main road out of town across marshes and through the forests towards St Petersburg. At one time it was the only proper road from the city.

Parks and art: To say the old city is an island is rather fanciful, but it is entirely surrounded by water. The old moat which encircles it on the landward side is now a small canal running through a series of attractive parks from the ferry terminal in the north on the far side of the castle, to the railway station and market in the south. To the north, on Kr Valdemāra Street, is the **National Theatre**. To the south, between Brīvības and Kr Barona Street, is the magnificent 19th-century **Opera House**, formerly known as the German Theatre, which has been undergoing thorough renovation with money donated by exiled Latvians. Richard Wagner was director of the opera for a year in 1837.

In the park just to the north of Brīvības is **Bastejkalns** the high spot of the city and not much more than a hiccup with little waterfalls and a pleasant café by the canal. Nearby are five inscribed stones which commemorate the film cameramen and policemen killed during the Soviet attack on the Ministry of the Interior around the modern Rīdzene Hotel in January 1991 (bullet holes remain inside the hotel where the prime minister was staying).

The rallying point for the nation is the **Statue of Liberty** on Brīvības, the elegant lady locally known as **Milda**, who holds aloft three golden stars representing the three regions of Latvia: Kurzeme, Vidzeme and Latgale. She was designed by K. Zāle and put up in 1935. Somehow she managed to survive the occupation of the Soviets who officially described her as a memorial to the Soviet saviours of the city. The first post-war public demonstration was held here, in June 1987.

Raiņa Boulevard runs along the top side of these parks and this was the diplomatic street of embassies during the years of independence, some of which have returned. Brīvības continues up past the Post Office and Sakta

Cheese stall, Riga market.

souvenir shop, opening into a boulevard and dominated by the Latvija Hotel.

On the left is the **Russian Orthodox Church**, now reclaimed from its Soviet use as a planetarium, though many locals still say "Meet you at the Planetarium," as it is used to house one of the best cafés in Riga called *Dieva auss* (God's Ear). The Esplanade park behind it leads to the 19th-century **Arts Academy** and the **Fine Arts Museum**, which contains the best of the national artists' works and is well worth a visit.

Elisabetes Street at the top of the park should be followed for a while to appreciate its **art nouveau** and **romantic nationalism buildings** (*see page 234*). Nos. 10 and 33 were designed by Michael Eisenstein, father of Riga's most famous film-maker, Sergei Eisenstein. But most of his work can be seen in Alberta Street (second right and first left after Kr Valdemāra) where he was responsible for the houses up to No. 8, plus No. 13 opposite. Step inside the entranceways to see the painted interiors, but be prepared to hold your nose: a

fair bit of drinking goes on around here. At the end of the street is Strēlnieku Street, with another Eisenstein masterpiece at 4a, which has his typical bright blue touch. On the corner of the two streets was the house the Latvian architect Konstantins Pēkšēns built for himself. Two other famous people lived there: the writer Rūdolfs Blaumanis (1863–1908) and the artist Jānis Rozentāls (1866–1916). A museum on the top floors contains their respective study and studio.

Rozentāls' work can also be seen on the facade of the former **Latvian Society building** near the university on the opposite side of Brīvības in Verķeļa Street. This street continues across Kr Barons, one of the main shopping streets, and down past the permanent **circus**. After independence the circus could not maintain itself, and while the animals languish in cages out the back, discos have been put on in its arena.

The market: Beyond the railway station are the humps of the five 39-ft (35-metre) high Zeppelin hangars, brought here in the 1930s to house the market which is one of the wonders of Riga. It used to be Europe's largest market, and must still be a contender for the title. It is built over a large underground storage system, and each hangar has its speciality: meat, dairy products, vegetables. Cream is sold in plastic bags, there are barrels of sauerkraut, fancy cakes, pickled garlic, dried herbs and mushrooms, smoked fish and whole stalls selling nothing but tins of sardines. On the way in via the station there are baskets of kittens and puppies, and wooden kiosks and stalls surround the hangars. Down by the waterfront the old flea-market spreads itself over acres of pavement. It is open every day, and is at its busiest on Fridays and Saturdays.

Beyond the market is the squat, brown, Empire-State building replica belonging to the **Academy of Science** and just beyond, in Jesus baznīca Street, is a fascinating octagonal wooden **Lutheran Church of Jesus** made of solid boards a foot wide. Built in 1822, it is the seat of the Lutheran bishop of the Commonwealth of Independent States.

Left, accordion player by the old city wall. **Right,** the view upriver beyond the market's Zeppelin hangars to the TV tower.

AROUND RIGA

Beyond the Old Town and the centre of Riga there are several diverse sites and entertainments that require public transport or a car. They are, in fact, so diverse it is hard to think that a visitor would be interested in all of them, but all of them, from the cemeteries to the seaside, will be of interest to somebody.

Perhaps of greatest general appeal is **Brīvdabas Muzejs**, the **open-air ethnographic museum** at Berǧi, 6 miles (10 km) northeast along Brīvības Street. More than 100 buildings are set out in a 250 acres (100 hectares) of woodland beside Lake Jugla. (A swim in the lake at Bergi is recommended in prefernce to use of public swimming pools in Riga.) The idea for the museum arose in the wake of the desolation of the countryside after World War I and work began on it in 1924.

The most impressive building is the 18th-century Lutheran church just to the left of the entrance. The whole building, including its figurative wood carvings, was made with an axe. There is a special seat, as fancy as a theatre box, beside the altar for the local German landlord and the front pews were reserved for imported German workers. Church was then obligatory for all workers and those caught skiving were put in the stocks or the pillory exhibited outside. Before the 19th-century organ was installed, music would have been an accompanying drum.

The display is divided into Latvia's ancient regions and it shows the contrasts between the rich Kurzeme farmers and those of poorer Latgale, but by and large the farmsteads were built solely for the family unit, which usually meant three generations. Costumed figures people the village and a blacksmith, potter and spoonmaker often perform. Sometimes there are folk gatherings and a major craft fare is held here on the first week in June and should not be missed.

In the same direction as this museum is the **Motor Museum**. Smerļa Street leads down to it from Brīvības, passing the city's large **film studios**, which have an open-door policy. Just beyond it, the street forks right into Sergei Eizenštein Street where the Motor Museum's facade stands out like a Rolls-Royce radiator grille.

Riga has been no slouch in motor manufacturing: its Russo-Balt factory presented Russia with its first car and tank. But the fruits of its labours are poorly represented. The high spots are waxworks figures of the famous with their vehicles: Lenin in his 7.3-tonne bullet-proof car which had hydraulic glass windows 3 inches (8 cm) thick; Maxim Gorky with his 1934 Lincoln; Brezhnev at the moment of impact when he crashed his 1966 Rolls-Royce, together with the subsequent press cuttings saying that his non-appearance was due to a "sudden bad cold".

The Forest Park: To the north of Brīvības is **Mežaparks** (Forest Park), a suburb of former well-to-do wooden villas and houses occupied by many Germans before 1939 when Hitler demanded they went back home. This is

Preceding pages: Jūrmala beach. Left, homestead in the Open-Air Museum. Right, Heroes' Cemetery.

where the city **zoo** was founded in 1912 to show all the animals of Latvia, though some of them, such as the beaver and wolf, are no longer there. In all there are 350 kinds of animals, including an elephant, and the largest herd of Tibetan wild asses (*kiangs*) in captivity. There are about 50 of them, all descended from a pair given to the zoo by China in the early 1960s.

The main **open-air concert stadium** is also in Mežaparks, and it is here that choirs gather in their thousands. Just to the south are the three great cemeteries of the city: the **Cemetery of Heroes** for the seemingly infinite casualties of 20th-century wars, but particularly from World War I and the War of Independence; **Raiņa Cemetery** for the great and the good Latvian literati; and **Meža Kapi**, the old forest cemetery.

High times: On the opposite side of the city is the **television tower** rising above the Daugava to the south. This is built on the upstream end of an island called **Zaķusala**, and is reached over Salu bridge. On the north side of the island is a modern office block where the television company operates from. There are plans for various nations to build theme parks and gardens on the barren land beneath. At 907 ft (368 metres), the tower is the 10th highest building in the world, as the guide will tell you as you are whisked by lift to the viewing-room halfway up. From a restaurant on the same level you can see Riga Bay.

Opposite the tower the only gold dome in the city peeks out from a clump of lime trees in Riga's **Moscow District**. This is the place of worship for the **Old Believers**, a sect expelled from Russia in the 17th century, and this church now has the largest parish of the faith in the world, with a congregation of perhaps 25,000. It has a unique collection of 17th- and 18th-century icons, and a rich and contemplative atmosphere broken only by the rather incongruous chimes of a grandfather clock. Services are at 8am and 5pm every day and there are four-hour services on Saturday evenings and Sunday mornings.

The Moscow road, the A215, follows

Old mansion house in Mežaparks.

the right bank of the Daugava for 10 miles (16km) to **Salaspils** where the Livonian Order built its first palace, in the 14th century, and in 1412 signed an important agreement with the Bishop of Riga, sorting out how they would mutually rule over the capital. On this site in 1605 the Swedes suffered a crushing defeat by the Poles who then ruled Lithuania. An atomic power station was built here in 1979. But Salaspils is destined to go down in the history books primarily as the site of a nightmarish World War II concentration camp where 53,000 died.

A 100-acre (40-hectare) **memorial park** was opened in 1967, centred on a long sloping, concrete building inscribed: "The earth moans beyond this gate". On the far side are half a dozen monumental statues and a lengthy, low black box where wreaths are placed. It emits a continuous and eerie ticking noise, supposed to represent a beating heart. The sites of the former barracks are marked and an inscribed stone marks the place of the gallows. There were

7,000 children killed among the Latvians, Belorussians, Poles, Czechs, Austrians, Dutch and Germans who died here. On the opposite side of the highway is a memorial to 47,000 Soviet prisoners of war who perished under the Nazis.

The seaside: The word *jūrmala* in Latvian means simply seaside, and it is the name given to the Baltics' most famous resort. It is stretched along a narrow strip of land, pressed against the beach by Latvia's second largest river, the Lielupe, which follows the coast for about 5 miles (8 km) before emptying itself into Riga Bay just west of the mouth of the Daugava. People do swim here, but it is not ideal. If you are desperate for a dip it is healthier to go further from the city.

There is a good road to Jūrmala from Riga, which leaves the city over the distinctive suspension bridge nicknamed "**Voss's guitar**" after the last local party boss who had it built, it is said, so he could get to his seaside home all the more quickly. Anyone driving to

Memorial to Nazi victims at Salaspils.

the resort, or even through it, needs to buy a permit for the day from the roadside offices on its outskirts: these are not given to cars with high exhaust emission, though rumour has it that palms can be greased. A ferry service to Jūrmala may also be running from Riga.

This is where to look for amber, especially after a storm. Here, in pine woods behind the sand dunes that so typify the whole Baltic coast, are some beautiful wooden villas of Edwardian elegance, with stained-glass windows and fancy duckboards still intact. Apart from the wooden homes, a whole Soviet holiday structure was built up. Factories and unions provided rest homes and apartments (some only for workers, without their families) and they included places for mud, peat and spa-water cures.

It has long been a popular bathing spot. Peggie Benton, an English diplomat's wife, was in Riga at the outbreak of World War II and like many people from the city rented a villa at Jūrmala for the summer, enjoying the women and children-only hours of the day. "The

Latvians kept up the delightful Russian custom of bathing naked," she wrote in *Baltic Countdown.* "One soon learned not to worry and got used to strolling up to a policeman, tightly buttoned into his uniform, to ask how much longer until the red flag went up and we had to put our clothes on again." Parts of the beaches in all three Baltic countries still have single-sex areas for all-over tans.

Although independence has resulted in a dramatic drop in tourism from the former Soviet interior, in high season Jūrmala seems quite full enough. The crowd swells at weekends as well as on summer weekday evenings, since the train from Riga takes only 30 minutes or so. In August there is a pop competition of the most popular kind devised by Raimonds Pauls, the composer and piano-playing Minister of Culture. Undignified? They say he doesn't care what anyone thinks of him.

There are a dozen train stops to choose from, between **Lielupe** and **Kemeri**, a spa town set back from the sea. In its heyday the grand Kemeri hotel had a cosmopolitan air, hosting international chess championships and social events. **Majori** is the central stop and the main pedestrian road has ice-cream parlours, souvenir shops and an outdoor concert hall, all within easy reach.

One of the only buildings to protrude over the beach is the Jūras Pērle (Sea Pearl) restaurant in **Bulduri**, just to the east, and it has wonderful views. Other restaurants include the Seven Sisters, a hang-out for some of the bad lads and minor villains who are attracted here, as they are to any resort.

The cultural high of Majori is the attractive wooden house lived in by the poet Jānis Rainis in a street called J. Plieksana iela, which was his real name. He lived here during his last three years, from 1926 to 1929, and a museum preserves his effects. His wife, the poet Aspazija, is also commemorated.

A Westerner won't find an abundance of expected seaside entertainments but just strolling around brings such rewarding sights as the renovated Lutheran church in **Dubulti** and the bright blue wooden Orthodox church nearby.

Left, Russian church, Bulduri. **Right**, statue to Rainis and Aspazija, Jūrmala.

KURZEME

Kurzeme is the westernmost region of Latvia, healthy agricultural land half surrounded by sea. This was once Courland (Kurland in German), named after the Curi or Kuri, the amber-rich seafaring people who dominated the coast before the arrival of the German crusaders. In 1561, after the break-up of Livonia, Courland came into its own. It became a duchy under the sovereignty of Poland, and included the region of Zemgale (formerly Semigallia) to the south of Riga, plus a small corner of modern Lithuania.

Its dukes enjoyed a degree of independence, building castles for themselves and Lutheran churches for the people. They became rich and powerful, notably Jēkabs Kettlers (1642–82), who went empire-building and collected a couple of outposts, one in Gambia, West Africa, the other the Caribbean island of Tobago.

The empire was built largely on the pines that grow exceptionally tall and straight. The most impressive forests are in the Slītere Nature Reserve (see page 110) and along the sandy coastal region, which was once below the sea. Trees grow to around 110 feet (35 metres) and may be up to 500 years old.

Kurzeme's thriving shipbuilding and trading activities were conducted at the two important ice-free ports of Ventspils and Liepāja, though neither of these modern industrial centres bears any sign of those years of greatness today.

The coast around Kurzeme is a continuous white sandy beach, from just north of the major Lithuanian resort of Palanga up to the Kolka peninsula and down to the fishing village of Mērsrags and Lake Engure in the Bay of Riga.

Beyond this is Jūrmala, Latvia's riviera, and Zemgale, or the Central Region. For 45 years, until 1991, most of this coast was used by the military and was therefore inaccessible: today, even in the heat of summer, much of it remains completely deserted. Between the coastal lowland in the west and Riga Bay in the northeast, towns, villages, churches and estates are tucked in the valleys and wooded corners of a landscape that rolls between rivers and hills. Kuldīga and Talsi are the principal inland provincial towns.

The town of **Kuldīga** is 100 miles (160 km) west of Riga, and is a good centre for exploring the region. A castle was first built here in 1242, and in 1561 the town was made the capital of Courland by the first duke, Gottard Kettlers. The castle was built beside the River Venta, which was navigable all the way to Ventspils and the sea.

The city declined after the Great Northern War and the castle was reduced to little more than a ruin: a park remains where it stood. The churches are worth exploring: the Baptist church has a striking clock-tower, St Catherine's Lutheran church, recently renovated, has a fine wooden altar and pulpit from 1660, and there is a grand view over the town from the top of its 85-ft (25-metre) tower. The altar of the Holy Trinity Catholic Church in Raiņa Street also

Preceding pages: Nogales manor house. Left, Courland countryside. Right, Liepāja.

has an impressive altar, donated by Tsar Alexander I in 1820.

Part of the town's charm is derived from the Alekšupīte, a tributary to the Venta, which runs by a mill and between wooden houses that date back to the 16th century. Most of the old buildings are centred around the square overlooked by the 19th-century town hall, but the main street today is Liepājas, which runs back from Raiņa Street (try the fresh raspberry cakes at the café on the corner) a few streets back. This street, with a wooden building that looks as if it might be a Wild West saloon, leads to the main modern square and the modern Kursal hotel.

At the old bridge over the Venta, which is now closed to traffic, you can see the **Kuldīgas rumba**, a shallow waterfall that runs the 360-ft (110-metre) width of the river. Grooms carry their brides across it for luck. In the fast-flowing waters beneath the bridge, people try to catch fish in their hands.

Around Kuldīga there are plenty of excursions to be made. The countryside is riven with streams and small lakes. The River Venta, which rises in Lake Vene in Lithuania and twists down to the sea at Ventspils, is popular for water-borne activity.

A pleasant drive leads northeast of Kuldīga, to **Sabile** and **Kandava**, towards **Tukums** in the Vidzeme region (*see page 269*). These villages are known for their gypsy population. Vina Kalns, **Wine Hill**, in Sabile is in the record books as the most northern place in Europe where vines are grown.

Between Kuldīga and Ventspils is the small town of **Piltene**, the seat of a bishopric that retained its independence from 1234 to 1583. The remains of its castle of the Livonian Order lie behind the church, built in 1792. Overlooking the lake are the original church and nunnery dating from 1254.

At the end of the Livonian Wars, when the rest of western Latvia became the new Duchy of Courland, the lands of the Bishop of Piltene and Oesel (the old name for the island of Saaremaa, now in Estonia) were not included in the sale,

Sand dunes by the beach, Liepāja.

and the bishop, Johann von Munchhausen, sold them in 1559 to Frederick II of Denmark. Frederick then gave them to his brother Magnus, who married the sister of Ivan the Terrible. The tsar crowned him "king of Livonia", a dubious title which he relinquished in 1578; he then retired to Piltene, where he founded Latvia's second school. He was buried in the castle, but in 1640 his remains were returned to Denmark.

Ancient churches: Danish craftsmen were imported via Piltene and art historians detect their hand on the robust folk carvings of the altars and pulpits of local churches. But the principal carvings at Piltene, which have not survived, were by the 18th-century master carvers from Ventspils, Nicolas Soeffrens, the older and younger, ship carvers who turned their skills to church work.

Among other local churches with fine carving is **Zlekas**, between Piltene and Kuldīga. This is the largest church in Courland and it has a fine black and gold baroque pulpit and altar which were carved by local Latvians. At **Ēdole** on the opposite side of the main Ventspils road and about 12 miles (20 km) northwest of Kuldīga, there is a church that dates from the 17th century. It has also a recently restored 13th-century castle. The keys of both the church and castle are to be found at a nearby house called Saules Lejas.

One of the most interesting churches is at **Ugale**, directly north of Kuldīga on the road between Tukums and Ventspils. Built in 1697, its organ was installed four years later, making it not only the oldest in the Baltics, but also unique in Europe, with 28 stops, including the only surviving baroque register. It was built by Cornelius Rhaneus from Kuldīga, who may have been Dutch.

The beautiful, unpainted lime wood carvings by Michael Markwart from Ventspils include stars that once revolved and angels' wings designed to flap. The pastor, a "charismatic" Lutheran, Jānis Kalniņš, is a musician and master organ restorer and he gives guided tours which are liable to include a few tunes (tel: 71475). The neighbouring

Good and bad women, Zlekas pew.

village of **Usma** is where the 18th-century Lutheran church in Riga's open-air ethnography museum comes from.

The Piltene bishops were not intolerant and they attracted a prosperous Jewish population. **Aizpute**, a town to the south, was known as "Klein Danzig" by the Jews who had their own municipality, citizens' guard and uniform. The town makes a pleasant stop and has a church dating back to 1254.

Aizpute is on the main road from Riga to Liepāja and around here there was military activity under the Soviets. Just north of **Skrunda** was the USSR's most westerly, and therefore most important tracking station, and there is a good view of it from **Valtaiki**, on the road to Embute, where there is a Lutheran church from 1792. The key is with the nearby little shop. One of the German barons from the family for whom it was built is depicted in the stained-glass window of 1902 designed by a local Latvian artist.

Around Talsi: The region northeast of Kuldīga is Talsi, centred on the town of the same name. Like a picture on a chocolate box, it is a pretty, tranquil idyll tucked under hills beside a large pond. Not surprisingly, it has long been an artists' haunt.

The oldest wooden church in the Baltics is 10 miles (16 km) northeast of Talsi at **Iğene**. It has been a working church since 1555, though most of it dates from 1752 and the altar is original. It was moved here from a nearby plague-stricken village. Approach it from Vandzene along a gravel road, taking the first left after the village pond. There is a ruined wooden church of a similar age just to the south, at **Lauciene**.

North of Talsi is a series of former large country-house estates. The palace at **Nogale** is typical and particularly fine. It was built in 1880 for Baron von Firks as a summer residence and hunting lodge, and from 1920 to 1980 it was a school. It has now been well restored. The ceiling paintings in the bedrooms, allegories of music and dance, are intact and an attractive conservatory has been repaired. The two-storey neoclassical

The country town of Kuldiga.

building, which is open to the public, overlooks a lake and 170 acres (70 hectares) of parkland. It has plans to become a cultural and residential centre. The adjacent village has a public sauna and a stone windmill with a church-steeple roof.

The neighbouring village to the west is **Valdemarpils**, where the main estate is still in the process of reconstruction. It takes its name from Krišjānis Valdemārs, one of the leading lights of the National Awakening, who was born in nearby **Cīruli** in 1825. He became enchanted by the sea near here at Roja and went on to found Latvia's first seamen's school at Ainaži, right up by the Estonian border.

Outside his country manor in Valdemarpils is one of the oldest elm trees in the country, a huge and crippled beast that is in need of support. **Lake Sasmaka** is nearby and the village has a church dating from 1646 and a small museum of local history in Statcijas Street.

The largest estate in the whole of the Baltics was **Dundaga**, the northernmost

village of any size on this cape. In the 18th century the castle's lands stretched for 270 sq. miles (700 sq. km), and today some attempts are being made to restore some of its former glory. The crozier and sword, symbols of the Church and the Sword Bearers, are inscribed on its entranceway and the main door inside the courtyard is guarded by a statue of a bishop and a crusader. The estate belonged to the bishops of Courland, the last of whom was Herzog of Holstein, brother of Germany's Frederich II.

There are seven coats of arms on the castle, belonging to owners going back to 1245, and they include those of the von Bülows and the Osten-Sachens, the subsequent inheritors of the **estate**. Today the building is a weekly boarding-house for schoolchildren who live too far away to bus in daily. In a first-floor bathroom still in use is a bath supposedly used by Duke Jēkabs, but it doesn't look anything special.

Like all Latvian castles, it is surrounded by stories of devils and ghosts:

Neoclassical Nogales.

it was built on a magic grey stone, and the sister of a local baron is meant to walk here during a full moon. There is an attractively-sited open-air concert venue in the grounds behind.

The local church, dated 1766, has wood carvings by Soeffrens and an altar painting by Latvia's great 20th-century artist, Jānis Rozentāls. The confessional possesses a definite Scandinavian flavour (keys from Inta Biezbarde, tel: 42231). Memorials to several members of the Osten-Sachens family are scattered in the church grounds.

The secret coast: On the Riga Bay side of the cape, the road from Jūrmala continues through pine trees of extraordinary stature, and it is not surprising that they provided masts for many western ships throughout the ages. A barrier, now abandoned, marks the point where the Soviet army held sway. People living in these small villages were heavily vetted, and as on all the coast fishing was simply banned.

Around **Roja**, the tarmac runs out, and is replaced with a bright carpet of white stones, but all around this peninsula, which encircles the carefully controlled **Slītere Nature Reserve**, there is scarcely any sign of life.

At the top of the peninsula, just beyond Kolka, is a point where the waters of Riga Bay meet the Baltic. It is a fabled sight, which Latvians had heard about but until recently never seen. The marked line where the seas meet runs out past the half washed-away lighthouse to the horizon, and when the wind blows, the waters are whipped up into a great crashing wall.

Land of the Livs: Continuing down the western, Baltic side of the coast are a further series of former fishing communities. Typical is **Mazirbe**, where farmlands stretch back from the dunes of the bleached sand which is strewn with small cockle and mussel shells. A white wooden hall has recently been built, with help from Estonia, as a meeting-place for the last of the Livs.

Latvians are very proud of this pure, all-but-lost tribe who have inhabited this coast since prehistory, and who

Café and chat in Aizpute.

were the first settlers of Riga. Being Finno-Ugric by origin, their language is more like Estonian than Latvian and they have their own ancient flag, which is green white and blue. Estonians and Finns contribute funds for their continued well-being.

There are scarcely more than 100 Livs left, scattered throughout the country and the world. In fact, only one old woman in Mazirbe speaks Liv and their leader lives just down the coast, at **Mikelbāka**. A small museum of Liv life is being prepared in an ancient barn in Mazirbe.

The heyday for **Ventspils** was enjoyed under Duke Jēkabs who launched his ships for the Caribbean and West Africa from here. But, after his death, Ventspils went into decline and was reduced to just seven families after the plague of 1710. It enjoyed a cultural renaissance during the years of independence, however, and after the war the Soviet Union built it up as an industrial centre. It was the main terminal for Soviet oil exports and the late Armand Hammer's Occidental Petroleum has chemical factories here.

Controls, however, were lax, and though there is no visible evidence of pollution, towards the end of the Soviet era it was so bad that children went to school wearing masks. It is an industrial town, certainly, and the river mouth is filled with shipping activity, though high walls and furtive, dead-end alleys frustratingly obstruct views of the river and wharfs.

The Old Town has the kind of run-down feeling often associated with ports: its wooden houses are in bad repair and its four-storey **castle**, much billeted and little loved, has recently been abandoned and is now just a tip.

But walk down Pils Street from the castle towards the 18th-century town hall and see the brighter side of the place: the architecture of the lowly houses and the touches of art nouveau give a hint of a rather grand little port. Here, with a lighthouse-sized lantern, is a sparklingly cleaned Lutheran church dated 1833 and dedicated, in German,

Kolka, where Riga Bay meets the Baltic.

to God and the Kaiser. In the nearby **Regional Museum** all is revealed: photos of the swish port of the turn-of-the-century; the swank Royal Hotel; emblems from the Norwegian and Swiss embassies from the 1920s and '30s; a bourgeois drawing-room. There are also Liv national costumes and customs, and a general feeling of far more prosperous and happy times.

A **Maritime Museum** in the modern part of town consists of an open-air exhibition of the coast and its fishing industry, with examples of pitch-black boats dating back 300 years. There are beach houses and drying huts, and an explanation that it was not until the 19th century that fishing moved away from the river and on to the sea, and it was not until 1863 that peasants were allowed to own land.

The other significant port on this coast is **Liepāja**, which is located 80 miles (130 km) south of Ventspils and has more than twice its population (114,900). Liepāja is a centre of metal smelting and has been a major Soviet military base with submarine pens. Trawlers, which travel as far as West Africa, are moored in its harbour, and commercial traffic is beginning to come back again. On the dockside in front of the old customs house in 1919, the British navy formerly recognised the state of Latvia when it disembarked Prime Minister Ulmanis, escaping from Riga.

The Old Town is spread out and tidy and its green, two-storey wood buildings, though in need of paint, sit attractively in the lanes of lime trees that give the town its name. The cafés and bars from the pre-war years are run down, but they have not been destroyed and a pedestrian mall has been added, based on Moscow's Arbut Street. A large neoclassical building in front of the Hotel Liva is one of the country's principal teacher-training colleges.

The town has two sturdy churches, Catholic **St Joseph's** from the 17th century and, behind the attractive market, Catholic **St Anne's**, with an altar carved by Nicolas Soeffrens.

Past the yellow former British consulate where Karlis Ulmanis was hidden for a while in a garden shed, Kurmajas Prospekts leads down to the sea. On the right is an unusual **Art Gallery and Museum**, with a garden full of sculptures. The house was built by Hakels Nelsons, a wood carver, in 1901 and it has beautiful panelled ceilings and patterned parquet floors as well as fine carvings. It passed to Nelsons' daughter on his death, but she hanged herself here, and her widower, a compulsive gambler, lost the home in a card game. The state took it over in 1935.

At the bottom of the boulevard, perched on the dunes, is a monument dedicated to the sea. For a mile or two to the south, a pleasant shady park rests among the trees with a few scattered grand old villas and an amusement park for children.

To the south, the immaculate beach continues its drift towards distant Lithuania, passing eroded sandbanks and the highest dune on the coast (125 feet/35 metres) near Nica before crossing the border and arriving at the next large resort, **Palanga**.

Left, the pulpit in Ugale church. Right, a carving on its rare organ.

ZEMGALE AND RUNDALE PALACE

The region of Zemgale was for a time linked with Courland, and it borders the modern region of Kurzeme from Lithuania in the south to Lake Engure halfway up the west side of Riga Bay. Skirting Riga, it then slips below the River Daugava and slides along the length of the Lithuanian border tailing away to the far southeast. Apart from the northerly area around Tukums, most of Zemgale is characterised by a dead flat, fertile plain, part of the central lowlands that in places actually sink below sea level. This is considered to be the breadbasket of Latvia.

There are comparatively few lakes, and the main river is the Leilupe, which flows through the ancient towns of Bauska and Jelgava, Zemgale's capital which the dukes of Courland and Semigallia made their home. There are a number of large 18th- and 19th-century estates in the region, but this was the front line in World War I, and many were burnt by the retreating Russian army. One that has been restored is the castle at Rundāle near Bauska, the finest palace in the Baltics. All of these places are within easy striking distance of Riga.

A step west: The region of Tukums lies to the west of Riga and Jūrmala, and is a stepping-stone into Kurzeme and the Baltic coast. Heading west from the capital, the A218 passes through scenes of World War I conflict, notably at **Ložmētejkalns**, site of an heroic attack by the Latvian Riflemen on a strong German position in 1918.

Tukums is the first town of any size on this road. It has a castle mound and was originally a Liv settlement. On the outskirts are a military airport and large animal feed factory, and it is an important centre for furniture manufacture. It has a pleasant old centre, and a tradition of ceramics which is carried on in the factory in Talsa Street. In Darzau Street is the **regional museum** which has a collection of works by the most important 20th-century Latvian artists, including Rozentāls and Svemps. The Lu-

theran church dates from 1670. Just to the north of the town is **Milzkalne**, the highest spot in the region, which has a view over Riga Bay.

A few miles past Tukums on the Ventspils road is **Jaunmokaspils**, a newly refurbished hunting lodge. It was built in 1901 by Wilhelm Bockslaff, who designed the Art Society building in Riga, for George Armitstead, who owned the hippodrome in the capital. Its most striking features are its ceramic stoves, built by the firm of Celms & Bems, especially one imprinted with old postcards of Riga from the city's 700th anniversary celebrations in 1901. On the first floor is a **Museum of the Forests of Latvia** and it includes a collection of around 40 different animal horns from all over the world. The lodge provides facilities for hunters' holidays in the area.

From here the road continues to the attractive towns of **Kandava** and **Sabile** on the way to Kuldīga (*see page 250*).

From **Lapmežciems** to **Bērzciems**, most of the communities on the coast

see page 250

Preceding pages: the grand gateway to Rundāle. **Left,** portraits of Birons and Anna in the Green Room. **Right,** the White Hall and Oval Porcelain Study.

have names ending with -*ciems*, meaning village. There attractive farm buildings stand near the sea and lurk in the wood. Just beyond the new buildings at **Ragaciems** is a well-established campsite. The **Engure lake and nature reserve** lie beyond the thatched church tower roof at the little port of Engure. Some 50,000 birds visit this long (12-mile/18-km), shallow lake every year. An ornithologist from Salaspils is the only resident and it is closed to the public, though licenced hunters and fishermen come here from September to April. Camps have been organised here for exiled Latvians who have not known their grandparents.

South of Tukums, on the road to **Dobele**, is **Juanpils,** a village with a lakeside manorial castle and church dating back to the 16th century. This was the estate of one Baron Reke, whose coat of arms is over the church altar. The manor at Dobele was built for a Swiss, Jānis Berlics, in 1820.

Dukes' domain: south of Riga, the only town of any size is **Jelgava**, home of RAF, makers of the Latvija minibus. Though you would not know it to look at it, Jelgava is an historic town, formerly called Mitau, that once rivalled Riga. The history of the town, and of the 11 dukes of Courland and Semigallia, the Kettlers, the Madems and Herzogs who were friends of the Russian Romanovs and influential at court in St Petersburg, is laid out in the **History and Art Museum**. This is housed in the Academia Petrina, built in 1775 and once an important educational and scientific centre. It lies just behind the landmark tower of the ruined Holy Trinity church. Most of the exhibits, which include gold and silver ducats minted here, and a waxwork of Duke Jēkabs at home, have full explantions in German. Also in the old part of town is **St Ann's church**, from 1619, which has an altar painting by Jānis Rozentāls.

The wide, slow Lielupe, which slips north into Riga Bay, has always carried river traffic. Today pleasure-boats ply the waters and there are small craft for hire on the left of the bridge that brings

Left, arcaded corridor. **Right**, the Gilded Hall.

the road in from Riga. On the right is **Rastrelli Palace**, a large and solid Italianate building on the site of the town's original, 1265 **castle**. Since 1957 this three-storey, brick-red and cream building set around a square has housed an agricultural college. It is an impersonal resting-place for the dukes of Courland and Semigallia.

Frederick-Wilhelm, the penultimate of the Kettlers dynasty of dukes, altered the family's fortunes when he married Ivan V's daughter Anna Ivanova, in St Petersburg in 1710. The 17-year-old newlyweds had just started back to the young duke's palace in Jelgava when he became ill and died. Reluctantly Anna was obliged to continue her life in Jelgava. Bored and confined in what to her must have seemed something of a backwater of wooden homes and flat farmlands, she began an affair with Johannes Ernst Birons, an ambitious Courlander on the palace staff.

In 1727 Anna became Empress Anne of Russia, peopling her court with German Balts and making Birons a count.

Within nine years he was wealthy enough to employ Bartholomeo Rastrelli (1700–71), the architect of St Petersburg's Hermitage or Winter Palace, to build a manor for himself at Rundāle, to the south of Jelgava.

Rundāle Palace is an imposing, well-restored palace of 138 rooms, approached through a grand drive flanked by twin semi-circular stables. Above the east wing a double-headed German eagle rises over the motto: "Faithfulness and Jealousy". At the height of its construction between 1736 and 1768 it employed 1,500 labourers and artisans. Work on the building and grounds, which still have to be restored, was interrupted first in 1738, after Birons had achieved his ambition of becoming Duke of Courland and diverted Rastrelli into turning Jelgava Castle into Rastrelli Palace. The second interruption was more serious when, after becoming regent of Russia for a year following the empress's death, Birons was banished to Siberia for 23 years.

Privately owned until 1920, Rundāle

The semicircular palace stables, housing the Ventspils carvers' work.

was damaged and fell into disrepair after World War I and has been under reconstruction since 1972. Its stairways, galleries, landings, rooms and halls are gracious and well decorated. The wall paintings are by the Italians Francesco Martini and Carlo Zucchi and the exquisite decorative moulding is by Michael Graff from Berlin. His oval **Porcelain Study** is particularly striking. On the ground floor there is a collection of period furniture and ornaments, including a guitar made from wood taken from the ruined palace by Andris Kārkliņš, who emigrated to America and became a flamenco player. The finest rooms are upstairs, where some interesting Dutch, Flemish and Spanish paintings from the 17th and 18th centuries are hung.

The dukes' throne stood in the **Gold Hall**, which is matched in magnificence by the **White Hall** or ballroom where the intricate stucco work includes a delicate heron's nest on the ceiling. In 1992 royalty returned when the Queen of Denmark was entertained here.

At the entrance to the palace is an exhibition of Ventspils **church wood carvings** by Nicolas Soeffrens, whom Peter the Great invited to work on his ships. The pieces are all carved from ships' timbers.

Rundāle was the apogee of the fusion of German and Russian society which came together and flourished in the region in the 18th and 19th centuries. A number of important manors were built in this accessible area. The one at **Mežotne**, which was given by Tsar Paul I to his children's governess, Charlotte von Lieven, in 1797, has been restored, but like Rastrelli Palace it has become an uninspired-looking institution. One of the grandest houses otherwise was at **Elija**, due south of Jelgava on the main road to Vilnius, but it is now just a forlorn ruin.

Semigallian roots: The flatlands of Zemgale were originally inhabited by the Semigallians, who in the 13th century produced one of the greatest Latvian leaders, Viesturs. The centre of his domains was to the west of Rundāle in **Tērvete**, but the tribe was pushed south by the German crusaders who built a castle on the site of their stronghold, some of which still remains. Nearby is the **Meža Ainavu Park** which has a museum to a children's writer, Anna Brigadere, who lived here from 1922 to 1933. The park has Latvia's tallest tree.

To the east of Rundāle is **Bauska**. On arrival there is a car-park just beyond the bridge over the River Mūsa. The river shortly converges with the Mēmele, helping to form half a moat for the **Livonian Order's castle w**hich did not survive the Great Northern War. Climb the tower: there is a good view from the top. Bauska itself is a pleasant little rural textile town. Several German painters settled here in the late 17th century, including Joachim Henning, Niklaus Tabin and Dietrich Seitz, who became mayor in 1706. Some of their work can be seen in **St Anne's church**.

From Bauska the road leads directly north back to Riga, past Brencis, a high-class hotel, restaurant and garage, just beyond **Iecava**, which is best known for its large chicken factory.

Left, an ornament from Jelgava Castle. Right, Bauska's old castle.

VIDZEME

Lying to the east of Riga, Vidzeme is the largest of the country's four regions. In the north it stretches from the Bay of Riga all along the Estonian border, and in the south it lies beside the right bank of the Daugava from the capital to the eastern region of Latgale. Beside the river's banks, scattered castles and signs of ancient settlements give a clue to the power this highway bestowed.

At the heart of the region is another riverine highway which, though less exalted, is just as ancient and rather more beguiling. This is the River Gauja, which runs through a deep gorge at the centre of the Gauja National Park. It is Latvia's showcase rural attraction, rich in wildlife, full of prehistoric hill forts and containing one of the most important archaeological sites. They call it "little Switzerland", and have installed a bobsled run, but "little" is the key word. The Baltics' highest point is in Vidzeme: it is 1,025 ft (312 metres).

The **Gauja National Park** begins at **Sigulda**, 30 miles (50 km) northeast of Riga and is an easy day-trip from the capital by road (A212) or by public transport. On the roadside just before Sigulda is one of the country's best known restaurants, the Sēnīte (Little Mushroom), where a canteen and smarter restaurant have a reputation which is considerably more attractive than the dull Soviet slab they inhabit.

From Sigulda the park extends north through **Cēsis**, the main centre for excursions, to **Valmiera**. It covers around 350 sq. miles (900 sq. km) along more than 60 miles (100 km) of river and is divided into sections with varying degrees of access. Boating is popular on the river, and organised parties embark in inflatables for overnight camps, taking three days to travel from Valmiera to Sigulda. Logging on the river was ended when the area was designated a national park in 1973.

Cultural retreat: There is something rather sedate about Sigulda: it is a pristine and airy little town which hides its affluent past beneath a film of cleanliness. It became popular during the National Awakening, as a place where Latvians from Riga could discover their rural roots. It has more recently become a winter sports centre, with a bobsled run and ski slopes on the far side of the railway crossing, to the left. The **castle** is through the town on the right.

The deeply moated castle, which included a convent, is now a crumbled ruin. It was built by the Crusaders' Order of Sword Bearers who came here as soon as they arrived in Latvia in 1207. They used large boulders and stuck them together with mortar mixed with eggs and honey. Today, there is a open-air concert hall in its midst.

The large and not particularly attractive country house beside it is the modern "castle" built in 1878. Artists and writers of the Awakening used to come for inspiration, and Rozentāls and other painters used to like to hike up to **Gleznotāju kalns**, Painters' Hill, just to the east, which has one of the best views over the Gauja (walk from the car-park

on the far side of the old castle). Kronvaldu Atis (1837–75), a teacher of Latvian, is remembered by a statue outside the new castle, and some of the stained glass produced then is still *in situ* in what is now a sanatorium. The town also has an information centre, near the white Lutheran church. Even if it looks closed, walk in and ask for whatever advice you need. It has a room full of stuffed animals culled from the park, from wild boar and beaver to the various deer from roe to elk.

One of the best places to see wildlife and natural scenery, with possibilities of sighting at least a deer, is just beyond Sigulda in **Līgatne**. There are also some rare plants here, such as Lady's Slipper orchids, Linnaea and woodland tulips, and in spring it is carpeted with lily-of-the-valley. Turn left to Līgatne through **Āuglīsgante** on the Sigulda to Cēsis main road, turning left again just before the river, where there are two parking spots and day tickets to the parks can be bought. Nature trails are mapped out, and a ferry takes cars over the river.

From Sigulda there are two ways across the Gauja. The road goes over a bridge, and every 30 minutes a cable car swings alongside it, 135 ft (40 metres) above the river, taking 3½ minutes to cover the half-mile (1 km) distance. On the far side, the road falls away to the right to reach the side of the river where day tickets to the park can be bought in the car-park.

Castles and caves: The banks of the Gauja are characterised by red sandstone cliffs and caves, the deepest of which is **Gūtmanis' Cave**, found opposite the car park. Scratched by graffiti more than 300 years old, it is 35 ft (14 metres) deep and the fresh spring water that wore it away still bubbles up into it, tasting strongly of iron. The cave is named after a healer called Gūtmanis who first used the water as a cure.

Some 10 minutes' walk further up the road is **Turaida castle**, a fort of red bricks and a single remaining round tower which breaks up through the forest heights. At the foot of the maple-lined approach is a stable with some fine

Picnic above the River Gauja.

horses for hire. Or you can hire a horse and carriage to take you up to the castle. In the language of the ancient Livs who first settled this valley, Turaida means the Garden of the Gods. Inside the castle there is a gallery and a small museum of its history. On the path from the stable is a Lutheran church from 1750, and a small restaurant in an old drying kiln which serves grey peas and other good local dishes.

A few yards away, beneath a large elm tree, a black marble slab marks the grave of Maija, the Turaida Rose who was killed in Gūtmanis' Cave in 1620. This 19-year-old local girl was in love with a castle gardener, and when a Polish officer approached her in the cave she devised a scheme whereby he would kill her rather than submit her to a fate worse than death. She had a magic scarf, she said, and he could have it if he promised to leave her alone: to prove the scarf's effectiveness, she put it around her neck and told him to try to cut off her head.

From Turaida the road continues to Inciems where it meets up with the road to Valmiera. The next small town along this road is **Straupe**, where there is something familiar about the old castle. The square tower which rises in a dark dome and lantern, and the scrolled and stepped gable of the building below, are reminiscent of the cathedral in Riga. It dates from 1263. The castle is in a pleasant setting beside a large pond and near the Brasla river, and today it is used as a clinic for rehabilitating alcoholics. Knock on the door to get shown round. There is not much to see in the castle itself, except for some wood panelling and several grand ceramic stoves. Parties may be shown up the main tower.

In the grounds is a bell-tower and a **Lutheran church** which has some interesting 17th-century painted panels. Tombstones and tablets mark the passing of generations of the von Rosen family, owners of the castle and fierce protectors of the German Baltic way of life. The present generation is scattered, though some have helped in its restoration. It has an organ made in Riga in

Turaida Castle.

1856 by the firm of Martin, and the acoustics make it a good recital venue.

Another German monument is nearby at **Ungurmuiža**, on the way to Cēsis. This belonged to the von Campenhausens who had it built in 1751. In 1938 it became a school and currently money is being sought for its restoration. Many of the fine wall paintings have disappeared, though paintings of Tsar Alexander guarding the baron's bedroom are still intact. In the grounds is a tea-room folly and a school the baron had built for local children, which has been used as a kitchen for the local collective.

Between Ungurmuiža and Cēsis is **Raiskums**, beside a lake of the same name, where there is threshing barn, school house and curious wood and stone chapel from the 19th century.

Excursion centre: Cēsis is a pleasant, wide-open town which was a popular cultural centre during both the National Awakening and First Independence. Its attractive yellow-and-white, two- and three-storey buildings date back several centuries, and a Lutheran church, St John's, was started in 1281. There are several hotels and good places to eat include Saieta nams and the more expensive Pie Raunas Vārtiem.

Cēsis has seen its fair share of bloodshed. It was a walled town and a member of the Hanseatic League and its history is well laid out in a good **museum** in the building next to the old **castle**. The castle is a chalky-white fortified convent which served as a power base for the Livonian Order. The old red-brick factory nearby is a brewery.

Cēsis was inhabited by Baltic Finns until the Letgallians moved in around the 6th century, and it has provided much archaeological information. But the most impressive digs have been in the **Araišu** area of the park just to the south. It was here that Letgallians built a large lake fortress in the 9th century, and its excavation has been one of the most important finds of this kind in northern Europe. Burial barrows have been uncovered as well as graves, and a scheme has begun to reconstruct some **Milk seller.**

272

of the ancient buildings on the lake. A stone castle built by the Livonian Order has also been excavated.

Beyond Cēsis is **Valmiera**, which also has an ancient castle and was a member of the Hanseatic League. An observation tower near the castle gives a good view of the valley. North of the town up towards **Strenči**, is one of the most picturesque stretches of the River Gauja. To the northwest is **Mazsalaca**, an attractive, out-of-the-way resort on the River Salaca.

Coastal route: The Gauja was strategically important as the main highway to Tallinn and St Petersburg. Today, the most pleasant way to drive to Tallinn is up the scenic coast, around the eastern edge of Riga Bay, which allows views of the Baltic through the pines. Unlike the rest of Latvia's coast, its sandy beaches are scattered, not unattractively, with boulders and stones. From Riga the M12 goes up past summer villas up to **Saulkrasti**, beyond which lie small communities, such as **Kumrags**, which has fine views and a good beach.

Salacgrīva provides a convenient stopping-point, and between here and **Ainaži**, the coast takes on a different aspects as meadows push out into the sea. Ainaži is right up by the border, and its interest is as the port Krišjānis Valdemārs put on the map in 1864 when he founded Latvia's Maritime Academy. Ainaži flourished for a while as a port and shipbuilding centre, but now it has returned to being a backwater, with a small museum explaining its moment of seafaring glory.

Along the Daugava: To the southeast of Riga the Moscow Road, the A215, follows the north bank of the Daugava, leaving Riga through the **Moscow District** with its Old Believers and traditional Russian community, a district that was pulled down and rebuilt in the 1960s. Just beyond it is **Rumbula**, where the big weekend market draws people for miles around. Bigger than Riga's market, it is the main place for buying and selling cars – often stolen.

The road continues towards the big textile town of **Ogre**, past **Ikškile**, which

Gauja Park deer.

in the Liv language was called Üxküll Ykescola. This is an island on the Daugava, inaccessible to the passing traveller, and it bears the remains of the oldest stone church in Latvia, built in 1186. The riverbank here is a good picnic spot and a stone monument gives a brief history of the church so frustratingly just out of reach.

At **Kegums**, just beyond, the country's first hydro-electric scheme, built between the wars, has pushed back the river's banks and created a long lake. The change of landscape, the submerging of small cliffs of the former riverbanks, is a source of regret to the historians and traditionalists who converge at its centre, around **Lāčplēsis**.

Magic belt: Lāčplēsis is the home of a Latvian legend, from a 19th-century epic written by Andrējs Pumpurs who used the names of real places for his characters. Lāčplēsis was brought up by a bear and on one occasion tore apart a rogue bear with his hands, giving him the soubriquet "bear-slayer". He was last seen in a fatal struggle with the Black Soldier of Death: but he will return, it is said, to throw the enemy into the sea and make the land free again.

The father of Lāčplēsis was **Lielvārdis** (named after the neighbouring village), who possessed a magic belt decorated with symbols which could tell personal fortunes. A copy of this belt is kept in the **Andrējs Pumpurs Museum** at Lāčplēsis, a village steeped in history. There was a Liv settlement here 3,000 years ago and the site is on a hill next to the museum overlooking the river. A sacred oak is at **Kaibala** nearby.

The museum, begun in 1970 under Edgars Kauliņš, the last, enlightened boss of the local Lāčplēsis collective farm, has an exhibition dedicated to Pumpurs, who was an officer in the Russian army. It also gives an introduction to the literature of the National Awakening, to which Vidzeme's sons made a considerable contribution.

Lielvārdis' belt, some 15 ft (5 metres) long, is brought out mainly on weekends when children and newly married couples come to Lāčplēsis to be blessed.

Folk-dancers in Cēsis.

A hand passing over it may come upon a warm spot, and when the symbols here are read they may reveal something of the person's destiny.

Before the Moscow road turns north to Madona, away from the Daugava river, it is worth noting the Swedish castle a **Koknese**. Following the river downstream past a white Lutheran church set on a wide sweep in the river, the road comes to the ruins of the two-storey castle, where the Perse meets the Daugava, a point appreciated by the teenagers who dive in to the green waters off the old walls. A Swedish grave from the Northern Wars lies in the surrounding woods.

Madona, is the next town of any size, a quiet spot with a renovated inn from the 16th-century Swedish days. Just north of Madona is **Cesvaine**. Its late 19th-century "castle", a mix of neo-Gothic with an art nouveau interior, was the hunting lodge of Baron Adolf von Wolf, who had no fewer than 99 estates in the Baltics. A hybrid statue has the tail of a fox, the mane of a lion and the face of a wolf, while another statue of a wolf has its tail pointed towards Gulbene, whose baron Wolf had argued with. The estate has a 60-acre (25 hectare) park which supposedly sustains 200 animal species. A squat tower to the left of a summer house is all that remains of a 14th-century **Bishop's Palace**.

Just outside Cesvaine, is **Gaizinš**, the highest hill in the Baltics, a stunningly low 1,025 ft (312 metres). In case you might miss it, a 15-storey red-brick lookout tower of graphic ugliness has been built on top of it. Its summit provides a 360-degree view of the lakes, pastureland and the acres of deep green forest. The most popular resort in the area is at **Mežezers**, a lakeside complex of boating and camping facilities with A-frame cabins in the woods, which is sorely in need of holidaymakers.

North of Madona is **Gulbene** where a manor house with a fine portico is in ruins: bullet holes still pepper its facade. In 1944 the Germans blew up the church tower before the advancing Russians, to deprive them of a viewing platform: it

First-aid for a veteran vehicle.

fell on to the church, destroying the roof. Beside it is the only statue of Martin Luther in the Baltics.

Just north of Gulbene at **Ate** there is a small **open-air museum** of around a dozen buildings. It is a popular place for weddings and a room is devoted to famous sons and daughters of Vidzeme. There are also souvenirs on display from the family of Baron Wolf, the man of many mansions.

From Gulbene a narrow-gauge railway runs up to the attractive town of **Alūksne**, which has one of the most pleasant hotels in Latvia. The town is centred on a ruined 14th-century Livonian castle on a lake. It sits on an island reached across a small wooden bridge and is devoted today to sports activities. Follies dedicated to Greek gods are scattered in what is now the cemetery in the surrounding woods. These were put up by the Nietinghoff family to honour the dead of the Great Northern War.

One of the town's main claims to fame is that its pastor, Ernst Glück,

adopted the daughter of a Lithuanian grave-digger, Martha Skavronska, who went on to marry Peter the Great and become Catherine I of Russia. Glück also produced the first Latvian translation of the Bible, in 1689, and a copy of it, one of only a dozen left in the world, is kept along with many others in the **Bible Museum**. The earliest Latvian religious tract, *God's Word*, dates from 1654 and is also in the museum.

When Glück first arrived in Alūksne, he lived in the castle, but he later moved to a single-storey wood manse behind the Lutheran church, and his plantation of oaks is still standing.

Literary trail: Between these eastern towns and the Gauja National Park, a number of Latvian literary figures are remembered in a pastoral setting that can have changed little since they knew it more than 100 years ago. Beneath shady trees are wood barns, cottage gardens, and small platforms for the delivery vehicles to collect and return milk-churns.

Beside **Lake Alauksts** is the **Skalbe Museum** which contains local painted furniture. Kārlis Skalbe (1879–1945), a writer of fairy-tales, died in Sweden where he had emigrated. His remains were returned in 1992 and buried beneath a stone overlooking the lake.

The museum at the nearby village of **Vēcpiebalga** celebrates the Kaudzītes brothers, Reinis and Matīss, who jointly wrote Latvia's first major novel, *The Time of the Land Surveyors* (1879). Vēcpiebalga also has a museum dedicated to the writer Jānis Subrabkalns and the composer Emils Darzins, with an exhibition of writers and composers who have emigrated.

At **Ērgli** there is a museum where the playwright Rūdolfs Blaumanis was born. **Indrāni** nearby is the setting of his most famous play.

Between Ērgli and Sigulda is **Malpils**, a clay manor house rebuilt just after it was set alight in 1905. It is now used as a school and houses a **Museum of Agriculture and Irrigation**. On display are some rather fine paintings and the first map of Latvia, from 1688, drawn by Swedish engineers.

Left, sledge-happy. Right, Lutheran church, Alūksne.

LATGALE AND THE BLUE LAKES

Latvia's easternmost region is "The Land of the Blue Lakes". A larger proportion of deciduous trees makes it not just bluer, but greener, too. It is the most remote of the regions, the most poor, and its people, who speak a dialect some regard as a separate language, have larger families and are more gregarious. They sometimes like to think of themselves as the Irish of Latvia. If there is any festival or gathering here it is bound to be lively. Traditionally, alone in Latvia, the people of Letgale had homesteads adjoining each other rather than isolated country homes. They continue their established crafts, especially ceramics, making big, chunky jugs and candelabra which are thickly glazed, and seen everywhere in the country.

Rubbing up against Russia, Belorus and Lithuania, Latgale's geography has given it a different history, too. While Kurzeme and Zemgale were being recruited to the Lutheran cause by the dukes of Courland, the Swedes in Riga and Vidzeme were banishing practising Catholics, and many of them came to Latgale, where Catholic Poland held sway. They left their mark in the baroque Jesuit style of their grand churches: St Peter's in Daugavpils, St Ludwig in Krāslava, the Holy Cross of Pasien and the huge, white, country church at Aglona where Catholics from all over Europe gather on Ascension Day.

But among these slightly distant lands is Daugavpils, Latvia's second largest city, a cosmopolitan place tucked in the far southeast 140 miles (224 km) from Riga, and the best part of a day's train ride away.

River road: The town of **Plavinas** is the last on the A215 Moscow Road from Riga before Latgale. Here the River Daugava has a serious reputation, especially at Lāčbedre (the Bear's Den) where men and boats have disappeared into the maw of a particularly voracious whirlpool. Just beyond Plavinas the A215 turns inland to Madona.

Taking the right fork, the road follows the Daugava upriver to **Jēkabpils**, named after the Courland duke. Beside the road on this north bank is **Krustpils castle**, occupied by the army but with plans to open for tourists. The town of Jēkabpils, marked by the dome of a Russian Orthodox church of 1887, lies on the far bank of the river and is one of the three sugar manufacturing towns in Latvia: "Three spoons of sugar in your coffee," people used to be urged: "One for Liepāja, one for Jelgava and one for Jēkabpils." There is a Regional Museum in the town and a Maritime School is a sign that it has been a stop on the river route to the hinterland since Viking times.

The town is famous as the birthplace of Jānis Rainis (1865–1929) the most important literary figuire of the National Awakening. His father was an estate overseer and he built Tadenava, the house where he was born, which is now the **Rainis Museum** containing the family's household items.

A bustling country market is held at weekends and everything from car boots

full of piglets to tsarist gold roubles are offered for sale.

Līvāni, the next town upstream, is on the map because of the cheap glass-fibre two-storey houses made here and bearing the town's name. They have a reputation for catching fire and burning to the ground in 10 minutes flat, which is what happened to the one belonging to the chess grandmaster Anatol Karpov, who has one as a country home near Plavinas. The Party immediately rebuilt it. In post-Soviet times they have been sold off to their occupants for as little as a few hundred pounds.

Daugavpils, near the Lithuanian and Belorus borders, is at a crossroads between the Baltic-to-Black Sea route, and the highway and railway from Warsaw to Moscow. This former capital of the Duchy of Pārdaugava, known as "Polish Livonia", has a sprinkling of 18th- and 19th-century mansions and the odd bright splash of art nouveau. Around the town, doors, shutters and whole wooden houses painted bright blue are signs of Russians in residence.

In its streets and in its markets, Latvian is rarely heard. The city has been attracting "foreigners" for centuries, from the Old Believers, the sect exiled from Moscow in the 18th century, to others just coming to this relatively prosperous town to find work.

It is an industrial town, a textile town, and Russification under the Soviets was intense. Before World War II one-third of the 40,000 population was Russian or Polish. Now there are 120,000 inhabitants, only 12 percent of whom are Latvian. The industries the Soviets built up – textiles, bicycle manufacture and locomotive repair sheds – have suffered in the aftermath of independence.

Like other large towns in Latvia, Daugavpils is bereft of road signs, and drivers may take a while to find the centre of this drawn-out conurbation. The rump of the church spires are scattered over an area away from the centre, which is set around the Hotel Latvija, a mini-version of its namesake in Riga, and the stunning white Catholic **Church of St Peter's** behind. This mid-18th

Left, Feast of the Assumption, Aglona. **Right**, festival in Rēzekne.

century former monastery building is an example of a fortress church and its twin-towered facade is a mark of the Jesuit baroque which was brought in from Lithuania. It is a basilica with three naves, the middle one rising to an impressive tunnel vault.

Beside it, an attractive tree-lined shopping boulevard, formerly Lenin Street, runs up to the station, with little bookshops and the lively Darts café. On the corner of the big square in front of the Latvija is the main shopping store, worth checking out for ceramics, Latvian linen and Russian hats. In the same street in the opposite direction, just beyond the gloomy grey culture centre, is a small **town museum** which has contemporary exibitions of art and crafts. In Gogola Street nearby there is a dashing example of art nouveau, and a café that has delicious cakes.

Some 30 miles (45 km) east of Daugavpils is the town of **Krāslava**, and in its centre is **Krāslavas pilsmuiža**, a fine old Polish house under restoration. It also has a distinguished church in St

Ludwig's, built in 1673 and radically altered into its present towerless baroque shape in 1763.

The stretch of river between the two towns is particularly enchanting, and it was here that the Soviets wanted to install a hydro-electric power station, causing protests that helped to fuel calls for independence. Since independence, the lack of a sufficient power supply in the country has led to the question tentatively being broached again. What is certain is that a petrochemical plant just over the border in Belorus has been polluting the Daugava for some years.

Lakeland: Rolling lands of rivers and lakes spread north from Krāslava, towards **Rēzekne**, Latgale's capital. Just above Krāslava, lying next to the Hill of the Sun, **Sauleskalns**, is **Dridzis**, probably the most beautiful and certainly the deepest of Latvia's lakes at 313 ft (65 metres). Its resort at **Komburi** has been a favourite for tourists from the former USSR.

Ežezers (hedgehog) lake, full of little islands, is to the northeast, and used to

Land of the Blue Lakes.

have a fine school nearby. **Rēzna**, just south of Rēzekne, is the country's largest lake at 21 sq. miles (56 sq. km), and there is a camp-site, though camp-site in the Baltics means solid buildings rather than tents. Until the Soviets drained half of it and ruined an important stork habitat, Latvia's largest lake used to be **Lake Lubāns** northwest of Rēzekne.

The traditional wooden architecture in this part of the region is particularly attractive, with splashes of colour and embellishments on doors and window shutters. Small sauna sheds are stuck out in all the gardens which are planted with fruit trees and bushes and beds of bright flowers.

Pilgrims' progress: Northeast of Daugavpils, down stony tracks on the east side of the road to Rēzekne, is the village of **Aglona** which is much too small for its grand baroque church to which thousands of pilgrims make their way every year. During the Reformation, when the Dom in Riga was taken over by the Lutherans, it became the country's principal Catholic church, a role it resumed under the Soviet system when the Dom was used as a concert hall. But whatever the vicissitudes of history, pilgrims have continued to come here on the Feast of the Assumption (15 August) each year, on foot, by gypsy cart, car and charabanc.

The object of their veneration is a picture of the Virgin Mary, kept behind the altar, which is said to have healing powers. The picture is reported to have been presented by Manuel of Byzantium to Lithuania's Vytautas the Great some time between 1325 and 1340. In 1700 the picture was copied and either the copy or the original, depending on which camp you follow, remained in Lithuania while the other came here to Aglona the year that the church was founded. Money came from Jeta-Justine Sastodicka, a local Polish aristocrat, whose portrait hangs on the present basilica's west wall.

The church was built to accommodate Dominicans from Lithuania whom Sastodicka invited to teach, heal and convert. This is the second church on **Filming time.**

the site. The first one was made of wood and built just to the north. In 1787 it burnt down and the present shining white, two-towered, Italianate creation rose up around the original organ, which was saved. A monastery and cloister are attached to the church and Dominicans lived here for 150 years until the tsar forbade people becoming involved in the church, and its life died.

In 1992, when a visit by the Pope to Aglona was announced, five Lithuanian-trained Latvian novices took up residence, while the grounds in front of the church were completely levelled to pave the way, literally, for the hullabaloo of a papal visit.

Rēzekne, 38 miles (60 km) north of Daugavpils, is a good centre for exploration. Although its population of 42,900 is about one-third that of Daugavpils, Rēzekne is the captial of Latgale. The **Regional Museum** is just up from the trio of churches in the main street. The statue in the middle of the road was erected for the third time on this spot in 1992, amid much celebration of costume-clad Latgalians. The Rēzna restaurant in the old Soviet eating-house block just beyond it has been pleasantly refurbished with a jolly mural of a country wedding, the food is good and the staff know how to smile.

Rēzekne is one of many ceramics centres in the region. Some families – the Paulāns, the Ušpelis – have been working potters for up to eight generations. The first pottery owned by the Ušpelis family, who have been in the business for six generations, is in Riga's Open-Air Ethnography Museum.

To the east of Rēzekne is **Ludza**, another good base for exploring the blue lakes of the region. From here the road goes east to Russia at **Zilupe**. To the south is the fourth of Latgale's great Catholic churches. **Pasiena Church** echoes that of Daugavpils, a twin-towered wedding cake built in 1761, 67 years after a Dominican mission was founded. From here there is a magnificent view across the plains of Russia.

To the north is the region of **Abrene** which Russia still claims.

Feeding time.

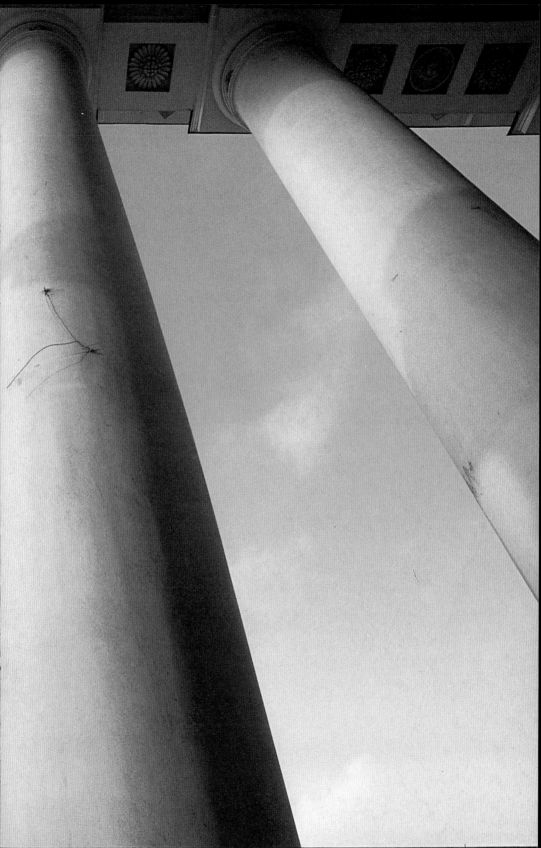

The largest of the three republics is a Catholic country, a fact that is impossible to miss. Vilnius, its capital, owes its splendid baroque flavour to the Jesuits who built its fine university as well as many of its churches. Throughout the country are roadside wooden shrines, and the Hill of Crosses just north of Šiauliai is an extraordinary symbol of a nation of believers. The shrines are part of a folk tradition of wood carving, which can be seen all over the country from the Witches' Park on the Neringa Spit to the monuments to the victims of World War II: Vilnius had a vibrant Jewish community and was a centre of Yiddish publishing.

Like Latvians, Lithuanians are originally Indo-Europeans and speak a Baltic language. In spite of their dedicated Catholicism, they were the last nation in Europe to convert to Christianity. At the height of their glorious history their Grand Duchy stretched from the Baltic to the Black Sea. Such grandeur can be glimpsed at the dukes' principal residence, the restored red-brick castle of Trakai set in the natural moat of Lake Galvė, west of Vilnius. For some time the Grand Duchy's southern border was along the River Nemunas, where many castles were built.

Lithuania's second city is Kaunas, which was a temporary capital between the wars. This is a business centre, and it also has the museum of Lithuania's towering artistic figure, M. K. Čiurlionis. From Kaunas the River Nemunas runs down to a lagoon kept from the sea by the Neringa Spit. This exceptional sand bar of small fishing villages stretches down into Lithuania Minor, formerly Königsburg, where the kings of Prussia were crowned. It is now the Russian enclave of Kaliningrad.

Deutschemarks are currency in many of the shops on the spit's southernmost resort town of Nida. Though the coast is shorter than those of its Baltic state neighbours, like them it has rest homes, bath houses and sanatoriums, chiefly to the north around the bustling resort of Palanga.

Preceding pages: Trakai Castle; the belfry of Vilnius Cathedral; rye fields. **Left**, a good day's catch.

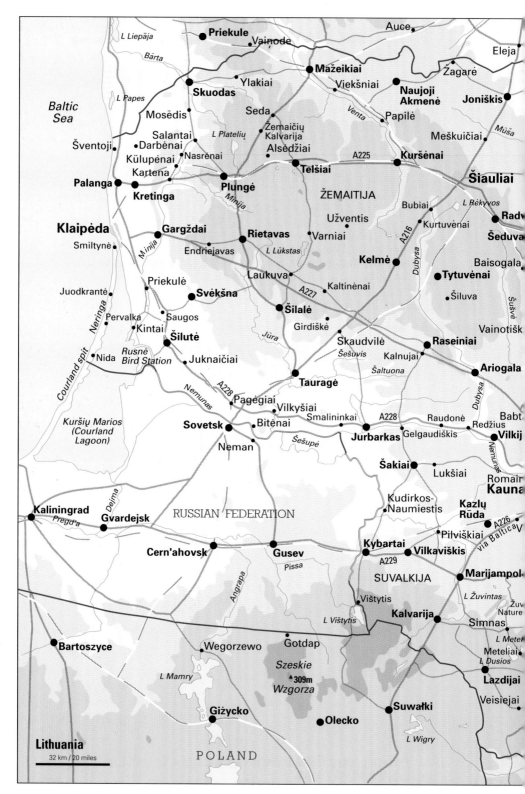

Auce

Eleja

L Liepāja

Priekule
Vainode

Žagarė

Bārta

Mažeikiai

Ylakiai

Viekšniai

Naujoji
Akmenė

Joniškis

L Papes

Skuodas

Seda

Venta

Papilė

Baltic
Sea

Mosėdis

Žemaičių
Kalvarija

L Platelių

Meškuičiai

Mūsa

Šventoji

Salantai
Darbėnai

Alsėdžiai

A225

Kuršėnai

Kūlupėnai

Nasrėnai

Telšiai

Palanga

Kartena

Plungė

ŽEMAITIJA

Šiauliai

Kretinga

Minija

Užventis

Bubiai

L Rėkyvos

Radv

Klaipėda

Gargždai

Rietavas

Varniai

Kurtuvėnai

A216

Šeduva

Smiltynė

Minija

Endriejavas

L Lūkstas

Kelmė

Dubysa

Baisogala

Juodkrantė

Priekulė

Laukuva

A227

Kaltinėnai

Tytuvėnai

Šiluva

Šušvė

Pervalka

Saugos

Šilalė

Girdiškė

Jūra

Vainotišk

Nida

Rusnė
Bird Station

Juknaičiai

Skaudvilė

Šešuvis

Kalnujai

Šaltuona

Raseiniai

Dubysa

Ariogala

Courland spit

Nemunas

A228

Pagėgiai

Vilkyšiai

Tauragė

Smalininkai

A228

Raudonė

Redžius

Babt

Kuršių Marios
(Courland
Lagoon)

Sovetsk

Bitėnai

Šešupė

Jurbarkas

Gelgaudiškis

Vilkij

Neman

Šakiai

Lukšiai

Nemunas

Romair

Kauna

Kaliningrad

Deima

Pregd'a

Gvardejsk

RUSSIAN FEDERATION

Kudirkos-
Naumiestis

Kazlų
Rūda

A226

via Baltica

Cern'ahovsk

Gusev

Pissa

Kybartai

Vilkaviškis

Pilviškiai

A229

SUVALKIJA

Marijampol

L Žuvintas

Žuv
Nature

Vištytis

Kalvarija

Simnas

Bartoszyce

Wegorzewo

Gotdap

L Vištytis

L Metel

Meteliai

L Dusios

Lazdijai

Angrapa

Szeskie
▲309m
Wzgorza

Veisiejai

L Mamry

Giżycko

Suwałki

L Wigry

Lithuania

Olecko

POLAND

32 km / 20 miles

294

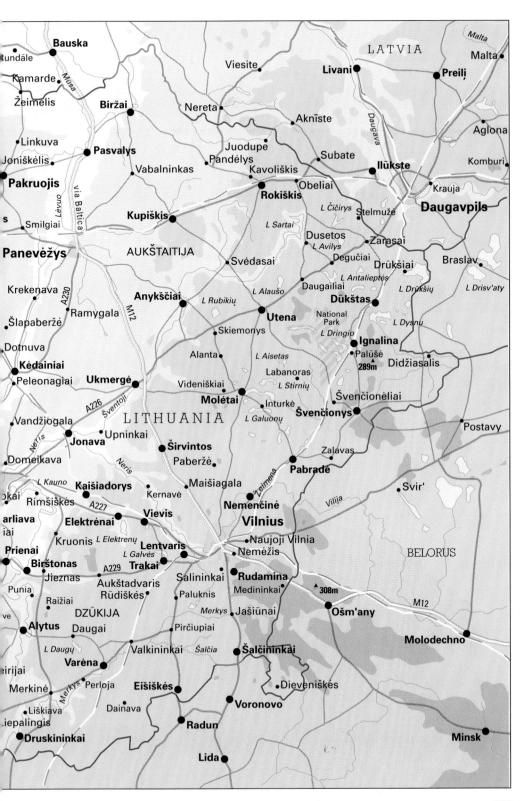

Bauska
Kundāle
Kamarde
Žeimelis
Linkuva
Joniškėlis
Pakruojis
Smilgiai
Panevėžys
Krekenava
Šlapaberžė
Dotnuva
Kėdainiai
Peleonagiai
Vandžiogala
Domeikava
arliava
iai
Prienai
Birštonas
Jieznas
Punia
Raižiai
ve
Alytus
eirijai
Merkinė
Liškiava
iepalingis
Druskininkai

Biržai
Pasvalys
Vabalninkas
Kupiškis
AUKŠTAITIJA
Ramygala
Anykščiai
Ukmergė
Jonava
Upninkai
Kaišiadorys
Rimšiškės
Elektrėnai
Vievis
Kruonis
Lentvaris
Trakai
Aukštadvaris
Rūdiškės
Daugai
Varėna
Perloja
Dainava
Radun
Lida

Viesite
Nereta
Juodupe
Pandėlys
Kavoliškis
Rokiškis
Obeliai
Svėdasai
L Rubikių
L Alaušo
Utena
Skiemonys
Alanta
Videniškiai
Molėtai
Širvintos
Paberžė
Maišiagala
Kernavė
Nemenčinė
Vilnius
Naujoji Vilnia
Nemėžis
Salininkai
Rudamina
Medininkai
Paluknis
Jašiūnai
Pirčiupiai
Valkininkai
Šalčininkai
Eišiškės
Voronovo
Dievēniškės

LATVIA
Livani
Aknīste
Subate
Ilūkste
Stelmužė
L Čičirys
Dusetos
L Avilys
Degučiai
Drūkšiai
Zarasai
Daugailiai
L Antalieptės
Dūkštas
National Park
L Dringio
Ignalina
Palūšė
289m
Labanoras
L Aisetas
L Stirnių
Inturkė
Švenčionėliai
Švenčionys
L Galuonų
Zalavas
Pabradė
Svir'
Osm'any
308m

Malta
Preiļ
Malta
Aglona
Komburi
Krauja
Daugavpils
Braslav
L Drūkšių
L Drisv'aty
L Dysnu
Didžiasalis
Postavy
BELORUS
M12
Molodechno
Minsk

LITHUANIA
DZŪKIJA
L Sartai
L Galvės
L Elektrenų
L Daugų
Šalčia
Merkys

295

Lithuania is now a country of 25,000 sq. miles (64,750 sq. km) with a population of 3.5 million, its very existence snatched back by the events of 1989–91 from the jaws of the Soviet Union. It is a country which has experienced unbelievable swings of fortune and, with hindsight, the turning-point was in 1385 when 11-year-old Princess Jadviga of Poland was due to marry young Wilhem von Habsburg, whom she had known and been betrothed to since infancy.

The wedding was to take place in Cracow, then capital of Poland, and the prisoners were released from the city dungeons as part of the celebrations welcoming Wilhem's arrival at the castle to claim his bride. The festivities were in full swing when, unexpectedly, a delegation of Lithuanian nobles arrived in Cracow and went into urgent conference with their Polish counterparts. The outcome was the archbishop going to the castle with unsettling news for little Jadviga. The wedding was off; she was going to marry another.

For the Polish nobility, if not for Jadviga, the proposal just put forward by the Lithuanian delegation made more sense than her marrying a Habsburg. A conjugal union between Poland and Lithuania with its huge, albeit rather ramshackle, empire would create a force capable of seeing off the Teutonic Knights who were grabbing ever more of the Baltic lands.

Jadviga must have seen things differently; at least the Habsburgs were Christians. The Lithuanian Grand Prince she was now supposed to marry was an outright pagan. The Lithuanians had resisted every attempt to convert them to Christianity, beginning with Bishop Adalbert of Prague in 997 who was murdered for his trouble. Moreover, Prince Jogaila was three times her age and it was known that he had already murdered a number of close relatives. Little Jadviga watched helplessly as the Castellan of Cracow entered the castle, seized the downcast von Habsburg and banished him from the kingdom.

Left, Grand Duke Vytautas, symbol of an empire. Right, the new parliament.

For his part, Jogaila had no more love for the Poles than he did for their religion. The Lithuanians were proud to be pagans. Their warrior elite claimed descent from Perkūnas, the god of thunder. Jogaila had distinguished antecedents. They included Mindaugas, the first to unite the peoples of Lithuania in 1230. He joined with the neighbouring Letts in attacks on the German crusaders and briefly decided to become Christian so that Pope Innocent would crown him king. Afterwards, he cynically sacrificed a Christian

princess to Perkūnas, and attacked the knights again.

The next strong leader to emerge was Gediminas (1316–41), the founder of the Gedimaičiai or Jogaillian dynasty which ruled Lithuania and Poland for the next 250 years. He founded Vilnius where he built his hilltop castle overlooking the Neris and Vilnia rivers. Though he remained pagan he brought in Dominican and Franciscan teachers and he encouraged immigration of artists and craftsmen.

By the time he died, Gediminas had so successfully fought against the Tatars of the east that the Lithuanian empire reached down as far as Kiev and the Black Sea. In the west the coast around Klaipėda (Memel in German) had been seized by Knights of the Livonian Order in 1225. Before the orders merged they had to fight the Teutonic knights of the southern lands that became Prussia, as well as Lithuania's dukes.

One of Gediminas's grandsons was Jogaila. He had become embroiled in a bloody family feud and was as vulnerable to the acquisitive Teutonic Knights as Poland itself was. The Lithuanian nobles had calculated the strength of a dynastic union with Poland, hence the delegation's trip to Cracow to seek out Jadviga.

Poland was very much Rome's champion both Poland and Lithuania. The marriage, alas, did not have a fairy-tale ending. Jadviga hated her husband from beginning to end and sought consolation in burying herself in good works for the poor. She died childless at 24, pointedly leaving her fortune to the educational establishment which later became the Jogaillian University.

King Ladislaus V – Jogaila's full title – fulfilled one of his contractual obligations by going straight to Vilnius and smashing Perkūnas's statue. What followed was the usual fusion of old pagan beliefs and new-fangled Christianity. Perkūnas's mother was transformed into the Lithuanian Madonna. A bishop was appointed and mass baptisms

and the marriage was not agreed without conditions. First, Jogaila would have to become a Christian. Second, he would have to convert his whole empire to Christianity. The terms of the marriage also required Lithuania to make some territorial concessions to Poland and release all Polish prisoners and slaves.

On 15 February 1386, Jogaila bowed his head for a splash of baptismal water, assumed the Christian name Ladislaus (the Poles afterwards called him Władysław-Jogiełło), and three days later he married a still confused and unhappy Jadviga. The following month they assumed the crowns of were organised at which converts were presented with a white smock and given a Christian name. Vilnius itself was given a new name, Christianised as well as Polonised into "Wilno".

The new king's previous position as Grand Prince of Lithuania *per se* was given to his cousin Vytautas, another grandson of Gediminas, who showed every inclination to preserve the greatest degree possible of Lithuanian independence within the dynastic union. The rivalry between the cousins focused on retaining the support of the Lithuanian nobility. The Polish nobility then enjoyed a considerably better living standard than their Lithuanian counterparts, and it was extending the Polish rights to the Lithuanians that won the day for the king. Vytautas was compensated by being made Grand Duke of Lithuania for his lifetime.

Vytautas was the last of the great Lithuanian rulers. He built the impressive red-brick island castle at Trakai after the nearby castle of his father, Kęstutis, had been attacked once too often by the German crusaders. He drove back the Turks and mustered a bodyguard of Turkic Karaites whose descendants live by the castle today. In 1410 he and Jogaila decisively defeated the German crusaders at Grünwald (Tannenberg) and under Vytautas's rule the Grand Duchy became

the union was solidified by two sets of "Lithuanian Statutes" and finally written down in constitutional form agreed in 1569 at the Union of Lublin. The two countries were to share a king and a two-tiered government, but Lithuania kept a separate administration and its name.

Although Lithuania was territorially the larger of the two partners, Poland exerted the greater cultural influence. The Lithuanian nobility were Polonised and spoke Latin at court and Polish at other times. For the other social strata, the effects of the union were more painfully felt. The Polish social order was rigorously imposed throughout the joint empire. Unlike the nobility, the Lithuanian

one of the largest states in Europe, occupying Belorus and the Ukraine.

Even with shared privileges, the rivalry between the Polish and Lithuanian nobilities see-sawed for many years. The union, which came perilously close to falling apart, was considerably strengthened by Jogaila's son Casimir (by a later wife), who held the position of both King of Poland and Grand Duke of Lithuania. There were times when the titles again went to different individuals, but

Left, the German knights vanquished at Tannenburg, or Grünwald. **Above**, confirmation of the Polish-Lithuanian union, 1569.

bourgeosie did not assume the status of their Polish counterparts. They were summarily demoted, disenfranchised and lost the right to own land.

The Lithuanian peasant had even more reason to rue the Polish take-over. "Common cruelty was an established feature of social life," says the distinguished historian Norman Davies. "Faced with the congenital idleness, drunkenness, and pilfering of the peasantry, the nobleman frequently replied with ferocious impositions and punishments. The lash and the knout were the accepted symbols of noble authority. The serfs were beaten for leaving the estate without permission, for brawls and misdemeanours, and for non-observance of religious practices. A dungeon, together with chains, shackles, stocks, hooks, and instruments of torture, were part of the regular inventory."

The history of Lithuania right up to the partition of the union by Prussia, Russia and Austria at the end of the 18th century is therefore tied to Poland's. Lithuania's separate identity had grown progressively weaker, and the partitions made matters worse. "Little Lithuania" or "Lithuania Minor" which included Kaliningrad and the coast, was detached and given to Prussia; Russia took the rest. Tsar Alexander I toyed with the idea of reconstituting the Grand

dox Russia. The Russian administration responded by decreeing that only Orthodox subjects were to be employed by the state, even in the most menial capacity.

From 1864 onwards, the tsars did their utmost to Russify their Lithuanian holdings, and it was the declared policy of Muraviev, the Russian governor, to eradicate the traces of ancient Lithuania once and for all. That generally took the form of imposing Russian Orthodoxy. Non-Orthodox nobles could not buy property. They could rent it, but only for 12 years. Peasants could not buy land without a "certificate of patriotism", for which one of the qualifications was that they were Orthodox. An otherwise qualified land-

Duchy – with himself as Grand Duke – but was prevented from pursuing it by Napoleon's invasion.

To begin with, it was the Lithuanian nobility and educated classes who fretted under the Russian yoke. They joined the Polish uprising of 1831, and paid dearly. Next time round, about 30 years later, it was a stirring among the peasants, which the Russian government quelled with reforms giving peasants the right to hold up to 120 acres of land each. This satisfied some of them, but others were firmly under the thumb of the Roman Catholic clergy and could not accept with good grace anything on offer from the Ortho-

owner could lose his privileges simply by taking a non-Orthodox wife. Land for Jews was completely out of the question.

The programme of Russification reached its extreme in education. The university was closed down and only Russians were admitted to schools above the elementary level. The use of the Lithuanian language was banned for all official purposes, and the Latin alphabet, in which Lithuanian was customarily written, was also proscribed. It was a punishable offence to be in possession of a prayer book written in Latin characters.

The Russian Revolution of 1905 gave the Lithuanians a chance to reclaim some of their dignity, if not their independence. Resolutions were passed demanding the creation of an autonomous state with a "Seim" or National Assembly and with Vilnius as the capital. Threatened with a campaign of passive resistance, concessions were made like the reintroduction of the Lithuanian language in schools. National literature sprouted with astonishing rapidity, but the great symbolic victory was that Vilnius, effectively part of Poland for five centuries, was restored as the Lithuanian capital. Just as it seemed that the country might be climbing out of its cobwebbed grave, World War I broke out.

Driven out of East Prussia, the Russian

Military Governor announced that the city would be returned to Poland. He called it "the Pearl of the Polish Kingdom". Germany's subsequent defeat meant all its plans for Lithuania were shelved, and the question of the country's future was transferred to the Paris peace conference.

The various claims submitted to the conference by a Lithuanian delegation were made to look irrelevant as the Russian revolutionary war, not to mention the activities of a renegade German force under General Bermondt, overflowed into Lithuania. A combined force of Estonians, Poles and Lithuanians managed to repel a Bolshevik invasion, but while they were thus engaged

army retired through Lithuania, burning, plundering and taking away all Lithuanian men of military age. The German troops in pursuit were received almost as liberators, but it was quickly apparent that Germany also considered Lithuania a source of cheap labour. Any remaining hopes of independence were dashed when it emerged that longer-term German policy was to re-integrate Lithuania into occupied Poland. The cruellest blow fell in September 1915 when, having occupied Vilnius, the German

Left, Vilnius in the 16th century. **Above**, Vilnius's Great Synagogue in 1944.

another Polish force made a run to seize Vilnius. They held on to it even as the Bolsheviks swept towards Warsaw. In the end they surrendered it to the Bolsheviks rather than to Lithuania and Kaunas became the capital. It was a small compensation when Lithuania reclaimed Klaipėda (Memel) and the coast from Germany in 1923.

The possession of Wilno-Vilnius bedevilled relations between Poland and Lithuania. The city was undoubtedly the ancient capital of Lithuania, but over the course of 500 years it had become overwhelmingly Polish in every other respect, or so Poland claimed. A Russian census in 1910 broke down the population as 97,800 Poles, 75,500 Jews and only 2,200 Lithuanians.

The argument – which can't be settled here – involves the issue of whether language determines nationality. After five centuries of Polonisation and enforced Russification, the Lithuanian language tended to be spoken only in country areas and among peasants. The national revival did not take off until the first quarter of the 20th century. In any case, the transfer of Vilnius to Lithuania by the Red Army in 1940 was mourned in Poland as a national tragedy.

The Red Army occupied Lithuania in 1940 under the terms of the secret Nazi-Soviet Pact. "Whether you agree or not is

irrelevant," Molotov told the Lithuanian government, "because the Red Army is going in tomorrow anyway." The invading troops had an approved "government" trailing in their wake. The existing parties were dissolved, and those leaders who had not already fled were sent to Siberia.

The Soviet propaganda machine then went into action. The previous government, it said, was "indifferent to the real interests of the people, has led the country into an impasse in the fields of both domestic and foreign policy. The vital interests of the Lithuanian people have been sacrificed to the mercenary interests of a handful of ex-ploiters and rich people. The only thing left to working people in the towns and in the country has been unemployment, insecurity, hunger, indigence and national oppression…" Lithuanians steadfastly denounced the Soviet annexation as illegal.

Lithuania, together with Latvia and Estonia, was occupied by the Germans in June 1941. The 150,000 Jews in Lithuania – Vilnius was then the Jewish capital of Eastern Europe, as the statistics quoted above imply – all but vanished in Hitler's grim "final solution". In common with all the Baltic areas reoccupied by the Red Army in 1944, Lithuania lost another 200,000 people to Stalin's deportation orders. By 1950 Lithuania itself had all but vanished as an incorporated unit of the Soviet Union.

The three Baltic states moved almost in unison out of Soviet control in the late 1980s. In Lithuania, the lead was taken by the Sajudis, a breakaway movement drawn largely from the Institute of Philosophy of the Lithuanian Academy of Sciences. Its objective was full independence. There was no need to consult the Soviet Union, it said cheekily, because no one had ever recognised the 1940 annexation. This was too provocative even for the easy-going Gorbachev and, on the day that the parliament voted for unilateral independence, Soviet tanks drew up outside. Despite the freezing temperatures, thousands found themselves on the streets, and there were shootings at the TV tower in Vilnius where 14 were killed and 700 injured. It appeared that once again Lithuania's future was to be decided by a powerful neighbour. Western television viewers saw Vytautas Landsbergis, a musician who had been elected president, appear increasingly fatalistic.

Within weeks, however, it was equally apparent that the Soviet Union was beset by greater priorities. The threat to Lithuania's long-delayed independence passed, and Landsbergis could get on with his job. But it was not an easy one, particularly on the economic front, and in the elections of 1992 Landsbergis and the Sajudis were voted out of office by the Democratic Labour Party, heirs to the pro-independence wing of the former Communist Party.

Left, victims of Soviet Army, 1991. **Right**, painting in the parliament shows a 1991 rally in Vilnius.

VILNIUS

Lithuania's capital lies rather inconveniently in the far southeastern corner of the country only a couple of dozen miles from Belorus. It grew up on a hill beside the River Neris, near the point where it is met by the smaller River Vilnia. It was a stronghold against first the German Teutonic Knights, then the Crimean Tatars.

The Neris flows westwards to Kaunas, Lithuania's capital earlier this century when Vilnius and the surrounding area belonged to Poland and for 17 years the two countries were not on speaking terms. Poland and Lithuania were joined by marriage in 1397; in 1795 Vilnius was swallowed into the Russian empire. Russification followed Polonisation and many of the churches the Jesuits had so elaborately built, evolving a local baroque style which peaked in the 18th century, were given over to the Russian Orthodox belief.

In spite of many decades of neglect, Vilnius has one of the largest old towns in Eastern Europe, bristling with the confident and robust baroque towers of churches that seem too large and too numerous for the half a million population. Today they are mainly Catholic and since independence money and missionaries have been pouring in to reclaim the buildings for the faithful.

About half the population is Lithuanian, 20 percent Russian and 19 percent Polish. Before the war Vilnius was one of the great Jewish cities of Europe, and the centre of Yiddish publishing. New streets and buildings in its centre mark the site of their ghetto: 150,000 were killed by the Nazis.

In spite of the imposing architecture, there is a lack of important museums and galleries, and most pleasure is to be had from inspecting the churches and simply walking the cobbled streets. These are brightened by flower stalls (*gėlės*), antique shops and bars. There

Preceding pages: the spires of Vilnius. <u>Left</u>, Pilies Street, heart of the Old Town.

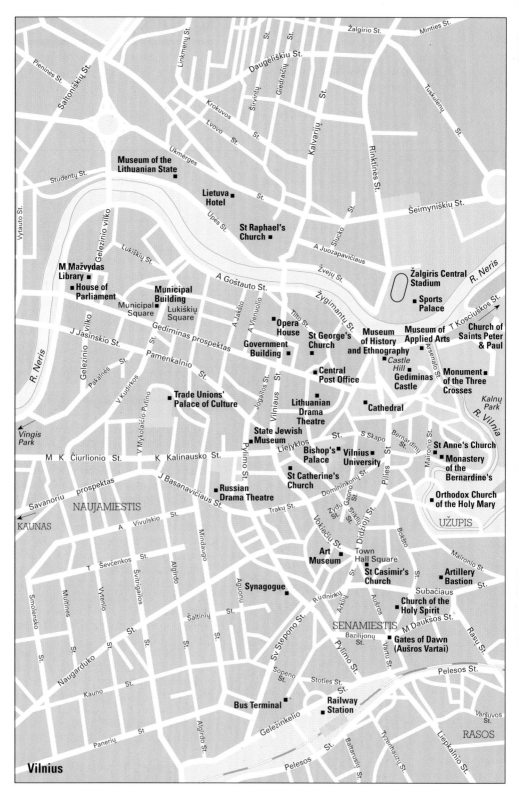

Vilnius

308

are some good restaurants such as the Stikliai, the first to be privatised and popular even during Soviet times, and the beer bars, often cavernous cellars, are a speciality.

The best place to start a tour of the city is from the top of the **Gediminas Tower**, overlooking the red-tiled roofs and the church towers of the Old Town, the cathedral, the administrative buildings along the main avenue, Gediminas prospektas, and the modern housing blocks on the right bank of the Neris stretching from the Lietuva Hotel to the television tower in the Lazdynai suburb.

The castle on **Castle Hill**, the oldest settlement of Vilnius, was built by Grand Duke Gediminas (1316–41) at the confluence of the Neris and Vilnia rivers. It was to this spot that he invited merchants, artisans and friars. According to legend, Gediminas dreamt of a powerful iron wolf howling from a hill at the mouth of the Vilnia, a dream which signified that at this spot a magnificent fort and a town would arise.

Today only the ruins of the southern part and the western defence tower (Gediminas Tower) are left. The 14th-century, three-storey octagonal brick tower houses a small exhibit of archaeological findings and the history of the castle which is one of the symbols of Lithuania's independence. The independence movement scored its first victory when the old Lithuanian yellow, green and red tricolor was raised on the observation platform on 7 October 1988.

On the nearby **Hill of Three Crosses** are the symbols of Lithuanian mourning and hope which were rebuilt and unveiled on 14 June 1989. The first crosses were erected on the hill in the 17th century in memory of martyred Franciscan monks. During Stalin's time they were removed and buried.

At the foot of Castle Hill lies the **Lower Castle** which was constructed in the 16th century. The palace built in the reign of Zygmunt August was levelled in the end of the 18th century to make way for a market, and only the drawings of P. Smugliewizc are left as a reminder of its beauty. Excavations at the Lower Castle, which later served as the city's

Gediminas Tower, a high point of the city.

law courts and a prison, are currently being undertaken.

The settlement's original church, which became the **cathedral** was commissioned in 1387 by Grand Duke Jogaila (Jagiello), and it was built to mark Lithuania's conversion to Catholicism. It occupied the northern part of the Lower Castle and it was rebuilt 11 times.

The present white neoclassical building by Laurynas Stuoka-Gucevičius dates back to 1777–1801 when it was given its dominating portico of six doric columns and a facade with large baroque statues depicting Abraham, Moses and the four evangelists. The interior has three naves of equal height divided by two rows of massive pillars. The main altar is classical and there are several interesting chapels on the right, especially the baroque chapel of St Casimir (1623–36), which contains the mausoleum of kings Alexander Jagiellon and Vladislav IV.

In the Soviet era the cathedral served as a picture gallery. As a symbol of national revival, it was the first church

to be reconsecrated, on 5 February 1989. The 170-ft (52-metre) **belfry** which stands to the front and to the right of the cathedral was originally part of the Lower Castle's defence walls. Although closed to visitors, it is a distinctive landmark and a good meeting-point.

On the left of the cathedral is the **Museum of Lithuania's State Culture and History**, the country's biggest museum. It was founded in 1855, closed by the tsarist authorities and reopened in 1968. Its 270,000 exhibits illustrate the history of the people of Lithuania from the Stone Age to 1940, with re-created interiors of houses from different regions. Further round the hill on the right at No. 2 Arsenalo is the **Museum of Applied Arts**. Beneath it are the excavations of Vilnius's first settlements at the foot of the hill, which can be visited. In the spacious halls on the ground floor are German and French porcelain and furniture from the 14th to the late 19th century. The museum's top floor is devoted to contemporary ceramics and tapestries from Lithuania.

The Old Town: Covering 665 acres (269 hectares), Vilnius's Old Town is one of the largest in Eastern Europe. The main artery running through the medieval city was Pilies (Castle) Street, which begins at the southeast corner of Cathedral Square and runs into Didžioji (Big) Street, past Town Hall Square to the **Gates of Dawn**, the only remaining gates of the town fortifications built against the Tatar invasions in the early 16th century. Only a few parts of the **town wall** remain in Bokšto, the street with the **Artillery Bastion** which is open to visitors.

On the cobble-stoned Pilies Street lie numerous historical buildings and from the balcony at No. 26 Lithuania's independence was declared in 1918. It is well worth venturing into the side streets and courtyards for a glimpse of the 19th-century city. There are a number of antique shops, cafés and cellar bars tucked away down these quiet lanes.

Bernadinų Street at the northern end of Pilies leads to **St Anne's church**, one of the best examples of Gothic architec-

Left, votive offerings. **Right,** Altar of the Sacred Heart in the cathedral.

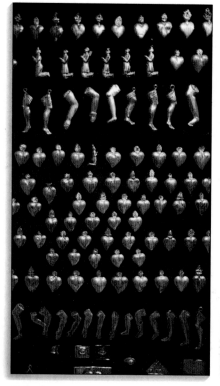

ture in Lithuania. Its western facade is patterned with 33 different varieties of bricks, making it amazingly graceful and harmonious. The original chapel was built in the 16th century during the reign of the Jogaillian king Zygmunt August (1520–72). Without any foundations the church rests on alder logs. The original interior was destroyed by fires and is of little interest. Napoleon Bonaparte is said to have been so enraptured by St Anne's that he exclaimed his desire to bring the church back to France in the palm of his hand and set it down next to Notre Dame.

Napoleon stayed in Vilnius on the way to Moscow in 1812, at the **Bishop's Palace** in Daukantas Square behind the university. Stendhal was in charge of food and provisions and it was in Vilnius, he said, that he learned to drink like a Russian. The euphoria that greeted the French army's arrival evaporated on their retreat when the city was plundered by the hungry troops. The palace was built for merchants in the 16th century and redesigned at the end of the

18th century by Laurynas Stuoka-Gucevičius, whose monument stands nearby. In tsarist times it was the residence of the governor general, and under the Soviets it was the Palace of the Art Workers. The French Embassy now occupies one wing of the building; a concert hall uses the other.

Next to St Anne's is the **monastery of the Bernardines** who came here from Poland in 1469. It has a Gothic roof and a baroque belfry, and being built on the edge of the town it was fortified with gun ports. The nearby statue represents the Polish-Lithuanian writer Adam Mickiewicz (1798–1859), born in Lithuania and educated at Vilnius University, who wrote the brilliant epic *Pan Tadeusz* about Lithuanian society.

Across the River Vilnia from here lies **Uzupis,** the first "suburb" outside the fortified city walls. This old and shabby district is considered one of the worst parts of town and it can be a dangerous place at night.

Facing St Anne's is **St Michael's church**, built between 1594 and 1625 in

the style of the Lublin Renaissance, as a family mausoleum for Leo Sapieha, Chancellor of Lithuania. The interior, burnt and desecrated by Cossacks in 1655, is light and spacious. To the left of the altar is the funerary monument of Sapieha and his two wives, while in the catacombs are the mummified Sapieha family.

Numerous churches in the old town are signs of Vilnius's geographical situation on the border of Catholicism and Orthodoxy. The **Orthodox Church of Paraskovila Piatnickaya** on Didžioji Street was built for the first wife of Grand Duke Algirdas in the 14th century and Peter the Great baptised Pushkin's grandfather here. A little bit further up the street in the former Slav quarter, the **Orthodox Church of the Holy Mother of God** belonged to Algirdas's second wife.

Town Hall Square was the political, cultural and economic centre of Vilnius. The original 15th-century town hall didn't survive frequent fires, and the present one, which was designed by Stuoka-Gucevičius, the architect of the city's cathedral, was completed in 1799 in the classical style. In the 19th century it was frequently used for cultural events and it became the first town theatre in 1845. In 1940 it was turned into the **Art Museum** and its two floors of galleries contain a good collection of Lithuanian paintings and sculptures from the 19th and early 20th centuries.

Past the Town Hall square up Didžioji Street lies **St Casimir's**, the oldest baroque church in Vilnius, built in 1604–15 and named after the patron saint of Lithuania. The saint, who was the son of King Casimir IV of Poland, is buried here and the crown on the church roof represents its royal connections. The church has long been an object of persecution. Under the tsars it was converted into the Orthodox Church of St Nicholas and the crown of St Casimir was replaced by an onion dome; during World War I the German occupation regime turned it into a Protestant church and the Soviets made it the Museum of Atheism and History of Religion. St Casimir's

View from the university tower.

was reopened to public worship in 1989.

Didžioji Street leads into Aušros Vartų Street where the 1902 **Philharmonic Concert Hall** is at No. 69. The street rises to the only remaining city gate, the **Gates of Dawn** (Aušros Vartai; Ostra Brama in Polish). In 1671 Carmelites from neighbouring **St Theresa**'s built a chapel above the gates to house a holy image of the Virgin Mary, the **White Madonna**, said to have miraculous powers. Its artist is unknown and it has been encased in gold and silver by local goldsmiths, leaving only the head and hands uncovered. The chapel's interior was refurbished in the neoclassical style in 1829, and the Virgin and the pilgrims filing past can be seen from the street below. Thousands of votive offerings decorate the walls and many pilgrims come to pray, queueing up on the stairs which were installed in the 18th century to connect the chapel to the adjacent Church of St Theresa. Mass is said in both Polish and a Lithuanian.

On the way up to the Gates of Dawn, in the courtyard of the only **Russian** **monastery** to operate during the Soviet era, stands Vilnius's most important Orthodox church, the **Church of the Holy Spirit**. It was built in the 17th century to serve the Russian Orthodox community, and it bears similarities to Catholic architecture. Before the altar a flight of steps leads down to a chamber with a display-case containing the well-preserved bodies of saints Anthony, Ivan and Eustachius, martyred in 1347 because of their faith, at the behest of Grand Duke Algirdas. The three saints are clothed in white during Christmas, black during Lent and red on all other occasions.

Seat of learning: A tour of the Old Town is not complete without a visit to the **university**, founded in 1570 by the Jesuits and one of the most important centres of the Counter-Reformation. For almost 200 years the Jesuits' college was the source of enlightenment, science and culture. It was closed under the tsarist regime in the 19th century. Today some 16,000 students study at its 15 faculties. The university complex has

Left, the university rector's room. Right, Arsenal Tower and St Casimir's.

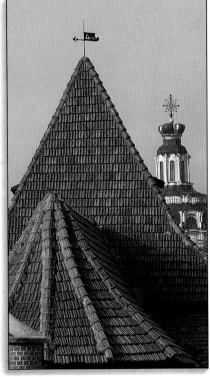

more than 10 courtyards. The four-storey building with an **observatory tower** dates back to 1569 and its windows are rococo. The **library** contains nearly 5 million volumes, making it the richest collection of Lithuanian books, as well as 180,000 manuscripts from the 13th to the 16th centuries. Soon after it was founded, it became one of the best known libraries in Eastern Europe.

Through the university courtyard a flight of stairs leads into St John's courtyard. Building began at **St John's church** soon after Lithuania's conversion to Catholicism in 1387. It was granted to the Jesuits in 1571 and transferred to the university following the abolition of the Jesuit Order in 1773. The present, late baroque church dates from restoration work carried out after a fire in 1737. Converted into the Museum of Scientific Thought during the Soviet occupation, St John's was reopened to public worship in 1991. Portraits of famous academics, part of the former museum's collection, adorn the walls. The 225-ft (68-metre) **belfry**,

added in the 16th century, is still one of the tallest buildings in the Old Town.

The oldest of the university courtyards is the small courtyard of the **observatory** built in the middle of the 18th century. At that time it ranked third in importance in Europe after Greenwich and the Sorbonne. The top of the observatory's facade is crowned with the signs of the zodiac.

The Jewish city: An essential part of pre-war Vilnius was the Jewish ghetto and the Jewish population which made up nearly half of the city. Today nothing remains of the "Jerusalem of Lithuania", as Vilnius was called. As a centre of Jewish culture Vilnius had 96 synagogues stretching from Gaono to Pylimo streets and Trakų to Rudininkų streets, all of which were razed during the war.

In 1941 some 50,000 Jews were herded into two ghettos. The small ghetto around Stiklių Street lasted for 43 days from 9 June to 29 October. Its 15,000 inhabitants were sent to labour and concentration camps. The bigger ghetto, established on 6 September around

Pilgrims's goal, the Gates of Dawn.

Žemaitijos and Rūdininkų streets, was liquidated two years later. Most of the 50,000 Jews were killed in **Paneriai** southeast of Vilnius. In the eerie forest you can still see the holes where men and women were shot and burned by Germans and local Nazis.

The **Great Synagogue** and the **Schulhoyf**, the traditional centre of Jewish culture around Vokiečių, Žydų and Antokolskio streets, suffered heavy damage during the war. The ruins of the synagogue, which dated back to 1661, remained for some years before the Soviet authorities decided to reconstruct the quarter, dynamiting what was left of the synagogue to make way for a kindergarten and a basketball field. The Jewish cemetery was levelled to build a concert and sports hall, the Palace of Concert and Sport. Its gravestones were subsequently used to make the steps leading up to the white Trade Union House on Taurakalnis Street.

The **synagogue** at 63 Pylimo Street, near **Halė**, the main food and flower market, was situated outside the ghetto, and is the only remaining prayer house for the small surviving Jewish community, which today numbers about 5,000, most of whom hope to start a new life in Israel. The recently opened **Jewish State Museum** at 12 Pamėnkalnio tells the tragic story of the community in Vilnius and is the only Jewish museum in the former USSR.

Commercial Street: New Vilnius unfolds along the central avenue Gedimino prospektas, opposite the cathedral. This is where most of the administrative buildings have been built and it is also the main shopping area. The **Opera House** is at the lower end on the right in Viennolio Street, near the overblown **Opera Café**, a meeting place for gays. The government is housed in the former building of the Central Committee of the Lithuanian Communist Party on Savivaldybes Square and the hated former KGB building is situated on Lukiškių Square where the leaders of the 1863 uprising were executed.

The mile-long (1.5-km) avenue ends at the modern **parliament building**

Concert-bound kettle-drums.

which was surrounded by barricades for a long time years after the Soviets attempted to storm the building in 1991. The great concrete blocks, flowers and graffiti were a constant reminder of the struggle for independence.

Although the street names have been changed and their Russian translations erased, Vilnius still bears many signs of its Soviet years. The Lenin statue which faced the KGB building on Lukiškių Square was taken off in the aftermath of the aborted putsch and is now tucked away in the Vilnius Art Workshop side-by-side with the statues of the Lithuanian communist leader Vincas Kapsukas and Joseph Stalin. Stalin's statue, which stood in front of the railway station, was removed in 1958.

The new grey housing districts on the outskirts are also the work of Soviet-Lithuanian architects. In 1974 the designers of the new **Lazdynai District** received the Order of Lenin for their grey pre-fabricated ferro-concrete housing blocks. The **Karoliniškės District** to the west of the city is dominated by the **television tower,** which has become infamous for the massacre in the night of 12–13 January 1991 when the Soviet tanks crushed and shot 14 unarmed civilians who were defending the building. The memory of the **"defenders of freedom"** is preserved in a small hall of fame at the foot of the tower as well as in the Lithuanian State Museum.

The 1,070-ft (326-metre) television tower is the tallest structure in Lithuania and has a restaurant halfway up from where there is a breathtaking view of the capital below.

Around Vilnius: One church outside the Old Town but worth making the effort to reach is the **Church of Saints Peter and Paul** which lies beyond the cathedral on the far side of Kalnų Park. It is the best example of baroque architecture in the city and was commissioned in 1668 by Michael Casimir Pac, a Lithuanian army commander. His tombstone, inscribed *Hic jacet peccator* ("Here lies a sinner"), is embedded in the wall to the right of the entrance. Despite a deceptively plain facade, the

Verkiai Palace, just outside the city.

baroque interior is breathtakingly beautiful with more than 2,000 undecorated stuccoed figures crowding the vaults, representing mythological, biblical and battle scenes.

Beyond the this church to the northeast of the city, is the **Antakalnis Cemetery** which symbolises Vilnius's tormented history. In the Soldiers' Cemetery German, Polish, Russian and Lithuanian soldiers lie side by side. In a clearing at the back four giant Soviet granite soldiers guard the eternal flame next to a hall of fame where the dignitaries of Soviet Lithuania are buried. In the centre of the cemetery lie the graves of the seven border guards and the civilians killed during the fight for independence by the same Soviet army.

Further out of town in the same direction is the **Verkiai Palace**, a singular neoclassical manor house now used by the scientific community.

The other major cemetery is to the southwest of the city. **Rasų Cemetery**, founded in 1801, is known as the "Pantheon of the famous". Prominent politicians, academics (Joachim Lelewel), poets (Ludvik Kondratowicz), and painters (Franciszek Smuglewicz, 1745–1807) are among those buried here. Of particular interest are the graves of the artist and composer Mikalojus Konstantinas Čiurlionis (1875–1911), the writer Balys Sruoga and author Jonas Basanavičius (1851–1927).

The adjacent **Military Cemetery** is dedicated to Polish Marshal Pilsudski whose heart rests here under a black granite slab.

Just out of town to the southeast, on the far side of the Markučiai District, is the **Pushkin Memorial Museum** in the home of Alexander Pushkin's son, built in 1867. One room contains the poet's possessions and in its 47-acre (19-hectare) grounds the anti-tsarist uprising of 1863 was hatched.

To the west of the city along the meandering Neris river is **Vingis Park**, which dates back to the 16th century when it was part of the aristocratic Radziwell family's estate. It is reported that Tsar Alexander I was at a ball in

Summer at Trakai.

Vingis when he received the news of Napoleon's invasion in 1812. The first National Song Festival took place here in 1947 and a special stage was built in 1960 to absorb the 20,000 singers, dancers and musicians who still flock here every five years to take part in one of the country's great celebrations.

Trakai: The former capital of the Grand Duchy of Lithuania, 18 miles (27 km) to the west of Vilnius, is a favourite place for an outing. The resort village is surrounded by some five lakes up to 158 ft (48 metres) deep. In the summer people swim and sail in the lakes around **Trakai Castle** situated on a peninsula in the midst of Lake Galvė.

Lithuania's most famous and most photographed castle was the heart of the Grand Duchy until 1323 when Grand Duke Gediminas moved the capital to Vilnius. The five-storey, red-brick fortifications were constructed by Vytautas and have been undergoing reconstruction since 1952.

The **Trakai Castle Museum** in the rooms around the internal courtyard offers an exhibition on prehistoric findings and the splendour of Lithuania's Grand Duchy which extended from the Baltic to the Black Sea. In the outer buildings there are items of furniture, ceramics and glassware from the feudal houses of later centuries. The ruins of the dukes' earlier castle can be seen in the town park.

In the 14th century Grand Duke Vytautas invited his bodyguard of Tatars from Crimea to Trakai where they settled around the castle. Their descendants, the Karaites – a Turkish ethnic group – still give the royal town its distinctive touch. The smallest ethnic minority in Lithuania, they number some 200 people.

The traditional Karaites' food is the *kibinai*, a meat-stuffed pastry which is served in the **Kibinine restaurant**, a traditional wooden Karaite house. A **Kinessa,** a prayer house of this fundamentalist Judaic sect which adheres strictly to the Law of Moses, is at 30 Karaimų, the main street.

Right, crossing the moat, Trakai Castle.

KAUNAS

Kaunas is the heart of Lithuania. More than any other city it has preserved its Lithuanian identity: 87 percent of its 422,931 inhabitants are ethnic Lithuanians, and Russians account for only 8.2 percent. It was relatively unscathed by World War II and large parts of the old city remain untouched, in spite of the grand designs of Soviet planners who had their hearts set on an eight-lane highway through the Old Town.

The country's second largest city has a long-lasting rivalry with Vilnius dating back to 1920 when it became the "provisional capital" after Vilnius fell to Poland. During its two decades as Lithuania's interim capital it developed rapidly from a Russian garrison town to a European city and many of the elegant buildings from that period remain. It is the major commercial centre of the country, manufacturing textiles and food products, and if Vilnius now provides the country with intellectuals, Kaunas provides it with smart dealers and businessmen. The two cities are connected by the River Neris which at Kaunas joins Lithuania's great river, the Nemunas. This river, once Lithuania's southern border, was on the German traders' route and Kaunas became a Hansa town. Today, the river is dammed on the east side of the city, turning it into a recreational area, and pleasure-boats are still able to make the journey from Kaunas to Klaipėda and the seaside.

Around the cobbled square: The city was first mentioned in 1361 and its historical heart is **Town Hall Square** (Rotušės aikste), surrounded by numerous 16th-century German merchant houses. In the middle of the cobble-stoned open area is the Town Hall, known as "The White Swan" for its elegance and 175-ft (53-metre) tower. Late baroque and early classical, it was begun in 1542 as a one-storey building. The second floor and the tower were added only at the end of the 16th century. The Gothic vaulted cellar of the tower served as a prison and a warehouse, the ground floor was reserved for traders and prison guards, and the first floor housed the magistrate's office, the treasury and the town archives.

Part of the building was destroyed during the Swedish-Russian war (1655–60). After reconstruction in 1771 it housed the local government. In 1824, under the tsarist regime, an Orthodox church was established there and later it became the warehouse of the artillery. It served as the provisional residence of the tsar (1837) and as a theatre (1865–69). Under the Soviet regime it was used by the engineering department of Kaunas polytechnic (1951–60). Renovated between 1969 and 1973, it now serves as the "wedding palace", and happy couples and their entourages often line up for photographs in the square outside.

Some 30 percent of the 545 houses in the Old Town have so far been renovated. The 16th-century **warehouse and pharmacy** (2 Rotušės) has a Gothic facade and vaults, and is a unique example of a Kaunas apartment house. The **Gildija House** (No. 3), built in the 16th

century, is the oldest on the square. Today it is the **Gildija restaurant**, an airy place with high-backed baronial chairs and a beer bar in the cellar which formerly served as a warehouse.

The Jesuits started to buy land and buildings in Kaunas in the early 17th century. The construction of the **St Franziskus Xavier church** and the **Jesuit monastery** was finished in the middle of the 18th century. After 1812 it served as a hospital and in 1824 it became the residence of the bishop. In 1924 it was returned to the Jesuits who used it for a boys' school. The church, which has a basilica layout, fine marble altars and wood carvings, was built in 1666 and was frequently destroyed by fires. In 1825 it became the Alexander Nevski Orthodox church and under the Soviets it was transformed into a vocational school. In 1990 it was returned to the church.

The house at 10 Rotušés, which has a Renaissance facade, was once a hunters' inn. A statue for the great Lithuanian poet and priest J. Mačiulis-Maironis

has been erected in front of No. 13, where he lived from 1910 until his death in 1932. In 1936 the **Maironis Museum of Lithuanian Literature** was set up here. On display are his study and living rooms as well as an exhibition on other Lithuanian writers. The baroque building from the late 16th century served as a military hospital in 1812. During the 1861 uprising against Russia its cellars were used as prisons.

In the northwest corner of the square is the **Bernardine monastery**. Renaissance with elements of Gothic, it dates back to the late 16th century, when the first house was bought by nuns. Its church, **Holy Trinity**, built in 1668 was rebuilt in baroque style. In the 19th century it possessed nine wooden altars but these were lost during World War I. In 1978 it was given back to the Catholic seminary.

In 1933–34, the late-Renaissance belfry was incorporated into the seminary which is located between the church and the belfry. The building was given back to the seminary in 1982.

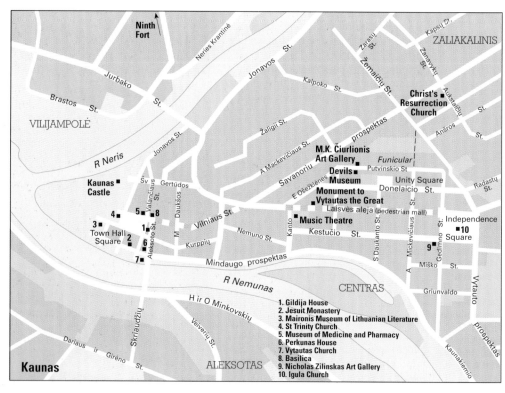

1. Gildija House
2. Jesuit Monastery
3. Maironis Museum of Lithuanian Literature
4. St Trinity Church
5. Museum of Medicine and Pharmacy
6. Perkunas House
7. Vytautas Church
8. Basilica
9. Nicholas Zilinskas Art Gallery
10. Igula Church

The **Museum of Medicine and Pharmacy** is at 28 Rotušės, a 17th-century building where there used to be a pharmacy. On display are old instruments and a reconstructed interior of a Lithuanian pharmacy at the turn of the century.

To the river: From Town Hall Square walk down Aleksoto Street to the banks of the Nemunas. At 6 Aleksoto Street is **Perkūnas House**. Historians cannot agree if the original purpose of this picturesque 15th-century Gothic brick building was a Jesuit chapel or the Hansa office. The more romantically-minded maintain it was the temple of Perkūnas, the god of thunder, since during renovation in 1818 workers found an 11-inch (27-cm) statue in the building, of a town and temples with three fishes which came to symbolise the rivers Nemunas, Neris and the god Perkūnas. The statue was lost but the name remained.

Similar to St Anne's church in Vilnius, the Perkūnas House is one of the most original examples of late Gothic in Lithuania and its rich architecture is a monument to the economic power of the Hansa and Germany. After reconstruction in the early 19th century it served as a school and in 1844 the first Kaunas Drama Theatre was established there. After 1863 the house fell into ruins. Renovated in the end of the 19th century it served as a religious school, and returned to the Jesuits. It now houses the **Museum of Ceramics**.

On the banks of the River Nemunas stands **Vytautas church**, built in the beginning of the 15th century and belonging to the Franciscan monks. Here foreign merchants celebrated Mass. It was built in the Gothic style and a tower was added at the end of the 15th century. French troops used it to store their ammunition in 1812 and in 1915, when the German army occupied Kaunas, it was used as a potato warehouse. In 1990 the church, with its sober white interior, was reopened for worship. The grave of priest and writer Tomas Vaižgantas (1869–1933), who organised the renovation of the church in 1920, is in the outer walls on the left.

A pathway leads to the confluence of

Town Hall Square.

the Neris and the Nemunas rivers. From the bank where they meet there is a good view of the Old Town spires, the Town Hall and the Jesuit and Vytautas churches. Midsummer Eve (St John's) on 21 June is celebrated every year on this piece of ground.

On the banks of the Neris lies **Kaunas Castle**. First mentioned in the 13th century, it was the earliest stone castle in Lithuania. The surrounding walls, 7 ft (2 metres) wide and 43 ft (13 metres) high, could not fend off the crusaders who destroyed the castle in 1362 after a three-week siege. Six years later a stronger castle was built with walls 12 ft (3.5 metre) thick and four towers. Nevertheless, over the centuries it was washed away by the Neris and the northern walls with the towers collapsed. Today, only part of the castle remains.

Through Valančiaus Street walk back to the Town Hall and turn right into Vilniaus Street at the **basilica** which towers 138 ft (42 metres) above the corner. The first church was built here in the early 15th century but its original shape is unknown. The naves were added in the 15th and 16th centuries and the construction was completed in 1655. Of especial interest are the baroque high altar of 1775 and the neo-Gothic chapel to the right. It belonged to Augustine monks until 1895 when it became a **cathedral**. It was elevated to the rank of basilica in 1921.

Little Champs-Elysées: Continue along Vilniaus Street to Birštono Street on the left. In a small yard is the **Presidentūra**, the residence of the Lithuanian president during the inter-war period. The one-storey building now serves as a teachers' residence.

Vilniaus Street leads into **Laisvės aleja (Freedom Avenue)**, the main thoroughfare of the New Town often optimistically compared to the Champs-Elysées in Paris or Unter den Linden in Berlin. Kaunas residents love to stroll along the mile-long (1.6-km) pedestrian street, designed in the late 19th century. In 1982 it was closed for traffic and the central tree-lined pathway was dotted with numerous benches. Repos-

Flowers of peace from the Lithuanian army.

ing and green in the summer, it can be quite grey and depressing in winter. Between the wars a number of administrative buildings were put up along this classy avenue now lined with shops.

At the crossing of Sapiegos Street stands the **Monument to Vytautas the Great.** The bronze statue of "the creator of Lithuanian power" stands proudly over four defeated soldiers: a Russian, a Pole, a Tatar and a German crusader holding a broken sword, symbolising the defeat of the Teutonic Knights. A bronze plaque pictures a map of medieval Lithuania extending from the Black Sea to the Baltic Sea.

In the park facing the statue in front of the **Music Theatre** lies a small granite slab, marking the spot where the 19-year-old student Romas Kalanta immolated himself on 14 May 1972 in protest against the Soviet system.

The large pedestrian mall ends in Independence Square (Nepriklausomybės aikste) which is dominated the the central **Igula (Saints Peter and Paul) church**. The imposing blue neo-Byzan-tine building which is perfectly symmetrical was built in 1893 by Russian architects as the Orthodox church for the army at Kaunas Castle. It was closed in 1960 and transformed into a permanent exhibition of stained glass and sculpture but after independence it reopened to public worship. Inside are several interesting frescoes of the evangelists and Orthodox saints and the stained glass represents the Assumption. In autumn, which is the favourite time for weddings in Lithuania, couples queue up outside the church to be married.

On the right-hand side of the square is the modern building of the **Mykolo Žilinsko Dailės Galerija (Nicolas Žilinskas Art Gallery)**. The avant-garde glass-and-granite building houses 1,670 works of art donated by Lithuanian-born Žilinsko (1904–92), a former head of security in East Berlin. It has Chinese, German and Dutch porcelain, Italian paintings of the 16th and 18th centuries, including Rubens, Rafael and Tiepolo, and an interesting collection of 20th-century Belgian art.

Left, city phone booths. **Right**, windmill at Rumšiškes Open-Air Museum.

Museum medley: Kaunas has the country's best museums. Parallel to Laisvės Street on Donelaičio Street lies Unity Square (Vienybės aikštė) where the symbols of Lithuanian statehood have recently been re-erected. A **hall of fame** with the portraits of famous Lithuanian politicians and writers leads from the **Liberty monument** to the **eternal flame**, flanked by traditional **wooden crosses** for those who died for Lithuania's independence.

The entrance to the **Military Museum of Vytautas the Great** is on Unity Square. Lithuania is shown through the ages from prehistoric times to the present day. There is the wreck of the *Lituanica*, the plane in which Steponas Darius and Stasys Girėnas attempted in 1933 to fly non-stop from New York to Kaunas (*see page 338*). Other exhibits show the history of the **Vytautas Magnus University** founded in 1922, closed in 1940 and only reopened in 1990.

The **M.K. Čiurlionis Art Gallery** is situated in the adjoining building and has its entrance at 55 Putvinskio. Built in 1936, the gallery has some 360 works of the outstanding Lithuanian painter and composer, and it should not be missed. The mystic and modernist Čiurlionis (1875–1911) saw nature as an inexhaustible source of beauty. Of his musical poem *In the Forest*, he wrote: "It begins with soft and wide chords, as soft and wide as the sighing of our Lithuanian pines."

Čiurlionis wrote some 20 preludes, canons and fugues for organ and harmonised around 60 folk-songs. In a special listening hall, visitors can hear some of his symphonies and orchestral works. (Concerts are also sometimes put on in his former home, now a museum, in the spa town of Druskininkai, 77 miles/ 124km to the south.) The museum also has an exhibition of Lithuanian crosses and spinning implements.

A few houses away, at 64 Putvinskio, is the A. Žmuidzinavičius Collection, better known as the **Devils Museum** for its impressive number of wooden devil statues that the folk-artist amassed during his lifetime (1876–1966). It has grown over the years as new foreign devils have been added, and there are now more than 1,700, including Hitler and Stalin seen dancing over Lithuania.

From Putvinskio you can either take the **funicular** or climb 231 steps up to the Žaliakalnis District which offers a splendid view of the city. One of the most interesting architectural monuments is the **Church of Christ's Resurrection** at 4 Aukštaičių. It was started in 1932 but never completed. With the annexation by the USSR in 1940, the unfinished church, rising to 205 ft (63 metres) was confiscated and in 1952 it was incorporated into the Banga radio plant which installed a workshop. In 1988 the building was given back to the Catholic church and restoration began. Being one of the symbols of national rebirth and liberation, it will eventually house a chapel for those who died in the struggle for independence.

Outside the town: A visit to Kaunas is not complete without a tour of the **Ninth Fort**, situated on the road to Klaipėda. It was built at the end of the 19th century as part of the outer town defences on the

Pažaislis monastery, a baroque treasure just outside Kaunas.

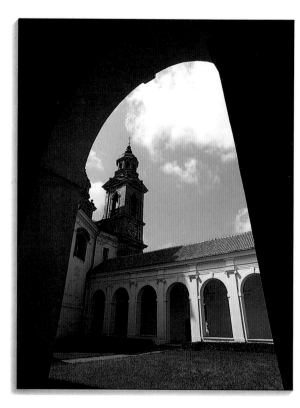

orders of Tsar Alexander II to fortify the western border of the Russian empire. It became infamous as a concentration camp during the Nazi occupation.

In the fort you can visit the former prison cells where Jews from all over Europe were herded together awaiting execution. A silent reminder of the horrors are the inscriptions preserved on the walls of the cell. "We are 500 French" (*Nous sommes 500 Français*), wrote Abraham Wechsler from the French town of Limoges before being killed.

The **Way of Death** (Mirties kelias) leads to the place where some 30,000 Jews were shot. A monumental concrete statue overlooks the mass graves where most of the inhabitants of the Kaunas ghetto were buried.

The **museum** housed in a concrete hall near the fort describes the deportations of Lithuanians by the NKVD (the predecessor of the KGB), the Nazi and the Stalinist terror, and the resistance fighters under the Soviet occupation who fought on until 1952.

To the east of the town, above the dam, is the **Pažaislis monastery**, one of Lithuania's architectural gems. Isolated in the countryside, it was built in the 17th century with orchards and gardens which are still cultivated. Entrance is through the Holy Gate and the church has a fine 150-ft (45-metre) cupola which on the inside has a painting of the Virgin Mary. The marble and oak interior is enriched with frescoes which are in the process of being restored under the aegis of the Čiurlionis Gallery which became responsible for it in 1966.

Before the war the monastery was run by nuns from Chicago but the houses they inhabited in the grounds no longer exist. Restoration work is continuing, and the sacristy and refectory have already been completed.

Nearby, between the dam and the A227, 8 miles (12 km) east of Kaunas, is **Rumšiškes**, site of Lithuania's main **open-air museum**. This makes a good half-day out, with collections of old buildings from all over the country. One of the large barns has been turned into an excellent café and restaurant.

The Ninth Fort, a vivid reminder of Nazi atrocities.

AUKSTAITIJA AND THE NORTH

The northern part of Lithuania, which lies above Kaunas and Vilnius, between the Nemunas and Neris rivers and the Latvian border, is called Aukštaitija, a name first recorded in the 13th century. In the west it abuts Žemaitija (*see page 357*) and it is higher than the coastal region. The communities of Aukštaitija grew up around uniform, one-street villages and the small homesteads were created as land has been divided up among the owners' descendants.

The region was once known for growing flax and still has the largest flax mill in the Baltics. Aukštaičiai cultivate their land by the calendar, working together when necessary. A traditional breakfast will be pancakes made of flour or potato starch, lunch will be hearty and supper something light and dairy-based. The people have a reputation for being talkative, friendly and fond of songs, and the women are known for flax spinning and ornament-making.

Aukštaitija has two distinct regions: a rather flat western region, accessible from Kaunas, and a hilly eastern region which has the greatest snowfall in the country and is best approached from the direction of Vilnius.

The Castle Road: The willow-lined banks on the right-hand side of the A228 Castle Road, which follows the River Nemunas from Kaunas to the coast, are dotted with red-brick fortified manor houses looking out over the wide valley towards Lithuania's southern neighbours. Just beyond Jurbarkas the river forms the border with Kaliningrad. Castles were originally built all along here when the river marked the border between the Grand Duchy and the lands of the Teutonic Order. From the 17th century, merchants and aristocrats made their castle homes here.

The castle at **Raudonvaris** at the start of the castle road on the outskirts of Kaunas was built in the 17th century and remodelled in the 19th century by the Tiškevičiai family who embellished it with a picture collection and a fine

library. In the park there is an old manor and the town is a centre for agricultural research. The 19th-century church was built by Lorenco Anichini, who is buried here, and the interior statuary is by Lorenco Pompaloni.

At **Seredžius** there is a hill fort named after a legendary hero, Duke Palemonas, who is supposed to have been descended from Roman nobility. Nearby is the Belveder old manor on a high slope, but it is rather neglected, as is the park it lies in. To the north of the manor there is a plain that served as an airfield for the French Normandy-Neman air squadron in World War II. Not all of the aeroplanes that took off from here returned.

Veliuona is a small town high on the river bank with a park and two hill forts: the Castle Mountain and the Gediminas Grave – it is thought that Lithuania's Grand Duke died here in 1341. The town has a 17th-century Renaissance church restored at the turn of the century and this is the burial place of Joazas Radavičius (1857–1911), a famous organ master, and Antanas and Jonas

Juška, Lithuanian folklorists whose remains were brought back here from Kazan in Russia in 1990.

A few miles further on is **Raudonė**, a town in a similarly elevated position. Its park is full of ancient oaks. The 17th-century red-brick palace, in a mix of Renaissance and neo-Gothic, was built for a merchant, Krispin Kirschenstein. It was rebuilt in the 19th century and today it houses a school. There is a wonderful view from its tower.

The 17th-century **Vytėnai Castle** was also built by a merchant, Janush Eperjesh, who came from Hungary, though it is sometimes called Gelgaudai Castle after its 19th-century owner. A park with ponds is near the castle, which is being restored.

Beyond **Skirsnemunė**, which used to be called Christmemel by the Germans, is **Jurbarkas**, where there is a hotel and garage facilities. It has a population of 15,000 and the biggest employers are the gravel extraction company, a ship repair yard, a logging concern and a flax mill. There is an interesting 19th-century part of the town and the local park has a farmstead museum which is devoted to the distinguished Lithuanian sculptor Juozas Grybas, who lived here from 1926 to 1941.

Kaunas to Latvia: The Žemaičiai Highway leaves Kaunas past the Ninth Fort (*see pages 328–29*). After a few miles, at the Cinkiškis crossroads, the A230 turn-off leads up to **Kėdainiai**, an administrative centre with chemical works and a sugar industry.

The Old Town is comparatively large and dates back to the 15th century when it was owned by the dukes of Radvilos, under whose patronage industry expanded, schools and publishing houses grew up and Lutheran, Roman Catholic and Reformed churches and a synagogue, all still standing, were built. The Kėdainiai estate with a manor and park, together with a local museum, tell the story of the town.

From Kėdainiai the road travels north in two directions: the 127 to the west goes up through **Pakruojis** to the border; the A230, running almost parallel

Golden teeth, silver smiles.

to the east passes through Panevėžys, joining the M12.

The 127 continues northwards through a land of farmers and artisans, past undulating plains, small brooks and villages. At **Dotnuva** a 17th-century abbey is being restored and the local manor, which before World War I belonged to the Russian minister Piotr Stolypin, is now an agricultural research centre. Similarly, the Komarai manor in **Baisogala**, 37 miles (60 km) north, is now used as a centre for research into livestock farming.

A few miles further on the road reaches the Panevėžys-Šiauliai road next to **Šeduva**. This is a small town with an old-fashioned air and a pleasant restaurant situated in a windmill. There is a local museum and a church dating back to the 17th century. A couple of miles (5 km) to the west is a rest place on **Lake Arimaičiai**. On the eastern side of Šeduva is the notable restored Raudonvaris manor, which in the 19th century belonged to the powerful local landlord, Theodor von Rop. Three miles (5 km)

further on is another manor, currently being restored, called Burbiškas.

Von Rop also had a country estate in **Pakruojis**, the region's administrative centre to the north. The manor house is still in good repair and there are a number of outbuildings, including a windmill and an arcaded bridge. **Linkuva**, between Pakruojis and the border, had a notable landlord in the noble Karpiai family, who in the 19th century had a reputation for caring for the land, for cultivating it and keeping it well-drained. The town has a typical 19th-century layout and the architectural ensemble of church and Carmelite monastery is intact. **Žeimelis** up by the border dates back earlier, and has a number of distinctive pubs.

Up the Via Baltica: From Kėdainiai the A230 is the right-hand of the two roads leading north. Just before Panevėžys it picks up the M12 and the Via Baltica continues on its way to Riga. **Panevėžys** is Lithuania's fifth largest city with a bishop's see and a population of 120,000. It dates from the middle of the 16th

Left, Pelusė's 250-year-old altarpiece. Right, Šeduva restaurant.

century when there was a community and a manor house on the River Nevezis where a park is laid out today. Its rapid expansion as an industrial centre, including the Baltics' largest textile mill turning flax into linen, has not improved its attractiveness. Since the 1960s its name has been linked with the Panevėžys Drama Theatre, which has built up an impressive reputation. There are usually a number of exhibitions on in the city and the local museum has a collection of butterflies and insects.

The karst region around **Pasvalys** 24 miles (38 km) north of Panevėžys, has created underground caverns and in the town park there are signs where some of these have caved in. Southwest of Pasvalys on Road 142 is **Joniškėlis** where the Karpiai family had another manor which lies in a park. Branching off the M12, the 59 leads up to **Likėnai** and **Biržai** where the landscape is pockmarked with small lakes and holes caused by the karst.

The old town of Biržai was built up around an artificial lake created in the 16th century at the confluence of the Aspasčia and the Širvena. The castle that stood here was destroyed in the 18th century but restored in the 1980s and there is a small museum inside. In the 19th century, under the rich and influential Tiškevičiai counts, the Catholic and Evangelical Reformed churches were erected. There is a monument in the town to a local poet, Julius Janonia (1896–1917). Also beside the lake is the Astravas manor with a palace and park now used by a textile enterprise. Biržai is famous for its beer.

Kaunas to Rokiškis: This route goes through the eastern edge of the Aukštaitija plains, following the River Šventoji. It leaves Kaunas on the A226, the former Warsaw-St Petersburg postroad which was paved in the early 19th century. It is a straight road, lined with old trees and still has a few remaining post-houses.

Jonava on the River Neris is an industrial town producing fertiliser and furniture. The 17th-century church in the old Skaruliai district has been marred

The manor house at Biržai.

by industry, but the main church is of interest, built in the 19th century by the distinguished Vilnius architect Laurynas Stuoka-Gucevičius. The turrets were added in 1935.

As the road enters **Ukmergė** there is a neoclassical post-house from 1835 on the right. On the south side of the town at **Vaitkuškis** is the former country home of the Koskovskiai family, arts patrons with a taste for literature who corresponded with Balzac.

At **Anykščiai**, where wine is blended from imported grapes and made from cherries, apples and black currants, there is also a literary tradition. On the outskirts is the farmstead of the writer Antanas Vienuolis (1882–1957), but the most famous work from the town was a lyric poem written by Antanas Baranauskas (1835–1902) in response to the felling by the tsar of Anykščių šilelis, the 700 sq. miles (1,812 sq. km) pine forest 3 miles (5 km) to the south. It became a milestone in the idea of conservation and the countryside. In the forest is the **Puntukas boulder**, one of

the largest in the country, weighing 265 tonnes. These big rocks, brought by glacial drift, are scattered throughout the Baltics, and are sometimes called "presents from Scandinavia". The sculptor Bronius Pundzius turned the boulder into a monument to the transatlantic flyers Darius and Girėnas in 1943 (*see following page*).

To the north of Anykščiai is the old village of **Niūroniai** and the memorial farmstead of the writer Jonas Biliūnas (1879–1907), who is buried at the nearby Liūdiškiai hill fort. The village also has a small track for trotting horse races, a stable with horses to rent and a huge barn housing a collection of carriages and other horse-drawn vehicles.

From **Svedasai** beside a lake 15 miles (24 km) further on, Road 62 goes northwest to **Kupiškis**, which is surrounded by manor houses, windmills and rural churches. Continuing 20 miles (33 km) on the 67 is **Rokiškis**, a regional centre with a hotel. Beside the main square is a country estate dating back to the 17th century and now housing a museum of

Left, rich woodland. **Right**, Juozas Puzinas, folk artist.

BASKETBALL'S HIGH-FLYER

The game at which Lithuania excels is basketball. It long provided the best players for the Soviet team and the Kaunas team Žalgiris has twice been USSR champions. Seven Lithuanians have Olympic gold medals and the national team took home a bronze in Barcelona in 1992. A handful are top players in the US, including Sarúnas Marciulionis who has put his money into a successful small hotel in Vilnius.

The history of the game here begins with one of the country's great heroes, Steponas Darius. The village of Rubiškė near the coast where he was born in 1896 has since changed its name to Darius. In 1907, with his mother and step-father, he emigrated to the US and as a student he excelled at baseball and football as well as basketball. He signed up for the army in 1917 and fought in France where he was wounded and he returned to the US with two decorations.

In 1920 he was one of the US volunteers for the Lithuanian army and as a pilot he took part in the liberation of occupied Klaipėda. He was a champion sportsman in his native country where he introduced basketball and laid down a sporting tradition that has continued ever since.

He returned to the US in 1927 and worked in civil aviation, founding a Lithuanian flying club, called Vytis. Five years later he and a colleague and mechanic, Stasys Girėnas, set out to bring fame and glory to their newly independent nation by embarking on an epic flight from New York to Lithuania. They had great trouble scraping together the money, but eventually had enough to buy an old plane they called *Lituanica*. There was no money left over to buy any radio equipment.

The plane left New York on 15 July 1933 and flew across the Atlantic, covering 3,984 miles (6,411 km) in 37 hours 11 minutes. Nobody knows exactly why but it never reached Lithuania and crashed at Soldin in Germany. At the time there was friction between the two countries, and rumours that the plane might have deliberately been brought down did not improve international relations. Their bodies were brought to Kaunas, then the provisional capital, and 60,000 turned out for their funeral.

Their death was not in vain: many felt the flight had put Lithuania on the map. The duo's portraits appeared on postage stamps and 300 streets, 18 bridges and eight schools were named after them and many of these survived the Soviet period.

One of the most popular monuments to the heroes is near Anykščiasi on a huge boulder called Puntukas. This is one of the country's mythical stones which has been a landmark from time immemorial. In 1943 a Lithuanian sculptor, Bronius Pundzius, was in the countryside hiding from the Germans and he made himself a shelter beside the boulder. To while away his vigil, he began to sculpt a relief of the faces of the two pilots into the stone, adding the text of their will which had been written before they embarked on the historic flight.

Remnants of their aeroplane and some of their personal effects are on display in the Historical Military Museum in Kaunas, in the same building as the M.K. Čiulionis Art Gallery. On the main road 4 miles (6 km) from Klaipėda, a signpost marked "S. Darius tėviškė" leads to the village of Darius and a new memorial museum. ■

Darius immortalised in the village that has taken his name.

wooden sculpture by a local master, Lionginas Šepka, and nearby is a former school for organists. The 19th-century church on the opposite side of the square is one of the most richly decorated in Lithuania. Its benefactor was the Tyzenhaus family.

The Aukštaitija Uplands: The main M12 highway which runs out of Vilnius towards Riga and Tallinn is a recent construction and it bypasses towns until it reaches Panevėžys. On its western side, on the banks of the Neris 20 miles (32 km) from Vilnius is the town of **Kernavė**. Forming a triangle with Vilnius and Trakai, this was the capital and major trading centre of Lithuania in the 13th and 14th centuries. Now a village of just 200 people, the historic site includes four hill-fort earthworks, evidence of the defences against the crusaders, which give a beautiful view over the Neris valley.

On the eastern side of the M12, the Molėtai highway (Road 1) heads due north through the **Green Lakes**, a popular, hilly area of summer homes, where the deep lake waters, tinted green, are a place for people from Vilnius to cool off. After 16 miles (26 km) up the main highway there is a signpost directing you down a dirt track, then along a footpath to a black granite stone. You are now standing at longitude 25° 19', latitude 50° 54', which is calculated to be the **centre of Europe**.

Molėtai itself is a base for exploration in all directions. To the west is **Videniškiai** where a richly decorated 17th-century church was built for the Giedraičiai, a rich local family who gave their name to a small town directly to the south. Road 42 northwest to Anykščiai is picturesque, passing through the pleasing villages of **Alanta** and **Skiemonys**. To the east is a landscape of forests and lakes. **Inturkė** has an 18th-century wooden church and near **Mindūnai**, on Road 40, there is a chain of comfortable places to stay.

The wooden village of **Labanoras** has authentic folk architecture and a wind instrument, the Labanoras Dūda played like the bagpipes, comes from

Crowns of rue and daisies.

here. On 8 September there used to be a colourful church festival in the village. Traditionally the people have not been rich. "If it weren't for mushrooms and berries," runs a saying, "Labanoras girls would have nothing to wear."

To the north of Molètai, at **Virinta**, there is a signposted turn-off to the right to the **Observatory and Museum of Astronomy** which is worth a visit. **Utena** is a light industrial town which has a Coca-Cola plant and, more importantly, the best beer in Lithuania. There is also a 19th-century church and museum.

At **Daugailiai** a left-turn up Road 57 leads through attractive countryside, passing **Antaliepté**, a village completely hidden in the **Šventoji valley**, where there is an 18th-century church and abbey and an old stone watermill by the river. The road leads along the banks of the 432 sq. miles (1,117 sq. km) **Lake Sartai**, shaped like a back-to-front E. The surrounding forests are a nature reserve and the lake attracts people from all over the country every February when horse races are held on the ice. Continu-

ing past Daugailiai to **Degučiai**, on the opposite side of the road, is another resort area of lakes, around **Salakas**, some of which were created when the Antaliepté dam was installed in 1959. Beyond Degučiai the road rises to a high point from which rivulets flow south to feed the Nemunas and north to feed Latvia's Daugava. The road then falls as it nears **Zarasai**, a town of broad streets and wide squares surrounded by lakes. There is a local museum, 19th-century church and a cemetery of German soldiers from World War I.

The road to **Smalsai**, southeast of Zarasai, passes through a wonderful hilly land of lakes, while to the north Road 52 goes to **Avilys**, **Čičiris** and **Stelmužè** on the border. Stelmužè has the largest oak in Lithuania, 66 ft (20 metres) high and 33 ft (10 metres) in circumference and supposedly 1,000 years old. There is also an 18th-century manor and 17th-century wooden church with original artwork inside.

Napoleon's Route: Road 2 runs from Vilnius up the eastern borders of Lithua- **Farm work for sun-seekers.**

nia, and this is the way Napoleon and his army moved into Russia in 1812. From the capital the road leaves through pine forests to **Nemenčinė**, an area full of summer houses on allotments still called "collective gardens". Each one measures 6,480 sq. ft (600 sq. metres) and their commodious and comfortable self-built shacks and houses, many of them made of brick, have been turned into second homes.

From **Pabradė**, with its rather neglected 18th-century coaching inn by the river, the road heads east to **Pavoverė**, where there is a wooden belfry and church with artworks, dating from 1769. The next village, **Zalavas**, is the birthplace of Poland's patriot and pre-war president, Józef Pilsudski (1867–1935). The road contiues through the old villages of **Miežionys** and **Modžiūnai. Švenčionys** is in a glacial valley and the original settlement was near the hill fort. Down the centuries Tatars, Russians, Belorussians and Poles have settled here.

From Švenčionys a pleasant detour

north can be made via **Švenčionėliai** in the west, though even here there is memory of war, with a grave of several thousand local Jews from the region murdered by the fascists and buried on the edge of the Labanoras Wood.

Road 51 continues north into the **Ignalina National Park**, an area of 1,750 sq. miles (4,530 sq. km) of which 15 percent is lakes. Most of the land is forested and there is a great diversity of flora and fauna, with more than 700 species of plants, 100 species of mammals and 78 species of fish. The park's administrative centres are at **Meironys** and the more interesting **Paluse**, where there is a 19th-century wooden church and belfry, and where boats can be hired for a better view of the lakes. **Ginučiai**, **Šuminai**, **Strazdai** and **Salos** are all pleasant villages and at **Stripeikiai** there is a bee-keeping exhibition.

Ignalina itself is not far from the park and the Švenčionys Uplands on its eastern side are an attractive hilly area. It snows more in Ignalina than anywhere else in the country and the snow stays

Messing about in boats.

longer, which make it a popular centre for winter sports.

Some 17 miles (27 km) further north on Road 2 is the new town of **Dūkštas**. The old town, sometimes called Pažemiškas, is on the far side of the adjacent Lake Dūkštas (sometimes called Lake Pažemiškas), but the places of interest here, the 18th-century buildings, are neglected, and the burnt-out church with a graveyard of noblemen has not been renovated. The local manor house is used for agricultural research. Road 47 east of Dūkštas leads to **Rojus** (Paradise), a farm museum and garden of the scientist and gardener Adam Hrebnicki (1857–1941).

To the north is Snieckas, which in 1992 changed its name to **Visaginas**. Most of the 33,700 who live here are Slavs. The town itself is situated in a picturesque area of pine forests near a lake, but to the east is the **Ignalina Atomic Power Plant** on the south bank of Lake Druksiai. It was built in 1974, to the same design as Chernobyl, and has been the subject of some controversy

(*see Environment chapter, page 113*). Two of the four reactors are operating.

On Belorus's border: Vilnius is only 15 miles (24 km) from the border and there are several places of interest in between, and the roads can be followed into the neighbouring country. The M12 has been the main highway to the east since the Middle Ages, and it goes to the Belorus capital of Minsk. **Nemezis** is the first village on the road, settled by Tatars in Vytautas's time, and they have their own chapel and cemetery here. On the opposite side of the valley are the remains of a 19th-century country estate and park. A few miles further, on the right, is **Boreikiskes**, where a manor belonging to the Tiškevičius family was rented by the writer and Vilnius publicist Vladislav Sirokomla (1823–62). Today it houses a museum.

The road is now in the **Medininkai Uplands**, an area of wide valleys, fewer depressions and fewer forests, formed in an earlier glacial age than other uplands in the country. The customs post at the frontier here is still fresh in local people's minds as the place where seven young Lithuanian border guards were massacred in July 1991. Just before the border an old track goes down to the right to Medininkai and the remains of **Medininkai Castle**, a stone defence work from the 14th century which is being restored. A museum gives a history of the place.

Just over a mile (3 km) to the south there is a signpost to **Juozapinės Mountain**, the highest point in Lithuania above sea level, at a meagre 963 ft 4 inches (293.7 metres). The A234 runs due south from Vilnius. Just beyond **Jašiūnai** at the River Merkys, an 18th-century classical palace and grounds are being restored. It belonged to the distinguished Balinski and the Sniadecki scientific families and many eminent scientists from Vilnius University are buried here.

Just over the border there are castles of ancient Lithuania at **Lyda**, like the one at Medininkai, and at Navagrudak (Naugardukas in Lithuanian), where there is an exhibition about the history of the two countries. The poet Adam Mickiewicz was born here in 1798.

Left, carved figure at a bee museum, Stripeikiai. Right, country picnic.

THE SOUTH

South of Kaunas and Vilnius, the country is divided into two by the River Nemunas which flows down the middle from the Belorus border. To the west, up to the river's southern bank after it has turned west to the sea, is **Suvalkija**. To the east, up to the southern bank of the Neris, is **Dzūkija**. Suvalkija was the land of the Sūduva and Jotvingiai tribes until it was joined to the Grand Duchy of Lithuania after the Teutonic Order was crushed in 1410. In the ensuing years of peace, people from Žemaitija and other neighbouring regions came to settle here, but the main villages and townships were not founded until the 17th and 18th centuries.

From 1867 to 1915 it was part of the Russian province of Suvalkai and although the region still bears the name, the town of Suvalkai is in Poland today and the capital of the province is now Marijampolė. After serfdom was abolished in the 19th century, peasants settled in farmsteads and a great number educated their own children. Their standards were so high that the local dialect became the basis of the modern Lithuanian literary language.

People of Suvalkija are supposed to be stingy and thrifty. They are used to working hard, waking early to a hearty breakfast of meat and soup, lunching on the warmed-up left-overs and and having a light supper. "It would be better if father fell off the roof than a grain or a drop be lost," is how a local joke sums up their attitude.

The Suvalkija plain: The first town in Lithuania encountered on the A226 from Poland is **Kalvarija** on the Šešupė river. The old part is attractive with a post-house (1820) and the remains of a large jail built in 1810 to contain 1,000 prisoners. The classical-style church was built in 1840 and rebuilt in 1908 and it has some good paintings inside. A large Jewish community settled here in the 17th century and most were exterminated by the Nazis. Their burial place is near Orija Square. **Marijampolė** (pop.

40,000), the principal town, lies in a rather dull plain relieved only by the Šešupe, the region's main river. The town manufactures car parts and woollen fabrics, canned vegetables, milk, sugar and mixed feed. It takes its name from an 18th-century monastery of the Marian Fathers and in the 19th century it was a centre of enlightenment. There is a good local museum and the 19th-century church is well-known for its fine paintings.

From Marijampolė the A229 leads 94 miles (150 km) eastwards to Vilnius. To the north is one of the most fertile plains in the country. After 31 miles (50 km) on the A226 towards Kaunas is **Sasnava**, marked by the belfry of its 1938 church. On the left of the road lies the forest of **Kazlū Rūda** and the town of the same name. Sulvakija is a land of farms on clay soil: forests are left where the soil is light. Further on is **Veiveriai**, which has a post-house and 19th-century teachers' training college.

To the west of Marijampolė, the A229 leads to the border, passing through

Vilkaviškis, a local centre which was burnt to the ground in World War II. Nearer the frontier is the Paežeriai manor, a 18th–19th century palace set in a park with a lake. Beyond it is **Kiršai**, birthplace of a famous Lithuanian poet, Salomėja Nėris (1904–45).

To the south is a hilly, attractive corner of the country. In the southwest corner on Road 95 is **Vištytis**, a border town by a large lake (70 sq. miles/180 sq. km) of the same name. At **Kudirkos Naumiestis**, on Road 89, Vincas Kudirka, author of the Lithuanian national anthem, was born (1858) and buried (1899).

Sūduva land: The southen part of Suvalkija, often called Sūduva, is a picturesque region of lakes and hills. Near the border with Poland is **Lazdijai**, the centre of the district, which has a late 19th-century church. The 82 continues for 11 miles (18 km) towards hills, dry forests, valleys and an attractive labyrinth of lakes around **Veisiejai**, which has a number of pleasant corners to stop for a rest. The old part of the town has a beautiful park and an early 19th-century church. Lazar Zamenhof (1859–1917), a physician from Warsaw who created Esperanto, lived here in 1886–87.

The A223 leads after 8 miles (12 km) to **Leipalingis** and on through pleasant countryside towards Drusininkai in the neighbouring province of Dzūkija (*see page 351*). From Lazdijai the 75 heads north towards Alytus and Vilnius, passing through **Šventežeris,** where Evangelical Lutherans settled. The present church, with interesting paintings, was built in the 19th century.

Next is the small town of **Seirijai**, with an Evangelical Reformed church built in the 17th century when the Electors of Brandenburg became owners of the town. The German settlers made their living by spinning and commerce. Today the town has a woollen and yarn industry and sewing workshops.

North from Seirijai, the 77 goes through forests and around the largest lakes in the region. The biggest of these is the 50 sq. mile (139 sq. km) **Lake Metelys** which has clear water going

Why do farmers seldom smile?

down to 50 ft (15 metres) and is teeming with fish. **Meteliai**, near the lake, has a 19th-century church with good interior decoration, as does the 16th-century church in nearby **Simnas**. To the north is **Lake Žuvintas**, which is 40 sq. miles (100 sq. km) and surrounded by a large **nature reserve**, a boggy area which supports more than 600 species of plants and more than 250 species of birds. A natural history museum has details of what can be seen.

Alytus is 15 miles (24 km) east of Simnas on road 76. It lies in a deep valley of the Nemunas, surrounded by dry forests and deciduous woods on the heights above and its attractive position has led to the development of good hotels and visitors' facilities. Because the ancient town straddled the river, it developed slowly. Half of it belonged to the province of Suvalkai and half to Vilnius, and in the late 19th century the Russians turned it into a frontier fortress. Today it has a population of 70,000 and up-to-date industries in building materials, machinery, textiles and food

processing. It is also the cultural centre of Dzūkija. There is a local museum, two 18th/19th century churches and a third being built. In **Vidugiris**, a forest in the southern part of the city, a monument has been erected to 35,000 Nazi victims. The bridge over the Nemunas is called after Antanas Juozapavičius, an officer killed here during the battle for independence in 1919. During World War II a French airforce squadron, Normandy-Neman, was stationed nearby.

Sūduva to Vilnius: From Alytus the 108 leads 38 miles (60 km) north to Kaunas. Just outside the town, two bridges cross the Nemunas, one going south to Druskininkai (A231) and the other east to Varėna (23), passing through a picturesque landscape and by the small town of **Daugai**, an old settlement with a stone neo-Gothic church.

The A231 north of Alytus leads to Vilnius across hilly, wooded country. After 6 miles (10 km) on the right is **Raižiai**, a small village of 100 Tatars. These Turkic-speaking Asian people began to settle in Lithuania in the 14th

Rural living.

century after serving Grand Duke Vytautas who gave them privileges.

On the opposite side of the road is **Punia**, a village built on a precipice. The impressive hill fort here, called **Margiris Mountain**, is often identified with the legendary Pilėnai, which was defended by Duke Margiris against the crusaders in 1336 until it was finally burnt, along with all who were in it when they refused to surrender. The town has a church reconstructed in the 19th century with some older sculptures. The pine forest of **Punia**, which is almost completely surrounded by a meander in the Nemunas, is a valuable **nature reserve**.

To the north, on the far side of the River Verknė, is **Jieznas**. In the 17th century this town was owned by the Pacai family who built a sumptuous palace based on the calendar, with 12 halls, 52 rooms and 365 windows. Only a few remains can be seen in the park. The church at Jieznas is a wonderful 18th-century baroque monument, with interior decoration and paintings by

Nikodemas Silvanavičius (1834–1919). The picture on the high altar of the Archangel Nicholas is a copy of a work by the Italian master Guido Reni.

To the west of Jieznas is **Birštonas**. Surrounded by forests, this 15th-century town is a holiday resort and its 3,000 population is added to by nearly 100,000 visitors a year. It became famous because of its mineral-water springs on the banks of the Nemunas. There is a park, a hill fort called **Vytautas's Mountain** and several comfortable places to stay.

From here the River Nemunas makes its longest loop, winding round 37 miles (59 km). At the far side of it stands **Prienai** where German craftsmen settled in the 18th century, establishing a cotton mill, and some of their buildings remain. There is a monument to Grand Duke Kęstutis, built in 1937, destroyed in 1954 and restored in 1989. The 18th-century wooden church is decorated by Nikodemas Silvanavičius, the town's distinguished local son, who decorated the churches at Punia and Jieznas. At nearby **Pociūnai** there is a flying club.

East from Jieznas, the A229 to Vilnius goes through some interesting places, among them Stakliškės, which has an attractive 18th-century baroque church and an old brewery where they make mead. The town used to be a resort, with mineral water sources, but it has never fully recovered from a fire which devastated it in 1857.

Further down the road is **Lapelioniai (Napoleon) Mound**, though the emperor never visited the place. Fortified settlements or castle hills are called *piliakalniai* in Lithuanian and they used to be inhabited by local people who could defend themselves against a common enemy. The word for citizen in Lithuanian, *pilietis,* comes from *pilis,* the word for castle.

Aukštadvaris, the next town, lies among lakes, and has a trout-fishing industry and agriculture school. There is also a hill fort, the remains of a manor house and an interesting church. **Strėva**, another small settlement among the lakes, is a good place for a stop. From here the road leads to the magnificent

Carving along Čiurlionis Way, representing the composer's father and mother.

castle at Trakai (*see Vilnius chapter*) and the capital.

Dzūkija's forests: The woodland of Dzūkija is often called Dainava (from *dainucti*, meaning to sing). The Dzūkai who live here are known for their cheerfulness and their great singing voices, as well as for an ability to scratch a living out of poor soil. They used to be said to have no saws, only axes; no bricks, only clay. But one saying is "A Dzūkas is a kind man – as long as he is poor."

The A231, which leads up from Warsaw via Grodno in Belorus, enters the country through the wide **Raigardas valley** of the Nemunas river. The bottom of this valley is 200 ft (60 metres) below the road and it is filled with meadows and groves and with little lakes where the river used to run. The disappearance of the town of Raigardas, swallowed by the earth and replaced by a swamp, is told in a legend. M.K. Čiurlionis used to come here, and he painted a triptych called *Raigardas*.

Čiurlionis's town: Lithuania's best known artist and composer, Mikalojus Konstantinas Čiurlionis (1875–1911), grew up in **Druskininkai**, the first main town on this road, 96 miles (150 km) south of Vilnius. It is a spa town and resort of wide boulevards and old and new villas, attracting around 100,000 people a year, many of them Poles, though visitors have dropped off since independence and smart restaurants like the Astra marble emporium are not as crowded as they once were.

The spa began in 1832 when salty mineral water was first used for treatment: the name Druskininkai comes from *druska* meaning salt. Every litre of water contains 3 grams of minerals and it arrives at the surface, both tepid and hot, from a depth of 235 ft (72 metres) There are several parks, and treatments are offered in the **Remedial Gymnastics and Climatotherapy Park**, where visitors queue up with their special cups to sample the waters in doses often prescribed by their doctors. Near the health park is a wonderful riverside walk, the **Sun Path**, which traces the Ratnyčia river for 4 miles (7 km) past carved seats

Raigardas National Reserve.

and follies inscribed with poems and sayings. At one point the river is wide and deep enough to swim.

The middle of the town has a 20th-century neo-Gothic church and nearby is a memorial to Čiurlionis. His family came here when he was three and until the age of 14 he lived in the family home in the street named after him (No. 41) to the south of the town. This timbered, single-storey house is now preserved as a museum and concerts are held around the piano in the sitting room, while the audience sits outside in the shade of the pretty garden.

Tucked in the woodlands around Druskininkai, which are abundant with mushrooms in autumn, there are some ancient farmsteads: at **Grūtas**, for example, and **Latežeris**. Upstream is **Liškiava**, a 15th-century hill fort with the remains of a castle and an 18th-century church, monastery and manor, part of which has been bought and turned into a rest home.

Merkinė, 17 miles (27 km) to the north, is at the confluence of the rivers Nemunas and Merkys. Russia's Peter I stayed here and Vladislav Vaza, the king of Poland, fell ill and died here in 1648. Though a little off the tourist track, Merkinė is worth visiting. It has a hill fort and 17th-century church which amalgamates Gothic and baroque. The local museum is in the Orthodox church where the town hall used to stand. In 1989 a memorial for the victims of Stalin was set up with wooden crosses decorated in typical Dzūkai style.

Lying just north of Merkinė, is the village of **Subartoniai**, which has a memorial museum to Vincas Krėvė-Mickievičius (1882–1954), the classical Lithuanian writer.

Forests cover the light plains on both sides of the road from Druskininkai and the route, lined with more than 20 traditional wooden sculptures, is called the **Čiurlionis Way**, for it leads 31 miles (50 km) from the family home to **Varėna**, his birthplace. The sculptures, by various local masters, were put up on the centenary of his birth, in 1975. Before Varėna, in woodland beside the **Mother and daughter.**

Merkys river, is the small town of **Perloja** (pop. 100), a place of independent-minded people. It came to fame as the Perloja Republic, which it declared itself to be in 1918, a status it stubbornly maintained for five years with a government and an armed guard of 50 men, defiant against Russians, Poles, Germans and both red and white Lithuanian factions.

In the centre of the town square is a hugely patriotic statue to Vytautas, Grand Duke of Lithuania, which was sculpted by Petras Tarabilda in 1930. The interior of the town's neo-Gothic church was painted in 1943 by professor Jerzy Hoppen and his students.

The old town of **Varėna**, also on the Merkys river, was completely burnt during World War II, and a church is now being built to mark its site. The modern town, the administrative centre of this woodland area, is 2 miles (5 km) to the south. From Varėna roads lead to the farmsteads of **Dainava** and to the **Čepkeliai Nature Reserve**.

Heading towards Vilnius, the road passes more hilly, sandy woodland and the village of **Akmuo**, with an 18th-century wooden church and separate belfry and arrives after 15 miles (25 km) at **Valkininkai**. There are signs of the town's ancient layout and a 19th-century stone church.

A little way beyond, at the resurrected village of **Pirčiupiai**, is a monument called the Sad Mother, by the sculptor Gediminas Jokūbonis. It was installed in remembrance of the village which was completely burnt, along with all its 119 inhabitants, on 3 June 1944 by the Nazis. The memorial is inscribed with each of the victims' names and the village has since been restored.

The road continues through **Paluknis**, past a sports airfield where gliders can be hired for $25–$30 an hour, on the right. Just before hitting the main Vilnius–Trakai road is the manor of the powerful local Tiškevičiai family, called Trakų Vokė, with a palace and a park designed by the French architect Eduard André. For some time the building has been used by an agricultural institute.

Left, Liškiava church, near Druskininkai. **Right**, the spa town's lake.

ZEMAITIJA AND THE COAST

The province of Žemaitija (pronounced *jam-i-tee-yer*), which includes all the coast, covers about a quarter of Lithuania and roughly corresponds with the Žemaitija Upland. Although the ancient tribes probably took their names from the places they came from, the Žemaičiai lived not in the Upland but around the mouth of the Nemunas, trading with the Aukštaičiai towards the river's source. On this coast there is also archaeological evidence of Romans and Vikings, and of Bronze-age trade with Britain and the Mediterranean.

For 200 years the Žemaičiai had a running battle with the German crusaders of the Livonian Order who had established their Baltic base in Riga, and with the Teutonic Order who harried them from the west. Between 1382 and 1404 the Dukes of Lithuania ceded Žemaitija to the Order, but in the 15th century it became a self-governing district and duchy, known in the west as Samogitia. To outsiders it long seemed a rather mysterious and wild, pagan land, an image enforced by Prosper Mérimée's novel *Lokis*, and reinforced by the modern novel *Samogitia* by the French writer Charles Pichel.

The Žemačiai maintain a strong regional dialect and keep their links with the past. Inhabited by men of few words, this is not a land of songs. Most of the countryside is rather severe, and the western slope of the Upland is windier, foggier and wetter than elsewhere. The trees are mostly firs and once-sacred oaks, and the landscape is dotted with old wooden crucifixes in roadside shrines and cemeteries. Three main arteries cross the region: the A225 goes over the top leaving the M12 at Panevėžys; from Kaunas the A228 follows the Nemunas valley to the sea; but the main highway runs between the two, from Vilnius to Klaipėda, the main town on the coast.

The Žemaičiai highway: The A227 from Vilnius via Kaunas to the coast is a breezy, uninterrupted 133 miles (214 km). It was completed in 1987 and replaced the old 159, built in 1939, which stops at all towns en route. The first of these that falls within the Žemaitija region is **Raseiniai**, 53 miles (86 km) west of Kaunas. It is an old city with a 17th-century church and abbey.

Ten miles (17 km) beyond Raseiniai is **Šiluva**, which has a beautiful church and chapel to the Virgin of Šiluva. Just to the north is **Tytuvėnai**, set around an 18th-century church and abbey which has a number of valuable paintings. The surrounding forests and lakes are popular recreational areas.

Westwards from Raseiniai the old road (159) continues 20 miles (32 km) to the A216 at Kryžkalnis. Not far from here is a sign on the road: **"Bijotai – Baubliai Museum of D. Poška"**. This local worthy lived here at the beginning of the 19th century and in 1812 he cut down a number of huge dry oaks and in their rotten insides he created a museum reflecting pagan Lithuanians' traditions of worship.

A few miles further west is **Girdiškė**

preceeding marginnote
Preceding pages: the Maritime Museum in a fishing cottage, Nida, Neringa. **Left**, the Baltic side of the shifting sands. **Right**, on holiday.

which has a church with unusual wooden altars. Just beyond it is **Upyna** which has a 19th-century wooden church and a rich country-life museum, and then **Vytogana** where the transatlantic pilot Stasys Girėnas was born. Every July on the anniversary of the fatal crash that ended his 1933 transatlantic bid, people gather at a farmstead in the village.

This is now approaching the highest point of the highway, marked with a roadside stone where it reaches 590 ft (180 metres) above sea level. There are pleasant settlements in the hills around here, such as **Kaltinėnai** on the northern side of the highway, which has cosy farmsteads and a newly rebuilt church.

Laukuva is 9 miles (15 km) further on, with a typical 19th-century stone church and square. The road north from here leads, after 11 miles (18 km), to **Varniai**, an ancient regional town with a population of 2,000. It has a wooden church and 18th-century cathedral and priest seminary. Nearby is a picturesque resort at **Lake Lūkstas**.

On the opposite side of the highway is **Šilalė**, an administrative centre with a petrol station and hotel. A more interesting detour is **Rietavas**, the next town on the right. This ancient settlement (population: 4,000) is centred around an old square. But the main attraction is the manor house and estate of the Oginskiai family. From 1812 to 1909 they ruled over their own autonomous domain, with their own laws and even their own currency. In 1835 they granted civil rights to their peasants, organised agricultural exhibitions, promoted Lithuanian culture and written language, and started publishing the Lithuanian calendar. They established a music school in the town and in 1872 mustered a famous brass band.

They helped introduce electricity and the telephone system to the town of Plungė, to the north, (*see North Žemaitija, page 365*) and it was Irenejus Oginskis who in 1951 started building the Žemaiciai highway. In 1874 a beautiful church in the Venetian style was built on their orders by the German architect Friedrich Augustus Stüler. To-

Ablinga memorial carvings.

day the manor is an agricultural college.

Back on the highway is the village named after Lithuania's great 20th-century hero, Steponas **Darius,** who was born in 1896 (*see page 338*). He left a small library on sports training and a museum has recently opened.

The road continues through 30 miles (50 km) of uninhabited forests. At **Endriejavas** there is a small lake and 4 miles (6 km) to the north is the former village of **Ablinga**. On 23 July 1941, it was totally burnt and obliterated by the Nazis, and all its 41 inhabitants with it. In recent years research has been undertaken on those who died, and large wooden sculptures have been made to portray every one of them. The next town of **Gargždai** was also completely destroyed in the war.

Klaipėda and the coast: The coastal plain, Pajuris, is 10–13 miles (15–20 km) wide and rises to around 132 ft (40 metres). The landscape is diverse: fertile clay soils, dunes, sandy forests and wet bogs. In the south is the swampy Nemunas delta and the 618-sq. mile (1,600-sq. km) and 13-ft (4-metre) deep Kuršių marios (Courland Lagoon). The coastline has urbanised resorts, around Palanga in the north, and in Neringa along the Kuršių nerija, or Courland spit, (Kurische Nehrung in German). Neringa is not actualy a town, but an adminstrative area with its capital at Nida, at the southern end of the spit. The area has many miles of empty beaches and some nature reserves.

Klaipėda is the main town on the coast, situated at the mouth of the Danė river on the Kuršių marios lagoon. It suffered heavy damage during World War II when it was used by the Germans as a submarine base. Since the 1970s when investment was ploughed into local industry, its population has dramatically grown and it now stands at around 200,000, making it the third largest city in Lithuania.

In 1252 the Livonian Order built a castle here, called Memelburg, and the city became known as Memel in German. Klaipėda otherwise finds its etymology in the words *klaips*, meaning

Art nouveau, Klaipeda.

THE AMBER COAST

There is amber everywhere in the Baltics. At any opportunity, stalls are set up to sell bargain bracelets, necklaces, earrings, keyrings and brooches of this ancient mineral, which has given its name to its golden colour. In its raw state, buffeted by tides and exposed to the elements, these are dull stones, scattered like pebbles the length of the beaches. People are always on the lookout for them, particularly after storms, though most of the amber bought today will have been dug out of the ground by excavators in Kaliningrad.

Amber is not in fact a stone, but fossilised resin of primeval pine trees. The amber deposit, dating back 40 million years, forms a seam 2–3 ft (60–90 cm) thick beneath the clay surface of the seabed. The jagged bottom of icebergs are thought to plough up the seabed and chunks of amber then become caught up in seaweed which is ripped out and dragged ashore by storms. In spring fishermen in waders used to comb the beaches with what look like large shrimping

nets to pull in flotsam that might contain amber. The Kuršių Lagoon was also a great source of it and in the 19th century Juodkrantė was known as Amber Cove: the Stantien and Becker company used to dredge up to 85 tons of it here every year.

The stone's peculiarity is that, while it was sticky resin, insects were attracted to it, and it often solidified while they were trapped by its surface. The result is that you can often hold an opaque, polished stone to the light and see flies, mosquitoes, gnats and other insects perfectly preserved inside. They intrigued the 18th-century English poet Alexander Pope, who wrote:

Pretty! in amber, to observe the forms
Of hairs, or straws, or dirt, or grubs or
worms;
The things, we know, are neither rich
nor rare,
But wonder how the devil they got there.

Amber gave the Baltics their first taste of wealth. It was a commodity with which the earliest tribes could easily trade and barter: according to Tacitus the price it fetched astonished them. It travelled far. Some has been found in the tombs of the Mycenae and the Egyptian pharoahs: Tutankhamun's treasure included an amber necklace. The Baltic shoreline was first called the Amber Coast by the ancient Greek poet Homer, who was probably thinking of the material when he described the brilliant "electron" on his warriors' shields.

The best place to see amber in the Baltics is at the Amber Museum in Palanga. A local legend tells how "Lithuanian gold" was created. There was once a queen of the Baltic named Jūrate who lived in a submarine palace made out of amber. She was to be the bride of the god of water, Patrimpas, but she fell for a mortal fisherman called Kastytis whom she visited in his hut on the banks of the Nemunas near Klaipėda at sunset every night for a year. The liaison eventually came to the attention of Perkūnas, the god of thunder, and in a rage he threw down bolts of lightning, one of which killed Jūrate and shattered her amber palace into 10,000 pieces. Perkūnas then punished Kastytis by binding him to a rock on the seabed.

Now when the west wind blows Kastytis can be heard moaning for his love, and when the wind dies down the shore is strewn with fragments of Jūrate's palace. ■

A beachcomber's dream: Lithuanian gold.

loaf of bread, and the verb *ėda* to eat. It was a Hansa port and it had a flourishing shipbuilding industry from the 18th century. Today it has a modest fishing fleet and ferries serve German and other Baltic harbours.

What is left of the old town is strung out along a couple of cobbled streets running along the left bank of the Danė, where there are some attractive bars and a floating restaurant, the three-masted *Meridianas*. There are a few remaining half-timbered (*Fachwerk*) buildings. The old post office, rebuilt with German bells in 1987, is now a concert venue. The city also has two theatres (Hitler spoke from the balcony of the one in Theatre Square), a university, and a museum devoted to the history of Lithuania Minor.

The northern coast:: 25 miles (40 km) north of Klaipėda on the A223 are the two popular resorts of **Palanga** and **Šventoji**. An old settlement of fishermen and amber-gatherers, Palanga became popular in the early 19th century when it developed as a spa and health resort. Today, it is still popular and at a sign marked "Leidimų Įsigijimas" motorists must pay a toll to drive in.

There are a number of sanatoriums still in use and the old Kurhaus, a fine wooden structure with elegant balustrades which was the resort's social centre, remains unchanged. Restaurants, cafés and ice-cream parlours serve a variety of needs, and there is altogether the bustling air of a seaside town. On summer evenings its wide boulevards are full of strolling holidaymakers, ducking into cafés or buying bottles of beer and portions of garlic toast. Most will head for the short wooden pier that projects into the sea just below the women-only bathing beach, hoping for a glimpse of the "green sky", a momentary phenomenon that sometimes lights the horizon at sundown.

The pier's builder and benefactor was Count Tiškevičius who owned the 495-acre (200-hectare) Tiškevičius Park, a formal country estate in the centre of the resort. Its large stately home houses the **Amber Museum**, and this is the best

place to see the pine-resin fossils and to learn about the story of the Amber Coast. The park, which includes Birutė's Hill where rituals were performed in pagan times, holds concerts and exhibitions throughout the summer.

A quieter resort is **Šventoji**, 12 miles (18 km) north on the A223. On the mouth of the small River Šventoji, it is also famous for its sand dunes, beach and bogs. It is mentioned on Hansa maps and it became a resort at the beginning of this century, with good places of rest and recuperation, small cottages and simple houses. Accommodation is better than at either Palanga or Klaipėda.

The Courland Spit: The spit, which is called **Kuršią Nerija** in Lithuanian, is named after the Curi who came here from Latvia. It was formed about 5,000 years ago and geologically it is the youngest part of the country. It has no rivers, a few lagoons and along its shore lies a chain of man-made beaches and dunes. A bird's eye-view is a wonderful picture of white, sandy hills against a dark blue background, and it was the sight of these extraordinary dunes that inspired the German naturalist Alexander von Humboldt to write in 1809: "Courland Spit is such a peculiar place as Italy or Spain. One must see it to give pleasure to one's soul."

Winds formed the long, narrow coastal spit no more than a mile wide and 200 ft (60 metres) high. It runs 60 miles (98 km) from just north of Klaipėda down to Kaliningrad; 32 miles (51 km) of it are in Lithuania. The lagoon on the inland side is formed by the mouth of the Nemunas.

On the tip of the the spit opposite Klaipėda is **Smiltynė**, reached by regular ferries from the port. This is a popular spot, centred on **Kopgalis Castle** where seals glide round the moat. This is a **marine world** and **sea museum** and dolphins give regular shows. Nearby is Klaipėda Yacht Club where members sailed the Atlantic in 1989 as part of the Columbus celebrations, and every June a traditional sea festival takes place.

But most of the peninsula lies to the south, where tourist traffic is curtailed **Making a splash in a safe sea.**

by a toll. All the little villages along here face the lagoon: until 1992, the white sandy coast, now deserted, was occupied by the Soviet army. **Juodkrantė** is a typical fishing village with 15 old houses and a harbour once known as Amber Cove because of the amount of the material that was dredged up for the local industry.

Shifting sands have meant many of the villages have constantly been on the move. During the 18th and 19th centuries more than a dozen were affected, some of them covered over by sand. **Pervalka** and **Preila** are typical shoreside communities. Raganų Kalnas, **Witches' Hill**, is a sculpture park filled with fabled figures, such as the main pagan god, Perkūnas, and Neringa, a local girl who became a giant and helped sailors in trouble.

At the southern end of the spit, just before the border with Russian Kaliningrad, is **Nida**, which has moved several times to escape the mobile sand. This is the largest of the resorts (pop. 1,500, rising to more than 10,000 in summer),

with the best facilities, and the sunniest and most famous place on the Lithuanian part of the peninsula.

It has a distinctive landscape, created by the wind and the sea. White sand dunes stretch away like a desert to the south, and trunks of trees show where ancient forests once flourished. The town has a statue to David Gotlieb Kuvert, who first began plantations to protect the dunes. In an old fisherman's cottage is a **museum of fishermen's life** and the house where Thomas Mann lived from 1930 to 1932 can be visited.

The Nemunas delta: From Klaipėda the A228 runs southeast through **Šilutė** and **Pagėgiai**, following the north bank of the Nemunas all the way to Kaunas. From the typical small town of **Priekulė** the 221 goes south, past the fishing village of **Kintau** and ending at the tip of the **Ventės Ragas peninsula**, marked by a lighthouse built in 1863. The main reason for coming to this backwater is the wildlife. An important **bird ringing station**, which keeps track of the many coastal migrants, has been operating

The Neringa Spit's extraordinary sands.

here since 1929. Some 8 miles (12 km) east of the A228, beyond **Saugos** on the 183, is the small town of **Švėkšna**. Its impressive neo-Gothic church contains valuable paintings and it has a memorial park and mansion now used as a college. A mile (2 km) outside town is another manor with a park, at **Vilkėnas**.

From Saugos the A228 falls down into the Nemunas delta plain, passing through **Šilutė** on the River Šyša. A town with a population of 2,000 and good tourist services, it was until 1923 called Heyde Krug. In the 17th century there was just one inn in the area, run by Richard Kant, grandfather of the philosopher. There is also a memorial museum to the German dramatist and novelist Hermann Sudermann, who was born in the former manor house of Macikai in 1857. In World War II there was a concentration camp in Macikai, and up until 1954 it was was used by the KGB for imprisoning Lithuanians.

Just west of Šilutė in the Nemunas delta is the 17 sq. mile (45 sq. km) **island of Rusnė** which rises just 5 ft

(1.5 metres) above sea level. It has a community of around 3,000 who earn a living by fishing and cattle breeding.

The next town of any size on the A228 is **Pagėgiai**, 22 miles (38 km) beyond Šilutė. During World War II, in the forest to the west behind a tangle of barbed-wire, the Germans kept prisoners of war under the open sky: 10,000 of them died. The ground is very hilly because the prisoners tried to bury themselves to escape the cold.

From Pagėgiai the A216 goes 20 miles (32 km) northeast to the turn-off to **Tauragė**, which gave its name to the Tauragė Convention, signed in 1812 between General Yorch for Prussia and General Diebitsch for Russia in Požėronys mill, and a monument records the event.

Back on the A228, just beyond the turn-off to Tauragė, is **Bitėnia** where the Lithuanian enlightener Martynas Jankus (1858–1946) was born, lived and worked. He made a notable contribution when there was a ban on printing Lithuanian books. In 1991, the remains

of Lithuania Minor's great philosopher, Vydunas, were brought back from Germany and re-buried here.

The next village is **Vilkyšiai**, set on a high point. There are a few hill forts just to the south. In the 18th century, after an outbreak of the plague in Europe, a number of Scots and Austrians from Salzburg settled in Vilkyšiai, but the surviving characteristic buildings from that time are rather neglected.

At **Viešvilė** on a river of the same name there is a water mill, pond, park and manor house, and in the past it had a wood trade. The road and river then close around **Smalininka**, where there was once a port for river traffic. The river's oldest hydrometric station still functions here. Six miles (10 km) further on is **Jurbarkas**, which has a hotel. The road follows the river another 54 miles (86 km) to Kaunas.

North Žemaitija: The northern part of Žemaitija can be explored around the A225 which runs 85 miles (137 km) from **Kretinga** near Palanga on the coast, to Šiauliai, 99 miles (159 km) north of Kaunas. Industrial Kretinga has many 18th-century buildings including a Catholic church and Minorite abbey. There are interesting chapels in the cemetery, a watermill and a manor house in a park still in good repair. In the 19th century this was cultivated by the Tiškevičiai family who built up a valuable art collection and were substantial benefactors to the town. There is a museum of local folklore.

Between Kretinga and the next main town of **Plungė** is **Kartena** in the beautiful valley of the Minij. It has a 19th-century wooden church and an 18th-century inn. Plungė is a little larger than Kretinga and a centre of light industry and administration, with a long tradition of folk-art. It became rich after the Oginskiai family arrived to buy up the local manor. They enlarged and cultivated the 18th-century "Thunder Oak" park and in 1879 entrusted the architect Karl Lorens with the building of a neo-Renaissance palace imitating the 15th-century Palazzo Vecchio in Florence. In 1889 they also sponsored the education

Dead wood in the Kuršių.

of the great Lithuanian painter and musician M. K. Čiurlionis.

To the north, on the 226, is **Salantai,** a typical Žemaitija town famous for its historical layout, neo-Gothic church and park. Nearby is the **Museum of Nonsense** at the **Orvidai farmhouse**, though overseas visitors are charged a high entry price. All around this area are roadside shrines, wooden sculptures mounted on crosses and on roofed poles.

Mosėdis, 8 miles (12 km) north of Salantai on the 101, is a curious town dominated by the enthusiasm of a local doctor, Vaclovas Intas. He has spent his life collecting boulders and stones. They line the road leading past the 17th-century church to his house, where there is a sunken stone garden and rockery. All shapes and sizes, the boulders lie everywhere around the town, and some huge ones are scattered over the garden at the back of an attractive watermill which is a restaurant and hotel.

Due east of **Salantai** is **Plateliai**, the heart of the **Žemaitija National Park**. Though 480 ft (146 metres) above sea level, there is a large lake beside it: Lake Plateliai is nearly 5 sq. miles (12 sq. km) around and 150 ft (46 metres) deep and it has seven islands. There are boating facilities on its its western side near the town, where there is an 18th-century wooden church and a ruined manor. The owners of the manor were French, called Choiseul de Gouffier, and some of their heritage is in Alka Museum in Telšiai. Other attractive small towns in this region, which is rich with festivals and calendar customs, include **Žemaičiu**, **Kalvarija**, **Alsėdžiai** and **Seda**.

Telšiai is an industrial town with a population of 30,000, but before the war it was an important religious and cultural centre with a bishop's see and seminaries for priest and Jewish teachers. It still has a school of applied art and the **Alka Museum of Žemaitija Culture**. The 18th- to 19th-century classical cathedral, where a number of well-known Lithuanians are buried, was designed by Fulgent Rimgaila a century after the Bernardine abbey was built.

On the southeast of the town is **Rainiai forest** where 73 people were executed by the KGB in 1941; 50 years later a chapel was built in their remembrance. East from here is **Luokė**, famous for its folklore festivals, and **Lake Germantas**, where there are holiday facilities and an airfield for pleasure flights.

Place of pilgrimage: There is little reason to stop between here and **Šiauliai**, Lithuania's fourth largest town. This is an industrial centre, of shoes, textiles and, notably, bicycles and there is a **Bicycle Museum**. There is a also a museum of photography and radio. To the south are picturesque hills and lakes around **Bubiai** and **Kurtuvenai**.

But Šiauliai is most famous for the **Hill of Crosses**, which lies in the countryside about 9 miles (14 km) to the northeast on the A216. Nobody is sure of its origins, but for centuries it has been a religious site. People come from all over the world to add their crosses to the thousands already here. The hill itself is only a small hump and it used to be much larger. This is because the Soviets bulldozed it three times. Each time the crosses reappeared.

Left, street corner, Šiauliai. **Right**, the Hill of Crosses just to the north of the city. **Overpage:** Dundaga Castle in Latvia.

TRAVEL TIPS

GETTING THERE

GENERAL INFORMATION

The three Baltic States offer a variety of entry points, by land sea and air, and the kind of a journey may depend on where the visitor is coming from. None of the capitals is far from the others, and it is possible to travel from one to another by public transport in a day, overnight, or in a brief flight. Flights into the countries from outside are becoming increasing accessible and cheap, but they still present a bewildering variety of choices and price structures. It is essential to shop around, and inquiries should involve information about changing from regular carriers to local carriers within sight of the destination.

A major deterrent to the would-be road traveller has been the bottleneck at the Polish-Lithuanian border crossing at Lazdijai, which most people travel through to get to the Baltics from the West. Customs inspection is selective, and those who refuse to pay bribes sometimes end up waiting several days to get through. A nightmare for tourists. The opening of another Polish-Lithuanian post at Kalvarija may ease the traffic at Lazdijai. Otherwise one can take a detour through Belarus (which may require a visa). Customs between the Baltic States themselves also produce long queues as they insist on stamping passports.

Anyone contemplating travelling to the Baltic States through Russia, including the enclave of Kaliningrad in the south, is advised to apply for a visa three months in advance.

TOUR OPERATORS

These offer a relatively stress-free alternative to independent travel, and may help getting to places where language may be a problem. The following agents all have experience in arranging travel to the Baltics.

AUSTRALIA
Baltic Travel, Box 108 Rundle Mall, Adelaide, SA5000.

CANADA
Pedersen World Tours Inc, Park Place Corporate Centre, 15 Wertheim Court, Suite 402, Richmond Hill, Toronto. Tel: 416-882 5470, fax: 416-882 5472.

DENMARK
Pedersen World Tours, H.C. Andersens Boulevard 12, Copenhagen. Tel: 33-93 86 87, fax: 33-93 44 20.

FINLAND
Tallink, Eteläranta 14, 00130 Helsinki. Tel: 602 822, 635 822.

FRANCE
Baltica Voyages, 24 Rue du Quatre Septembre, Paris 75002. Tel: 147-42 58 58, fax: 142-65 18 01.

GERMANY
Baltisches Reisebüro, Bayerstr. 37, 8000 München 2. Tel: 89-59 36 94, fax: 89-52 59 13.
Greif Reisen/Rossgärtner Tours GmbH, Universitätsstr. 2, 5810 Witten. Tel: 02302/24044, fax: 02302/25050
Hein Reisen, Zwergerstr. 1, 8014 Neubiberg/München. Tel: 089-637 39 84, fax: 089-679 28 12.
Intourist Reisen GmbH, Kurfürstendamm 63, 1000 Berlin 63. Tel: 30-88 00 70, fax: 30-88 00 71 26.
Ost Reise Service/Fachreisebüro für Ost-Touristik, Artur Landeck str. 139, 4800 Bielefeld. Tel: 521-14 21 67/8, fax: 521-15 25 55.
Rautenberg Reisen, Blinke 8, Postfach 1909, 2950 Leer. Tel: 0491/4288.
Schnieder Reisen, Harkortstr. 121, 2000 Hamburg 50. Tel: 40-38 02 06 71, fax: 40-38 02 06 88.

GREAT BRITAIN
Gunnel Travel Service, Stratford St Mary, Colchester, Essex, CO7 6JW. Tel/fax: 0206-322 352.
Intourist, 219 Marsh Wall, London E14. Tel: 071-538 3202.
Martin Randall Travel. Tel: 081-994 6477. Art and architecture tours.
Regent Holidays UK Ltd, 5 John Street, Bristol BS1 2HR. Tel: 0272 211 711, fax: 0272 254 866. Individual and group tours.
Swan Hellenic, 77 New Oxford Street, London WC1A 1PP. Tel: 071-831 1616. Art treasure tours of the three capitals plus St Petersburg.
Trailfinders, 47-50 Earls Court Road, London W8 6EJ. Tel: 071-937 5400.

UNITED STATES
Union Tours, 79 Madison Avenue, New York, NY. Tel 212-683 9500, fax: 212-683 9511. Baltic specialists of long standing, Union Tours offers both group tours and individual itineraries.
Academic Travel Abroad, Washington, DC. Tel: 202-333 3535, fax: 202-342 0317. Special interest groups.
American Express, Norcross, Georgia. Tel: 404-368 5202, fax: 404-368 5391. Escorted tours.
American Travel Service, 9439 S. Kedzie Avenue, Evergreen Park, Chicago, ILL. Tel: 708-422 3000, fax: 708-422 3163. Tours and individual itineraries.
Baltic Tours: 77 Oak Street, Newton, MA02164. Tel: 617-965 8080.
General Tours, 245 Fifth Avenue, New York, NY. Tel: 212-685 1800, fax: 212-685 2011. Escorted tours.
ITS Tours and Travel, College Station, Texas. Tel: 409-764 9400, fax: 409-693 9673. Tours and individual itineraries.

UNIONTOURS

B E S T T O T H E B A L T I C S

INDIVIDUAL AND GROUP TRAVEL ARRANGEMENTS

INSIGHT GUIDES

COLORSET NUMBERS

160 Alaska	135F Düsseldorf	158 Netherlands
155 Alsace	204 East African	100 New England
150 Amazon Wildlife	Wildlife,	184E New Orleans
116 America, South	149 Eastern Europe,	184F New York City
173 American Southwest	118 Ecuador	133 New York State
158A Amsterdam	148A Edinburgh	293 New Zealand
260 Argentina	268 Egypt	265 Nile, The
287 Asia, East	123 Finland	120 Norway
207 Asia, South	209B Florence	124B Oxford
262 Asia, South East	243 Florida	147 Pacific Northwest
194 Asian Wildlife,	154 France	205 Pakistan
Southeast	135C Frankfurt	154A Paris
167A Athens	208 Gambia & Senegal	249 Peru
272 Australia	135 Germany	184B Philadelphia
263 Austria	148B Glasgow	222 Philippines
188 Bahamas	279 Gran Canaria	115 Poland
206 Bali Baru	169 Great Barrier Reef	202 Portugal
107 Baltic States	124 Great Britain	114A Prague
246A Bangkok	167 Greece	153 Provence
292 Barbados	166 Greek Islands	156 Puerto Rico
219B Barcelona	135G Hamburg	250 Rajasthan
187 Bay of Naples	240 Hawaii	177 Rhine
234A Beijing	193 Himalaya, Western	127A Rio de Janeiro
109 Belgium	196 Hong Kong	172 Rockies
135A Berlin	144 Hungary	209A Rome
217 Bermuda	256 Iceland	101 Russia
100A Boston	247 India	275B San Francisco
127 Brazil	212 India, South	130 Sardinia
178 Brittany	128 Indian Wildlife	148 Scotland
109A Brussels	143 Indonesia	184D Seattle
144A Budapest	142 Ireland	261 Sicily
260A Buenos Aires	252 Israel	159 Singapore
213 Burgundy	236A Istanbul	257 South Africa
268A Cairo	209 Italy	264 South Tyrol
247B Calcutta	213 Jamaica	219 Spain
275 California	278 Japan	220 Spain, Southern
180 California,	266 Java	105 Sri Lanka
Northern	252A Jerusalem-Tel Aviv	101B St Petersburg
161 California,	203A Kathmandu	170 Sweden
Southern	270 Kenya	232 Switzerland
237 Canada	300 Korea	272 Sydney
162 Caribbean	202A Lisbon	175 Taiwan
The Lesser Antilles	258 Loire Valley	112 Tenerife
122 Catalonia	124A London	186 Texas
(Costa Brava)	275A Los Angeles	246 Thailand
141 Channel Islands	201 Madeira	278A Tokyo
184C Chicago	219A Madrid	139 Trinidad & Tobago
151 Chile	145 Malaysia	113 Tunisia
234 China	157 Mallorca & Ibiza	236 Turkey
135E Cologne	117 Malta	171 Turkish Coast
119 Continental Europe	272B Melbourne	210 Tuscany
189 Corsica	285 Mexico	174 Umbria
281 Costa Rica	285A Mexico City	237A Vancouver
291 Cote d'Azur	243A Miami	198 Venezuela
165 Crete	237B Montreal	209C Venice
184 Crossing America	235 Morocco	263A Vienna
226 Cyprus	101A Moscow	255 Vietnam
114 Czechoslovakia	135D Munich	267 Wales
247A Delhi, Jaipur, Agra	211 Myanmar (Burma)	184C Washington DC
238 Denmark	259 Namibia	183 Waterways
135B Dresden	269 Native America	of Europe
142B Dublin	203 Nepal	215 Yemen

You'll find the colorset number on the spine of each Insight Guide.

GETTING TO ESTONIA BY AIR

Estonia's international airport (*lennujaam*) is on the outskirts of Tallinn by the shores of Lake Ülemiste. It was built during the boom that came with the 1980 Moscow Olympics when Tallinn was the venue for the yachting events. The terminal is relatively clean and offers the usual facilities including car hire, post office, cash exchange and an information desk. Three international carriers, Lufthansa, FinnAir and SAS, along with the state airline, Estonian Air, currently fly out of Tallinn. If travelling with an airline other than these it is most convenient to fly to Helsinki from where it is just a 30-minute flight on to Tallinn and connections are frequent. Alternatively, a ferry may be taken from Helsinki. It is possible to get cut-rate airfares to Tallinn, so check with a travel agency before booking any flight.

From the airport: If your baggage isn't too cumbersome ignore the predatory taxis on the airport forecourt and take a bus instead. The forecourt is a terminus for bus 22 which arrives every 20 minutes. It is a 10-minute ride down into the Old Town. The bus stops at the radio building, the Estonia Theatre, Vabaduse väljak, the Hotel Tallinn and the railway station. Carriers phone numbers in Tallinn are:

Estonian Air (to Helsinki, Stockholm, Frankfurt, Copenhagen, Moscow, Kiev, St Petersburg, Riga, Vilnius, Minsk): Tel: 446 382.
Finnair (via Helsinki): Tel: 683 771/423 538.
Lufthansa (via Frankfurt): Tel: 215 557/444 037.
SAS (via Stockholm): Tel: 212 553/455 610, fax: 210 354.

BY SEA

A flotilla of all shapes and sizes eases in and out of the harbour at Tallinn ferrying passengers by various routes across the Baltic. From Helsinki passage can be taken at almost any hour of the day. There are several hydrofoils making early morning crossings with a journey time of between one and two hours depending on the particular craft and the weather. *M/S Jaanika, Liisa* and *Monica,* owned by the Estonian New Line, all cross daily between 9am and 11am. Two more crossings are made later in the day. Two other hydrofoils, the *M/S Sinilind* and *Luik,* owned by Helta, also make three crossings a day between them. Three larger ships take a more leisurely 3½ hours to cross each day, but offer restaurants, bars, videos and cabins to help pass the time. Of these *M/S St Patric II* and *M/S Tallink* are owned by the company Tallink and *M/S Linda* (Corbiere) is owned by the Estonian New Line. Estline operates the *m/s Nord Estonia,* a similar kind of vessel that sails every second day from Stockholm to Tallinn. If you are planning to sail from Sweden then you may want to consider as a cheaper alternative sailing to Helsinki and picking up the

ferry from there. Two lines, Silja and the Viking line, operate the Stockholm-Helsinki route. Tickets bought in Finland are subject to a travel tax of 30 Finnish marks and so it is wise to book in Tallinn.

From the harbour: The harbour (*sadam*) is 15 minutes' walk from the Old Town. On trams 1 or 2 it is the next stop after Viru väljak, or from the opposite direction, two stops from the railway station. Estonian New Line operates courtesy buses to the major hotels for its passengers on Linda.
Estline: in Stockholm, Tallinnterminalen, Frihamm, 115 56 Stockholm. Tel: 8-667 0001/8-613 1950, fax: 8-660 7439. Booking office in Tallinn, Aia 5a. Tel: 666 579/443 524.
Tallink: in Helsinki. Tel: 602 822/635 822, fax: 635 811, telex: 126 102. Booking office in Tallinn, Pärnu mnt. 16. Tel: 442 440/666 379.
Helta: in Helsinki, Etäläranta 7, the harbour. Tel: 664 141. In Tallinn, the harbour. Tel: 428 701.
Estonian New Line (Inreko): in Helsinki, Yrjönkatu 23A2. Tel: 680 2499. In Tallinn, the harbour building. Tel: 428 382.
Viking Line: Bookings through Estravel Ltd, Pikk 37, Old Town, Tallinn. Tel: 601 886.
Silja: 1st floor, Teenindusmaja, Viru väljak, Tallinn. Tel: 430 663.

BY RAIL

There is a twice-daily train from St Petersburg, which is preferable to the bus. The overnight train from Riga has four bunks to a compartment (pay for all four if you want peace and quiet) and is preferable to the bus, though you don't get the view.

BY ROAD

Entering by car one gets a sense of just how seriously Estonia takes the idea of being seen to be a separate country. Elsewhere in Europe borders are coming down but in the Baltics they are being enforced with a vengeance. Coming from Latvia the wayward notion of the Baltics as a single unit is painfully dispelled by a lengthy wait in no-man's land before a heavily guarded border installation. By comparison the main Russian-Estonian border at Narva is almost convivial; a high bridge spans the River Narva and the Russians stand at one end, the Estonians at the other. You can probably stroll over the bridge without a visa but almost every vehicle receives a cursory search, making the crossing a slow one. Public transport may be used to enter Estonia. There is a weekly coach to Tallinn from Warsaw, via Riga, and there is a daily bus from St Petersburg. The St Petersburg bus is not particularly recommended as the border is reached in the early hours of the morning and everyone must disembark to complete immigration formalities.

GETTING TO LATVIA BY AIR

Flying is by far the most convenient, but also the most expensive way to get to the Baltics. There are direct flights with SAS from Helsinki, Stockholm and Copenhagen to Riga. Lufthansa, Hamburg Airlines and Baltic International Airlines have regular flights from Germany (Frankfurt, Dusseldorf, Hamburg or Munich). CSA has a Riga–Prague line. Latvian Airlines flies from Stockholm, Copenhagen, Helsinki, Frankfurt, Düsseldorf and Vienna. Finnair has flights from Helsinki. Travellers arriving from other countries can transfer to the above European cities and then on to Riga. (Riga Airport address: Skulte, Riga, LV 1026. Tel: 207 009, fax: 348 654.)

Riga airport has an information booth on the ground floor and is open 24 hours a day. Various cafés and bars are open from 7am–11 pm and a hard-currency bar is on the second floor of the international terminal. Convertible currencies can be exchanged from 9am–7pm on the ground floor where newsstands and kiosks are open 7am–5pm. Hertz car rental is open Monday–Friday 10am–7pm, Saturday 10am–2pm, Sunday 9am–2pm. Tel: 207 131. The duty-free shop in the international terminal operates from 8am–6pm. Baggage can be stored 24 hours a day on the ground floor. Local phone calls can be made from any public phone. They need a special token, which can be bought at any of the airport's many kiosks. There is also a mobile telephone station. The airport hotel is located only a few minutes away. For reservations, tel: 207 149.

From the airport: Riga airport is a 30-minute ride from the centre of the city on the 22 bus. Public transport tickets can be purchased at kiosks. Although taxis cost 20LVR (about 50 sentīms) per kilometre and the official rate should be just over 1 lats, you will most likely be asked to pay in hard currency, regardless of whether or not you are a native Rigan. Drivers have been known to ask as much as $100 for a ride into town. However, you should be able to get by with less than $20. Always negotiate the price with the driver before getting into the cab.

Baltic International Airlines (BIA) (For Dusseldorf, Frankfurt, Munich): 4 Pils laukums, Riga. Tel: 212 460/327 296, fax: 35 849 348 676. Weekdays 9.30am–6pm.

CSA (For Prague): Riga Airport, 2nd floor. Tel: 207 636/207 337. Monday and Wednesday 7am–2pm, Tuesday 2pm–8pm, Thursday and Friday 10am–4pm, Saturday 10am–2pm, Sunday 2–8pm.

Finnair (FA) (For Helsinki): Riga Airport, 2nd floor. Tel: 207 010. Weekdays 9am–5pm.

Latvian Airlines (LA) (For Helsinki, Copenhagen, Stockholm and Vienna): 54 Brīvības iela. Tel: 207272. Weekdays 8.30am–6.30pm.

Lufthansa (LH) (For Frankfurt): Riga Airport, 2nd floor. Tel: 207 183. Weekdays: 10am–5pm, weekends: noon–5pm.

SAS (For Stockholm): Riga Airport, 2nd floor. Tel: 207 055. Monday–Saturday 10am–5pm.

Latvian Airlines and Baltic International Airlines Ticketing: 54 Brīvības iela. Tel: 207 272.

BY SEA

A regular service runs between Riga and Sweden, weekly from Stockholm, and more frequently from Norrköping, taking just over a day and a half. There is also a weekly service to Kiel in Germany, which also takes about 41 hours. Boats are less expensive than flying but prices vary, depending on the on-board accommodation.

Baltic Tour Riga (for Sweden): Riga Passenger Terminal, 1a Eksporta iela, Riga, LV 1080. Tel: 329 514.

Latvia Tours (for Kiel): 25 Peldu iela, Riga. Tel: 227 349.

BY RAIL

The Berlin–St Petersburg line, which passes through Riga, is the most common route used from the West to get to Latvia. Reserve tickets in advance. Previously, it was necessary for Westerners to get an expensive transit visa for the short trip through Belarus. The visa can now be obtained at the border for $20.

Riga Central Railway Station: Tel: 007 or 232 122.

BY ROAD

Customs posts between Estonia and Lithuania should present no problems to visitors, and the roads are generally good. High-grade petrol is not always available outside Riga, and petrol is leaded. Road-side hotels and rest stops are a rarity outside the larger cities. Although good road maps can now be bought, try to get one before you enter the country. The speed limit on highways is 55 mph (90 kph), 35 mph (60 kph) in residential areas. Seat belts must be worn by front-seat passengers who must be no less than 12 years of age. The driving age is 18.

A Helsinki-Warsaw-Helsinki coach passes through Riga three days a week. The vehicles are made in the West and are equipped with toilet facilities. There are also daily bus routes from Lithuania and Estonia.

Riga bus station: Prāgas iela. Tel: 213 611.

GETTING TO LITHUANIA BY AIR

Vilnius has frequent direct flights to some nine major European cities: Berlin, Budapest, Copenhagen, Frankfurt, Hamburg, London, Vienna, Warsaw and Zürich. (Paris and Amsterdam should be added shortly.) Lithuanian Airlines also serves major eastbound directions with daily flights to Moscow and frequent flights to Kiev and St Petersburg. The

following airlines now serve the Lithuanian capital:
Austrian Airlines, SAS and **Swissair**: Airport 1st floor. Tel: 66 20 00/66 02 02, fax: 66 01 39.
Lietuvos Avialinijos (Lithuanian Airlines): Ukmerges str. 12. Tel: 75 25 88/75 32 12, fax: 35 48 52.
LOT (Polish Airlines): c/o Hotel Skrydis, room 104. Tel: 63 01 95.
Lufthansa: Airport 1st floor. Tel: 63 60 49/63 76 99.
Malev (Hungarian Airlines): c/o Hotel Skrydis, room 103. Tel: 63 08 10, fax: 26 68 23.
For **Estonian Airlines** and **Hamburg Airlines** enquire at the Lithuanian Airlines office: Airport ground floor. Tel: 63 01 16/63 78 17.

BY SEA

Two ferry lines link the Lithuanian port of Klaipėda to Germany. The boat-trips across the Baltic Sea last more than a day but save the ride across Poland. Book at least one month in advance.
Klaipėda–Kiel (30 hrs). *Mercury I* runs weekly and is operated by the German travel agency Schnieder Reisen, Harkortstr. 121, 2000 Hamburg 50. Tel: 40-38 02 06 71. Information in Klaipėda: Tel: (261) 57 849, fax: (261) 53 466. Advance booking in Klaipėda: Tel. (261) 55 549.
Klaipėda–Mukran (16 hrs). Departs every two days but has very limited passenger capacity. Information: Tel: (261) 17 825. Advance booking: Tel: (261) 99 936, fax: (261) 16 681.

BY RAIL

Direct rail links from Vilnius to Warsaw still go through Belarus and Belorussian border guards require a transit visa to cross their country.
The European standard railway line from Sestokai (Lithuania) to Suwalki (Poland) has been reopened after being closed for 47 years allowing direct daily connections from Vilnius to Warsaw with change of trains in the two villages.

BY ROAD

The entry into Lithuania by car is the most difficult approach because the Lithuanian-Polish border crossing of Lazdijai/Grodnicki tends to be jammed by local traders and dealers. Over-zealous customs officials on both sides still work according to the Soviet pace of one car every half hour. A second border crossing has been opened for lorries at Kalvaria. As it is becoming more and more difficult to bribe one's way into the country, it is advisable to possess an official letter from the Polish and Lithuanian authorities to pass the first checkpoints.
By bus: Daily coaches circulate between Warsaw, Gdańsk and Bialystok as well as Riga and Tallinn to Vilnius.

TRAVEL ESSENTIALS

VISAS & PASSPORTS

ESTONIA

Citizens of Great Britain, Bulgaria, the Czech and Slovak Republics, Hungary and Poland do not need a visa to visit Estonia. Citizens of the United States, although they must have a visa, are exempt from the cost. Theoretically, anyone may enter Estonia but there are easy ways of doing it and then there are the other ways. The easiest and surest way is to obtain your visa from an Estonia embassy or consulate in your own country before travelling. The visa costs US$10 and invitations are no longer required. However, individuals arriving without an invitation must show that they have sufficient funds for their stay – the minimum is US$8, or its equivalent in other currencies, per day of your visa (a strange figure really, because $8 is not going to get you a room in any hotel in Tallinn). Invitations are necessary for stays of over six weeks. An invitation may be issued by any legal citizen or institution of Estonia. For longer stays you must also take an AIDS test. An Estonian visa is also good for stays of up to 30 days in Latvia and Lithuania. Once in Estonia visas can be extended at the immigration office at Lai 38-40 in the Old Town, Tallinn.

LATVIA

Valid passports are required but visas are no longer needed for citizens of Great Britain, Denmark, Hungary and Poland. Those who do need them can obtain them at the border, but it is better to get them at Latvian representations abroad in order to save time and money. A Latvian visa is also good for stays in Estonia and Lithuania.

LITHUANIA

Entry to Lithuania requires a valid passport and citizens of Great Britain, Hungary, Poland and Denmark are exempt from visa requirements. Others need to buy a visa via any Lithuanian representation abroad, though they can also get one directly at the border or the airport in Vilnius. A Lithuanian visa is also good for stays in Estonia and Latvia.

ESTONIA

Individuals entering and leaving Estonia are permitted to carry with them most articles, personal property and other valuables in unlimited quantities with some notable, and occasionally odd, exceptions. Not permitted are weapons and ammunition of any kind, drugs and pyschotropic substances, poisonous substances, hormone preparations and preparations of blood, animals and plants, military badges and insignia, paper currency withdrawn from circulation and postage stamps. The last two require written permission from the Ministry of Culture. Blood and hormones need permission from the Ministry of Health.

Import and export of tobacco and alcohol is limited, for persons over 21, to 1 litre of spirits, 1 litre of wine, 10 litres of beer and 200 cigarettes or 20 cigars or 250g of tobacco. For persons aged 18 to 21 the limits are the same but no spirits are allowed and instead the wine allowance is increased to 2 litres. Persons under 18 may only have cigarettes, cigars or tobacco.

LATVIA

Customs is generally trouble-free when travelling into the country. Leaving can be just as simple, but there have been cases of tourists coming across rigorous customs agents who insist on going through your belongings with a fine-tooth comb until they find something to "confiscate".

Private persons may bring in unrestricted hard currency, up to 1 litre of alcohol and 200 cigarettes. Foodstuffs may not have a total value exceeding one subsistence minimum monthly salary, set by the Council of Ministers of Latvia (currently it is 15 lats). Any articles that are not prohibited or restricted (*see below*) can be brought in as long as their total value does not exceed 15 minimum monthly salaries (22.5 lats, or approximately $250 at current exchange rates). People must fill out customs declarations upon entering and leaving Latvia if they are carrying items which they consider declarable.

Private persons may export duty-free foodstuffs or other articles, as long as there are no more than three pieces of each type, and as long as their total value does not exceed 10 minimum monthly salaries. Any amount of hard currency can be taken out, as well as all articles (including cultural objects, works of art, handicraft, etc.) purchased in Latvia for hard currency, providing that the purchase receipts are shown at the border. Items deemed to be of cultural or historical value may be brought out of the country only according to the regulations set by the Ministry of Culture.

It is prohibited to import or export the following items without special permission: firearms and their components, ammunition explosives and other weapons; dangerous chemical substances and appliances for their use (except tear gas pistols and canisters); narcotic and psycho-active substances and appliances for their use; pornographic materials.

Further information: Customs Department of the Finance Ministry of the Republic of Latvia, 1a Kr. Valdemara iela, Riga. Fax: 322 440, tel: 226 246 (information); 320 928 (duty person).

LITHUANIA

Lithuanian customs regulations are constantly changing and do not correspond to Western standards. You can bring to Lithuania duty free: 1 litre of alcohol, spirits or liqueurs or 2 litres of champagne. A 100 percent of customs tax is levied on every extra bottle. An unlimited amount of cigarettes may be brought in. Although any amount of currency may be imported, it is advised to fill in the customs declaration on entry stating the amount of currency and any valuables you carry with you. Although it will not be checked on leaving the country, you avoid any complications.

Export regulations are constantly changing. For the moment basic foodstuffs such as sugar, salt, meat are subject to limitation. Export is duty free for cigarettes and alcohol as long as the total value does not exceed the equivalent of two minimum salaries. (This amounts approximately to 2½ litres of vodka yet the Polish customs allow only the import of 1 litre of vodka.) A 100 percent customs duty is levied for every bottle exceeding this amount. Art works less than 40 years old are duty free: art works over 40 years old need a permit from the Cultural Heritage Inspector who will evaluate it and tax it with a 200 percent duty.

Further information: Customs Department, tel: 61 30 27/22 22 65.

HEALTH

Unless you have a specific health problem you are just as safe in the Baltic States as anywhere in Western Europe. The water in some places may taste funny but is perfectly fine. In Riga, Latvia, however drinking unboiled water can be risky. Some of the food may look suspect, if so, don't eat it – there is enough decent food around that you won't have any trouble finding better. If, however, you are particularly susceptible to upset stomachs, suffer from migraines or fall prey easily to any other ailment, then take along any medication you might require. Even basic drugs such as painkillers can be difficult to find. If you are here during summer bring something effective against mosquito bites.

No vaccinations are compulsory, but a hepatitis A injection is advisable. Anyone camping or spending some time in the countryside should consider a vaccination for tick-borne encephalytus, which requires a course of injections over some weeks.

ESTONIA

The official currency of Estonia is the Estonian kroon (abbreviated to EEK and pronounced *krone*). The notes are printed in the denominations 1, 2, 5, 10, 25, 100 and 500. Coins are minted at the values of 5, 10, 20 and 50 sents with one hundred sents to the kroon. US$1 is equivalent to around 13 kroons. All transactions within Estonia must be made in kroons. Trading in any other currency, the Russian rouble and US dollar included, is illegal.

Exchange points exist at the harbour, the airport, all the major hotels, the central post office, the department store and in numerous other locations. Exchange rates are set by the Bank of Estonia and are posted daily. A commission of around 2 percent is generally charged on all transactions. Changing money on the blackmarket is a punishable offence.

Although many outlets claim to cash travellers' cheques, in practice the cashier will often refuse. Your chances seem to be slightly improved if your travellers' cheques are issued by American Express. Except at the larger hotels and their associated restaurants, credit cards are not widely accepted.

LATVIA

In 1993 the lats replaced the Latvian rouble (LVR). The rate of the Latvian rouble was one for one against the Russian rouble, but in six months after its inception in 1990, the rate of the Russian rouble fell to about 50 percent of the Latvian rouble. When introduced, one lats equalled 200LVR or roughly 1ECU. The lats (plural lati) is made up of 100 sentīms and is freely convertible internally (within the country) as bank notes. In the centre of Riga, exchange points can be found on almost every other street corner. They are less frequent in the suburbs and in other Latvian cities, but generally, finding an exchange point should be no problem. Opening hours are usually Monday–Saturday 10am–6pm.

If exchanging large amounts of money, it is worthwhile shopping around, because the rates vary slightly from place to place and from day to day. Hotels give lower rates, so don't change your hard currency there unless you really have to.

The US dollar and German mark have higher value in Latvia than they do abroad *vis-a-vis* other foreign currencies. This means that if you are a citizen of the UK, for example, you should change your pounds into dollars in the UK and then exchange your dollars into lats once you arrive in Latvia. You will get more for your money this way.

LITHUANIA

Lithuania is introducing its own national currency, the Litas, replacing the so-called *talonas* (coupons), an intermediate monetary unit introduced on 1 October 1992. The *Zveriukai* (little animals) as Lithuanians call the small-sized bills sporting animals, exist in two different sizes. The 1, 10, 50, 100, 200 and 500 notes are smaller in size than the 1, 3, 5, 10, 25, 50 and 100 *Vagnorkes* bills introduced by former prime minister Gediminas Vagnorius in 1991 and reissued in October 1991.

Currency can be changed in banks and their outlets in a number of shops. Changing money on the street is illegal and might be dangerous for the little profit you can achieve.

Credit cards are only accepted in major hotels and just one restaurant. Money withdrawal with credit cards is only possible with Visa cards in Vilnius Bankas, Gedimino pr. 12, Vilnius.

GETTING ACQUAINTED

ESTONIA

The official title of the country is the Republic of Estonia (*Eesti Vabariik*). The highest office in the land is that of president (in Estonian *Riigivanem*, literally state elder) a position currently held by Lennart Meri. Meri gained the office after the first elections since independence, held in September 1992. The parliament (*Riigikogu*) is the highest body in the land and the president represents the parliament in internal and international contacts. The parliament is responsible for all national legislative matters. Parallel to the parliament is the Government of the Republic of Estonia, headed by a parliament-approved prime minister (Mart Laar was elected for a five-year term in 1992), responsible for the day-to-day running of the country.

LATVIA

After the June 1993 elections the Saeima, or parliament, replaced the Supreme Council established in March 1990, when the pro-independence Popular Front gained slightly more than two-thirds of the seats. Pro-Soviet Communists (mostly Russians) took the other third. On 21 August 1991, the SC declared full independence, and Soviet recognition soon followed. By the end of the year, the Popular Front also began to fragment and while still the largest faction in parliament, it no longer had the majority of seats.

The government is the executive branch of the state. It answers to the new 100-member Saeima which must confirm the appointment of ministers, as well as government decrees and resolutions.

LITHUANIA

Lithuania is a parliamentary democracy and the government is subordinate to parliament, the Seimas, which came into being with the elections in October 1992, after which a new constitution was adopted. At these elections the pro-independence communist party, the Democratic Labour Party, won a surprise victory over the centre-right Sajudis party of Vytautas Landsbergis, who had steered the country to independence. The government is headed by Adolfas Šleževičius Lubys and following a referendum to create an executive presidency, the DLP party leader Algirdas Brazauskas was elected for a five-year presidential term in February 1993. Brazauskas became leader of Lithuania's Communist Party in 1988 and in 1989 became the first republican communist leader to split from the Soviet Communist Party.

GEOGRAPHY & POPULATION

ESTONIA

Estonia is the northernmost of the three Baltic States. To the south it shares a land border with Latvia but for the most part its borders are denoted by water. The eastern border is with Russia, much of it running through the 1,350 sq. mile (3,500 sq. km) Lake Peipsi. To the west is the Baltic Sea which becomes the Gulf of Finland as it laps the northern coastline. Estonia is the smallest of the Baltic States and covers around 17,375 sq. miles (45,000 sq. km) which makes it larger than Denmark, Holland or Switzerland. The country is pocked with lakes just as the surrounding coastline is dotted with more than a thousand islands. The landscape is remarkably flat and over 40 percent of the country is covered with dense forest.

The population of Estonia is a little over 1.5 million with almost a third (484,400) living in and around Tallinn, followed by Tartu (115,400), Narva (82,300), Kohtla-Järva (76,800) and Pärnu (54,200). Ethnically the composition of Estonia is approximately 60 percent Estonian, 30 percent Russian with the remainder composed of other ex-Soviet nationalities such as Ukrainians and Belorussians. The composition of the populace in any particular region varies greatly. In the industrial towns of northeastern Estonia, Russians account for some 95 percent of the population while in rural areas Estonians form over 90 percent of the population. There is concern at the continuing trend of a decreasing birth rate among Estonians while the birthrate among the Russian population steadily increases.

LATVIA

The Republic of Latvia, the middle of the three States, lies on the eastern coast of the Baltic Sea, less than an hour's flight from Stockholm or Helsinki. It is bounded by Estonia to the north, Lithuania to the south, and Russia and Belorus to the east. The territory covers 24,950 sq. miles (64,600 sq. km). Average north-south distance is 130 miles (210 km) and the greatest east-west distance in a straight line is 255 miles. The 640-mile (1,030-km) River Daugavpils enters the Baltics in Riga Bay and the dune-backed coast runs for more than 310 miles (500 km). The country is generally flat and forested, with uplands in the northwest and in the east, where most of the lakes lie. The highest point in the Baltics is in Latvia: Galziņkalns reaches 1,025 ft (312 metres).

The population of Latvia is 2,686,000, of whom 916,500 live in Riga: Latvia's second city is Daugavpils (128,200), followed by Liepāja (114,900), Jelgava (75,100), Jūrmala (66,400) and Ventspils (50,400). Latvians make up 52 percent and are in a minority in the five largest towns: in Riga they represent just 35 percent. Overall, Russians account for 34 percent of the population. Latvians are a minority in the country's larger cities (35 percent in Riga, only 13 percent in Daugavpils), but a majority in the smaller towns and countryside.

LITHUANIA

Lithuania is the largest of the three Baltic countries, covering 25,175 sq. miles (65,200 sq. km), twice the size of Belgium. It borders Latvia in the north, Belorus in the east and south, and Poland and the Russian enclave of Kaliningrad in the southwest. It also likes to boast that it is the centre of Europe: the dead centre of the continent lies near Bernotai, 15 miles (25 km) north of Vilnius. The countryside is slighly more undulating than its northern neighbours and it is riven with rivers and lakes, 2,833 of which exceed an acre. It has the shortest coastline, covering 60 miles (99 km), much of which is taken up by the extraordinary sand dunes of Neringa Spit, where the 582 mile (937 km) River Nemunas reaches the sea via a large lagoon.

Lithuania has a population of 3,752,000. Vilnius, the capital, is the biggest city with 591,000 inhabitants, followed by Kaunas (430,000), Klaipėda (206,000), Šiauliai (148,000) and Panevėžys (129,000). Lithuanians make up the majority of the population: 79.6 percent. The second largest ethnic group is Russian (9.4 percent) followed by Poles (7 percent) who mainly inhabit the southeastern part of the country.

CLIMATE & CLOTHING

By far the best time to visit the Baltic States is in June. During this month the days are longest with the most hours of sun. The following month of July the rain can start and it may increase as the summer progresses. By June the temperature has also become quite clement, the last of the icy spells of spring having ended in May in Estonia, earlier in Lithuania. July is the hottest month when mid-summer temperatures can reach up to 86°F (30°C), but generally they are a pleasant 63°F (17°C).

In winter temperatures have been recorded as low as –22°F (–30°C) in Estoinia, –4°F (–20°C) in Lithuania. That is still cold, especially when accompanied by piercing coastal winds. In recent years winter temperatures have tended to be milder, seldom falling below around the 23°F (–5°C) mark, and temperatures inland are generally lower than near the coast. Snow is most prolonged in Estonia where it can fall from January through to March though the amount has been decreasing and often there is no lasting snow cover. More than snow, rain or the cold, the biggest drawback for a winter visitor is the lack of sunlight. From early November through until late March darkness never seems to completely lift, and the weeks go by with just a filmy greyness for six or seven hours to pass for a day.

What to wear: People do dress up for concerts and the theatre, but unless here on official business, there is little else to dress up for – apart, that is, from the cold. From November to April minimum requirements are a heavy woollen jumper, thermal underwear, leggings and something thick-soled and waterproof on your feet. During January, February and March gloves and a scarf are a must and a woollen cap is also advisable.

For the summer months lightweight garments and even shorts and T-shirts are adequate. Nights can get cold, so bring a sweater and jacket for the evenings. It is advisable to have something waterproof along, too, and perhaps an umbrella. Sensible, comfortable footwear is also highly recommended as the cities' cobbled streets are uncomfortable in thin-soled shoes and treacherous in high-heels.

LANGUAGE

Each of the three countries has its own official language – Estonian, Latvian and Lithuanian – and each uses the Latin alphabet. Estonian is based on the Finno-Ugric family of languages, while Latvian and Lithuanian are the last remaining of the Baltic family of Indo-European languages, which Estonians cannot understand. A Latvian and a Lithuanian can roughly understand what each other is trying to say but cannot hold a deep conversation.

Although Russian is common to all three countries, it is not now being taught as a first language and out of national pride many Balts prefer not to speak it. However, large populations of Russians, particularly in Latvia and Estonia, keep the language alive in bookshops and some roadsigns. Many Russians work in the service industries in Latvia and Estonia, though a minimum working knowledge of the local language is a prerequisite for citizenship.

In theory every Balt under the age of around 45 should be able to speak Russian as under Soviet occupation the language was a compulsory part of schooling. In practice, however, few choose to speak Russian and as a visitor if you do speak some Russian yourself it is usually tactful to try to converse in your own language first. Estonians are often multilingual, speaking English as well as Finnish. In Latvia English has become the language of choice as a third language for students, followed by German and French. In Lithuania German is more commonly understood.

A more comprehensive guide to the languages, plus some useful words and phrases, appears on *page 415.*

RELIGION

ESTONIA

The state church is the Estonian Evangelical Lutheran Church which has held sway since the Reformation in the 16th century. The Orthodox and Baptist churches also draw large congregations, mainly from the Russian community. Estonians have never been a particularly religious people. However, at the present time there is a renewed interest in the church and attendances are rising. Since the church has become re-established, many are now searching for spiritual fulfilment. A little curiosity and some intellectual vanity has caused congregations to swell. The principal churches now open for services in Tallinn are:

St John's church, Vabaduse väljak (Lutheran).
St Charles's church, Kaarli pst (Lutheran).
Alexander Nevski Cathedral, Lossi plats 10, Toompea (Russian Orthodox).
St Olaf's church (Oleviste kirik), Lai 50, (Evangelist-Baptist).
Church of St Peter and Paul, Vene 18 (Catholic).
Church of the 7th Day Adventists, Mere pst.
Jewish synagogue, Lastaia 9.

LATVIA

Before the war, 55 percent of the population was Lutheran, 24 percent was Catholic (concentrated in Latgale, the eastern region). The rest were Russian Orthodox, Baptist and Jewish. The religious revival which began in 1988 has tapered off somewhat. Many of the younger generation are agnostic and, as the economy deteriorates, are more concerned with making ends meet than going to church. Religious groups from abroad (Hare Krishnas, Moonies and various Christian churches) have been moving in to try to gain ground. The principal churches in Riga are:

Dome cathedral, 1 Doma laukums (Lutheran).
St Peter's church, 23 Skārņu iela (Lutheran).
St John's church, 7 Jāņa iela (Lutheran).
Old St Gertrude's church, 8 Gertrūdes iela (Lutheran)

Church of Jesus, 18 Odessas (Lutheran).
St Jacob's cathedral, 2 Klostera iela (Catholic).
Mater Dolorosa church, 5 L. Pils iela (Catholic).
Orthodox cathedral, 126 Kr. Barona iela.
St Alexander Nevsky church, 56 Brīvības iela (Orthodox).
Grebenschikov's church, 73 Krasta iela (Russian Old Believers).
Union of Latvian Baptist Congregations, 50b Matīsa iela.
Jewish synagogue, 6-8 Peitavas iela.

LITHUANIA

Mainly Catholic, Lithuania is the most religious of the three countries, a flame that was kept alive throughout the communist era by the church in Rome. Most of its churches were converted to other uses during the communist years, but since February 1989, reconsecration has begun and a lot of money has been pouring in to churches, monasteries and seminaries to re-establish Vilnius in particular as a major Catholic centre in Europe. These are the principal churches in the city:
Cathedral, 23 Cathedral Square (Catholic).
St Casimir's, 34 Didžoji (Catholic).
Gates of Dawn, 12 Aušros Vartų (Catholic shrine).
St Anne's, 8 Maironio (Catholic).
Church of Sts Peter and Paul, 1 Antakalnio (Catholic).
Orthodox Church of the Holy Spirit, 10 Aušros Vartų.
Reformed Evangelical church, Pylimo 20.
Jewish synagogue, 39 Pylimo.

WEIGHTS & MEASURES

The Baltics use the metric system, and everywhere calculations are made on traditional abacuses. Vodka is ordered in grammes – 50g equates to a single, 100g is a double.

ELECTRICITY

The mains is 220v AC, 50 Hertz and sockets take a two-pronged, continental-style plug. It is not possible to buy plugs, adaptors, leads or most any kind of electrical accessories. Batteries are available at photographic supply shops though only the standard sizes and not special items such as watch cells.

TIME

The Baltic States are in the Central European Time Zone, which is two hours ahead of GMT. That means when it's noon in the Baltics it is:
1pm in Moscow
11am in Warsaw
noon in Tel Aviv
6pm in Tokyo
8pm in Sydney

2am in Los Angeles
5am in New York
10am in London
Daylight Savings Time, during which the clocks are set one hour ahead of standard time, lasts from 2am on the first Sunday of April to the last Sunday of September.

BUSINESS HOURS

ESTONIA

A European 9am–6pm five-day working week is standard with Saturday and Sunday as the weekend. Lunch hours tend to begin around 2pm. Shops operate a little differently. Their opening hours tend to be from 10am–7pm with a lunch break either from 1–2pm or 2–3pm. Many close early on Saturday, especially food shops. However food shops are generally open on Sunday when all other shops are closed. In Tallinn the Comex store, on Pärnu mnt., close by the Palace Hotel, and the Lembitu store in the Teenindusmaja on Viru väljak, are the only late shops, both open until 11pm every night of the week. A number of shops, noticEably bookshops, are also closed on Monday. Museums and galleries generally close on Monday, and often on Tuesday too. Instead they open through the week-end. (This is not a rule so check individual entries in the listings). Restaurants open at around midday and close at 11pm, the kitchens usually closing a half hour before. It is not possible to get a late meal unless you resort to a late-night pizza takeaway, and only for those in dire need, one of the 24-hour burger kiosks that are dotted around town (Vabaduse väljak, Viru väljak, at the intersection of Liivalaia and Tartu mnt.).

LATVIA

Business hours vary and can make life confusing. On weekdays some shops and stores open as early as 8am, others as late as 10am. The lunch hour, during which shops and restaurants close, also varies among businesses. In some places it is from noon–1pm, in others from 1–2pm, and in still others from 2–3pm. Most offices close at some time between 5 and 6pm, although on Friday people tend to leave earlier. Most stores close at 5pm, although some close as late as 7pm and on Friday they tend to close earlier. New 24-hour stores and kiosks have sprung up selling mostly imported cigarettes, alcohol and confection-ary. Saturday hours also vary, opening between 8 and 10am and closing between 4 and 7pm. On Sunday almost all businesses are closed.

LITHUANIA

Lithuanians works from 9am–1pm and 2–6pm. Most shops and restaurants close for one hour around lunch time. Once a month all museums, shops and restaurants close for the traditional *sanitarine diena* (sanitary day) devoted to a thorough clean-up.

TIPPING

Estonia: Service is not included on most bills presumably because so few people seem to place any value on good service. However on the off-chance that you feel especially well-treated nobody is going to be insulted by a tip.

Latvia: The Soviet tradition was simply to round up the sum of the bill. But in private restaurants tips probably should reach about 10 percent. Local porters and taxi drivers also expect tips.

Lithuania: Tipping is becoming widespread habit. Taxi drivers and children at petrol stations will ask you for a "dollar". In restaurants you should leave a 10 percent tip. Sometimes waiters will come back to your table to explain that you left too much.

PUBLIC HOLIDAYS

Since independence there have been a number of new holidays made official and a number of former days of national remembrance, such as 7 November "October Revolution Day", discreetly allowed to lapse. Public holidays are marked differently in Estonia from those in most other parts of Europe. The roads are jammed with traffic, shops crowded with holiday-sale bargain-hunters and streets made lethal with school-freed kids are all absent. On a public holiday city streets appear deserted. But if there are no people there are flags by the thousand. From almost every building there hangs a blue, black and white tricolor. (All buildings in Latvia must, by law, have the Latvian flag displayed prominently on their facades near the front door).

This display of national pride is not restricted solely to public holidays but occurs perhaps a dozen or more times a year. On public holidays however, combined with the eerie absence of people, the effect is not of a country celebrating but of a country in mourning. The most celebrated event in the Estonian calendar. Jaanipäev is a festival of pagan origins, deeply rooted in peasant culture. The date marks mid-summer and the end of Spring labours in the fields. It always used to be considered a night of omens and sorcery. One tradition firmly linked with Jaanipäev, which still exists to this day, is that of leaping over bonfires. A successful clearance of the flames used to indicate similar success for the year ahead. On the days leading up to this festival Tallinn is drained of people as they all head out into the countryside where the fires flicker and Jaanipäev is still best celebrated. In Latvia, Jāņi, midsummer's eve, is also of pagin origin and the most important festival of the year. Lithuania is reviving many village celebrations.

ESTONIA

1 January: New Year's Day.
24 February: Independence Day, first secession from Russia, 1918.
23 June: Victory Day, battle of Vannu, 1919.
24 June: St John's Day (*Jaanipäev*).
16 November: Rebirth Day Commemorating Estonia's 1988 Declaration of Sovereignty.
25/26 December: Christmas.

LATVIA

1 January: New Year's Day.
Good Friday
1 May: May Day.
24 June: Jāņi (summer solstice).
18 November: Independence Day.
25/26 December: Christmas.

MEMORIAL DAYS

25 March: mass deportation of Balts to Siberia in 1949.
14 June: first mass deportation of Balts to Siberia, 1941.
11 November: 1919 battle, during which invading German forces were repulsed from Riga.

LITHUANIA

1 January: New Year.
16 February: Restoration of Lithuanian statehood (1918).
Easter
May: Mothers' Day.
6 July: Crowning of Mindaugas, Day of statehood.
1 November: All Saints' Day.
25 December: Christmas Day.
26 December: Boxing Day.

CŌMMUNICATIONS

POSTAL SERVICES

ESTONIA

Although mail is no longer directed through Moscow, the postal service in Estonia is still at best erratic – and it is not often at its best. It is common to receive on the same day two letters posted from the same point but weeks apart. It is also equally possible never to receive them at all. Outward-bound mail fares better and most of it would seem to get through. To gain the best odds and speed things along, it is a good idea to post your letters only at the central post office. The central post office is also one of the few places stamps can be purchased. Other places include the large hotels.

Tallinn Post Office: Narva mnt. 1 (opposite the Hotel Viru). Tel: 442 347 or 441 803. Weekdays 8am–8pm, Saturday 8am–5pm.
Tartu Post Office: 29 Lai.
Pärnu Post Office: 7 Akadeemia.
Narva Post Office: 3 Tuleviku.

LATVIA

As in Soviet times, letters from the West are still known to disappear *en route*, but such events are relatively rare. Curious customs agents and postal workers still look for *valūta*, or hard currency. Such letters invariably end up being either "confiscated" or sent on without their monetary contents. Letters to and from Europe take anywhere between a week and a month to reach their destination. Average time is a week to 10 days. The Latvian postal index system begins with LV – followed by four digits, for example: LV – 1081.

Riga Central Post Office: 21 Brīvības bulv. Tel: 224 155.
Express mail: Stacijas laukums (near the central railway station). Tel: 213 297. Weekdays 8am–8pm, Saturday 8am–6pm.
DHL (freight express): 5 Palasta iela (Old Riga). Tel: 210 973.
Kuldīga Post Office: 34 Liepājas.
Sigulda Post Office: 2 Pils.
Rēzekne Post Office: 81-5 Brīvības.

LITHUANIA

Allow at least one week for letters and postcards from Lithuania to western Europe. Express letters can be sent for hard currency from the post office and the major delivery services (Federal Express, DHL, and TNT) have opened shop in Vilnius and in Kaunas.

Vilnius Central Post Office: Gedimino pr 7.
Post Office: Vilniaus 33. Tel: 61 99 60.
Kaunas Central Post Office: 102 Laisves al.
Klaipėda Central Post Office: 16 Liepų.

TELEPHONE & FAX

ESTONIA

Pay-phones are being replaced to accept sents and a cardphone system has been introduced which accepts magnetic Alcatel cards (not credit cards), which can be bought nearby for 30 and 250 kroons. For long distance calls within Estonia (outside of Tallinn) and to Latvia, Lithuania, the CIS, Finland, Sweden, Canada and the US, you can dial direct. Dial 8 and wait for a long, constant tone; dial the code and the number then wait for about 50 seconds.

City calls within Estonia: Dial 8+ Haapsalu 47, Jõgeva 37, Kohtla-Järve 33, Kuressaare 45, Kärdla 46, Narva 35, Paide 38, Põlva 30, Pärnu 44, Rakvere 32, Rapla 48, Sillamäe 49, Tartu 34, Valga 42, Viljandi 43, Võru 41.

From abroad: The code for Estonia is 372, followed by area or city code (+2 for Tallinn).

Overseas calls: These must be booked. Call the operator on 007 (they speak English). Once you have booked your call replace the receiver and wait to be connected. This can take anything from five minutes to an hour. If you don't have access to a private phone then international calls can be made from the Central Post Office.

Fax and telex: In general, communications are stuck firmly in the Stone Age. If you are able to get hold of a fax machine it is going to take endless patience, some sweat and possibly even a few tears before you manage to get your document transmitted. A business service exists at the Palace hotel in Tallinn and the Taru in Tartu for guests but apart from that there are no business centres and the only place to send faxes and telexes from is the central post office.

LATVIA

Phone lines in Latvia, like everywhere else in the former Soviet Union, are notoriously bad. The new *žetoni* (pronounced zhe-toni), or public pay-phone tokens, can be obtained at most kiosks and at telephone exchange centres. Dialling to other cities within Latvia is frustrating. One has to dial 8 and wait for a dial tone, then the local city code and the local number. Consider yourself lucky if you get through on the first try. There are also inter-city tokens which can be obtained at the same places as the tokens for local calls. Inter-city phones can be found at most post offices and telephone exchanges. It is possible to dial direct to all parts of the former Soviet Union: dial 8, followed by the local code and the local number. Latkom offers telephone and fax service within Latvia and the CIS. Tel: 382 529.

Dialling to other countries is much more difficult, and can only be done with the assistance of an operator. In Riga, one can go to the main post office on 21 Brīvības Street in downtown Riga near the Freedom Monument. (Tel: 223 163.) After waiting some time in line, you tell the operator where you want to call and the length of your conversation. Then you pay him/her the required amount and wait... sometimes for up to two hours, or longer. It depends on what mood the operators are in. Sometimes you'll be told to come back at a fixed time the next day or the day after. If that happens, arrive about half an hour early and remind them you have placed a call. If you are lucky, you'll get it within two hours of the assigned time.

You can also call the international operator from a private phone. Often the international lines are busy, so keep trying. Once you get through, the operators usually take a long time to answer, so don't hang up in despair right away. Again, you may have to register your call for the next day or the day after at a fixed time. Be there at least half an hour in advance, just in case. About 15 minutes after the assigned time, call them to remind them that you have reserved a call.

For a fat fee, you can make direct calls from Riga's major hotels. Be prepared to pay at least $2 a minute. Latvian Mobile Telephone (39 Ūnijas iela, Riga, tel: 567 764) provides mobile telephone service from the Hotel Riga and Riga airport.

For faxes the same rules apply as for making calls. Bad connections are the rule, rather than the exception, but sometimes faxes do get through both ways. **Lattelekom**, 41-43 Elizabetes eila, Riga, also provides international telephone and fax service for local currency (tel: 210 610/332 815). The **Riga Business Centre** next door at 45-47 Elizabetes eila also sends faxes for hard currency (tel: 225 189). Faxes can also be sent through SIMSS at 4 Tallinnas eila (tel: 372 029).

Directory assistance in Riga: 09
City calls within Latvia: Dial 8 + Cēsis 241, Daugavpils 254, Jelgava 230, Kuldīga 233, Liepāja 234, Rēzekne 246, Talsi 232, Tukums 231, Valmiera 242, Ventspils 236. Inter-city telephone connections within Latvia: 282 222.
International calls: 8-191, 8-194,
From abroad: the code for Latvia is 371 followed by the area or city code (+ 2 for Riga).

LITHUANIA

Lithuania has the most advanced telephone system in the former Soviet Union and it is possible to dial major European countries as well as Israel and the US from any private phone in the country due to a new satellite hook-up installed in Kaunas. Dial the international access code: 8-10 followed by the country code, city code and the telephone number.

Whenever dialling outside Vilnius you must first dial 8 and wait for the dial tone to obtain a line. **City Codes within Lithuania**: Dial 8 + Druskininkai 33, Kaunas 7, Klaipėda 61, Nida 59, Panevėžys 54, Palanga 36, Šiauliai 14, Vilnius 2.
International operator: 8-194 (English spoken).
From abroad: the code for Lithuania is 370 followed by area or city code (+ 2 for Vilnius).

For even quicker and more reliable lines you can use cellular telephones in Vilnius, Kaunas and Klaipėda. In Vilnius the portable phones can be bought or rented from:
Comliet, Architektų 146. Tel: 26 98 48/26 96 90.

Since Lithuania has a different system than Latvia and Estonia it is impossible to roam through the Baltic countries.

Public phone booths require a 15 kopeck coin or special *žetonas* tokens. Both can be purchased at any post office.

Telegraph offices and fax services:
Central Telegraph Office, Vilniaus 33/2. Tel: 61 96 14.
Central Post Office, Gedimino pr 7. Tel: 61 66 14.
Lietuva Hotel, ground floor, Ukmergės 12.
Sajūdis Information Agency, Gedimino pr 1 (room 104). Tel: 22 48 96/22 49 09.
Kaunas Central Post Office, 102 Laisvės al. 102. Tel: 22 62 20.
Klaipėda Central Telegraph Office, 16 Liepų 16. Tel: 160 75.
Nida Post Office, 13 Taikos Tel: 525 25.
Šiauliai Post Office, 42 Aušros al. Tel: 306 20
Palanga long-distance telephone centre, Biliūno 1. Tel: 562 22. In summer also on Vytauto 39. Tel: 531 40.
E-Mail, Varicom E-Mail Services, Pilies 23. Tel: 61 62 20. Weekdays 10am–6pm.

THE MEDIA

ESTONIA

Print: There are a great number of dailies, both in the Estonian language and Russian, and they enjoy comparatively large circulations considering the size of the population. Among the most popular dailies are *Päevaleht* (Daily Paper), *Rähva Hääl* (Voice of the People) and *Äripäev* (Business Day). The tradition of the press as a mouthpiece for the ruling body is a hard one to break and journalism in Estonia lacks objectivity. The news is gradually improving and the weekly *Eesti Ekspress* runs some good investigative journalism, dipping into scandal and intrigue.

There are two English-language newspapers printed in Tallinn. Focusing on politics and economics *The Baltic Independent* is the highest circulation English-language weekly newspaper in the Baltics. *Tallinn City Paper* is a bi-monthly, full-colour publication that runs longer feature articles on current affairs and includes a comprehensive regularly updated guide section. There is also a useful listings magazine, *Tallinn This Week*, which is good on details of coming events. All three publications are available from hotels, the harbour and airport and the two newspapers are also sold throughout Estonia at news kiosks. A limited selection of foreign newspapers and journals are carried by some of the larger hotels. In Tallinn the best selection is at the kiosk on the first floor of the Viru hotel, in Tartu the best place to look is at the Pinguin kiosk on Vabaduse pst.

Radio: Estonian Radio (*Eesti Raadio*), the state radio station, and until recently the only radio station, has been broadcasting regularly since 1926. There are three channels and transmissions are made in eight languages including English. On the second channel, *Vikerraadio,* (290MHz medium wave), every weekday there is a 10-minute English-language news bulletin at 6.20pm local time. Also on the same frequencies every Monday and Thursday at 11.30pm local time there is "Estonia Today", a half-hour round-up of the current goings-on in and around Tallinn. It's all very dour stuff. Much more upbeat are the new independent radio stations. The best of these is *Raadio Kuku* (100.7MHz), daily 6am–8pm, which was the first independent, commercial radio station in Estonia. The programming is almost all in Estonian but there isn't much talk, just a lively mix of music.

Television: Estonia is remarkably well served by television though not as a result of its own output. Estonian TV, the state company, broadcasts one channel only, daily, 5pm–midnight. Most of the programmes are in Estonian with the occasional subtitled European documentary. However, Estonian TV is supplemented by three Russian channels and, in northern Estonia, by an additional three Finnish channels. Even if you don't understand them, the Russian channels are quite fascinating. The Finnish channels are substantially less fascinating but they are crammed with BBC series and American soaps, comedies and films. Many hotels offer satellite television which gives a further four channels of Finland compiled American soaps, comedies, films, CNN and erotica.

LATVIA

There is no government censorship on either radio, television or the press but most radio and TV stations are still state run, and some reporters and announcers do have a pro-government bias. But the state media is also in difficulty, due to budget restrictions.

Print: The state-founded and now privatised *Diena* is the most balanced and qualitative Latvian-language newspaper in the country, and it has a Latvian edition. *Latvijas Jaunatne* and *Neatkariga Cina* are the other two Latvian papers, the latter having the highest local circulation (160,000). *SM Segodnya* is the most widely-read Russian-language newspaper.

The 12–16-page English-language newspaper *The Baltic Observer* provides weekly coverage of current political, economic and cultural events in all three countries and is a good buy. Due to the astronomical rise in the price of newsprint, many newspapers have been forced to raise their newsstand and subscription prices, and some will inevitably be forced to fold. The *Herald Tribune* is on sale in the main hotels.

Radio: There are two radio stations in the capital: Radio Latvia, based in the cathedral square and Independent Radio "AA". News is sometimes, rather unsatisfactorily, broadcast in English.

Television: There are now two independent TV stations to provide balance news coverage. There is also a high English-language input with CNN *World Day* broadcast on Latvijas TV II at 5pm on weekdays, and CNN news on weekdays from 10.30pm–midnight on Channel 7. Channel 7 also broadcasts BBC news from 10–11.30pm on weekdays. The NTV-5 Evening News gives a complete report of Latvia's news, sport and weather at 9.30pm every weeknight on Channel 31 and Monday–Thursday at 11.50pm on Latvia II. The ITN World News Report is shown at 9.45pm on weeknights and 9.30pm at weekends on Channel 31. There is another station, Latvian TV3, and Latgale has its own station, Latgalian TV90, based in Rēzekne.

LITHUANIA

Print: Foreign newspapers of the previous day can be found in the newsstand of the Draugyste Hotel as well as in selected bookshops. For local news in English try the following publications: *Baltic News*, edited in Vilnius, is a weekly A-4 which seeks to provide "information and analysis" of the events in the Baltics and exclusively sold for hard currency, but there are better buys. *Lithuanian Weekly*, four-page weekly, gives an extensive round-up of Lithuanian news in English and is also sold exclusively for hard currency in selected stores.

Parliamentary Record is a monthly sold exclusively to subscribers and gives the major Lithuanian legal texts in English. *The Economist of Lithuania* is a quarterly magazine written in poor English, with articles on all aspects of business in Lithuania. Sold for hard currency in selected stores.

Vilnius in Your Pocket is the first and most successful English-language city guide. It is published every two months and provides thorough information about tourist attractions, things to do in town, complete opera and theatre programmes and helpful restaurant reviews. It is available in most kiosks and hotels. *Klaipėda Today* is a guide to where to go and what to do on the coast in English and German by the publishers of *Vilnius In Your Pocket*.

Radio: The external service of the state owned radio provides a daily 30-minute round-up of Lithuanian news in English at 12.30am local time on 666 KHz. Outside Lithuania you can find the half-hour broadcast at 11pm UTC on 9530, 17690 and 17605 KHz, tel. 66 05 26. Independent radio stations have flourished in Lithuania where you may find the following all-music programmes: M1, 106.4 MHz providing an English-language show *Breakfast in America* or *The Work Week* every day hosted by "Uncle Steve" from America; Radiocentras, 101.1 MHz, has music and news 24 hours a day; Radiofonas Vilniaus Varpas, 103.1 FM, has folk and jazz.

Television: Lithuania has two state owned channels (RTV I and RTVII) and one new private station, TV26. The second channel from Kaunas is splitting the airwaves with the former central Soviet television which is still partly aired in Lithuania as well as the Russian channel RTR. In Vilnius and the southeastern part of Lithuania you can tune into the Polish television, and a pirate satellite TV from parliament mainly transmitting Sky programmes. Most hotels have their own satellite dishes for visitors to keep up with events back home.

EMERGENCIES

CRIME

Economic hardship and chronically understaffed and ill-equipped police forces have contributed to a sharp increase in crime. It is certainly no New York but care should be taken. Violent crime tends to be gangland related and assaults on foreigners are rare. Much more common is theft. Anything you are not physically attached to is liable to walk. This applies equally to valuables left in hotel rooms – even those of some of the top hotels. Don't tempt the staff by leaving things out. Further good advice to visitors is to remain sober; nothing could present a more appealing target than an inebriated tourist staggering through dimly lit streets.

In emergencies: (no coins needed) dial 02.
Advertising lost items on TV: Tel: 200 340 (Riga).

MEDICAL SERVICES

If you're going to get sick, the former Soviet Union is not the best place to do so. In a place where cancer is still – in the opinion of many – caused by sitting in a draft, and gastrointestinal disorders are the result of getting one's feet wet in a cold autumn rain, it is not surprising that a visit to the corner drugstore will leave much to be desired for the average Westerner. The shelves tend to be overflowing with traditional remedies like herbal teas, mustard plaster and bee pollen. Even Soviet-made analgesics and antibiotics are in short supply, as are persons who could tell you what's in the packages, which are most often labelled in Cyrillic.

If you should happen to feel a little ill, your best bet is to visit one of the many private (for the most part hard currency) drugstores popping up in all three capitals. There you can often find most of what you might need to cure common, temporary ailments. Many of these stores carry everything from Pepto Bismol, Advil and antibiotics to such "trivial" goods such as Visine, condoms and Slim Fast.

If over-the-counter medicines do not do the trick, it is advisable to find help from a qualified physician. Unfortunately there are some people who prey on foreigners' gullibility and who are out to make a quick buck. Thus, when seeking assistance at an outpatient or emergency clinic, it is helpful to keep in mind the following details:

• Emergency medical care is free of charge in all three Baltic countries.

• Prices for simple medical procedures are fixed in Lithuania. In Estonia and Latvia they may vary, depending on the complexity of the procedure and, in the case of foreigners, the agreements between the two countries involved. For the time being, only Latvia and Poland have signed a formal agreement on mutual health care.

While the health care system is undergoing a deep crisis due to budget cuts, foreigners are generally well-treated. Doctors and nurses are grossly underpaid but still try to provide adequate service. Usually they will not refuse extra payment after treatment. Hospitals are spartan, but generally sanitary.

In emergencies: (no coins needed) tel: 03.

ESTONIA (IN TALLINN)

10 Sütiste, Mustamäe. 24 hour, seven days a week.
18 Ravi, close to the Hotel Olümpia. Weekdays 9am–6pm.

CHEMISTS

Apteek No. 1, Tõnismägi 5. Prescriptions made up. There is an information desk to advise on the kinds of medicines available in Tallinn.
Apteek No. 2, Pärnu mnt. 10, opposite the Drama Theatre. Prescriptions: weekdays 8am–8pm Saturday 9am–5pm.

Vanaturu Apteek, Vene1, close to the Town Hall Square. No prescription service. Weekdays 9am–7pm, Saturday until 4pm.

Apteek, Rävala pst.7. Prescriptions made up. Weekdays 8am–8pm, Saturday 9am–4pm. Contains a Medipharm counter selling a range of imported drugs, vitamins and sanitary supplies.

DENTISTS

Baltic Medical Partners, Toompuieste 4. Tel: 666 009, fax: 451 866. Monday–Friday 10am–8pm.

LATVIA (Riga)

HARD CURRENCY DRUGSTORES

21a Elizabetes iela. Weekdays 10am–6pm, Saturday 10am–5pm. Tel: 333 196.
15 Vāgnera iela. Weekdays 10am–7pm, Saturday 10am–6pm. Tel: 216 885.
Interpegro, 8 Matīsa iela. Weekdays 10am–6pm, Saturday 10am–5pm. Tel: 272 813.
Nord Composit, 28 Grēcinieku iela. Weekdays 9.30am–6.30pm. Tel: 227 273. *Also at:* 15 Stabu iela, Tuesday–Friday 9.30am–6.30pm, Saturday 9am–3pm; 5 Tērbatas iela, weekdays 9am–6pm; Central railway station, Monday–Saturday 8am–6pm and Sunday 10am–6pm; 82 Dzelzavas iela, weekdays 9am–6pm and Saturday 9am–3pm.

ALL-NIGHT DRUGSTORES

29 Audēju iela; 74 Brīvības iela; 211 Brīvības iela; 21a Elizabetes iela.

EMERGENCY MEDICAL CARE

Hospital No. 7 (eye care), 2 P. Dauges iela. Tel: 536 339.
Traumatologic and Orthopedic Institute, 12/22 Duntes iela. Tel: 393 197.
Children's Republican Clinical Hospital, 45 Vienības gatve. Tel: 622 997.
P. Stradins Republican Clinical Hospital, 13 Pilsoņu iela. Tel: 611 201.
Psychiatric Hospital, 2 Tvaika iela. Tel: 392 463.
Baltic Railway Children's Outpatient Hospital, 68 Lielvārdes iela. Tel: 576 255.

EMERGENCY DENTAL SERVICES

Republican Dental Outpatient Hospital 20 Dzirciema iela. Tel: 455 586.
9 Stabu iela. Tel: 274 546.
17 Blaumaña iela. Tel: 283 851.

SEXUALLY TRANSMITTED DISEASES

Republican Venereal Center, 2 A. Barbisa iela. Tel: 272 198.
Anonymous AIDS testing. Tel: 613 606.

ACCIDENTS

Hospital No. 1, 8 Bruņinieku iela. Tel: 296 734.
1 Gimnastikas iela. Tel: 622 168.

LITHUANIA (Vilnius)

PHARMACIES (HARD CURRENCY ONLY)

Apotheke German-Lithuanian pharmacy, 13 Didžioji. Weekdays 9am–8pm, Saturday 10am–6pm. Tel: 22 42 32.
Pharm-Tech, 21 Šeimyniškių. Weekdays only, 10am–5pm. Tel: 75 01 67.

HOSPITALS

Antakalnis Hospital, 124 Antakalnio. Tel: 74 60 41.
Emergency Hospital, 29 Šiltnamių, Tel: 26 90 69.
Medical Rehabilitation Centre, 21 Šeimyniškių. Tel: 75 00 36.
Red Cross Hospital, 6 Žygimantų. Tel: 61 62 58.
Santariškių Hospital, 2 Santaraškių. Tel 77 99 12.
SBT Private Clinic, 24 Seskines, Polyclinic No. 10. The only private clinic, English spoken. Weekdays 1–4pm. Tel: 46 85 83.
Vilnius Clinic No. 6, 57 Antakalnio. Tel: 74 45 19.

EMERGENCY NUMBERS

Fire: 01 (no coins needed).
Police: 02 (no coins needed).
Ambulance: 03 (no coins needed).

GETTING AROUND

ESTONIA

BY AIR

There is only one domestic carrier flying the pot-holed skies over Estonia and that is the state airline, Estonian Air. Estonian Air rose from the ashes of Aeroflot and operates 12 ex-Aeroflot Tupolevs. It has taken over many of Aeroflot's routes as well as the Tallinn office premises. Thankfully the standards of service have been improved. Estonian Air has a new computer ticketing system acquired from British Airways and the air hostesses are trained by SAS. Its domestic and Baltic flights include Kuressaare, Kardla and Riga and Vilnius. The flights are timesaving but the prices are high. Estonian Air operates a two-tier pricing system offering extremely low prices to those with a Russian or Estonian passport but asking rather too much from everyone else. (For comparison, a flight to Kuressaare on the island of Saaremaa is for an Estonian 30EEK, and for a foreigner 310EEK). Bookings can be made at the airports. In Tallinn the Estonian Air desk is in the domestic terminal but staff there sometimes only speak only Russian. More advisable is to book in advance at the office in the Old Town.
Estonian Air: Vabaduse väljak 10, Tallinn. Tel: 446 382.

BY RAIL

Lines radiate out from Tallinn railway station (*Balti jaam*) connecting the capital to all of Estonia's major towns and beyond. Though the service is frequent, it is slow. The information on trains is presented clearly on boards at all stations. No timetables are otherwise available. Travelling out of Estonia it is advisable to book your ticket in advance, especially so in the case of St Petersburg. If you know your date of return it is a good idea to book a return ticket to avoid difficulties at the other end – however chaotic booking a ticket may seem in Tallinn it is far worse in Riga, Vilnius or St Petersburg. There are ticket windows in the station concourse but they are often very busy and whichever queue you join, no matter what people around you may say, on reaching the counter you will invariably find it to have been the wrong one. Much easier is to use the adjacent but badly signposted booking office beside Platform 5.

Trains to Riga and St Petersburg are particularly good. They make the journey overnight, departing Tallinn shortly before midnight. Beds can be booked in four-berth coupés or for more privacy two-bed coupés are also available. The attendant gives a wake-up call around 7am shortly before the train arrives. For a small charge the attendant provides a pillow and sheets. No beverages are available but the carriage attendant has hot water continuously on the boil for passengers' use, so take a cup and a teabag.

BY BUS

For journeys within Estonia the bus is often a better alternative to the train. Buses depart more frequently, travel faster and provide a greater degree of comfort. The only drawback is that the buses have no luggage compartments or overhead racks inside. The only place to put large bags on the bus is behind the rear seats although often even this space is taken by standing passengers. Another possible problem is that many of the buses do not make any stops en route and they are not equipped with toilets. Most of the buses leave from the main bus stations but when booking your ticket check because there are other departure points in all towns. Tickets can be booked at the stations or in Tallinn also from the office at Pärnu mnt. 19, just behind the Palace hotel. Return portions of tickets cannot be booked at the point of departure so do this as soon as you reach your destination. If possible try to avoid travelling at weekends during the summer months.

Distances and journey times by bus:

Tallinn–Pärnu	80 miles/128 km	2½ hrs
Tallinn–Tartu	116 miles/187 km	3 hrs
Tallinn–Narva	132 miles/212 km	5 hrs
Tallinn–Kuressaare	138 miles/222 km	4 hrs
Tallinn–Riga	190 miles/307 km	5 hrs
Tallinn–Vilnius	377 miles/607 km	12 hrs

BY CAR

Having a car at your disposal is by far the best way to see Estonia. One of the rare benefits of the Soviet occupation is that the major routes connecting Tallinn's urban centres are very well defined and in a good state of repair. Another result of Soviet rule is that they are also fairly free of traffic. The real pleasure is in taking off from the main routes and following the minor roads as they wind between walls of towering dense forest. Make sure you have a full tank before setting out because petrol stations are scarce. It is also highly recommended that you carry a full spare can in the boot. The speed limit on open roads is 55 mph (90 kph). In built-up areas this decreases to 35 mph (50 kph). Front seat belts are required to be worn at all times. Parking is rarely a problem but it should be noted that cars are not admitted into the Old Town of Tallinn without a permit. When driving in Tallinn beware of the trams. They run along the centre of the road and when they stop to discharge their passengers all traffic must halt.

Traffic problems: In case of accident or emergency dial 02 for the police, or contact the Tallinn traffic police (*Tallinna Liikuspolitsei*), 31 Lastekodu, opposite the bus station. Tel: 445 450.

Car rental: A number of car rental agencies exist offering cars, and in some cases minibuses and vans, with or without drivers. Foreigners must have a valid licence and passport and are generally required to be over 22 years of age. Prices begin at around 480EEK per day without a driver.

Refit: Magasini 20, Tallinn. Tel: 661 046, 682 607, fax: 683 096. Also at the Hotel Olümpia service bureau. Tel: 602 434.

Ideal: Tallinn airport. Tel: 212 735/219 222, fax: 212 735. (Can also book from Sweden tel: 063 127 860, fax: 121 915; or Finland tel: 949 247 950.)

Baltic Limousine Service: 6th floor, Vabaduse väljak 10b, Tallinn. Tel: 666 672, fax: 444 725.

Taxis are expensive and not a good option for travelling long distances.

ORGANISED TOURS

A number of travel agencies offer daily sightseeing trips around Tallinn and excursions to other Estonian towns and places of interest. Most will also take care of flight and ferry bookings, car rental, provide guides and organise trips to the neighbouring Baltics and St Petersburg. As a hang-over of the old days, a number of agencies still offer such attractions as visits to local kindergartens, farms and factories but at least these are now just an option and no longer compulsory.

TALLINN

Estravel, Pikk 37, Old Town, Tallinn. Tel: 601 886/602 773, fax: 444 882, telex 173 223.

Estonian Holidays Ltd at the Viru Hotel, Viru väljak 4, Tallinn. Tel: 650 873, fax: 440 416.

Hermann Travel, Pärnu mnt, Old Town, Tallinn. Tel: 444 037, fax: 440 290.

Raetourist, Raekoja plats 18 (Town Hall Square), Old Town, Tallinn. Tel: 444 333, fax: 441 100.

WEST COAST & ISLANDS

Pärnu Travel Bureau, Kuninga 32, Pärnu. Tel: (244) 42 570.

SOUTHERN ESTONIA

A/s Real Tourist Company, Lipuväljak 4, Otepää, Valgamaa. Tel: (242) 54 042, fax: 55293.

TALLINN CITY TRANSPORT

Within Tallinn travel between the hours of 5am–midnight (6am–midnight on Sunday) is relatively painless. Although a little crowded at times public transport is very good with a system of trams, buses and trolleybuses covering the city.

Trams: There are four main tram routes, numbered, sensibly enough, 1, 2, 3 and 4. They run east-west across the centre of the city. Trams 1 and 2 originate in the district of Kopli and terminate at Kadriorg and Ülemiste respectively. Trams 3 and 4 originate at Tondi and again terminate at Kadriorg and Ülemiste. Trams 1 and 3 stop at the railway station and also pass close to the harbour. Trams 2 and 4 serve the main bus terminus.

Trolleybuses: Are those with the grasshopper antenna. They run beneath their electrified cables from either the train station or department store out to the residential districts of Mustamäe and Öismäe.

Buses: Cover all of the routes above plus everywhere else. Important is bus 22 which is the bus for the airport. It can be caught from Vabaduse väljak or across from the front of the Estonia Theatre.

For information about public transport:

Buses: Tel: 444 484

Trams: Tel: 556 903

Trolleybuses: Tel: 491 870

Tickets: Are purchased at special kiosks around town, usually sited next to major bus stops. They can also be bought from some news kiosks – the kiosks stick a wad of tickets in the window as an indication. One ticket is used each time you travel. The ticket must be punched using the small machines affixed in the interiors of the vehicles. The system relies on honesty though authorities do occasionally patrol to check on passengers' tickets. A fine is levied on those travelling unlawfully. An unlimited monthly travel card (*kuupilet*) is also available.

Maps: A very useful map exists called, explicitly, *Tallinn: City Plan with Public Transport*. Clear and up-to-date, it marks all the tram, bus and trolleybus routes and on the reverse gives further detailed information. The map is on sale at bookshops and some kiosks.

Elsewhere in Estonia: There are no trams or trolleybuses in towns outside of Tallinn, just buses. They all operate similar ticketing systems which are non-transferable. In rural areas the tickets are bought from the driver.

Taxis: There are three taxi firms in Tallinn, two private and a third, the largest, Taksopark, run by the state. All three offer 24-hour service and can be ordered to collect. It is always advisable to order a taxi over the phone or through a reception desk to avoid the illegal taxi mafia who have seized control of the most lucrative taxi ranks and who charge vastly inflated fares.

Tallinna Taksopark: Tulika 33. Tel: 444 856.

Tallinna Taksokeskus: Tulika 33. Tel: 603 044.

Esra: Püssirohu 6. Tel: 602 340/430 330.

THE COLOUR OF LIFE.

A holiday may last just a week or so, but the memories of those happy, colourful days will last forever, because together you and Kodak Ektachrome films will capture, as large as life, the wondrous sights, the breathtaking scenery and the magical moments. For you to relive over and over again.

The Kodak Ektachrome range of slide films offers a choice of light source, speed and colour rendition and features extremely fine grain, very high sharpness and high resolving power.

Take home the real colour of life with Kodak Ektachrome films.

LIKE THIS?

OR LIKE THIS?

A KODAK FUN PANORAMIC CAMERA
BROADENS YOUR VIEW

The holiday you and your camera have been looking forward to all year; and a stunning panoramic view appears. "Fabulous", you think to yourself, "must take that one".

Unfortunately, your lens is just not wide enough. And three-in-a-row is a poor substitute.

That's when you take out your pocket-size, 'single use' Kodak Fun Panoramic Camera. A film and a camera, all in one, and it works miracles. You won't need to focus, you don't need special lenses. Just aim, click

and... it's all yours. The total picture. You take twelve panoramic pictures with one Kodak Fun Panoramic Camera. Then put the camera in for developing and printing.

Each print is 25 by 9 centimetres. Excellent depth of field. True Kodak Gold colours.

The Kodak Fun Panoramic Camera itself goes back to the factory, to be recycled. So that others too can capture one of those spectacular phooooooooooootoooooooooooooos.

BY AIR

Since Latvia is a small country, few people take domestic flights, although this can be done. No flight takes more than 30 minutes. Foreigners will be charged in hard currency.
Riga Airport: Tel: 223 175

BY RAIL

Travel by train is extremely cheap by Western standards, and the seating is comfortable enough. Make sure you get ticket at least a day in advance, otherwise you may end up standing most of the way between frequently travelled routes on weekends. However, opting for the train also means spending more time getting from point A to point B. Even express trains stop in the larger urban centres along the route between the Baltic capitals, so keep that in mind if you are in a hurry: Riga to Ventspils, for example, a distance of 125 miles (202 km) can take more than five hours. Local trains travelling within Latvia have no toilets, but the international trains are fully equipped. One can reserve a place in a *kupē* (4 beds per car), and if that doesn't work out, try the *platskarte*, a whole train car set up with beds but with no partitions, like a dormitory. The electric commuter trains, however, are fast and convenient and an easy way to reach Jūrmala: in Riga tickets can be bought minutes before departure at the central train station section closest to the big clock in the square. The further section is for longer-distance travel.
Riga Railway Station: Tel: 232 134

BY BUS

Travel by bus is also inexpensive by Western standards and, as in the trains, the seating is comfortable enough. The same rules for getting tickets also apply: get them a day in advance or you may end up standing most of the way. Travelling by bus can be even slower than by train (unless one takes express routes). The lack of toilet facilities is only a minor inconvenience, since the facilities in the bus stations along the way can be used.
Minibuses also stop at the Riga bus station. They are faster and more expensive than the bigger buses. Another minibus terminal is located across the street from the Riga Central Railway Station.
Riga Bus Station: Prāgas iela. Tel: 213 611

BY CAR

Except for a small stretch between Riga and Jūrmala and another between Riga and Jelgava, there are no multi-lane superhighways running through Latvia but the road network is adequate for car and bus travel. The country's 30 major urban centres are all connected by two-lane paved roads, for the most part in good repair, but watch out for potholes and construction work because, more often than not, they are poorly marked. The streets in the cities, particularly Riga, are not always in good condition, and the cobblestones in older sectors are sure to give your shock absorbers a beating.

CAR RENTAL IN RIGA

Auseklītis, 13 Dzirnavu iela. Tel: 331 505. Opel, ORD, BMW and other cars. $50 a day plus 30 cents per kilometre.
Hotel Riga, 30 Aspāzijas bulv. Tel: 216 516. For Soviet cars with driver, tel: 216 516. For Western models, tel: 532 412 between 8am and 4pm. For minibuses, tel: 627 755 between 8.30am and 5pm.
Ventus, Hotel de Rome, 28 Kaļķu iela Tel: 216 268 (24 hours). Volvo, Ford and other cars for hard currency. Prices vary according to the distance and duration.
Hertz and **Avis** also rent cars from Riga airport, tel: 207 333; Avis: tel: 225 876.

TAXIS

Taxis are available in every urban centre in Latvia. One can order them by phone (which is more expensive) or catch them in the street. There are two types of taxis: state and private. Both can be recognised by a green light shining in the front windshield near the driver. State taxis are painted yellow and have a taxi light on the roof. As elsewhere in Eastern Europe, many taxi drivers in Latvia believe that all foreigners have money growing on trees in their back yards, so be prepared to get stung at the airport, bus depot, train station and at hotels. Although the official currency is the local currency, you will, more likely than not, be given a price in hard currency.

Elsewhere in the city the drivers are usually more honest, even to foreigners. Ask the driver his price before stepping in, and don't be afraid to bargain with him. Once you have verbally settled on a price, step inside. He won't suddenly ask you for more once you have reached your destination.

Private car owners are often willing to go out of their way and take you to your destination, for approximately the same rate as taxi drivers. Therefore, don't be afraid to flag down any car that's passing by, even if it doesn't have the telltale green light.

If you are a woman, however, stick to the yellow state taxis, especially at night. Women at night are advised to travel in pairs or be accompanied by men. Although cases of sexual assault are not as common as in major Western urban centres, they do occur nonetheless.
To order a taxi in Latvia: Tel: 334 041/333 354
Taxi vans: Tel: 225 551/272 769. 8-20

ORGANISED TOURS

A number of operators run excursions to the best-known sites and destinations, and many of them can be booked through the major hotels.

Intourist Travel Agency, Riga. Tel: 211 781. Bus and minibus tours go to Sigulda, Rundāle and Jūrmala.

Bureau of Tourism, 10 Smilšu iela, Riga. Tel: 224 903. By bus to Sigulda and Gaujas National Park, Rundāle, and Vecpiebalga. They also do a tour westwards to Talsi, Sabile, Kandava and Kuldīga.

Lattours, 29-31 Bruninieku iela, Riga. Tel: 274 952. They organise Old Riga walking tours and three or four-day excursion covering Riga itself, Jūrmala, Sigulda and Rundāle. A 10-day programme takes in a stay at Jūrmala.

Latvia Tours, 22-24 Grēcinieku iela, Riga. Tel: 213 652. Individual and group excursions, Old Riga walking tours, excursions to Riga Museums. Excursions by bus to Rundāle and Kuldīga, and to other Baltic towns: Tallinn and Tartu in Estonia and Klaipėda and Vilnius in Lithuania. It also organises **helicopter flights** for up to seven people and **air balloon** trips for three people at a time for $25 for 15 minutes.

CITY TRANSPORT

Like other state-funded services, urban transport is deteriorating in Latvia. Most of the city buses were made in Hungary and most trolleys were made in the former Czechoslovakia, and both countries are demanding hard currency for spare parts, which Latvia can little afford. Vehicles in the worst shape are being stripped for parts, reducing the number of vehicles on the road.

Several bus routes have already been cancelled, but otherwise, the remaining bus, trolley and tramway routes are adequately serviced, from around 6am to midnight. Service in Riga is still acceptable. The only problem is that routes may be overcrowded during rush hours. Tickets are inexpensive for Westerners and can be obtained at kiosks throughout the city. Fares are good for one trip of unlimited length, but tickets are not transferable, so another is needed if you switch vehicles. Children under 7 travel free. Monthly passes are also available.

Special services: Excursion by retro tram to Riga Zoo. Tel: 371 349.

WATERWAYS

River-borne traffic has been a common feature of the Daugava and Lielupe, though a fall off in tourism and increase in fuel prices have considerably reduced the available services.

One can take the *Liepāja* or *Misisipi* ferry from Old Riga to Majori, Lielupe, Dole, Jelgava, Lake Baltezers or Lake Ķīšezers (local currency).

Craft rental in Riga: Tel: 0132-615 095

LITHUANIA

BY AIR

In the summer Lithuanian Airlines has frequent flights from Vilnius to Palanga, the seaside resort near Klaipėda. Lietuvos Avialinijos (Lithuanian Airlines) has branch offices in major towns around the country.

Vilnius: 12 Ukmergės str., tel: 75 25 88/75 32 12, fax: 35 48 52. Airport inquiries: tel: 63 02 01/66 94 81.

Kaunas: 7-9 Gertrudes. Tel: 29 17 70. Airport inquiries: tel: 22 81 76; Airport booking office: tel: 22 97 06.

Klaipėda: 107 Taikos pr. Airport inquiries: tel: 304 09; Airport booking office: tel: 304 09.

Panevėžys, 15 Laisvės al. Tel: 332 98.

Palanga: Kretingos 1. Airport inquiries: tel: 530 31; Airport booking office: tel: 534 31; Booking office, 100 Vytauto, tel: 533 31.

Druskininkai, Čiurlionio 2a. Tel: 510 25.

BY RAIL

Frequent trains link Vilnius to Kaunas (2 hours), Klaipėda (10 hours), Panevėžys and other cities in Lithuania. Much the same conditions of travel apply in Lithuania as in Estonia and Latvia.

Vilnius Station: 16 Geležinkelio str. Tel: 63 00 88. Last-minute tickets for the same day and only for domestic destinations have to be bought at the station. Count on queuing for between one and two hours.

Reservation Bureau: 3 Šopeno str. (near the station). Tel: 62 30 44. For home delivery, tel: 62 69 56.

For foreign destinations you still have to go to the former Intourist travel bureau in the Lietuva Hotel, 20 Ukmergės str. Tel: 35 62 25.

Druskininkai 3 Gardino. Tel: 534 43.

Kaunas 16 Čiurlionio. Tel: 22 10 93. Booking Office: tel: 29 24 55. Advance booking: tel: 29 24 55.

Klaipėda 7 Prtiestoties. Tel 146 14. Booking office: 312 15. Advance booking, 107 Taiokos. Tel: 936 56.

Panevėžys Stoties. Tel: 630 51.

BY BUS

Travelling by bus is quite popular in Lithuania since trains do not serve every town and village. Bus is the cheapest way to get around but a long ride can be quite uncomfortable.

Vilnius Bus Station: 22 Sodų str. (next to the Railway Station). Tel: 26 24 82.

Advance Booking: Tel: 26 29 77

Same Day Booking: Tel: 26 22 93

International Booking: Tel: 63 52 77

BY CAR

Lithuania's roads and highways are comparatively well kept. The highway from Vilnius to Klaipėda and the M12 to Panevėžys are quite good. On secondary roads and in town watch out for treacherous potholes and sewers. Avoid driving at night and watch out for unexpected obstacles such as bricks and planks of wood. You are forbidden to drink and drive. You risk a hefty fine and the Lithuanian police may take you straight to the police station for a blood test.

Most petrol stations sell only low-grade A-76 octane or A-92 octane petrol but you can find Western leaded and unleaded high-grade petrol and diesel at a number of Western-style service stations that are being opened around Lithuania by the Lithuanian-Finnish joint venture Litofinn.

Hitching a ride is quite common in Lithuania. It is understood that passengers pay their share.

CAR RENTAL

Baltic Auto, 28 Žvejų. Tel: 73 13 85, fax: 73 21 60. Weekdays 9am–5pm
Eva Garage, 14 Jačionų. Tel: 64 94 28/64 94 19. Amex credit cards accepted. Monday–Thursday 8.15am–5pm, Friday 8.15am–4pm.
Litinterp, 10/15 Vokiečių. Tel: 61 20 40, fax: 62 34 15. Budget chauffeur-driven cars and minibus rental.
Balticar. Tel: 46 09 98, fax: 75 89 24. 24-hour.

TAXIS

You can find regular or private taxis at any taxi-stand. If you book one it will come within the hour. Taxis rarely possess functioning taximeters and very often the fare is subject to discussion. Foreigners are sometimes asked to pay in hard currency. Try to avoid it.
To book a taxi: Vilnius, tel: 22 88 88; Kaunas, tel: 23 44 44; Klaipėda, tel: 192 58; Panevėžys, tel: 666 56; Šiauliai, tel: 422 01.

CITY TRANSPORT

Public transport in Lithuania is well developed and the biggest cities have trolley-buses. Vilnius counts some 50 bus lines and some 20 trolley-bus lines criss-crossing the capital. Tickets can be bought in most kiosks, *spaudos kioskas*, and the passenger must punch one in the machine inside the bus.

WATERWAYS

In the summer you can take a boat on the River Nemunas from Kaunas to Nida on the Neringa Spit. The speedy passenger boat leaves every day from the Prieplauka, 107 Kaunas Raudondvario plentas, tel: 8-27-26 13 48.

Two ferries link Klaipėda to the Neringa Spit. The boats leave every half hour and the crossing takes barely 10 minutes. Tel: 122 24. Booking office for the boat *Rasketa* in Klaipėda. Tel: 144 88.

Boat trips on the River Neris from Vilnius to Valakampiai, Prieplauka (quai), T. Kosciuskos 4. Tel: 61 29 72.

ORGANISED TOURS

Lithuanian Tourism Association, Ukmerges 20. Tel: 35 61 91.
Lithuanian Tours, Seiminiskiu 18/1. Tel:/fax: 35 18 15.
Balticorp, Gedimino 26, room 217. Tel: 22 03 03, fax: 22 63 68.
Baltic Tours, Tumo Vaizganto 9/1. Tel: 22 78 78, fax: 22 67 67.
Baltic Travel Service, Liejyklos 2. Tel: 62 40 28, fax: 62 41 29.
GT International Travel Consultants, Kalvariju 223. Tel: 77 83 92, fax: 35 01 15.
Int Express, Dariaus ir Gireno 25. Tel: 26 71 56, 26 48 88.
Lietuva, Ukmerges 20. Tel: 35 60 14.
Litamicus, Jogailos 9/1. Tel:/fax: 22 44 74.
Liturimex, Gedimino pr 14. Tel: 61 00 50/22 60 63, fax: 62 17 70.
Okto-Piligrimas, Sevcenkos 19. Tel: 63 07 06, fax: 22 49 52.
Sputnikas, Jogailos 9/1. Tel:/fax: 22 48 84.
Villon, Sevcenkos 31. Tel: 65 13 85, fax: 65 13 85.

WHERE TO STAY

All three countries are poorly served by hotels and those in the capitals are often booked well in advance, so if is best to book if possible before leaving home, especially in summer, when it can also be difficult trying to extend a stay. There is also an enormous price discrepancy between the traditional main city hotels and their counterparts in other towns, where they are much less likely to demand the inflated hard currency rate. The smartest hotels are joint ventures, usually with German or Scandinavian partners, and though they are relatively expensive ($80–$120 a night) they are not as expensive as their counterparts in the West, nor, in general, are they as sophisticated. Small local-currency hotels can be one-tenth of the price. Visitors might consider alternative accommodation, such as through agencies which lodge people with local families.

ESTONIA
HOTELS

The lack of hotel space, led to a bizarre announcement in late 1992 by the Estonian Immigration Department to the effect that because of a shortage of hotels they were cutting back on the numbers of visas issued. Even more bizarrely they followed this up with a statement a few weeks later saying they were further cutting back on visas because not only were there too few beds available but hotel prices in Estonia were too expensive for visitors. They are half right; there are very few decent hotels and often guests are charged Western prices for all-too Soviet service. Salt is rubbed in the wound by the practice employed by many hotels of a two-tiered pricing system. Under this system people with Soviet or Baltic passports get to pay what approximates to a true rate while foreign guests are obliged to pay a rate of up to 10 times higher.

The system of room categorisation in Estonia includes *lux* and *super lux*. Definitions of these vary between hotels but in general *lux* indicates a suite, with *super lux* being a suite with a greater number of rooms. If you are offered *half lux* forget it; this means they string a curtain across your single room to create an impromptu reception area. The star-rating system may disappoint if you are comfortable with international standards. While the hotels given as ☆☆☆☆ are generally deserving, of those with ☆☆☆ only the Taru measures up. And while the

Emmi, Peoleo and Pirita may have some justification for their ☆☆ the Kungla doesn't come close.

Price rating system: Cheap = below 300EEK; Average = 3–500EEK; Expensive = 5–800EEK; Very Expensive = over 800EEK. All payment must be made in Estonian kroons.

TALLINN

Palace ☆☆☆☆, Vabaduse väljak 3. Tel: 443 461/444 761, fax: 443 098. After independence the Palace was home temporarily to at least three Western embassies. Run by a Finnish-Estonian company, no other hotel in Tallinn comes remotely close in quality. Rooms have private bars, televisions in every room receive MTV and Sky TV and the phones have international direct dialling. The hotel has a suitably high-class restaurant attached, the Linda, as well as a more modest pizzeria. On the top floor are a nightclub and casino. All credit cards accepted. Very expensive. Single: 1,890EEK, double: 2,390EEK, lux: 2,460EEK.

Olümpia ☆☆☆, Liivalaia 33. Tel: 602 600/602 438, fax: 602 492, telex: 173 165 HOOL SU. Another Soviet-era monster hotel that dubiously lays claim to being three star. Westernisation is well underway at the Olümpia with Finest, the people behind the Palace, being a major interest in the redevelopment. The Olümpia doesn't offer the number of facilities that the Viru does and it is a little further distant from the Old Town but nevertheless it is very popular with tour groups and is often full to capacity. There is a restaurant, two cafes and a bar as well as a nightclub. Also a gift shop, florist, beauty parlour and, on the second floor, a medical centre. Expensive. Single: 590EEK, double: 780EEK, lux: 950EEK.

Viru ☆☆☆, Viru väljak 4. Tel: 652 093/652 084. Possibly Tallinn's most infamous landmark with a reputation to match. This hotel is rapidly attempting to shed its Soviet trappings in a haste to embrace the Western tourist. Service aside it has much to recommend it. The views of the Old Town are wonderful and they make dining in the 22nd floor restaurant almost a pleasure. The Viru possesses two other restaurants as well as a ground floor café and a couple of bars. Amenities include a conference centre, beautician, hairdressers and fitness centre, florist, gift shop and news kiosk. All credit cards accepted. Expensive. Single: 650EEK, double: 800EEK.

Peoleo ☆☆, Pärnu mnt. 555, Laagri. Tel: 556 469, fax: 771 463, telex: 173 872 SOOTS. Another alternative to staying in the city proper. A 15-minute drive out along the Pärnu road the Peoleo is an attractive lodge-like motel, far more Scandinavian than Soviet. All the rooms contain two single beds, a bathroom, telephone and TV. Meals are served in the Vana Saku dining hall. There is also a quick-service diner, a barber, shop and conference rooms. Expensive. Single: 596EEK, double: 884EEK.

Pirita ☆☆, Regati pst 1, Pirita. Tel: 238 598/238 615, fax: 237 433. Built for the 1980 Olympic yachting events, the former Sport hotel is attractively located in a forested coastal strip. It is 3 miles (5 km) from the town centre but the adjacent beach, marina and forest walks may be adequate compensation. The hotel is reasonably self-contained with a restaurant, café, bar, conference rooms, fitness centre and pool. Average. Single: 405EEK, double: 510EEK.

Kungla, Kreutzwaldi 23. Tel: 421 460, 427 040. Only included because with so few hotels in Tallinn someone may have to resort to it one day. Even the receptionists have gone on record describing it as "horrible". Two-tier pricing. Average. Single: 500EEK, lux: 600EEK.

Tallinn, Toompuiestee 27. Tel: 0142-604 142/604 332. Well situated at the foot of Toompea and close to the railway station this hotel is however, rather grim and unappealing. Two-tier rates. Average. Single: 400EEK, double: 600EEK, lux: 800EEK.

HAAPSALU

Hotel Haapsalu ☆☆☆☆, Posti 43. Tel: 247-44 847, fax: 247-45 191. Extremely comfortable modern hotel in the centre of town. Restaurant, bar and conference hall. Average. Single: 400EEK, double: 500EEK, suite: 600EEK.

Pension Pipi, Posti 37. Tel: 247-45 174, fax: 247-45 191. Eight rooms some sharing showers and toilets. Café, boutique and a sauna. Average. Single: 300EEK, double: 350EEK.

Yacht Club, Holmi 5a. Tel: 247-97 172. Out of the centre on the headland. Basic but clean. Offers boat, yacht and bicycle hire. No prices available.

NARVA

Hotel Narva, Pushkini 6. Tel: 235-22 700. Like everything in Narva, more Soviet-style than elsewhere in Estonia. Average. Single: 300EEK, double: 420EEK.

Vanalinn, Koidula 6. Tel: 235-22 486. This is the best hotel Narva has to offer. Located in a quaint medieval building, which is the main attraction. Basic but clean. Single: 300EEK, double: 420EEK.

PARNU

Victoria ☆☆☆☆, Kuninga 25. Tel: 244-43 412, fax: 244-43 415. Very attractive belle-epoque hotel. Each room has a telephone, satellite TV, minibar and shower. Very good restaurant. Bar, sauna and gift shop. Very expensive. Single: 1,100EEK, double: 1,440EEK, suite: 1,880EEK.

Emmi ☆☆, Laine 2. Tel: 244-22 043. Beside the sea a mile (2 km) out of the town centre. Bar, sauna and restaurant next door. Cheap. Single: 200EEK, double: 300EEK.

Pärnu, Rüütli 44. Tel: 244-42 145. Centrally located dingy Soviet-era hotel. Cheap. Single: 230EEK, double: 300EEK, lux: 560EEK.

TARTU

Taru ☆☆☆, Rebase 9. Tel: 234-73 700, fax: 234-74 095, telex: 173 104 TARU SU. Luxury hotel, sister to the Palace in Tallinn. Ten minutes from the centre it has a very good restaurant, the Fox, and bar. Also offers business services, car transfer, sightseeing. All credit cards accepted. Expensive. Single: 790EEK, double: 980EEK.

Park, Vallikraavi 23. Tel: 234-33 663. Fine location on wooded slopes. Bar, café and sauna. Cheap. Single: 140EEK; with shower 400EEK, double: 180EEK; with shower 400EEK.

Pro Studiorum, Tuglase 13. Tel: 234-61 853/61 386, fax: 234-31 481, telex: 173 209 PTB SU. Converted apartment building 15-minutes' walk from the centre. Rooms are all triple or double bed suites. Pretty café/restaurant and small bar and handicraft shop. Pro Studiorum also has extensive experience organising tours. Average. Single: 290EEK, double: 430EEK.

Tartu, Soola 3. Tel: 234-32 091. Gloomy state hotel next to the bus station. Cheap. Single: 60EEK, double: 96–156EEK.

VILJANDI

Hotel Viljandi, Tartu 11. Tel: 243-53 852. Included not even as a last resort but as a warning. Complaints against include filth, bugs in the bathroom, poor sanitation and use by the locals as a party venue.

Kivi farm, Viljandi maakond, Kramsi. Tel: 243-91 457. A very hospitable couple welcome guests 3 miles (5 km) from Viljandi in the village of Ramsi. They offer a self-contained building of six bedrooms, lounge, dining room, shower and sauna. Very cheap. Single: 35EEK, double: 75EEK.

Sammuli, Männimäe tee 28. Tel: 243-54 463/94 713, fax: 243-53 104. Large lodge on the shores of Lake Viljandi, 4 miles (6 km) out of town. Rooms are basic with shared bathrooms but comfortable with balconies overlooking the lake. Meals are served and there is a bar. Good sports facilities with tennis courts, a basketball court and rowing boats for hire. Reduction for longer stays. Cheap. Single: 220EEK, double: 380EEK, room for four: 550EEK.

VORU

Võru Tourist Centre, Manniku 43, Võru. Tel: 241-71 489/31 354, fax: 241-31 757. Located on the pine covered shores of Lake Kubija 1 mile from the town centre. The complex includes the very large **Kubija Hotel** (50-rooms), beautifully situated, with bar and dining room. Chalet-style accommodation for families, plus camping facilities. Hiking and canoeing expeditions are easily arranged. An excellent base to explore southern Estonia.

MOTELS & CAMPING

Pesa ☆☆☆, Uus 5, Polva, a small town 26 miles (42 km) from Tartu. Tel: 230-90 086. All 32 rooms have telephones, satellite TV and shower. There is a restaurant and bar. The hotel has a good trade from organising hunting expeditions. Expensive Single: 600EEK, double: 820EEK.

Rootsa Camping ☆☆, Tuksi, Lääne maakond, 22 miles (36 km) from Haapsalu. Tel: 247-93 732. Luxury camping. A Swedish-Estonian venture offering 23 six-bed cottages in forest beside the sea. All cottages are heated and have a living-room, bedroom, WC, kitchenette, TV, telephone, fridge. The site has restaurant, bar, sauna, minigolf and tennis. Expensive.

Kernu, Harju maakond, 23 miles (37 km) from Tallinn on the Pärnu road. Tel: 771 630. Basic: shared showers and toilets, communal TV room. They also have four-person chalets. Cheap. Chalet per person: 100EEK, double room: 200–300EEK.

Mäha, Phajarve vald 7-4, Valgamaa. Tel: 242-54 003. About 2 miles (3 km) from the centre of Otepää, situated by a small lake, fine for swimming. Attractive, clean and restful, but only two showers and two toilets to 31 beds. Bar and lakeside sauna. Cheap. 100EEK per person.

Oru-Kolga, Kolga, Oru. Tel: 242-55 213. Handsome hillside site close to the Pühajarv lake and beach. Ten rooms and 20 beds. Reportedly lukewarm atmosphere and infrequent hot water. Cheap. Double room: 300EEK.

ALTERNATIVE ACCOMMODATION

There are a couple of other options for those looking for something different or something cheaper. The first option is to contact the **Family Hotel Association**, Mere pst, Old Town, Tallinn, tel:/fax: 441 187. This organisation claims to be the cheapest and one of the most interesting ways to stay in Estonia. It has a network of more than 300 family homes and seperate apartments throughout Estonia, including the islands, and also in Riga and Vilnius. The association places visitors in the spare rooms of local residents allowing them to make a little supplementary income and providing the tourist with a chance to get a real insight into life in Estonia. The amenities offered are dependent on the host but the minimum is a room, a bed with clean sheets and washing facilities. For those with no desire for such contact the FHA also has a number of unoccupied flats for rent on a nightly basis. The accommodations are not always central and their cleanliness varies but they are usually quite large and the hosts are generally well-educated, upper middle-class professionals. Prices range from 100EEK for a room to 300EEK for a complete apartment.

Part of the international youth hostels network, the **Estonian Youth Hostel Association** (*Eesti Puhkemajad*), was set up in 1992. They operate eight hostels: two on the west coast from Haapsalu to south of Pärnu, two in the Otepää region, three in Tallinn and one just west of Tallinn. The hostels vary considerably in form – from converted farmhouses to purpose-built camp huts – and amenities – bicycles, boats and skis are all for hire at different hostels. Rooming arrangements may be seven-bed dormitories or twin rooms. No membership of a hosteling association is required nor is there any restriction on age or group size. Rates can range up to 300EEK (at Lepanina, which is more a fully-fledged hotel than hostel) per night but are often less than 10. All bookings can be at the individual hostels or through the main Tallinn office. The Tallinn office can also make bookings for affiliated hostels in St Petersburg and Helsinki.
Estonian Youth Hostels, Liivalaia 2, Tallinn. Tel: 445 853.

NORTH COAST

Agnes, Narva mnt. 7, Tallinn. Tel: 438 870. Open: April–August.
Kloogall, Keila, Harjumaa. Tel: 743 242. Open: April–November.
Kuramaa, Kuramaa 15, Lasnamäe, Tallinn. Tel: 327 781/327 715. Open: all year.
Polyhostel, Liivalaia 2, Tallinn. Tel: 445 853. Open: all year.

WEST COAST

Lepanina, Häädemeeste, Pärnu. Tel: 244-98 477/ 40 230, fax: 244-40 773. Open: all year.
Virtsu, Hanila k/n, Läänemaa. Tel: 75 527/624 562. Open: May–September, though by arrangement will accommodate large parties out of season.

THE SOUTH

Otepää, Otepää linn. Tel: 242-55 934/40 230, fax: 40 773. Open: all year.
Taevaskoja, Polva maakond, Polva. Tel: 230-447 274. Open: all year.

LATVIA
HOTELS

The hotel industry is still underdeveloped in Latvia, but gaining momentum. Joint-ventures have successfully established Western-style accommodation within the quarters of existing hotels in Riga. The Hotel de Rome and the Metropole are the most expensive in Latvia. The star ratings beside each hotel's name are the researchers' and not official ratings.

RIGA

Eurolink ☆☆☆☆, 22 Azpāzijas bulv. Tel: 216 317. A joint-venture located on the third floor of the Hotel Riga. It has 56 rooms with refrigerators and cable TV. Brasserie, bar, restaurant, 24-hour laundry service, souvenir shop, conference rooms, translation services, free airport shuttle, safety box, luggage room. Single room: $135, double room: $160.

Fremad ☆☆☆☆, 55 Elizabetes iela. Tel: 221 611. Renovated by a Danish company on the 16th floor of the Hotel Latvija, it has 33 rooms with satellite TV, satellite phone, photocopy and typing services. Single room: 140DM, double room: 207DM.

Hotel de Rome ☆☆☆☆, 28 Kaļķu iela. Tel: 216 286. One of the smartest places to stay, it is centrally located on the edge of the Old Town. It has 90 rooms, restaurant, and two bars. Extras: sauna, massage, hairdresser, mobile phone, car rental, ticket reservations. Single room: 235DM, double room: 305DM.

Metropole ☆☆☆☆, Aspāzijas 36-38. Tel 216 184. Opened in 1993 as the best place in the Baltics to stay. It is in a fine old building centrally situated. 78 rooms, bar, restaurant, four conference rooms. Single room: $140, double room: $165, suite $265. All credit cards except Diners Card accepted.

Rīdzene ☆☆☆☆, 1 Endrupa iela. Tel: 324 433/ 324 596. A modern, central hotel where the party elite used to stay, but pleasant looking for all that. It has 49 rooms, satellite TV, sauna, swimming pool, conference hall seating 50 people, banquet hall, and billiards. Single room: $74, double room: $90, junior suites: $130, luxury suites: $190, all excluding breakfast.

Rīga ☆☆☆, 22 Aspāzijas bulv. Tel: 216 700. Very central and the more pleasant of the Intourist hotels. 300 rooms, three restaurants, three bars, sauna, hairdresser, plane and train ticket reservations, foreign newspaper and magazine kiosk. Single room: $50, double room: $70 excluding breakfast.

Latvija ☆☆☆, 55 Elizabetes iela. Tel: 212 503. You can't miss this landmark glasshouse, Intourist at its brassiest. Its 356 rooms have pretty thin walls. There are seven restaurants, express bar. Extras: sauna, hairdresser, massage, variety show, foreign newspaper and magazine kiosk, conference facilities, car parking, girls. Centrally located. Single room: $111, double room: $117.

LOWER BUDGET RIGA HOTELS
(spartan but clean)

Saulīte ☆☆☆, 12 Merķeļa iela. Tel: 224 546. Single room: 240LVR (1.20 lati), double room: 400LVR.

Baltija ☆☆, 3 Raiņa bulv. Tel: 227 461. Single room: 263LVR (5.25 lati).

Tūrists ☆☆, 1 Slokas iela. Tel: 615 455. Single room: 300LVR (1.5 lati) for 1 night, 200 (1 lats) thereafter.

Viktorija ☆☆, 55 A. Čaka iela. Tel: 272 305. Single room: 330LVR (1.65 lati), double room: 540LVR (2.80 lati).

BATS, 33 Raiņa bulv. Hostel with English spoken. $9 a night.

Laine, 11 Skolas iela. Tel: 287 658. Single room: $7, luxury apartment $14–$19.

JURMALA

The seaside resort of Jūrmala can be easily reached by electric commuter train from Riga in less than half an hour. It has white, sandy beaches and numerous sanatoriums for recuperation.

Jūrmala, 47-49 Jomas iela. Tel: 761 340, fax: 761 455. The main hotel has 258 rooms, a casino, and two hard-currency bars. Single room: $30–60, double room: $60–120.

Majori, 29 Jomas iela. Tel: 761 380.

Pumpuri, 2 Upes iela. Tel: 767 554. Summer hotel.

Vaivari, 1 Atbalss iela. Tel: 736 392. Summer hotel.

AROUND LATVIA

Bauska, 7 Slimnicas iela. Tel: 39-24705. Bar, café, TV in some rooms but no phones. 230LVR–380LVR (1.15–1.9 lati).

Brencis, on the M12 just north of Bauska, 22 miles (38 km) from Riga. Unusual and welcome motel acccommodation in rural setting. Satellite and video communications, gym, sauna, tennis court. Moderately priced.

Kuldīga, Hotel Kursa, 6 Pilsētas laukums. Tel 33-22430. Modern, the only place in town. 300–400LVR (1.5–2 lati).

Sigulda, 19 Televīzijas iela. Tel 973 121. Just 12 rooms. 200LVR (1 lats).

Talsi, 16 Kareivju iela. Tel 32-22689. No facilities, but pleasantly situated overlooking the lake. $15.

When travelling throughout Latvia you will find most towns have at least one hotel. Facilities will be very basic but acceptable.

CAMPING

Camping grounds usually have no water and only one poorly lit toilet. You are not expected to run up and pitch a tent, but use cabins already built. As in most countries the sites are often attractively situated by lakes and rivers, in the middle of forests, or by the sea. With the demise of the Pioneers and other state-enforcers of holiday many now lie rather empty. Among those worth pursuing are: **Starts** in Vaivari, **Sigulda** in Sigulda, **Mežezers** in Plaviņas, and **Sauleskalns** and **Ezernieki** both in the Rēzekne region. Camping holidays can be arranged by **Alternative**, Riga, tel: 270 369; and **Environmental Protection Club of Talsi**, tel: (Talsi) 232 23273.

LITHUANIA HOTELS

Vilnius is short of quality hotels and many of them are booked for months in advance. Some have been restored and re-opened with foreign management.

Others, especially the smaller ones, are brand new and make you really feel at home. Most hotels ask their guests to pay in hard currency. A large number of state-owned hotels remain and these have little incentive for quality, service or customer satisfaction. It is also worth bearing in mind that the word "luxury" still means nothing more than a door that actually locks.

VILNIUS

Astorija ☆☆☆, 32/5 Didžioji. Tel: 62 99 14; reservations: 22 40 31; fax: 22 00 97. This well located old-fashioned looking hotel is Norwegian run and one of the most comfortable in town. Single room: $30–$60, double: $40–$100, suites: $130.
Karolina Hotel ☆☆☆, Sausio 13-Osios 2. Tel: 45 39 39/26 91 87, fax: 26 33 41. Set in the Karolimiskes district this hotel, opened in 1993, offers pleasantly refurbished rooms, three conference rooms, sauna, pool and four indoor tennis courts.
Mabre ☆☆☆, 13 Maironio. Tel: 61 41 62, fax: 61 30 86. This is Vilnius's most exclusive hotel, in a former monastery. It is highly recommended if you can get in: there are only four suites. 119DM, with 30 percent reduction on additional persons.
Šarūnas ☆☆☆, 4 Raitininkų. Tel: 35 38 88; reservations: 35 48 88; fax: 29 00 72. Built by Lithuania's basketball star Šarūnas Marčiulionis, this is a popular, stylish hotel with a personal touch from the proprietor: sneakers hanging from the ceiling of the Rooney Bar.
Zebis ☆☆☆, 6 Sibiro. Tel: 69 07 07, fax: 69 08 90. This is a bit of a one-off, situated in the hilly landscape of the southeastern Markučiai district. There is a sauna and billiard room and breakfast is in the planetarium. There are only four rooms, $40–$50 each, one of them a luxury $90.
Draugystė ☆☆, 84 Čiurlionio. Tel 66 27 11, fax: 26 31 01. Once sought out as the best party hotel in the capital, but now just rubbing along. Single room: $50–$70, double room: $70, luxury suites: $110–$170.
Lietuva ☆☆, 20 Ukmergės. Tel: 25 60 16/35 60 90, fax: 35 61 56. The 23-storey, 335-room hotel is the old Intourist flagship. It still has full services, such as travel facilities, but is long overdue for a take-over by foreign management. Single room: $72, double room: $88, luxury suites: $122.
Neringa ☆☆, 23 Gedimino pr. Tel 61 05 16. Centrally located and booked for months. Single room: $63, double room: $80, luxury suite: $108.
Taffo ☆☆, 56 Saltoniskiu. Tel: 35 11 36; reservations: 73 89 29. Clean and pleasant, it has been restored by Swedish management. Single room: $30, double room: $55.
Žalgiris ☆☆, 21a Šeimyniškių. Tel: 35 34 28; reservations: 35 20 78; fax: 35 39 33. Clean, quiet, spacious apartment-style rooms with TV, phone and fridge. Single $35–$52, double: $80–$115.

BUDGET

Baltic Accommodation and Travel Service, 27 Geležinio Vilko. Tel: 66 16 92/66 76 80. Family hostel. $10.
Lithuanian Alternative Youth Hostels. Tel: 44 51 40/75 66 50. Summer camps in Vingis Park, plus information for budget travellers. $5 a night.
Litinterp, 10-15 Vokiečių. Tel: 61 20 40, fax: 22 29 82. Bed and breakfast accommodation in the heart of the Old Town, with other apartments to rent. Single room: $15, double: $25.

OUTSIDE VILNIUS

Villon ☆☆☆, 12 miles (19 km) north of Vilnius on the M12 to Riga. Tel: 65 13 85, fax: 61 65 82. A country club with swimming pool, tennis courts, boating and fishing. Single: $40, double: $70–$92.

DRUSKININKAI

Druskininkai, 41 Kudirkos. Tel: 525 66. Private showers, telephone and TV only in the three suites; the other 50 rooms without.

KAUNAS

Baltija, 71 Vytauto pr. Tel: 22 36 39/22 87 85. Six suites, 330 rooms, not all with TV and telephone.
Lietuva, 21 Daukanto. Tel: 20 569 92/20 98 28, fax: 20 62 69. Sister hotel is in 35 Laisvės al., tel: 22 17 91. Not all rooms with TV and phone, but nice luxury suites.
Nemunas, 88 Laisvės al. Tel: 22 31 02. Budget hotel with communal showers, no phones or TV.
Nėris, 27 Donelaičio. Tel 20 42 24. Former Intourist hotel of 320 rooms and all conveniences.

KLAIPEDA & THE COAST

Prusija ☆☆☆, 6 Šimkaus. Tel: 543 77; reservations: 559 63. Centrally located cosy private hotel with just seven rooms and two suites.
Klaipėda ☆☆, 1 Naujo Sodo. Tel: 169 71; reservations: 922 63; fax: 539 11. This former Intourist hotel has all facilities from sauna to a travel and service bureau.
Baltija, 4 Janonio. Tel: 149 67. Only three of the 57 rooms have showers and only the luxury suite has a telephone.
Pamarys, 28 Šiasulių. Tel: 199 43. Has 6 suites and 30 rooms.
Viktorija, 12 Šimkaus. Tel: 136 70. Budget hostel with one shower for 131 rooms. Local currency.

NERINGA

There are no hotels on the most popular part of the coast, but a number of rest homes offer full pension to individual tourists:

THE KODAK GOLD GUIDE TO BETTER PICTURES.

Good photography is not difficult. Use these practical hints and Kodak Gold II Film: then notice the improvement.

Move in close. Get close enough to capture only the important elements.

Frame your Pictures. Look out for natural frames such as archways or tree branches to add an interesting foreground. Frames help create a sensation of depth and direct attention into the picture.

One centre of interest. Ensure you have one focus of interest and avoid distracting features that can confuse the viewer.

Use leading lines. Leading lines direct attention to your subject i.e. — a stream, a fence, a pathway; or the less obvious such as light beams or shadows.

Maintain activity. Pictures are more appealing if the subject is involved in some natural action.

Keep within the flash range. Ensure subject is within flash range for your camera (generally 4 metres). With groups make sure everyone is the same distance from the camera to receive the same amount of light.

Check the light direction. People tend to squint in bright direct light. Light from the side creates highlights and shadows that reveal texture and help to show the shapes of the subject. If shooting into direct sunlight fill-in flash can be effective to light the subject from the front.

CHOOSING YOUR KODAK GOLD II FILM.

Choosing the correct speed of colour print film for the type of photographs you will be taking is essential to achieve the best colourful results.

Basically the more intricate your needs in terms of capturing speed or low-light situations the higher speed film you require.

Kodak Gold II 100. Use in bright outdoor light or indoors with electronic flash. Fine grain, ideal for enlargements and close-ups. Ideal for beaches, snow scenes and posed shots.

Kodak Gold II 200. A multipurpose film for general lighting conditions and slow to moderate action. Recommended for automatic 35mm cameras. Ideal for walks, bike rides and parties.

Kodak Gold II 400. Provides the best colour accuracy as well as the richest, most saturated colours of any 400 speed film. Outstanding flash-taking capabilities for low-light and fast-action situations; excellent exposure latitude. Ideal for outdoor or well-lit indoor sports, stage shows or sunsets.

INSIGHT GUIDES

160 Alaska	135F Düsseldorf	158 Netherlands
155 Alsace	204 East African	100 New England
150 Amazon Wildlife	Wildlife,	184E New Orleans
116 America, South	149 Eastern Europe,	184F New York City
173 American Southwest	118 Ecuador	133 New York State
158A Amsterdam	148A Edinburgh	293 New Zealand
260 Argentina	268 Egypt	265 Nile, The
287 Asia, East	123 Finland	120 Norway
207 Asia, South	209B Florence	124B Oxford
262 Asia, South East	243 Florida	147 Pacific Northwest
194 Asian Wildlife,	154 France	205 Pakistan
Southeast	135C Frankfurt	154A Paris
167A Athens	208 Gambia & Senegal	249 Peru
272 Australia	135 Germany	184B Philadelphia
263 Austria	148B Glasgow	222 Philippines
188 Bahamas	279 Gran Canaria	115 Poland
206 Bali Baru	169 Great Barrier Reef	202 Portugal
107 Baltic States	124 Great Britain	114A Prague
246A Bangkok	167 Greece	153 Provence
292 Barbados	166 Greek Islands	156 Puerto Rico
219B Barcelona	135G Hamburg	250 Rajasthan
187 Bay of Naples	240 Hawaii	177 Rhine
234A Beijing	193 Himalaya, Western	127A Rio de Janeiro
109 Belgium	196 Hong Kong	172 Rockies
135A Berlin	144 Hungary	209A Rome
217 Bermuda	256 Iceland	101 Russia
100A Boston	247 India	275B San Francisco
127 Brazil	212 India, South	130 Sardinia
178 Brittany	128 Indian Wildlife	148 Scotland
109A Brussels	143 Indonesia	184D Seattle
144A Budapest	142 Ireland	261 Sicily
260A Buenos Aires	252 Israel	159 Singapore
213 Burgundy	236A Istanbul	257 South Africa
268A Cairo	209 Italy	264 South Tyrol
247B Calcutta	213 Jamaica	219 Spain
275 California	278 Japan	220 Spain, Southern
180 California,	266 Java	105 Sri Lanka
Northern	252A Jerusalem-Tel Aviv	101B St Petersburg
161 California,	203A Kathmandu	170 Sweden
Southern	270 Kenya	232 Switzerland
237 Canada	300 Korea	272 Sydney
162 Caribbean	202A Lisbon	175 Taiwan
The Lesser Antilles	258 Loire Valley	112 Tenerife
122 Catalonia	124A London	186 Texas
(Costa Brava)	275A Los Angeles	246 Thailand
141 Channel Islands	201 Madeira	278A Tokyo
184C Chicago	219A Madrid	139 Trinidad & Tobago
151 Chile	145 Malaysia	113 Tunisia
234 China	157 Mallorca & Ibiza	236 Turkey
135E Cologne	117 Malta	171 Turkish Coast
119 Continental Europe	272B Melbourne	210 Tuscany
189 Corsica	285 Mexico	174 Umbria
281 Costa Rica	285A Mexico City	237A Vancouver
291 Cote d'Azur	243A Miami	198 Venezuela
165 Crete	237B Montreal	209C Venice
184 Crossing America	235 Morocco	263A Vienna
226 Cyprus	101A Moscow	255 Vietnam
114 Czechoslovakia	135D Munich	267 Wales
247A Delhi, Jaipur, Agra	211 Myanmar (Burma)	184C Washington DC
238 Denmark	259 Namibia	183 Waterways
135B Dresden	269 Native America	of Europe
142B Dublin	203 Nepal	215 Yemen

You'll find the colorset number on the spine of each Insight Guide.

Auksinė Kopos (Golden Dunes), Kuverto 17, Nida. Tel: 522 12. The best rest house in Nida.
Ažuolynas, Liudo Rėzos 54, Juodkrante. Tel: 531 10. TVs and bathrooms for all 120 beds. Excursions and sailing are organised by management.
Jūrate, Pamario 3. Tel: 526 18/52619. Half of the 500-bed rooms have TV, fridge and bar. Sailing on the Kuršių lagoon is organised by the management.
Rūta, Kuverto 15. Tel: 523 67/523 30. The 350-bed establishment is fully equipped with TV and fridges, but not phones.

PALANGA

Pajūris, 9 Basanavičiasus. Tel: 533 45. Communal showers. Some of the 60 rooms have TV and phones. Two luxury suites.
Žilvinas, 26 Kęstučio, Tel: 538 76/538 10. Its 21 apartments are fully equipped with fridge, telephone and TV.

SIAULIAI

Šiauliai, 25 Draugystės pr. Tel: 373 33. 337 beds and 14 suites. Not every room has phone and TV.
Salduva, 70 Donelaičio. Tel: 561 79/562 30. Shared showers, no phones and few TVs in this 430-bed hotel.

TRAKAI

Nakvynė Hotel Travel Service, 8 Kauno. Tel: 63 77 32/63 48 23. Family accommodation is offered in Trakai as well as in Vilnius. They also have houses with all conveniences, including saunas, in the woods near **Molėtai**.

CAMPING

Wild camping is not allowed in Vilnius but is acceptable in the countryside. Pitch a tent at your own risk.
Rukainiai: Rytu Kempingas, Murininku gvy, off the highway to Minsk. Tel 54 42 81. 15 miles (25 km) east of Vilnius, this offers small summer lodgings for three to four people, with communal showers and kitchens. Tents can also be pitched on this riverside campsite where there is a sauna and video-café.
Trakai: There is a campsite on the north shore of Lake Galvė 2 miles (4 km) from Trakai on the road to Vievis. Contact the Trakai Tourist Centre. Tel: 8-238 51 745.

FOOD DIGEST

ESTONIA

The situation is improving but eating out in Estonia is still no feast. Estonians are country people with little tradition of dining out. Tables at home have always been amply supplied with produce from the fields, forests and sea. Herring, potatoes and sour cream have been the basic staples of the Estonian diet supplemented by gathered garnishings such as mushrooms and berries. Townsfolk maintain summer cottages in the country with adjacent plots of land which they lovingly tend to provide for their winter larder. Berries are boiled into jams, mushrooms are sealed in brine and various herbs and grasses are dried, shredded and labelled in tins.

During Soviet times the standard restaurant followed the idea of food for sustanance and not delectation. Though higher-class establishments existed they were not common (or for the common) and the typical restaurant (the *püstijala kohvik*, or "on-foot" café) served one meal which invariably consisted of potato, meat of some form and a vegetable. The meal was consumed at midriff-high counters. A couple of these establishments still exist but they have taken the radical step of introducing tables and chairs. The attitude toward the menu is only just beginning to change. Until recently menus rarely went beyond meat (*liha*), served *gril* or *filee*, chicken (*kana*) and the ubiquitous goulash/stroganoff. The sole starter was always *soljanka*, a rich meaty soup and the dessert ice cream (*jaatis*), of which Estonians are inordinately fond. Now the change has begun it is progressing rapidly. New restaurants are appearing at a startling rate, the quality of food is improving and the choice of dish is expanding. However, there is still some way to go and even at the most expensive of restaurants don't expect that the kitchen can deliver everything on the menu. If there is no price beside the item then it is not available. Dining out still requires patience but the chances of your patience being rewarded are improving all the time. Do make reservations. Opening hours are generally from around midday to 11pm, later on Friday and Saturday.

Price rating system (starter + main dish + dessert): Cheap = below 20EEK per head. Average = 20–60EEK. Expensive = above 60EEK per head. Drinks will double the bill.

TALLINN

RESTAURANTS

Astoria, Vabaduse väljak 5, next door to the Palace Hotel. Tel: 448 462. A luxury restaurant with a captivating "Roaring Twenties" atmosphere and a nice dance floor. The service leaves a lot to be desired. Expensive.

Carina, Pirita tee 26, on the coast road out to Pirita. Tel: 237 475. Pleasant view of the sea while dining. A 1 mile (3 km) walk from town centre or bus 1, 8, 34 or 38. Average.

Eeslitall, Dunkri 4, off the Town Hall Square. Tel: 448 033. Tallinn's most popular restaurant. The food is good and the management occasionally imports cooks to add a little ethnic diversity to the menu. The biggest draw however is the atmosphere; the restaurant is totally untainted by the Soviet dourness that seems to linger in most other establishments. Reservations are a must to guarantee a table. Average.

Gnoom, Viru 2, Old Town. Tel: 442 288. A beautiful 16th-century townhouse with a choice of four different dining rooms but little on the menu and service that remains steadfastly Soviet. Cheap.

Kikas, Liivalaia 29, near the Olümpia Hotel. Chicken bar. Deceptively dingy exterior masks an interior that resembles a smart 1950s American diner. Average.

Linda, Vabaduse väljak 3, part of the Palace Hotel. Tel: 666 702. A luxury, Western-standard restaurant. The food is of a variety and quality to be found nowhere else in Tallinn. There are even a few possibilities for vegetarians. The wine list is excellent and the liqueurs delicious – if enough of them are downed it might even deaden the pain of the bill. Very expensive.

Maharaja, Raekoja plats 13 (Town Hall Square). Tel: 444 367. One of the few representatives of international cuisine in Estonia, the Maharaja serves Indian food that adds a little spice to the otherwise bland fare on offer in Tallinn. The food is good but the prices are high even by Western standards.

Margareta, Vabaduse väljak 3, part of the Palace Hotel. Tel: 666 702. High-class, Western-standard pizza restaurant. Average.

Peetri Pizza, Liivalaia 40, close to the Olümpia Hotel. Modelled on the standard self-consciously Italianate pizza parlours of the West, it is a fair copy though the pizzas are on the thin side. Cheap.

Sub Monte, Rüütli 4, behind the Niguliste church. Tel: 666 871. Impressively located in a medieval cellar with an upmarket menu. Expensive.

Toomkooli, Toomkooli 11, on Toompea close by the Dome church. Tel: 446 613. One of Tallinn's most attractively sited restaurants though the architecture fails to capitalise on it. The menu is very good offering an uncommonly large choice. They also have on draft Saaremaa beer, considered by locals Estonia's best. Average.

Vana Toomas, Raekoja plats 8 (Town Hall Square). Tel.445 818. Very popular with locals and inebriates. Cheap.

Viru, Viru väljak 4, 22nd floor of the Viru Hotel. Tel: 652 093. Any shortcomings are more than compensated for by the view over the Old Town. Average.

FAST FOOD

McDonald's open in the Baltics in late 1993 but local joint-venture enterprises gained a head start.

Bistro, Narva mnt. 6 and Estonia pst. 5 (both open 9am–9pm). Swiss-Estonian joint venture. Pastas, salads and ice cream. The portions are generous and it is doubtful whether you can eat more for less money anywhere else in town.

Peetri Pizza, Lai 4, Old Town (10am–11pm), Pärnu mnt. 22, close to the Palace hotel (10–3am); Liivalaia 40, close to the Olümpia Hotel (11am–11pm); Kopli 2, by the railway terminal (11–2am); Pirita tee, close to the Sport Hotel (half-hour drive away). Varieties of pizza baked while you wait.

Chick Inn, Aia 5, Old Town. Open: 10am–9pm. Burgers that tend towards being edible, and fries.

CAFES

Maiasmokk, Pikk 16, Old Town. Open: 8am–8pm. Tallinn's oldest coffee-house. It was in existence during the First Independence and probably looks no different now than it did then. Fine place to take breakfast with a great array of pastries to choose from to accompany the coffee.

Maiustused, Vana Turu 8, right beside the Town Hall. Open: 9am–8pm, Sunday 9am–2pm. Traditional style coffee house with the small café at the rear of a coffeeshop/patisserie.

Neitsitorn, Komandandi tee 1, occupying four floors of a fortified tower. Open: 11am–10pm. A tourist favourite. Care has been taken to keep the interior in character with the building down to the virtual absence of any light on the lower floors. During the colder months mulled wine is served in the cellar.

Pärl, Pikk 3, Old Town. Open: 9am–9pm, Sunday 10am–8pm. An almost post-modernist interior lifts this from being a run-of-the-mill café.

Samaaria, Vaimu 3, Old Town. Open: 11am–6pm, Saturday until 4pm. Christian vegetarian café.

Vesi Veski, Suur-Karja 17-19. Open: 9am–7pm. Located at a busy junction in the Old Town with large windows to take advantage of it.

TARTU

RESTAURANTS

Gildi Frahter, Gildi 7. Don't be deceived by the ostentatious decor – the food is fairly basic but very good and served in generous portions. Also a well stocked bar. Cheap.

Tarvas, Riia 2, next to the kaubamaja. Tel: 234-32 253. A clientele composed of nomenklatura and the newly rich.

Kaunas, Narva mnt. 2. Tel: 234-34 600.

Püssirohukelder, Lossi 28. Tel: 234-34 124. Unusual and attractive. The name translates to "powder cellar" and refers to the original function of the burrow in which the restaurant is situated. Expensive.

FAST FOOD & CAFES

Ekspress, Gildi 12, next to the police station. Open: midday–10pm. Smart and modern.

Bistro, Rüütli 2. Open: 9am–9pm. Pasta, salads and ice cream.

Peetri Pizza, Tiigi 9, behind the university library. Tel: 234-30 310. Open: 11am–10pm. Takeaway pizza.

PARNU

RESTAURANTS

Postipoiss, Vee 12, town centre. Tel: 244-40 204. Open: 11am–10pm. Old post station attractively converted into a restaurant/tavern.

◦ DRINKING IN ESTONIA

If there are few places to eat in Tallinn then there are even fewer places in which to drink. Estonians have often tended to do their drinking at home with a few friends and more than a few bottles of vodka. The proliferation of vodka (*viin*) is a result of Russification. The true national drink of Estonia is beer (*olu*). In rural areas beer drinking is still very much a part of daily life and it is often brewed at home. Cloudy and thick with sediment, it is not refined stuff. In certain areas, notably the islands, vast consumption of beer has led to the ruin of many farmsteads as many men have drunk themselves to early deaths. For a country with such a love of beer the local product is surprisingly difficult to find. The output of Estonian breweries is passed over by restaurants and hotels eager to serve their guests the more attractively packaged and promoted import brands. These imported beers, along with the imported wines and spirits, are expensive and you may find when dining that you are paying far more for the drinks than for the food.

Most hotels have bars though few have much to recommend them.

The **Sky Bar** on the top of the Palace hotel is an exception, albeit an expensive one.

Eeslitall, Dunkri 4, off the Town Hall Square. Open: 4pm–3am. Bar in a chain of cellar rooms. It can be quite a squeeze to get in some nights but there are cosy corners if you get there early enough. Often live jazz, traditional and modern.

Lucky Luke's, Mere pst 20, behind the Linnahall facing the sea. Open: until 3am. A large drinking,

eating and dancing place which often has live country music.

Von Krahli Theatre Bar, Rataskaevu 10, Old Town. Open late. Atmospheric bar with a clientele of the local bright-young-things. Live music most nights.

West End, Pärnu mnt. 19. Open: 7–5am. The nearest thing in Tallinn to a British pub. Very good large portioned meals available.

LATVIA

Latvian traditional meals are usually mild and never spicy. Latvians are fond of dairy produce – local cheese, cheese with cumin seeds, curdled milk. Potatoes are used as a separate dish, variously cooked. Latvia is famous for its numerous sorts of bread, the sweet and sour bread being the most popular. If you stay in Latvia you should taste some national Latvian dishes: pearl-barley soup with dried mushrooms, fried ham and tomatoes, grey peas with smoked pork, black bread layered with whipped cream. And no celebrations can do without *pīrāgi* – little croissants with bacon and onions. Some places do have good service and very good food, such as Jana (for lats), Lido and Jever (for hard currency). The hotels which cater to Westerners are generally a sure bet that one won't get complications later.

RIGA

Rīga, 22 Aspāzijas bulv. Tel: 216 699. Open: 11.30am–10.30pm. In the Riga Hotel. Also the **Senā Rīga** (Tel: 216 869. 1–5pm, 6–11pm). For quick inexpensive snacks late at night, the hotel also has a handy second-floor café.

Latvija, 55 Elizabetes iela. Tel: 212 380/212 381 There are several restaurants and bars in the old Intourist Hotel, many of them occupied by groups on package tours. The best one is Pie Kamīna on the 26th floor, with views out over the city.

Otto, Hotel de Rome, 29 Kaļķu iela. Tel: 216 572. Open: 7–11am, noon–midnight. A smart place to eat in town, especially for visiting businessmen. Hard currency only.

Lido, 6 Tirgoņu iela. Tel: 222 431. Open: noon–6pm, 8pm–2am. Spilling out on to the pavement, this has money written all over it. The food is good and the wine list reasonable, but you pay for it – in hard currency.

Lido, 53 Lāčplēša iela. Tel: 287 927. Open: noon–6pm, 8pm–midnight.

Pie Kristapa, 25-29 Jauniela. Tel: 227 590. Open: noon–6pm, 7pm–midnight. One of the most pleasant and atmospheric restaurants in town, behind an Art Nouveau facade. The ground floor sometimes has a band: to avoid it, dive into the basement. Pitchers of beer accompany good helpings of food.

Pūt vējiņi, 18 Jauniela. Tel: 228 841. Open: noon–11pm. You will probably have to book to get in – or so the flunky on the door will probably say. This is where the government ministers dine out.

Jever, 6 Kaļķu iela. Tel: 227 076. Open: 11–3am. This is an informal, elbow-rubbing bistro-style restaurant, one of the first hard currency places in town, and popular with foreigners, particularly Americans.
Jana, 16 Šķuņu iela. Tel: 226 258. Open: noon–11.30pm. A pleasant and intimate little restaurant with good food that deserves to do well.
Asia China Restaurant, 6/8 Mārstaļu iela in Old Riga.
Casinos Latvia, 24 Kaļķu iela. Tel: 212 322. Open: 6pm–4am.
Forums, 24 Kaļķu iela. Tel: 228 489. Open: noon–6pm, 7pm–midnight. A lively meeting place that also has a bar and live jazz.
Katrīna, 9 Šķuņu iela. Open: 1–11.30pm.
Pičērija, Doma laukums. Excellent pizza, deserts, beer on tap. Expensive by local standards but reasonable by Western standards.
Sēnīte, 9 Gertrūdes iela. Tel: 373 380. Open: 11am–11pm.
Tallinn, 27-29 Kr. Valdemāra iela. Tel: 332 480. Open: noon–5pm, 6–11pm.
Tūrists, 1 Slokas iela. Tel: 615 682. Open: 9–12.30am.
Vēja roze, the restaurant in the TV tower on Zaķusala island, with great views out over the city.

FAST FOOD

American Fried Chicken, 33-35 Tērbatas iela.
Fish and Chips, Kronvalda bulv., on the corner of Valdemāra iela.
Little Johnnie's Pizza, Central railway station.
Pārsla, 2 Audēju iela. Open: 10am–11pm. Central railway station.
Viking Burger, 16 Basteja bulv. Open: 10am–8pm.

CAFES

Arhitekts, 4 Amatu iela. Tel: 225 172. Open: 11am–5pm, 6–11pm.
Baltā roze, 27 Meistaru iela.
Luna, 18 Basteja bulv. Tel: 221 271. Open: 11am–6pm, 7–11pm.
Magdalena, 2-4 Smilšu iela. Tel: 224 378. Open: noon–11pm.
Māksla, 9 Vaļņu iela. Tel: 216 756. Open: 11am–11pm.
Možums, 19 Šķuņu iela. Tel: 223 943. Open: 11am–10pm.
Pils, 3 Pils laukums. Open: only in the summer 10am–10pm. This outdoor café beside the castle sometimes has barbecues.

Other summer cafés are located at the Dome Square, Filharmonijas Square and near the Freedom Monument opposite from the Hotel de Rome.

JURMALA

Jūras pērle, 2 Vienības av, Bulduri. The dining room juts out over the sea, giving one of the best views of the coast.

SIGULDA

Sēnīte, 8 miles (12 km) from Sigulda on the road from Riga, this institutional-looking restaurant has long had a reputation in the area.

DRINKING IN LATVIA

Like its neighbours, Latvia has delicious bottled beer (*alus*) which should be drunk within a few weeks of purchase. The beer lorries do the rounds of the towns and countryisde and people queue up with their jars and jugs. Local vodka is also good and drinking for many is rather more than a pasttime. But the most distinctive Latvian drink is Riga Black Balsam, *melnais balzāms*, a liqueur made of herbs and reminiscent of cough medicine. Don't drink tap water in Riga: buy bottled water, though you may have to shop around for brands such as Valmieras, which is not too salty. Fruit juices are the typical Eastern European sugar-and-water concoctions, though real fruit juice is available.

LITHUANIA

Vilnius has a wide selection of restaurants, cafés and tea-rooms although few match Western standards. Menus are long although the selection available is sparse. You will invariably find *karbonada*, *kespnys* and *kotletas* (pork cutlet, roast and meat balls) which seem to come from a central kitchen. The Lithuanian cuisine, mainly based on potatoes, is rich and somewhat fatty. The national dish, *cepelinai* (zeppelins), mashed potato rolls filled with meat and dripping in a bacon-butter sauce, is quite a mouthful. *Kijevo kotletas* (chicken Kiev) is a standard feature on most menus without being a national dish. Kitchens usually close early. After 8pm you will often find it difficult to find a hot meal or even get into a restaurant regardless of hours indicated on the door. Menus are generally written in Lithuanian or Russian, but in some restaurants you may find English, German or French versions. Smoking is prohibited in most restaurants and customers will generally go outside during a meal to have a smoke.

VILNIUS

Bočių, Šv. Ignoto 4. Tel: 62 37 72. Open: noon–11pm. Housed in a former monastery refectory with beautiful frescoes on the wall. The food is standard.
Ida Basar, Subačiaus 3. Tel: 62 84 84. Open: noon–1am. A top-class restaurant offering good food and large portions. German and English menu, hard currency only.

Juoda-Raudona, Gedimino pr 14. Open: 11am–midnight, Monday 5pm–midnight. This black-and-red restaurant is a high-class establishment dealing in local currency. The food and service are excellent.
Laura, Žirmūnų 147. Tel: 77 96 11. Inconveniently set in a northern suburb, Laura is definitely one of the better establishments with excellent food and service.
Literatų Svetainė, Gedimino pr 1. Tel: 61 18 89. Open: 11am–10pm. Centrally located in front of the cathedral, the small restaurant offers standard meals.
Lokys, Stiklių 8. Tel: 62 90 46. Open: noon–11pm. Set in a gothic cellar, Lokys is famous for the house speciality: *šerniena* (wild boar) and *briediena* (elk), subject to availability.
Medininkai, Aušros Vartų 4. Tel: 61 40 19. Open: noon–10pm. Grandiose setting and fairly good food but the service is patchy.
Neringa, Gedimino pr 23. Tel: 61 40 58. Open: 8am–noon, 12.30–10pm, Tuesday 8am–4pm. Formerly known as the literary café of Vilnius intelligentsia, the Neringa and its 1960s style has lost some of its lustre. Try the stroganoff or *blynia* (pancakes).
Seklyča, Lietuva Hotel. Tel: 35 60 69. Open: noon–midnight. Traditional Lithuanian cuisine and especially *cepeliniai*.
Senasis Rūsys, Šv. Ignoto 16. Tel: 61 11 37. Open: noon–11pm, Monday noon–5pm. Splendid, romantic setting and fairly good food, but the service leaves a lot to be desired.
Stikliai, Gaono 7. Tel: 62 79 71. Open: noon–midnight. Truly the best private restaurant in Lithuania, if not in the Baltics, tested by Caroline of Monaco and François Mitterrand. There is also food and beer in the bar.
The Golden Dragon, Aguonų 10. Tel: 26 27 01. Open: noon–3pm, 5.30–10pm. The first Chinese restaurant in Lithuania offers small portions but exotic food, a healthy change to the local kitchen.
Viola, Kalvarijų 3. Run by Armenians, Viola features spicy *shaslik* and kebabs in a nice setting but the live music is somewhat loud.
Žaliasis, Jankiškių 43A. Tel: 65 32 33. Open: noon–10pm. The second best restaurant is out of town but worth the trip for its excellent food, presentation and service.

CAFES

Arka, Aušros Vartų 7. Open: 11am–4pm and 5–11pm, Tuesday noon–11pm. Stylish interior, outdoor seating and live concerts.
Do-Re-Me, Aukų 3. Open: 10am–10pm. Popular youth hang-out. Videos and MTV screen in bars.
Geležinis Vilkas, Vokiečiu 2. Open: 11am–7pm. A favourite lunch spot, in the contemporary arts centre. Tasty salads, a little above average prices but great service.
Senas Grafas, Šv Kazimiero 3. Open: 11am–11pm. The best spaghetti in town. Pleasant outdoor courtyard setting and relaxing for a drink.

BEER BARS

Beer bars are a special part of the city and of Lithuanian culture and should be tried out: just remember that drunks don't like to be stared at.
Alaus Baras, next to the Lietuva Hotel. Open: 11am–3pm, 5–9.30pm. Small bar in comfortable setting.
Rūdininkai, Rūdininkų 14. Open: 11am–9pm. Cavernous brick arches and earthenware jugs give this a really authentic flavour.
Tauro Ragas, Jasinkio 2. Open: 10am–9pm. A big beer hall on two floors with train compartment type seating. Loud, seedy and full of atmosphere.

KAUNAS

Bernelių Užeiga, M. Valanciaus 9. Typical Lithuanian food in a country-style setting. Try the *gyra*, the Lithuanian version of the Russian *kvas* drink.
Gildija, Rotušės aikštė 2. Tel: 22 01 48/22 00 03. Centrally located in a historic merchant's house, the interior is clean with big wooden chairs and the meals are above average.
Kaukas, Šimkaus al 2. Tel: 73 01 90. Better than average restaurant with good cuisine.
Metropolis, Laisvės al 68. Tel: 20 44 27. Open: noon–5pm, 6pm–midnight. Set in a grandiose red hall, this is one of the town's better establishments and is a must for exiles who knew the restaurant before the war. Try the *kotletas baravykas*, a stuffed potato topped with a slice of meat.

KLAIPEDA

Kestučio Žilinsko Theatre Bar, Kurpių 1. Tel: 190 10. Jazz every night 9–11.30pm, except Monday. The bar above the small theatre is one of the best and it serves small meals.
Klaipėda, Naujo sodo 1. Tel: 199 60. The restaurant on the ground floor of the Klaipėda Hotel is not the best in town but it offers live music and a variety show in the evening.
Meridianas, Danės krantinė. Tel: 168 51. Open: 12.30–3.30pm, 6.30pm–12.30am, closed: Tuesday. Set aboard an old three-masted schooner, the Meridianas is considered to be one of the best restaurants in Klaipėda.
Vyturys, Laukininkų 13. Tel: 297 91. Open: noon–6pm, 7pm–1am. A German-Lithuanian joint venture, this is one of the best restaurants in town, inconveniently located on the outskirts in a new housing district some 5 miles (9 km) from the centre. Try the the pancakes with curd and jam.

PALANGA

Birutė, Vytauto 64. Tel: 525 91. A high spot of the resort, it includes an evening variety show.
Du Broliai, Daukanto 15. Tel: 512 70. The best restaurant in Palanga, for hard currency.

THINGS TO DO

TALLINN

MONUMENTS & SITES

The Old Town: The Old Town of Tallinn (*vanalinn*) is one of the best preserved collections of medieval buildings in Europe, east or west. The Old Town is well defined, wrapped around by a solid 16th-century city wall, with eight gates and 48 towers. Much of the wall remains and many of the towers are now converted into use as cafés, museums and galleries. Within the Old Town the cobbled streets jog and rise around irregularly shaped buildings which date mainly from the 15th and 16th centuries. Though individual buildings may be of particular architectural or historical merit the true beauty is in the whole.

Toompea: Toompea is the upper part of the Old Town, reached by the cobbled incline of Pikk jalg or the steps of Lühike jalg. It is the ancient seat of government, the site where in the 13th-century fortifications were first built to strengthen the Danes' hold on their newly conquered territory. Toompea still retains an air of detachment. Despite their narrowness its streets are much less intimate than in the lower town and the buildings are more austere. The garish colours of the **Alexander Nevsky catheral** (19th century) squatting outside the **parliamentary building** (18th century) seem something of an intrusion.

Pirita: Stark beside the mouth of the Pirita river are the skeletal remains of the **Convent of St Bridget**. They have stood in this ruinous state since the convent's destruction during the 16th-century Livonian wars. The ruins serve as a venue for occasional open-air concerts and performances. The walk from town to the ruins, along the sea front, is a pleasant one leading past **Kadriorg Park**, the **Song Festival ground** and the **Maarjamäe Palace museum**. Alternatively take a 1, 5, 8 or 34 bus from Narva mnt.

ART GALLERIES

The **state art museum** in Kadriorg is closed until 1994 while undergoing renovation but there are numerous other halls and galleries to provide compensation. Information on current exhibitions can be found in the listings magazine, *Tallinn This Week*, and most galleries also extensively promote their exhibitions with posters around the town centre.

Draakoni: Pikk 18, Old Town, Tallinn. Open: weekdays 11am–6pm, Saturday 11am–4pm. Print and graphic work by contemporary Estonian artists. Exhibitions change each month.

Kristjan Raud Museum: Raua 8, NõmmeTallinn. Open: Wednesday–Sunday 11am–6pm. The work of Kristjan Raud plus temporary exhibitions.

Kunstihoone Galerii (Art Hall Gallery): Vabaduse väljak 6, Tallinn. Open: Wednesday–Sunday noon–7pm, Monday noon–6pm. State exhibition gallery.

Luum: Harju 13, Old Town, Tallinn. Open: Wednesday–Sunday 11am–6pm.

Sammas: Vabaduse väljak 6, Tallinn. Open: Wednesday–Sunday noon–6pm. State exhibition gallery.

Tallinna Kunstihoone (Tallinn Art Hall): Vabaduse väljak 8, Tallinn. Open: Wednesday–Sunday noon–7pm, Monday noon–6pm. The main state exhibition space.

Tornigalerii: Pirita tee 56, Tallinn. Open: Wednesday–Sunday 11am–6pm. Part of the Maarjamäe Palace museum.

Vaal: Väike-Karja 12, Old Town, Tallinn. Open: Tuesday–Friday 2–7pm, Saturday noon–4pm. Tallinn's prestige gallery.

MUSEUMS

The admission price to most museums is next to nothing and, irrespective of any collection, is often worth paying just to get to look inside the building. Tallinn's City and History museums are in beautifully preserved medieval guild houses with creaking oaken galleries and stairs, the Applied Art Museum is in a renovated warehouse with large, almost Moorish, arched halls, and Kiek in de Kök and the Maritime Museum are both in restored medieval towers. The view from the upper floors of Kiek in de Kök is impressive, as is the panorama from the roof of the Maritime Museum which has been transformed into a viewing platform. This is one of the few places from where you can appreciate Tallinn as a coastal town and the view needs to be photographed. Another fine museum for open-air photography is the Rocca al Mare open-air museum. Scattered through woodland beside the sea are exact replicas of rural buildings from the 18th and 19th centuries. Many of the interiors have also been recreated. It takes at least a half day to wander through them all.

Adamson-Erik Museum: Lühike jalg 3, Old Town. Tel: 445 838. Open: Wednesday–Sunday 11am–6pm. Painting and applied art.

Applied Arts (Tarbekunstmuuseum): Lai 17, Old Town. Tel: 445 989. Open: Wednesday–Sunday 11am–6pm.

City Museum (Linnamuuseum): Vene 17, Old Town.

Tel: 445 856. Open: Tuesday–Sunday 10.30am–5.30pm. The history of Tallinn during the 18th and 19th centuries.

Health Museum: Lai 28, Old Town. Tel: 601 602. Open: Tuesday–Saturday 11am–5pm.

Historical Museum (Ajaloomuuseum): Pikk 17, Old Town. Tel: 443 446. Open: Thursday–Tuesday 11am–6pm. The early history of Estonia.

Kiek in de Kök: Komandani tee 1, Old Town. Tel: 446 686. Open: Tuesday, Wednesday and Friday 10.30am–5.30pm, Saturday and Sunday 11am–4pm. History of Tallinn's fortifications and photographic exhibitions.

Maritime Museum: Pikk 70, Old Town. Tel: 601 803. Open: Wednesday–Sunday 10am–6pm.

Maarjamäe Palace: Pirita tee 56. Tel: 237 071. Open: Wednesday–Sunday 11am–5pm. Neo-gothic, 19th-century summer residence, now a museum of Tallinn's recent history and art gallery. Buses 1, 4, 8, 12, 34 and 38.

Natural History Museum: Lai 29, Old Town. Tel: 444 223. Open: Tuesday–Saturday 11am–5pm.

Rocca al Mare, open-air museum: Vabaohumuuseum tee 12. Tel: 559 176. Open: Wednesday–Sunday 10am–6pm but only during the summer months. Dancing and folk displays on Sunday mornings. Roughly 6 miles (10 km) west from the centre of town, take buses 21 or 45.

Theatre and Music Museum: Müürivahe 12. Tel: 442 884. Open: Wednesday–Sunday 10am–5.30pm.

PARKS

To gaze on a summer's day from the viewing platforms on Toompea, it seems as though Tallinn is a loose collection of buildings scattered throughout a dense and verdant forest. Only the concrete masses of the Soviet suburbs give any real impression of urbanisation. The Old Town is surrounded by a green belt of parks laid out over what were once medieval bastions and moats. They bear such evocative names as **Hirvepark** (Deer Park), **Tornide väljak** (Towers Place) and **Rannavärava mägi** (Coast Gate Hill). Walking through them is a fine way to gain a view of Toompea as the fortress it was constructed to be. The largest of Tallinn's parks is **Kadriorg** created in 1718 by Peter the Great. The park was designed by an Italian architect, Niccolo Michetti, and its centrepiece is a baroque palace which now serves as the State Art Museum. Pathways meander through the trees connecting a lake, tennis courts, an ice rink and numerous statues and monuments. The park lies at the terminus of trams 1 and 3.

Beyond Kadriorg, interupted by the four lanes of Narva mnt. the parkland continues. Set into the slope of a hill so to form a natural amphitheatre is the enormous concrete shell of the **Song Festival Ground**. It is here that every five years a large proportion of the populace gathers with massed choirs in a celebration of Estonia. Visible further along the coast are the **Exhibition Grounds** where year round the halls are filled with trade fairs, art sales, car shows and all manner of other displays. A short ride on bus 1, 5, 8, 34 or 38 leads to the tranquil **Woodland cemetery** (Metsakalmistu). Although not very old it is the last resting place of many famous Estonians.

TARTU

TOURIST ATTRACTIONS

Stately and faded, the town of Tartu is styled in classicism, best exemplified by the **Town Hall** (1789) and the **University Building** (1809). Much of medieval Tartu was destroyed in the Great Fire of 1775 and most of the rest by the Nazis during World War II. Of the little remaining from that period are the **Jaani Church** (14th century) which has unique terracotta figures and the outer structure of the **Cathedral of Tartu Castle**, which now now forms a shell to the University History Museum. A great many of Tartu's attractions are linked to the university such as the **Botanical Gardens** (1803) and the **Observatory**.

MUSEUMS

Estonian National Museum: Veski 32. Tel: 34 279. Open: Wednesday–Sunday 11am–6pm.

Town Museum: Oru 2. Tel: 32 033. Open: Wednesday–Monday 11am–6pm.

F.R. Kreutzwaldi Literary Museum: Vanemuise 42. Tel: 30 053. Open: weekdays 8am–5pm.

Art Museum: Vallikraavi 14. Tel: 32 521. Open: Tuesday–Sunday 11am–6pm.

Zoology Museum: Vanemuise 46. Tel: 30 633. Open: Wednesday–Sunday 11am–4.30pm.

K.E. von Bauer Museum: Veski 4. Tel: 33 514. Open: weekdays 9am–5pm.

Oskar Luts Museum: Riia 38. Tel: 33 705. Open: Wednesday–Monday 11am–6pm, Sunday noon–5pm.

Classical Art and Antiquities Museum: Ülikool 18. Tel: 31 414. Open: Tuesday–Friday 11am–4.30pm, Saturday 10am–1.30pm.

Art Gallery – Sinimandria: Kompanii 2.

LATVIA

RIGA

MONUMENTS & SITES

Old Riga is rich in medieval, Renaissance and late 19th-century architecture. Another beautiful part of the city stretches along Elizabetes Street between Valdemara Street and the riverfront, and all the side streets along the way (L. Paegles, Alberta, Rūpniecības and others). In many parts of the city, entire neighbourhoods of old wooden houses, built late last century, are still standing. Although many of these dwellings are in a state of disrepair, they exude a rusticity which gives these parts of Riga a certain charm and character, an appealing lived-in, run-down look. Interesting and inexpensive (by Western standards) shops can also be found along many of these streets. Although Riga is safe compared to Western cities, be careful, particularly at night.

Freedom Monument (Brīvības piemineklis): on the corner of Raiņa bulv. and Brīvības bulv. Built between 1931 and 1935, it was designed by one of Latvia's greatest sculptors, Kārlis Zāle. To Latvians, it symbolises the country's struggle for freedom under centuries of occupation.

The National Opera (Nacionālā opera): 8 Aspāzijas bulv. A stately 19th-century building now under renovation, thanks to a $500,000 grant by Western Latvians.

Warehouses: Ventspils iela, Alksnāja iela and Vecpilsētas iela. Built in the 17th century, they are a reminder of Riga's history as a city of trade.

Reuthern's House (Reiterna nams): 17 Mārstaļu iela. Built in 1685. The building, also known as the Journalists' House, is a fine example of baroque architecture. It houses a café on the second floor and an exhibition hall.

Dunnerstern's House (Dunnersterna nams): 21 Mārstaļu iela. Another baroque building. It dates from 1696 and was built by Reuthern's son-in-law.

St George's Church (Jura baznīca): 10/16 Skirņu iela. Begun in 1208, it is the oldest stone building in Riga. It has been rebuilt several times, and now houses the Museum of Decorative and Applied Arts.

St Peter's Church (Pētera baznīca): 19 Skārņu iela. Also begun in the 13th century, it has elements of Gothic, Romanesque and baroque architecture. Until the steeple burned down in 1941 during the advance of the Germans and retreat of the Russians, it was considered the highest wooden edifice in the world. Visitors can take the elevator up to the first and second levels for a wonderful bird's eye view of the city. Services are held on Sunday at 1pm.

St John's Church and Court (Jāņa baznīca and Jāņa sēta): 24 Skārņu iela. This 13th-century church has suffered from storms and fires and been rebuilt many times and is now a working church again.

The Courtyard (Jāņa sēta): next to St John's is flanked on one side by a restored fragment of the old fortification wall which surrounded the city in the 13th century, and on the opposite side by the Jāņa sēta exhibition hall. Street musicians sometimes play there.

The Big and Small Guilds (Lielā un mazā gilde): Neighbouring buildings on 6 and 5 Amatu iela. The Leilā gilde now houses the Philharmonic Concert Hall, and the Mazā gilde can be rented for public and private events.

The Dome Cathedral (Doma katedrāle): Doma laukums. Begun in 1211, it unites elements of Gothic, Romanesque and baroque architecture and has been rebuilt several times. The organ in the cathedral was once ranked among the best in the world, and concerts are still held there. The Museum of the History of Riga and Navigation adjoins the cathedral, in the quarters of what used to be a monastery.

Riga Castle (Rīgas pils): 3 Pils laukums. Begun in the 14th century, it housed the German Order of the Brethren of the Sword. The President of Latvia resided there between the two world wars. It now houses the Museum of the History of Latvia, as well as some impressive rooms and hallways which can be rented out for public and private events.

Mater Dolorosa Church: This Catholic church next to the Rīgas pils displays early classical architecture.

The Three Brothers medieval houses (Trīs brāļi): 17, 19 and 21 Mazā pils iela. Built at the end of the 15th century, the white house on the right is the oldest surviving residential building in Riga.

St Jacob's Church (Jēkaba baznāca): Jēkaba iela. Begun in 1225, it is the site of the first Reformation service held in Latvia, in the 16th century. It is now a working Roman Catholic church.

Saiema (parliament) building (Augstākā padome.), on Jēkaba iela next to Jēkaba baznīca. It was built in the 19th century to house the Knights of Vidzeme.

Swedish Gate (Zviedru vārti): 11 Torņa iela. Built during Swedish rule in the 17th century, it is the only surviving gate into the Old City.

City Wall: Torņa iela. Begun in the 13th century, the city wall surrounded Riga until the mid-19th century, when it was torn down to make way for further expansion. The fragment on Torņa iela was restored by Polish workers in the late 1980s.

Powder Tower (Pulvertornis): 20 Smilšu iela. Begun in the 14th century, it is only surviving tower of the medieval city wall (there were 28 such towers in all). The 85-ft (26-metre) structure still bears battle scars: cannon balls can be seen sticking out of the 10-ft (3-metre) thick walls. The adjacent building houses the War Museum and the "Pulvertornis" art gallery.

Valdemāra iela: Walking along this street away from the old city (from Basteja bulv. or Jēkaba iela), one encounters some fine works of late 19th-century architecture.

The National Theatre (Nacionālais teātris): 2 Kronvalda bulv. This is where Latvia declared its independence on 18 November 1918. It has a fine, stately, late 19th-century interior.

Academy of Arts (Māklsas akadēmija): 13 Kalpaka bulv.

Open-Air Museum of Ethnography (Brīvdabas muzejs): 440 Brīvības iela. Open: every day 10am–5pm. The museum is located by the shores of Lake Jugla at the northern outskirts of Riga and it has authentic examples of rural, fully furnished Latvian architecture dating from the 17th to 19th centuries. Various events are held there in the summer, including an open-air craft market on the first weekend of June, which is attended by thousands of people from all three Baltic States and hundreds of Western tourists.

Cemeteries: The northern part of the city is testimony to Latvia's history of repeated warfare and occupation. The Brāļu kapi (Brethren Cemetery) was projected by the sculptor Kārlis Zāle, author of the Freedom Monument, from 1924 to 1936. It has some of Latvia's most impressive works of memorial architecture. The Raiņa kapi (Rainis Cemetery) and Meža kapi (Forest Cemetery) nearby are also worth visiting.

ART GALLERIES

Ars Longa: 4 R. Vāgnera iela. Open: Tuesday–Sunday 11am–5pm. Modern and classic Latvian art, including paintings, graphics, earth and glassware.
Kolonna: 16 Skūņu iela. Open: Tuesday–Sunday 11am–6pm. Modern Latvian and Baltic art.
Tēlnieku nams (Sculptors' House): 3 Pils laukums. Open: Tuesday–Sunday 11am–6pm.
Arhitektu nams (Architects' House): 11 Torņa iela. Open: Mon–Fri 10am–5pm. Modern Latvian art.
Mākslinieku nams (Artists' House): 35 11. novembra krastmala. Open: Wednesday–Sunday 11am–6pm.
Fotogrāfu nams (Photographers' House): 6 Mārstaļu iela. Open: Tuesday–Sunday noon–7pm.
Reiterna nams (Reuthern's House): 17 Mārstaļu iela. Open: Tuesday–Thursday 11am–6pm, Friday 11am–5pm, weekends 11am–6pm. Closed: Monday. Modern and classic Latvian art, including paintings, graphics, earth and glassware.
Bastejs: 12 Basteja bulv. Open: Tuesday–Sunday 11am–5pm. Modern Latvian art.
Centrs: 4 Kalēju iela. Modern Latvian art.
Ornamentica Lettonica: 21 Kalēju iela. Latvian art.
Pils: 3 Pils laukums. Open: Tueday–Sunday 11.30am–4.30pm.
Rol-Art: 2 Pils laukums. Russian art.
Salons A: 24 Kaļķu iela. Fashion design.
A & E: 17 Jauniela. Decorative and applied art.
Salons Lasītava: 2 Vaļņu iela. Decorative and applied art.

MUSEUMS & EXHIBITIONS

Museum of the Riga Dome Cathedral (Doma Baznīcas muzejs): 1 Doma laukums. Tel: 213 461. A tour of the inside of the cathedral. Open: Tuesday–Friday 1–5pm, Saturday 10am–2pm.
Museum of St Peter's Church (Pētera Baznīcas muzejs): 19 Skārņu iela. Tel: 229 426. Open: Monday–Saturday 10am–6pm, Sunday 10am–1pm and 2–6pm.
State Art Museum (Valsts Mākslas muzejs): 10a Kr. Valdemāra iela. Tel: 323 204. Early and modern Latvian and Russian painting. The best art museum in the Baltics. Open: weekdays noon–6pm (closed: Tuesday), weekends 11am–6pm.

Museum of Decorative and Applied Art (Dekoratīvi Lietišķās mākslas muzejs): 10-20 Skārņu iela. Tel: 227 833. Open: 10am–6pm, closed: Monday.
Museum of the History of Latvia (Latvijas Vēstures muzejs): 3 Pils laukums. Tel: 227 429.
Museum of Foreign Art (Aizrobežu Mākslas muzejs): 3 Pils laukums. Tel: 226 467. Open: Tuesday, Thursday, Saturday, Sunday 11am–5pm; Wednesday and Friday 1–7pm.
Museum of the History of Riga and Navigation (Rīgas Vēstures un kuĝniecības muzejs): 4 Palasta iela. Tel: 213 589. Open: Wednesday, Saturday 1–5pm; Thursday, Friday and Sunday 11am–5pm. The city's most important historical collection.
P. Stradiņa Museum of the History of Medicine (P. Stradiņa Medicīniskās vēstures muzejs): 1 L. Paegles iela. Tel: 224 396. Open: Wednesday–Friday noon–5.30pm, weekends 11am–4.30pm.
Latvian Museum of War (Latvijas kara muzejs), 20 Smilsu iela. Tel: 228 147. Open: Monday, Wednesday, Thursday 10am–5pm, weekends 11am–6pm. Memorabilia from the two World Wars and the 1917 Revolution.
E. Smiļga Museum of Theatre (E. Smiļga Teātra muzejs): 37-39 E. Smiļga iela. Tel: 611 893. Open: Wednesday–Saturday noon–7pm, closed: Monday and Tuesday. The history of Latvian theater.
Nature Museum of Latvia (Latvijas Dabas muzejs): 4 Kr. Barona iela. Tel: 213 291. Open: Wednesday, Friday, Saturday and Sunday 10am–5pm, Thursday noon–7pm, closed: Monday and Tuesday.
Riga Motor Museum (Rīgas Motormuzejs): 6 Eizenšteina iela. Tel: 537 730. Old and new cars, bicycles and other vehicles from different countries. Open: 10am–6pm, closed: Monday.
Open-Air Museum of Ethnography (Brīvdabas muzejs): 440 Brīvības iela. Tel: 994 510. Open: 10am–5pm, closed: Monday. A taste of Latvian rural life during the past three centuries.
Dauderi: 44 Tvaika iela. Tel: 391 780. Summer residence of Latvian President Kārlis Ulmanis in the 1930s. Open: 11am–5pm, closed: Tuesday.
Arsenāls exhibition hall: 1 Torņa iela. Tel: 229 570. Modern Latvian art. Open: weekdays noon–5.30pm, weekends 11am–5pm.
Latvia exhibition hall: 31 Brīvības iela. Tel: 222 461. Open: weekdays noon–6pm, closed: Monday; weekends 11am–6pm. Latvian art.
Ķīpsalas keramika, 34 Balasta dambis. Tel: 612 467. Ceramics.

WILDLIFE

Gauja National Park: Līgatne "Pauguri". Tel: 53323/53324. Open: (in season) 8am–8pm.
Slītere State Reserve: Dundaga. Tel: 42542. Open: (in season) 8am–5pm.
Riga Circus (Rīgas cirks): 4 Merķeļa iela, Riga. Closed: during the summer.
Zoo: 1 Meža prospekts, Riga. Tel: 213 479. Open: 10am–4pm, in summer 10am–8pm.

As in Estonia and Latvia, the enjoyment of the cities of Lithuania is to be had simply by walking their streets. Vilnius has special rewards in its great baroque churches, Kaunas has its old merchants' buildings and museums, and in summer the seaside towns are lively resorts. Like the other countries it also has a wealth of small museums scattered through the countryside, a number of which are mentioned in the Places section of this book.

VILNIUS

MONUMENTS & SITES

Castle Hill and Gediminas Tower: behind the Cathedral. The high point of the Old Town gives a view over the city. There is a small **Castle Museum** with archaeological finds and the history of the castle. Open: 11am–5pm, closed: Tuesday.
Hill of Three Crosses: on the hill of the same name northeast of Castle Hill. Originally erected for seven Franciscan martyrs, the newly re-erected crosses have become symbolic of the nation.
Cathedral: Cathedral Square. Tel: 61 07 31. The original church was commissioned in 1387 to mark Lithuania's conversion to Catholicism.
Gates of Dawn (Aušros Vartai/Ostra Brama): Aušros Vartų 12. The city's most famous shrine has Mass daily in Lithuanian and Polish.
St Anne's church (Šv. Onos): Maironio 8. This 16th-century brick church is the peak of gothic architecture in Lithuania.
St Casimir's church (Šv. Kazimiero): Didžioji 34. The oldest baroque church in the city, founded in 1604, is dedicated to the patron saint of Vilnius and bears a distinctive crown on its dome.
St John's church (Šv. Jono): Šv. Jono 10. A fine late baroque church that once belonged to the university.
St Michael's church (Šv. Mykolo): A.Volano 13. Early 17th-century church contains the mummified remains of the Sapieha family who had it built.
St Nicholas's church (Šv. Mikalojaus): Šv. Mikalojaus 4. The oldest standing church, from 1320 before the country became Christian.
Sts Peter and Paul church (Šv. Petro ir Povilo), Antakalnio 1. Worth visiting for its fine stucco work, depicting more than 2,000 figures.

MUSEUMS

Museums are inexpensive and most have free entry on Wednesdays.
Adam Mickiewicz Memorial Apartment: Bernadinų 11. In the house where Lithuania's most celebrated poet lived in 1822. Open: Friday 2–6pm, Saturday 10am–2pm.
Artillery Bastion: Bokšto 20/18. Open: 11am–7pm, closed: Tuesday. A 17th-century bastion with medieval armour and cannons.

Lithuanian Art Museum: Didžioji 31. Open: noon–6pm, closed: Monday. Permanent exhibition of 19th-century Lithuanian painters and sculptors.
Lithuanian State Jewish Museum: Pamėnkalnio 12 and Pylimo 4. Open: weekdays 10am–5pm. A permanent exhibition pays homage to the victims of the holocaust. (The **Museum of Genocide** is in the southwest of the city in the Paneriai Forest where 100,000 were executed by the Nazis.)
Museum of Applied Art: Arsenalo 2. Open: 11am–7pm, closed: Monday and Tuesday. A fine collection of German and French porcelain and furniture, contemporary Lithuanian ceramics and tapestry. Beneath the building are excavations of the earliest settlements in the city.
Museum of Communications: Pilies 23. Open: weekdays 3–7pm, Saturday 11am–2pm, closed: Sunday, Monday and Thursday.
Pushkin Memorial Museum: Subačaus 124. Open: 10am–6pm, closed: Monday and Tuesday. The house of Alexander Pushkin's son is a little out of town. The 1863 uprising against the tsar was hatched in its tranquil 47-acre (19-hectare) grounds.
Radvilu Palace: Vilniaus 22. The former home of the Radziwell aristocracy contains family portraits and etchings of Vilnius.

ART GALLERIES

There are dozens of art shops and galleries (*dailė*) in Vilnius. Listed are just some of them:
Andromeda: Ukmergės 12a. Open: weekdays 11am–6pm, Saturday 11am–4pm, closed: Sunday. Paintings, pottery and ceramics.
Arka: Aušros Vartų 7. Open: Tuesday–Friday 11am–7pm, Saturday noon–5pm, closed: Sunday and Monday. Exhibitions of contemporary works.
Dailė centrinis salonas: Vokiečių 2. Open: Tuesday–Friday 10am–2pm and 3–7pm, Saturday 10am–4pm, closed: Sunday and Monday. Contemporary painters, pottery, leatherwork.
Kuparas: Šv. Jono 3. Open: 11am–7pm. Folk art for hard currency.
Langas: Ašmenos 8. Open: 11am–7pm, Saturday noon–4pm. Modern gallery with contemporary local and foreign artists.
Medalių galerija: Šv. Jono 11. Open: 10am–6pm, Friday 10am–5pm, closed weekends. Magnificent hall shows sculpture at its best.
Paroda-pardavimas Sauluva: Pilies 22. Open: 10am–7pm. Wide range of traditional Lithuanian crafts: ironwork, ceramics, glass and leather, and *verba* dried flowers.
Photographic Society Exhibition Hall: Didžioji 19. Open: 1am–7pm, closed: Monday and Tuesday.
Russian Gallery: Bokšto 4/2. Open: 11am–6pm. Temporary exhibitions of contemporary painters.
Vartai: Vilniaus 39. Open: noon–3pm, 4–7pm, Saturday noon–6pm, closed: Sunday and Monday. Private gallery on the second floor of the House of Teachers. Contemporary exhibitions.

Vilnius Contemporary Art Centre: Vokiečių 2. Continually changing exhibitions of individual works. **Vilnius ir Dailė**: Barboros Radvilaites 6. Open: 11am–7pm, closed: Sunday and Monday. First private gallery selling landscapes and city-scapes by Lithuanian artists.

PARKS

The city is surrounded by a number of pleasant open spaces. At **Kalnų Park** at the foot of the Hill of Crosses is Song Valley, where folk dancing, singing and rock concerts are held, but the biggest music venue is among the pines in the 395-acre (160-hectare) **Vingis Park** on the west side of the city where a huge stage was built in 1960 and where the major festival takes place every five years (for events details, tel: 63 28 69). **Pasakų Park** in the Karoliskes district has large wooden statues of fairy-tale heroes and is delightful for children. **Burbiškių Park** near the Paneriai forest (5 miles/8 km southwest of the city) is dotted with wood carvings. **Sereikiškių Park** is the oldest in Vilnius. It borders the old town and used to house the university's botanical gardens. North of the city, along the banks of the River Neris, is the city's largest park, the 740-acre (300-hectare) **Valakampiai Park**.

Also worth mentioning as places of quiet reflection are the cemeteries, which Lithuanians hold in great respect. **Antakalnis Cemetery**, Karių kapų, is the soldiers' resting place, and communist leaders are buried alongside the seven border guards killed in July 1991. In **Rasų Cemetery**, Rasų 32, there is a pantheon of the famous, including the heart of Marshal Pilsudski.

KAUNAS

MUSEUMS

Ceramics Museum: Rotušės aikštė 15. Modern ceramics.
Composer J. Gurodis Memorial Museum: Salako 18.
Military Museum of Vytautas the Great: Donelaičio 64.
M.K. Čiurlionis Art Gallery: Putvinskio 55. The museum to Lithuania's most important creative genius should not be missed.
Museum of Lithuanian Folk Music and Instruments: Kurpių 12. An intimate museum about an important part of the country's folklore and life.
Museum of Lithuanian Medicine and Pharmacy: Rotušės aikštė 28. Housed in an original pharmacy in Town Hall Square.
Marionis Museum of Lithuanian Literature: Rotušės aikštė 13. In the house where the literary figure lived.
Ninth Fort (IX Fortas): Žemaičų plentas 73. Tel: 23 75 74/23 76 68. Memorial to the Nazi victims.
Picture Gallery: Donelaičio 16.

A. Žilinskas Art Gallery: Nepriklausomybės aikštė 12. Curious and enormous eclectic private collection donated to the nation.
A. Žmuidzinavičius Collection (Devils Museum): Putvinskio 64. Something of a one-off: devil figures from every quarter.
Zoological Museum: Laisvės al. 106.

ART GALLERIES

Gallery Al: Vilniaus 22.
Old Town Gallery: Valančiaus 3.
Photography Gallery: (Fotografijos galerija), Vilniaus 2.
Tautodailė: Vilniaus 25. Folk art.

KLAIPEDA & THE COAST

Clock Museum: Liepų 12. From the beginning of our time to the 20th-century quartz watch pen, an interesting exhibition on two storeys with a constant tic-toc.
Lithuania Minor Museum: Didžioji vandens 6. Archives and administration: Liepų 7.
Maritime Museum and Aquarium: This fully-fledged sea world is at Smiltynė on the Neringa Spit. Tel: 911 33. Guided tours: Tel: 911 25. Penguins, porpoises and other sea mammals and fish. The aquarium is set in an old fortress.

JUODKRANTĖ

Open-air Museum of Sculpture: Raganų kalnas. Otherwise known as the Witches' Museum. Full of carvings and folk tales of the region.
Fisherman's Museum: Located in a small thatched cottage at Nida on the Neringa Spit. Furnished as a typical 19th-century Lithuanian fisherman's cottage it also contains fishing memorabilia.

PALANGA

Amber Museum: Vytauto 17. The best place to learn all about this important mineral.

DRUSKININKAI

M.K. Čiurlionio Memorial Museum: Čiurlionio 41. The house where the artist/composer grew up. Concerts are still performed there.
Girios Aidas: Čiurlionio 102. Wildlife exhibition and wood carvings.

SIAULIAI

Bicycle Museum: Vilniaus 139. In the centre of the manufacturing industry.
Cats Museum: Zuvininku 18.

CULTURE PLUS

ESTONIA

THEATRE

The first professional theatre group, the Vanemuine Theatre, was formed in Tartu at the beginning of this century. It was followed shortly after by the Estonia Theatre in Tallinn. Although the Vanemuine still exists as a drama theatre, housed in an ugly, large gymnasium of a building in the centre of Tartu, during the early years of Soviet occupation the Estonia Theatre was transformed into a music theatre. The Estonian Drama Theatre emerged during the thaw of the 1950s as Tallinn's pre-eminent theatre. It was joined in the 1960s by the Youth Theatre. Along with the Endla Theatre in Pärnu and the Ugale in Viljandi these remain the major theatres in Estonia.

The theatre season is from mid-September until the end of May. Performances usually start at seven. Tickets must be booked beforehand. All performances, except those at the Russian Drama Theatre, are in Estonian. Many of the plays in the theatres' repertoires are familiar to a Western audience (Stoppard, Havel, Friel, Mrožek) and are, if you are at all familiar with them, worth going to see in their Estonian interpretation. It is particularly worth going to see any production at the Youth Theatre on Lai, if only because of its wonderful intimate auditorium.

Estonia Drama Theater: Pärnu mnt. 5, Tallinn. Tel: 443 378. Box office open: 1–7pm, closed: Monday.
Russian Drama Theatre: Vabaduse väljak 5, Tallinn. Tel: 443 716. Box office open: 11am–7pm, closed: Monday.
Youth Theatre (Eesti Noorsooteater): Lai 23, Tallinn. Tel: 448 579. Box office open: 1–7pm, closed: Sunday.
Old City Studio (Vannalinnastudio): Box office Kullaseppa 2, Tallinn. Open: 1–7pm, closed: Sunday.
Puppet Theatre (Eesti Riiklik Nukuteater): Lai 1, Tallinn. Tel: 441 252. Box office open: 2–6pm, closed: Tuesday and Wednesday.
Vanemuine Theatre: Vanemuine 6, Tartu. Tel: 32 968.
Vanemuine small hall: Vanemuine 45a, Tartu.
Endla Theatre: Keskväljak 1, Pärnu. Tel: 42 480.

CLASSICAL CONCERTS

Virtually every night of the week, except for the summer break between May and September, a classical performance is held at the **Estonia Concert Hall**. More often than not the performance is given by the Estonian State Symphony Orchestra though performances are also given by the Symphony Orchestra of the Tallinn Conservatoire or the Estonian Philharmonic Chamber Orchestra and Choir. Guest orchestras, choirs and ensembles are frequent and their countries of origin varied. A garden café adjacent to the concert hall often hosts smaller ensembles and solo artists. These performances usually transfer to other concert halls, notably to Tartu's Vanemuine Theatre and Pärnu's Endla Theatre. Details of the month's performances are posted on notice boards outside the theatre. In Tallinn there are a number of smaller venues where performances take place including the **Town Hall** (Raekoda), the **Niguliste church**, the **Olavi Hall** (Pikk 26) and the **matkamaja** (Raekoja plats 18, Town Hall Square). Check venues for details or consult *Tallinn This Week*.

OPERA & BALLET

With their great love of singing it is natural that Estonians should have a love of opera. It is quite amazing the number of people who are casually able to belt their way through an aria and, what's more, make a decent job of it. Surprising then that there is only one opera theatre in Estonia, the **Estonia Theatre**. Even more surprising is that opera in Estonia is in such a bad state. Many of the productions are old and they do not wear their age well. Similarly the cast of performers is in need of new blood but sadly there is a tendancy for the most promising of the newcomers to now look for their fortune outside the country. The biggest problem however is generally agreed to be the lack of good direction. Despite all, the musical *Fiddler On The Roof* is very popular.

Ballet is in a much better state with the current repertoire containing some very worthwhile performances. Recent successes have included Bartok's *Magic Manderin* and an adaptation of Dostoeyevski's *Crime and Punishment*, with music by the internationally renowned Estonian composer, Arvo Pärt. **Nordic Star** are a dance group splintered off from the Estonian Theatre troupe who perform a repertoire of short modern and avant-garde pieces. They often work with foreign choreographers. Their performances take place occasionally at the Russian Drama Theatre but more often at their erstwhile home, the Estonian Theatre.

Estonia Theatre (Ballet and Opera): Estonia pst. 4. Tel: 449 040. Box office open: 1–7pm, closed: Tuesday.

MUSIC FESTIVALS

Foremost in the Estonian musical calendar is the **National Song Festival** which takes place every five years. During the great period of intense Russification towards the end of the 19th century when the use of the national tongue was almost completely forbidden, the first Estonian Song Festival proved the means by which the steadily growing subterranean nationalist movement was kept alive. The Estonian love of singing was well known and so when a deputation of Estonians laid a petition to hold a festival of song near Tartu in 1869 the authorities saw no harm in allowing the natives of this province of Russia to go ahead. The first festival was ostensibly given in honour of the tsar, but Estonian leaders immediately realised how indispensible such meetings were as a form of national self-cognition and they determined to continue them. At the 1990 Song Festival, at the height of the drive to independence, there were 300,000 participants, a fifth of the whole population of Estonia. Also taking place at the song festival grounds and boasting an impressive audience, is the annual **Rock Summer** festival. Taking place in early July, Rock Summer is three days of international acts, including not just rock but blues, world music and even attracting the London Chamber Orchestra. Since 1984, under the guidance of the prominent Estonian organist, Andres Uibo, every year an **International Organ Music Festival** has taken place. The festival is held during early August and recitals are given in Tallinn and throughout Estonia. Early October is the **Jazz and Blues Festival**. The names are possibly not as high profile as those attracted by Rock Summer but nevertheless performances are world class.

CINEMA

Estonia is very poorly served by cinema. There are few screens and they tend to show poor copies of third-rate American movies. The films are subtitled in Estonian and overdubbed in Russian. The dubbing is done in a single monotone voice, the inflections of which never change whether the character on the screen is male or female, and suffering hysterics or terror. This can be amusing for the first 10 minutes. After that it is thoroughly irritating. In Tallinn the house of the cinema union (*kinomaja*), at Uus 3, operates like a club and has screenings of small independent features and documentaries from around the world – in short anything they can get their hands on. Details of forthcoming films are posted in the window.

LATVIA

THEATRE

Latvians, like other Eastern Europeans, have traditionally been a nation of theatre-goers. Under the Soviets, the theatre was the last fortress of the Baltic cultures and languages still left relatively unscathed, and actors almost filled the role of prophets in lands threatened by Russification. But since independence the situation in the theatres has deteriorated. New economic realities have set in, and the people have become more interested in the daily theatre going on around them and in their thinning wallets. Released from state subsidy and the claws of censorship, the theatre has gradually lost its audience. In a poor economy, theatres are being forced to fend for themselves and many are on the verge of bankruptcy. Several of the buildings are run down, and actors are finding it necessary to moonlight to support themselves. Tickets are becoming too expensive for people to go to the shows on a regular basis.

Nevertheless, new experimental troupes keep popping up, and some are managing to make ends meet. With luck, the *nouveau riche* businessmen will find some spare money not only for purchasing new Mercedes, but also to invest in culture.

Besides classical and Latvian authors, translated versions of world authors are also performed.
National Theatre (Nacionālais teātris): 2 Kronvalda bulv. Tel: 322 923.
Russian Drama Theatre of Riga (Rīgas Krievu drāmas teātris): 16 Kaļķu iela. Tel: 225 395.
A. Rūtentāls' Theatre of Movement (A. Rūtentāla Kustību teātris): 48 Kr. Valdemāra iela. Tel: 280 673.
New Riga Theatre (Jaunais Rīgas teātris): 25 Lāčplēša iela. The theatre is currently being reorganised from the former Latvian Youth Theater.
Teātra Studija "Kabata": 26-28 Grēcinieku iela. Tel: 225 334.
Riga Musical Chamber Theatre "In A Quiet Street" (Rīgas Muzikālais Kamerteātris "Teātris Klusā iela"): 3 Grēcinieku iela. 226 618.
Puppet Theatre: 16-18 Kr. Barona iela. Tel: 285 418.

OUTSIDE RIGA

Daugavpils Musical Drama Theatre (Daugavpils Muzikāli dramatiskais teātris): Gogoļa 23a, Daugavpils. Telephone from Riga: 8-254-267 00.
State Liepāja Theatre (Valsts Liepājas teātris): Teātra 4, Liepāja. Telephone from Riga: 8-234-201 45.
Valmiera Drama Theatre (Valmieras Drāmas teātris): Lāčplēša 4, Valmiera. Telephone from Riga: 8-242-249 43.

OPERA & BALLET

Riga had a pre-eminent name for ballet in the Soviet Union and many stars, including Mikhail Baryshnikov,

trained here. Like the theatre, however, it has declined since state funding has ceased to become available.
Dailes Theatre (Dailes teātris): 75 Brīvības iela. Tel: 279 566. Performances four times a month.
Operetta Theatre of Riga (Rīgas Operetes teātris): 96 Brīvības iela. Tel: 276 528. Performances four times a month.
National Opera (Nacionālā opera): 3 Aspāzijas bulv. Tel: 228 934. This is the major venue, where Wagner was music director for a year. It is presently under restoration.

CLASSICAL MUSIC

Dome Cathedral: 1 Doma laukums. Tel: 213 498. The cathedral's famous organ has a wonderful sound and visitors should not miss the chance of hearing a concert here. The booking office is opposite the cathedral.
Filharmonija: 6 Amatu iela. Tel: 213 793. The Concert Hall of the Philharmonic Society is in the old Great Guild Hall.
Ave Sol Concert Hall: 7 Citadeles iela. Tel: 327 391.
R. Wagner Concert Hall: 4 R. Vāgnera iela. Tel: 210 814. This charming building in the Old Town is a good place to hear chamber music.

JAZZ

Café Forums, 20 Kaļķu iela, Riga. Tel: 228 489. Open: noon–6pm, 7pm–midnight. Jazz played every day except Monday.
Hotel de Rome, 28 Kaļķu iela. Tel: 216 572. Piano music every night, jazz occasionally on request.

MUSIC FESTIVALS

Spring: Durvis rock festival, Riga.
June: Jazz festival, Riga.
July: Pop music festival, Jūrmala.
August: Liepājas Dintars, rock music festival, Liepāja.
Autumn: Bildes rock music festival, Riga.

CINEMA

The Baltic countries have produced some excellent award-winning films, particularly documentaries. Unfortunately, most of the films now shown in Latvian movie houses are pirated versions of the most popular (and not-so popular) Hollywood and other foreign films. Most of the films are poorly dubbed in either Russian or Latvian (usually in Russian), depriving one who doesn't understand either language of the pleasure of watching them. This is all perfectly legal, since Latvia has yet to sign international copyright agreements.
Riga cinemas:
Aina, 19 Vaļņu iela. Tel: 216 927.
Daile, 31 Kr. Barona iela. Tel: 283 854.
Riga, 61 Elizabetes iela. Tel: 210 166. (It's worth

taking a wander around this fading glory of Art Deco.)
Spartaks, 61 Elizabetes iela. Tel: 286 380.
Palladium, 21 Marijas iela Tel: 0132-280 917.
Etna, 72 Gertrūdes iela. Tel: 280 405.
Maskava, 2 Ed. Smiltēna iela. Tel: 255 106.

LITHUANIA

THEATRE

In spite of difficulties over funding, the main theatres in Vilnius continue to perform a broad range of plays. There is a tradition of acting throughout the country. The players at Panavėžys, for example, have for many years had a good reputation. Look out, too, for performances at the university, and by troupes such as the 15-strong Lithuanian National Theatre. Performances usually start at 7pm, and resumés are sometimes available in English.
Academic Drama Theatre (Akademinis dramos teatros): Gedimino pr 4. Tel: 62 97 71/62 64 71. There is also a small theatre at the back of the building.
Puppet Theatre (Lėlės Teatris): Arklių 5. Tel: 62 86 78. Fairy-tales for children, usually at weekends.
Russian Drama Theatre (Rusų dramos teatros): Basanavičiaus 13. Tel: 62 05 52. Plays performed in Russian.
Vilnius Small Theatre (Vilniaus mažaias teatras): Gedimino pr 4. Tel: 61 31 95.
Youth Theatre (Jaunimo teatras): Arklių 5. Tel: 61 60 12/61 61 26. Ambitious productions of classics and modern authors worldwide.

CLASSICAL CONCERTS

Tickets for most of the classical concerts can be purchased beforehand at the central ticket office of the National Philharmonic, Aušros Vartų 5. Tel: 62 71 65.
Artists' Palace: Daukanto Square 3-8. Tel: 61 69 68.
Baroque Hall: Daukanto Square 1. Tel: 61 99 26. The beautiful small 17th-century church, seating 100, offers excellent acoustics for classical organ concerts on Saturdays and Sundays at 7.30pm.
Music Academy: Gedimino pr 42. Tel: 61 26 91.
St John's church: Šv Jono 10. The University Girls' Choir and the "Virgo" sing every Sunday after mass at 3pm.

OPERA & BALLET

Productions are wide ranging but tend to be classical and safe.
Opera and Ballet Theatre (OBT) (Operos ir baleto teatras): Vienuolio 1. Tel: 62 06 36, fax: 62 35 03.

JAZZ

Jazz Club in the House of Teachers, Vilniaus 39. Tel: 22 27 58. Fridays at 7.30pm, jazz concerts with local and foreign bands.
Galerija Arka, Aušros Vartų 7. Tel: 22 12 10/22 11 85.

MUSIC FESTIVALS

May: Jazz festival, Birštonas.
August: Pop music festival, Palanga.
September: Griezyne folk music festival, Vilnius; International pop music festival, Vilnius.
Autumn: Grok Jurgeli, folk music festival, Kaunas
October: Jazz Festival, Vilnius
November: Italian opera week, Vilnius; Gaida Baltic Music Festival.
Every five years: "Dainu Svente" traditional song festival.

CINEMA

Every town has a cinema and there are more than 25 in Vilnius. Almost all films are dubbed in Russian with Lithuanian sub-titles. The major US and European productions eventually come to Lithuania.

SHOPPING

ESTONIA

WHERE TO SHOP

Shopping is not one of Estonia's major attractions. In fact shopping can often be a totally fruitless experience particularly if the object of your search is something mundane but essential like a lightbulb or kitchen knife. However, if the country is struggling to come to terms with the concept of supply and demand the concept of tourism has been more fully grasped. While there may be only one butcher in Tallinn's Old Town there are at least a dozen handicraft shops. With a little patience, some perseverance and the occasional surge of aggression, the shopper will be able to return home with spoils of his or her visit. The real delight of casual shopping is not in the goods for sale but rather in the shops themselves. Many shops, particularly those in Tallinn's Old Town, possess great character, derived often from the architecture, for example the chemist on the

Town Hall Square, or from the decor, as with the fish shop on Kuninga with its large colourful paintings above the counter. The Old Town in Tallinn is the only extended area of shops in Estonia.

WHAT TO BUY

ANTIQUES

Considered immoral by some because their popularity encourages unscrupulous dealers to remove them from isolated country churches, the trade in religious icons continues. Morals aside, purchasing an icon is difficult ground. Many people buy icons as investments but it is very hard to authenticate true ages and histories and thus gain a proper estimate of worth. Buy only on face value. Aside from icons, antique shops are especially strong on medals and distinctive metalworked items of jewellery. The following are in Tallinn's Old Town:
A/s Aigis Antiik Kunst, Rataskaevu 6.
Antiik and Sepis, Rataskaevu 22, Old Town.
Shifara Kunst and Antiik, Vana Posti 7, Old Town.

FINE ART & GRAPHICS

There is no great tradition of painting in Estonia and Estonian national art only truly came into being in the later part of the 19th century. It still remains for an Estonian painter of international impact to emerge. Estonia's most famous artist, Eduard Viiralt, though he did work on canvas is recognised much more for his skill in drawing and etching. Although there are currently some good artists in Estonia working with paint, print-making and graphics remain the strongest aspect of Estonian art. In some ways the production of graphic works for sale has become something of a cottage industry. The work is of high standard and reasonably priced although it is probably produced with the tourist in mind, a lot of local people also buy. An Estonian home is likely to contain pieces of original art.
Deco, Koidula 11, Tallinn. Open: Tues–Fri, 2–6pm.
Gallerii G, Narva mnt. 2, Tallinn. Open: Tuesday–Saturday, noon–6pm.
Galleriis Tokko and Arrak, Raekoja plats 14 (Town Hall Square), Tallinn. Open: noon–5pm, closed: Tuesday.
Hansa Ait, Sauna 10, Tallinn. Open: weekdays 11am–6pm, Saturday noon–4pm.
Matkamaja, Raekoja plats 14 (Town Hall Square), Tallinn. Open: Tuesday–Saturday, 11am–5pm.
Molen, Viru 19, Old Town, Tallinn. Open: Wednesday–Friday, 11am–6pm.
Munkadetagunetorn, Müürivahe 58, in a medieval tower, Old Town, Tallinn. Open: daily 9am–6pm, Saturday 11am–5pm.
Tallart, Aia 12, Old Town, Tallinn. Open: 11am–7pm, closed: Sunday.
   Many of those listed under *Art Galleries* also have work for sale.

BOOKS

There is nothing published in the English-language in Estonia. There has been very little work by Estonian authors translated into English, with the notable exception of Jaan Kross. The few translations that have been made were done a number of years ago and have long since disappeared. It is interesting to browse the titles on the shelves and discover which English-language authors have been translated into Estonian – the choice is eclectic to say the least. Books are printed on the cheapest of paper with little colour and no glossy pictures. This hasn't always been the case. At one time coffee-table volumes were quite common as were art folios. These books may still occasionally be found at one of the second-hand and antiquarian bookshops in Tallinn. Note that books published before 1945 require a licence before they can be taken out of the country.

Antikvariaat, Mündi, Old Town, Tallinn. Second-hand and antiquarian.

ARP Bookshop, Voorimehe 9, Old Town, Tallinn. Second-hand and antiquarian.

Lugemisvara, Harju 1, Old Town, Tallinn. Also sells original cartoons and caricatures by local artists.

Rahva Raamat, Pärnu mnt. 10, Tallinn.

Viruvärava, Viru 23, Old Town, Tallinn. A large selection of imported German books as well as tourist-orientated literature on Estonia.

HANDICRAFTS

Leatherwork and beautifully patterned, hand knitted pullovers, socks and mittens are specialities. Each parish in Estonia has its own belt and mitten designs. Similarly each district of Estonia wears a slight variation on the national costume and these sometimes find their way into handicraft stores. Different regions are also famed for particular craft; Haapsalu produces fine cobwebby shawls of woollen lace and the island of Muhu excels in colourful hand-embroidered floral patterns stitched on to slippers, blankets and sweaters. In addition to wool, linen too has been a traditional Estonian fabric. Tablecloths, doillies, place mats and towels of linen and are still produced in number combining age-old skills with modern designs.

TALLINN
ARS, Vabaduse väljak 8 and Pikk 18, Tallinn.

Hame, Pikk 7, Old Town, Tallinn.

Hansa Ait, Sauna 10, Old Town, Tallinn. Open: weekdays 11am–6pm, Saturday noon–4pm.

Käsitöö, Apteegi 2 and 3, just off the Town Hall Square, Old Town, Tallinn.

Maali, Kaarli pst. 7, Tallinn. Open: weekdays 9am–7pm, Saturday 9am–3pm.

Uku, Pikk 9, Old Town, Tallinn.

PÄRNU
Pärl, Supeluse 3, Pärnu. Open: weekdays 10am–5pm, Saturday 10am–3pm.

RECORDS

Records are ridiculously cheap but the drawback is the very limited selection. The Estonian devotion to choral singing and organ music is reflected in the stock. Also well represented are Russian classics. The big disappointment is that none of the highly evocative work of Estonia's internationally renowned composer Arvo Pärt is available. It is sometimes possible though to pick up recordings of the work of Veljo Tormis, another Estonian composer of great stature. The best work of Tormis is folk-based and employs to great effect an eerie chanting vocal technique. There are a growing number of local pressings available of Western artists and performances, from the Rolling Stones to Lloyd Weber's *Jesus Christ Superstar*. The sound quality, however, might offend those with CD-attuned expectations.

LATVIA

WHERE TO SHOP

Although the selection may not be as wide as in the West, goods are generally inexpensive by Western standards, and good buys may be found. Most imported items come from Germany and Poland. Latvians are well-known for their art and craftsmanship. Good buys are all types of art, paintings, ceramics, jewellery, glassware, porcelain, textiles, amber, leather, wood crafts and locally-made clothes. The traditional souvenir shops in Riga always seem rather empty, but close inspection shows that there are a number of bargains to be had. The city's old department stores are also worth a perusal, for among the poor-quality ex-Soviet products is the occassional startling bargain. As a general rule, if you see something you think you like, buy it. It is unlikely to be there next time you go by.

Central Department Store, 16 Audēju iela, Riga. Open: 10am–8pm, closed: Sunday. Food, clothing, luggage, household items.

Children's World (Bērnu Pasaule), 25 Matīsa iela, Riga. Open: weekdays 10am–7pm, Sat 10am–6pm.

WHAT TO BUY

FOLK ART/SOUVENIRS

Best buys are the locally-made woollen mittens and socks in bright patterns. Shawls are appealing, too. Linen in all shapes and sizes is really high quality, and the blouses, usually part of the folk costumes, are attractive. Traditional leather shoes with long thong laces make good slippers. Leather is also beautifully used in binding notepads.

Sakta, 32 Brīvības bulv. Open: weekdays 10am–8pm, Saturday 9am–6pm.

25 Valņu iela. Open: weekdays 10am–7pm, Saturday 10am–6pm.

30 Aspāzijas bulv. Open: weekdays 10am–7pm, Saturday 10am–7pm, Sunday 9am–5pm.
15 Kaļķu iela. Open: weekdays 10am–2pm and 3–7pm, Saturday 10am–5pm.

WATCHES/JEWELLERY

There are some well designed, locally-made pieces. Some of the most interesting modern jewellery incorporates ancient and pagan designs, including the distinctive designs of the interlocking Latvian ring. Amber is a fraction of the price it is in the West.
Rota, 15 Kaļķu iela. Open: weekdays 10am–2pm and 3–7pm, Saturday 10am–5pm.
Dimants, 66 Brīvības iela. Open: weekdays 10am–2pm and 3–7pm, Saturday 10am–5pm.
Tik-Tak, 4 Kaļķu iela. Open: weekdays 10am–2pm and 3–7pm, Saturday 10am–5pm.

BOOKS

The rule for books is as for everything else: if you hesitate, the chances are you will lose it. Having said that, book prices vary enormously, and it is worth checking out the proper stores before buying from a city centre stall, where as an obvious foreigner you will instantly increase the price by 20 times or more and be asked to pay in dollars – though chances are it will still be cheap by Western standards. If you are thinking of taking a trip around the country, before you go look out for some of the old guides and picture books of the place you may be visiting – the Gauja National Park for example – as information will not be easy to find once you get there. Other things to look out for are old postcards which are almost being given away.
Central Bookstore, 24 Aspāzijas bulv. Open: weekdays 10am–2pm and 3–7pm, Saturday 10am–5pm.
Globuss, 26 Aspāzijas bulv. Open: weekdays 10am–2pm and 3–7pm, Sat 10am–5pm. Foreign literature.
Music Shop, 3 Kr. Barona iela. Open: weekdays 10am–7pm.
Second Hand-Bookstore, 5 Tērbatas iela. Open: weekdays 9am–6pm. Foreign literature.
Central Second-Hand Bookshop, 46 Brīvības iela. Open: weekdays 9am–6pm.
Daina, 63 Elizabetes iela. Open: daily 9am–6pm. For hard currency.

PERFUMES

Lelde, 58 A.Čaka iela. Open: weekdays 10am–7pm, Saturday 10am–5pm.
Dzintars, 3 Kr. Barona iela. Open: weekdays 10am–2pm and 3–7pm, Saturday 10am–5pm.

RECORDS

These are very cheap but the range is limited. Perhaps souvenirs of *kokle* playing will bring back memories.

Sonate, 77 Elizabetes iela. Open: Tuesday–Saturday 11am–7pm.
26 Vaļņu iela. Open: Monday–Friday 10am–8pm, Saturday 10am–7pm.

FLOWERS

If you visit Latvians, they will be delighted if you bring them a small bunch of flowers. The best place to go is the flower market on the corner of Brīvības bulv. and Merķeļa iela. Open: 24 hours. Other places:
30 Brīvības iela. Open: weekdays 10am–2pm and 3–7pm, Saturday 10am–5pm.
60 Brīvības iela. Open: weekdays 10am–2pm and 2–7pm, Saturday 10am–5pm.
11 Vaļņu iela. Open: weekdays 10am–2pm and 3–7pm, Saturday 10am–5pm.

HARD CURRENCY SHOPS

More and more pop up every week. These are just a few of many.
Dzintarkrasts, 31 Brīvības iela. Open: weekdays 9am–1pm and 2–6pm, Saturday 9am–6pm.
Gerkens & Co: 10 Šķūņa iela. Open: weekdays 10am–7pm.
Spartacus, 5 Kr. Barona iela. Open: weekdays 10am–2pm and 3–7pm, Saturday 10am–2pm and 3–6pm.
Ruta, 11 Kr. Barona iela. Open: weekdays 10am–2pm and 3–7pm, Saturday 10am–2pm and 3–6pm.
Koblenz, 73 Dzirnavu iela. Open: Monday–Saturday 10am–8pm, Sunday 10am–7pm.

PHOTOGRAPHY & FILM

Latvian Photo Artists Society. Tel: 210 327.
Photo labs
69 Elizabetes iela, Monday–Friday 9am–2pm and 3–8pm, Saturday 3–8pm. Handles all kinds of colour films.
Kodak-Express, 40 Brīvības iela. Tel: 288 662. Open: weekdays 9am–2pm and 3–6pm, Saturday 9am–2pm and 3–8pm. Kodak and Fuji film.
77 Elizabetes iela. Open: weekdays 9am–2pm and 3–8pm, Saturday 9am–2pm. Black-and-white negative films.
Three companies in one building at 12 Blaumaņu iela. Tel: 281 878:
Konika, weekdays 9am–2pm and 3–7pm. Western films on Konika paper.
Rīgas foto kino laboratorija, weekdays 9am–2pm and 3–7pm. Orwo and ex-Soviet colour negative, slide and cinema film.
Rīgas foto diapozitīvs, weekdays 10am–2pm and 3–7pm. Orwo and ex-Soviet colour negative and slide film.

Do not expect fast service when placing film for development a week or longer is usual.

MARKETS

Every town has its market and these have among the widest selection of food and other trinkets and provide a fascinating view of local life. As in any market, watch out for pickpockets. In Riga the main venues are:

Central Market (Centrālais tirgus), 7 Nēģu iela. Open: Tuesday–Saturday 8am–5pm, Sunday and Monday 8am–3pm. This vast market in five old Zeppelin hangars spills down across a flea market towards the river, and is at its busiest on Friday and Saturday.

Vidzeme Market (Vidzemes tirgus), 90 Brīvības iela. Open: Tuesday–Saturday 8am–5pm, Sunday and Monday 8am–3pm.

Āgenskaln Market (Āgenskalna tirgus), 64 L. Laicēna iela. Open: Tuesday–Saturday 8am–5pm, Sunday and Monday 8am–3pm.

LITHUANIA

WHERE TO SHOP

Hundreds of private or co-operative shops and kiosks, known as *Komiso parduotuve* (commission shops), have mushroomed all over Vilnius, as well as in the other major towns, offering almost everything from inexpensive American cigarettes and Italian spaghetti to television sets and electrical heaters. But for a flavour of local products, it is worth looking at the department stores. Vilnius's department stores offer a wide selection of local products for bargain prices.

Vilniaus centrine universaline parduotuve (VCUP), Ukmergės 16. Open: weekdays 10am–8pm, Saturday 10am–6pm. The widest selection of clothes, shoes and household goods in Vilnius.

Vilniaus universaline parduotuve (VUP), Gedimino pr 18. Open: weekdays 10am–8pm, Saturday 10am–5pm. Three storeys of everything you could need but not necessarily want.

ANTIQUES

Vilnius is becoming quite a centre for antiques. Bear in mind customs regulations when buying. Icons, coins, stamps, furniture, amber, jewellery, fine arts and souvenirs (including Soviet memorabilia) can be bought at the following:

Antika kieme, Labdariụ 3. Open: daily 10am–7pm.
Antikvariniụ daiktụ komisas, Dominikonụ 14. Open: Tuesday–Friday 9am–2pm and 3–6pm, Saturday 10am–3pm.
Antikvarine komiso, Mėsiniụ 5. Open: Tuesday–Friday 10am–1pm and 2–6.30pm, Saturday 10am–3pm.
Juste, Justiniškiụ 62A. Open: Monday 2–8pm, Tuesday–Friday 11am–2pm and 3–8pm.
Kolekcionierius, Mėsiniụ 9. Open: Tuesday–Friday 11am–2pm and 3–6pm, Saturday 11am–6pm.

Solda, Dominikonụ 9. Open: Tuesday–Friday 10am–6pm, Saturday 10am–2pm.

BOOKS

Most of the books sold in Vilnius and throughout the country are in Lithuanian, Russian and Polish.
Aura, Gedimino 2. Open: Monday–Thursday 10am–2pm and 3–7pm, Friday 10am–2pm and 3–6pm. Large selection of Polish books.
Five Continents (Penki kontinentai), Vilniaus 39/6. Open: weekdays 10am–2pm and 3–7pm, Saturday 10am–3pm. Largest selection of foreign books, newspapers and magazines, for hard currency. English, French and German literature at bargain prices.
Littera, Šv. Jono 12. Open: Monday–Thursday 10am–6pm, Friday 10am–5pm. University bookshop.
Šilelis, Sėliụ 39/2. Open: Tuesday–Friday 10am–2pm and 3–7pm, Saturday 9am–4pm.
Vaga, Gedimino 50. Open: Monday–Saturday 10am–2pm and 3–7pm.
Vilnius, Gedimino 13. Open: weekdays 10am–2pm and 3–7pm, Saturday 11am–4pm.

FASHION

Shops here might not be on the sharp edge of fashion, but there are things to look out for, among them fur and woollen coats, hats and gloves. There is some design-conscious local clothing, too.
Alars, Pakalnės 3. Open: weekdays 9.30am–2pm and 3–6.30pm, Saturday 9am–3.30pm. Western and Russian fashion for hard currency.
Bei Eduardo, Aušros Vartụ 10. Open: Tuesday–Saturday 10am–6pm. Western clothes for hard currency.
Burda Moden/Big Star, Didžioji 11. Open: daily 10am–8pm. Western casual clothes for hard currency.
Nijole Fur Shop, Savičiaus 8. Open: Monday–Saturday 10am–6pm. Best collection of fur coats and hats.
Salonas 7, Pamėnkalnio 40. Open: weekdays noon–6pm. Owned by prize-winning Lithuanian fashion designers Snaigė and Raimonda, whose studio claims to be the "female protest against industrial levelling and the ignorant labour of craftsmen".
Vilnius Fashion House Commercial Centre, Rūdininkụ 2/33. Open: Tuesday–Friday 10am–2pm and 3–7pm, Saturday 10am–2pm. Custom-made national costumes.

FLOWERS

Lithuanians offer flowers on many occasions and for any reason. You can find flowers almost around the clock at the Flower Market on Basanavičiaus 42.

HARD CURRENCY SHOPS

Shops selling Western goods for hard currency generally have a wider selection than the state stores but presentation leaves a lot to be desired. Most of them sell Western items – sweets, spirits, tobacco, cosmetics, household appliances, hi-fi equipment and clothing – which are very expensive for locals.

Ida-Bassar, Subačiaus 3. Open: weekdays 11am–7pm, Saturday 11am–4pm.

Londvil, Vokiečių 6. Open: Tuesday–Saturday 10am–2pm and 3–7pm. Self-service with French foodstuffs, wines, Champagne and perfume at low prices with helpful service.

Rūta, Konarskio 17. Open: weekdays 10am–2pm and 3–7pm, Saturday 9am–4pm.

Vilbara, Pilies 2/1. Open: weekdays 10am–2pm, Saturday 10am–5pm. Good selection of quality amber but generally overpriced.

RECORDS

It is worth hunting out records of Čiurlionis's work, as well as local jazz and folk rendering for souvenirs.

Melodija, Tilto 15. Open: Tuesday–Friday 10am–2pm and 3–7pm, Saturday 9am–4pm. Good selection of local jazz recordings.

Muzikos prekės, Gedimino pr 33/17. Open: weekdays 10am–2pm and 3–7pm, Saturday 9am–4pm. Western compact discs.

SPECIALIST SHOPS

Souvenir shops are usually small and poorly stocked. You are likely to find amber, dolls and *verba*, dried flower and twig (willow and yew) bouquets, especially popular on Palm Sunday. Inexpensive amber, too, is on sale in many shops.

Amber: Aušros Vartų 15. Open: daily 11am–7pm, closed: Monday. Largest selection of amber in Vilnius.

Baby shop: Kotryna, Rudininkų 11. Tuesday–Friday 11am–7pm, Saturday 10am–3pm. Toys, puppets, nappies, for hard currency.

Drink: Gerimai, Kauno 1. 1pm–1am. Large selection of alcoholic drinks for both hard and local currency.

Honey: Bitinėlis, Šopeno 12/26. Open: weekdays 9.30am–1pm and 2–6.30pm, Saturday 9.30am–2pm. The "Queen of the Bees" is run by the Vilnius Beekeepers' Union and sells all kinds of homemade honey.

Photography and film: There is no one-hour film development laboratory but if you are anxious to get your Kodak, Agfa or Fuji films or slides developed try the following laboratories:

Ampco, Verkiu 22. Tel: 76 63 47.

Fotocolorexpress Aguona, Aguonu 10.

Minolta Trading Baltia, Didzioji 11.

Photo Laboratory, Kestucio 41.

MARKETS

Local markets are worth a visit for the wide choice of products on offer. **Gariunai flea market** outside Vilnius has everything you ever dreamed of finding in the former USSR. The big bazaar is the meeting point of Lithuanians, Poles, Russians, and Belorussians, selling items from cheap watches to toothpaste to cars and machine-guns. Beware of pickpockets. The private farmers' markets in Vilnius sell meat, milk, fruits and vegetables:

Halė, Pylimo 58/1. Open: mornings only, closed: Monday.

Kalvariju, Kalvariju 61. Best on Saturday and Sunday mornings. Azerbaijani traders sell exotic fruits and vegetables and are prepared to haggle. Beware of pickpockets and burly *babushkas*.

SPORTS

ESTONIA

SPECTATOR

In 1992 Estonia re-entered the international sporting scene. The country sent teams to both the Winter and Summer Olympics. In Barcelona Estonia picked up its first ever gold with a victory in the **sprint cycling** for Erika Salumäe (she had taken the gold in the 1988 Olympics but then she wore the colours of the Soviet Union). There was a bronze medal, too, in **yachting**. In 1992 Estonia played its first international **football** match, against Switzerland, in the first round qualifier for the 1994 World Cup. However, in general sporting events do not loom large in the Estonian calendar. The areas which in the past Estonians have excelled in, reflecting the Estonian character, have always been individual disciplines rather than team sports. As well as cycling and yachting, during Soviet times Estonians also did well in **wrestling** and **weight-lifting** and produced the world **chess-master**, Paul Keres. These days by far the most popular sport is **basketball** and the home games of the national team always draw a full-house. The **ice-hockey** games at Tallinn's Linnahall are popular and the rink is also the venue for **figure-skating** and **ice-dancing** performances.

Kalev sportshall: Juhkentali 12, Tallinn. Tel: 661 687.

Linnahall indoor arena: Mere pst. 20, Tallinn. Tel: 425 158.

PARTICIPANT

Yachting has returned and Estonia may become once again a popular destination for yachting. Facilities are being improved. A new port has recently been created at Lehtma on the island of Hiiumaa and facilities have been upgraded on Saaremaa and the mainland ports of Haapsaluu, Pärnu and Pirita (Tallinn). A shower, a meal and drinks are available at all and lodgings can be obtained at Pirita. Yachts can be chartered at Pirita, by the hour or for as long as a couple of weeks. Skippers can be provided for the inexperienced.

Ports: Pirita tel: 0142-238 044; Haapsalu tel: 01447-45 582; Lehtma 01446-49 214; Pärnu tel: 01444-41 948.

Hunting: With its vast tracts of virgin forest and profligate reedy lakes Estonia provides good hunting. Many hotels and travel agencies, particularly in southern Estonia, arrange trips with guides, beaters and guns provided.

Chess: Tallinna Malemaja: Vene 29, Tallinn.

Cycling: Cycling track: Rummu tee 3, Tallinn. Tel: 239 148.

Swimming: Kalev indoor pool: Aia 18, Tallinn. Tel: 440 545; Dünamo indoor pool: Aia 3, Tallinn. Tel: 446 617.

Tennis: Kalev courts: Herne 28 and off Vabaduse väljak, Tallinn. Tel: 442 169.

There are scant other facilities for those of a sporting nature. The Pirita hotel has a swimming pool and a gym for weightlifting, boxing and wrestling. The hotels Olümpia and Viru and the Fortius club (Toompuieste 4, Tallinn, tel: 666 553) offer fitness centres with aerobics, bodybuilding and solariums.

LATVIA

Tennis: Central Tennis Club, 7 Baldones iela, Riga. Tel: 612 604.

Horse Riding: There are a number of stables around the country, including one at the castle of Turaida. Riga Region, Kleisi Village, tel: (in Riga): 460 284.

Fishing: Ministry of Forestry, 1 Smilsu iela. Tel: 212 776. In Lake Kanieru, for hard currency.

Hunting: Special permission is needed to bring a firearm across the border. Special licences also need to be obtained, for hard currency, from:

Ministry of Forestry, 1 Smilšu iela, Riga.
Tel: 212 776.

State Hunting Enterprise, Kuldīga. Tel: 22641.

Sailing and Watersports: Central Yachting Club, 1a Stūrmaņu iela, Riga. Tel: 433 344.

Winter sports: Sigulda bobsleigh and sledging sports centre, 13 Šveices iela, Sigulda. Tel: 973 813.

ANNUAL SPORTING EVENTS

February: Ski Marathon from Cēsis to Līgatne.
May: Sport Festival of Riga.
July: International Riga Marathon; Seaside Volleyball in Vecāķi.
September: Riga Children's Cycling Festival.
October: Riga Folk Song Marathon.

LITHUANIA

Aeronautics: Aeroclub of Lithuania, Sporto 34. Tel: 75 24 40, fax: 73 01 57. Organises flights over Vilnius and Trakai. Aeroplane excursions over Klaipėda, tel: 544 14.

Balloon rides over Vilnius: Donelaičio 20-3. Tel: 63 75 42, fax: 62 48 72.

Tennis: Žalgiris Tennis Club, Barboros Radvilaitės 6. Tel: 61 25 34; Culture and Sports Hall of the Ministry of the Interior, Sporto 21. Tel: 75 10 30.

Horse riding: Traditionally horse races are organised every year on the second Saturday in January when riders qualify for the *Sartų lentynės*, the Republican races held on the first Saturday in February on Lake Sartų near Utena if it is frozen, otherwise in the city. For information tel: 8-239-54 346.

Fishing: Vilnus Society of Hunters and Fishers, Stiklių 6. Tel: 61 84 91.

Sailing: Every summer on the Lakes at Trakai. Neringa Yacht Club, Lotmiskiu 2.

Rowing club: Irklavimo Sporto Bazė, Žirmunų 1d. Tel: 73 20 31/75 07 16.

Swimming pools: Erfurto 13, Vilnius, tel: 26 90 41, indoor; Pakrantės 1, Vilnius, tel: 75 89 23/75 33 75, indoor; Rinktinės 3/19, Vilnius, tel: 35 10 13, outdoor.

Winter sports: The Travellers Club organises cross-country skiing trips in December and in January (if there is snow) or guided hiking tours around Vilnius. The club also organises the traditional *Snaige* (snowflake) marathon. Travellers Club, Didžioji 11. Tel: 62 98 71/62 71 18.

New Year's Marathon: the traditional marathon is organised every year at the end of December 8 miles (12.5 km) around Vilnius.

LANGUAGE

ESTONIAN

The Estonian language is the official language of the Republic of Estonia. It is closely related to Finnish and distantly to Hungarian. Though it uses a Latin alphabet and each letter represents only one sound, it is a difficult language to master. There are 14 different cases of any noun. Verbs also conjugate and as with nouns, they run out of things to tack on the end and have to change the vowel sounds in the root of the word to change its meaning. There are, however, no articles or genders in Estonian. Though in the Balto-Finnic group of the Finno-Ugric language, words have been borrowed from German and old German and there is a smattering of international, mainly English words. But the language was largely de-Germanised when it became the country's official language in 1919 and was standardised. There are 14 cases in which a noun can appear with myriad word endings, but this need not bother the visitor. There are however a few things worth knowing just to get around.

Vowels:
a – as in c*a*r
e – as in b*e*d
i – as in h*i*t
o – as in *o*n
u – as in *u*p
ä – a as in c*a*t
ö – o as in h*u*rt
õ – as in g*i*rl
ü – oo as in sh*oo*t.
   When a vowel is doubled its sound is lengthened.

Consonants:
Have the same sound values as in English with the following exceptions:
g – always hard, as in *g*ate never *g*in
j – as the y in *y*et
š – tch as in ma*tch*
ž – as in plea*s*ure

COMMON EXPRESSIONS

hello	*tere*
good morning	*tere hommikust*
good evening	*tere ohtust*
goodbye	*head aega*
see you	*nägemist*
thanks	*aitäh* or *tänan*

please	*palun*
sorry	*vabandust*
excuse me	*vabandage palun*
yes/no	*jaa/ei*
fine	*hästi*
as a greeting or a toast	*tervist*
bon appetit	*head isu.*

   The last two are frequently used but the most uttered phrase must be the general purpose negative – *ei ole* – that encompasses every inconvenience from "we're sold out" to "she's not here".

USEFUL WORDS

1	*üks*
2	*kaks*
3	*kolm*
4	*neli*
5	*viis*
6	*kuus*
7	*seitse*
8	*kaheks*
9	*üheks*
10	*kümme*
11	*üksteist*
12	*kaksteist*
13	*kolmteist*
20	*kakskümmend*
21	*kakskümmend-üks*
30	*kolmkümmend*
32	*kolmkümmendkaks*
100	*sada*
400	*neli sada*

Sunday	*pühapäev*
Monday	*esmaspäev*
Tuesday	*teisipäe*
Wednesday	*kolmapäev*
Thursday	*neljapäev*
Friday	*reede*
Saturday	*laupäev*
every day	*igapäev*
holiday	*puhkepäev*

closed (for a variety of reasons)...
suletud/avariid/remont/sanitaarpäev/inventuur/reserveeritud

AROUND TOWN

airport	*lennujaam*
train station	*raudteejaam*
in Tallinn the station is known as	*Balti jaam*
harbour	*sadam*
shop	*kauplus/pood*
town centre	*kesklinn*
market	*turg*
hairdresser	*juuksur*
pharmacy	*apteek*
street/road	*maantee (mnt.)/puieste (pst.)*

LATVIAN

Latvian is the native language of about 1,690,000 of the 2,686,000 people living in the country, and is on the endangered list of languages. It is one of two surviving Baltic languages of the Indo-European language group (the other being Lithuanian). The Baltic languages are remotely related to the Slavic languages (Russian, Polish, Ukranian, etc.). Latvian has 48 phonemes – speech sounds distinguishing one word from another – 12 vowels, 10 diphthongs and 26 consonants. Nouns can be used in a number of cases, changing their word endings. Street signs, for example, are in the genitive: K. Barons becomes K. Barona iela. Stress is always on the first syllable and there are several unusual diacritical marks.

Vowels:
These have the same sound values as in English, with several additions:

a – as in c*a*t
e – as in b*e*d
i – as in h*i*t
o – as in fl*oo*r
u – as in g*oo*d
  a line over a vowel lengthens it:
ā – as in c*a*r
ē – as in th*e*re
ī – as in b*ee* (Riga is spelt Rīga in Latvian)
ū – oo as in c*oo*l

Dipthongs:
au – ow as in p*ou*t
ie – e as in h*e*re
ai – I as in s*i*ght
ei – ay as in sw*ay*

Consonants:
Have the same sound values as in English with the following exceptions:

c –ts as in *ts*ar
č – ch as in *ch*in
g – always hard, as in gate
ǧ – as in logical. The accent can also be a "tail" under the letter.
j – as the y in *y*et
ķ – tch as in ha*tch*
ļ – as in fai*l*ure
ņ – as in o*n*ion
r – always rolled as in Spanish or Russian
š – sh as in *sh*oe
ž – as in plea*s*ure

COMMON EXPRESSIONS

hello, hi	*sveiki*
good morning	*labrīt*
good afternoon	*labdien*
good evening	*labvakar*
goodbye	*uz redzēšanso/visu laub*
yes	*jā*
no	*nē*
Please; You're welcome	*lūdzu*

Thank you	*paldies*
I am sorry! Excuse me	*Atvainojiet!*
That's all right	*Nekas*
May I ask a question?	*Vai drīkstu jautāt?*
May I come in?	*Vai drîkstu ienākt?*
Where can... be found?	*Kur atrodas...?*
How much is it?	*Cik tas maksā?*

Would you please tell me/show me
Vai Jūs lūdzu mannepateiktu/neparādītū?
Pleased to meet you.
Patīkami ar Jums iepazīties.
Let me introduce myself.
Atļaujiet stādīties priekšā.
My name is...
Mani sauc...
Do you speak English?
Vai Jūs runājat angliski?
I don't understand/speak Latvian
Es nesaprotu/nerunāju latviski.
We need an interpreter
Mums ir vajadzīgs tulks.

USEFUL WORDS

1	*viens*
2	*divi*
3	*trīs*
4	*četri*
5	*pieci*
6	*seši*
7	*septiņi*
8	*astoņi*
9	*deviņi*
10	*desmit*
11	*vienpadsmit*
12	*divpadsmit*
20	*divdesmit*
30	*trīsdesmit*
100	*simt*
1,000	*tūkstotis*
Sunday	*svētdiena*
Monday	*pirmdiena*
Tuesday	*otrdiena*
Wednesday	*trešdiena*
Thursday	*ceturtdiena*
Friday	*piektdiena*
Saturday	*sestdiena*
closed	*slēgts*
open	*atvērts*

AROUND TOWN

doctor	*ārsts*
hospital	*slimnīca*
first aid	*ātrā palīdzība*
hotel	*viesnīca*
restaurant	*restorāns*
shop	*veikals*
airport	*lidosta*

bus station	*autoosta*
railway station	*dzelzceļa stacija*
petrol station	*degvielas uzpildes stacija*
post office	*pasts*
street	*iela*
boulevard	*bulvāris*
square	*laukums*

LITHUANIAN

Lithuanian and Latvian belong to the Baltic family of the Indo-European languages. It is one of the oldest surviving languages related to Sanskrit and it has kept its sound system and many archaic forms and sentence structures. When the language was first formalised, in 1918, there were a variety of distinctive dialects across the country and Suvalkiečų, the southern "sub-dialect" of Western High Lithuania, was adopted. But these local dialects have largely been assimilated. There are 32 letters in the alphabet, and one of its idiosyncracies is the tail that appears beneath its vowels. For summer language courses contact the Lithuanian Language Department at Vilnius University, Universiteto 3. Tel: 61 07 86.

Vowels:
a – as in *a*rm
e – as in th*e*re
ė – as in m*a*ke
i – as in s*i*t
o – as in sh*o*t
u – as in sh*ou*ld
ū – *oo* as in st*oo*l
y – *ee* as in s*ee*

a, ę, į and ų appear in special cases and have to be pronounced a bit longer.

Dipthongs:
ai – as in *I*
au – as in n*ow*
ei – as in m*a*ke
ie – as in *ye*llow
uo – as in w*o*nder

Consonants:
c – ts as in ticke*ts*
č – ch as in *ch*in
j – as in *ye*s
š – sh as in *sh*e
z – as in *z*oo
ž – as in vi*s*ion

COMMON EXPRESSIONS

hello	*laba diena*
hello Mr…	*laba diena, pone…*
hi	*sveikas*
good morning	*labas rytas*
good evening	*labas vakaras*
good night	*labanakt*
goodbye	*Viso gero*
welcome	*sveiki atvykę*
How are you?	*Kaip sekasi?*
Pleased to meet you	*Malonu su jumis susipažinti*

See you later	*Iki pasimatymo*
yes/no	*taip/ne*
okay	*gerai*
perhaps	*galbūt*
when?	*kada?*
where?	*kur?*
who?	*kas?*
why?	*kodėl?*

Do you understand me?	*Ar mane suprantate?*
I don't speak Lithuanian	*Aš nekalbu lietuviškai*
I understand Lithuanian	*Aš suprantu lietuviškai*

Do you speak English, German, French, Russian, Polish?
Kalbate angliškai, vokiškai, prancūziškai, rusiškai, lenkiškai?

I speak English, German…
Aš kalbu angliškai, vokiškai…

May I have…?	*Prašyčiau…?*
bread	*duona*
butter	*sviestas*
cheese	*sūris*
beer	*alus*
wine	*vynas*
tea	*arbata*
coffee	*kava*
the bill	*sąskaita?*
May I smoke?	*Ar galima užsirūkyti?*
What time is it?	*Kelinta dabar valanda?*
At what time?	*Kuriuo laiku?*
How much is it?	*Kiek kainuoja?*

Where is the nearest shop, hotel, restaurant, café, bar, toilet?
Kur artimiausia parduotuve, viešbutis, restoranas, kavine, baras, tualetas?

thank you	*ačiū*
thank you very much	*labai ačiū*
please	*prašom*
excuse me	*atsiprašau*
sorry	*apgailestauju*
left	*kairė*
right	*dešinė*
straight	*tiesiai*

NUMBERS

0	*nulis*
1	*vienas*
2	*du*
3	*trys*
4	*keturi*
5	*penki*
6	*šeši*
7	*septyni*
8	*aštuoni*
9	*devyni*
10	*dešimt*
11	*vienuolika*

12	*dvylika*
13	*trylika*
15	*penkiolika*
20	*dvidešimt*
21	*dvidešimt vienas*
22	*dvidešimt du*
30	*trisdešimt*
40	*keturiasdešimt*
50	*penkiasdešimt*
100	*šimtas*
200	*du šimtai*
1,000	*tūkstantis*
1,000.000	*miliionas*

USEFUL ADDRESSES

TOURIST INFORMATION CENTRES

ESTONIA

TALLINN
Tallinn Tourist Board, Raekoja plats 6 (Town Hall Square). Tel: 666 959.

WEST COAST AND ISLANDS
Westra, Postimaja 67, Haapsalu. Tel: 247-45 649, 45 648, fax: 247-45 191.
Tourism Development Centre, Supeluse 18b, Pärnu. Tel: 244-45 533/45 633, fax: 244-45 266/43 415.
Thule Tourist Firm, Pargi 1, Kuressaare, Saaremaa. Tel: 245-59 686/59 328, fax: 245-54 104.
Dago Tourist Firm, Vabriku väljak 1, Kardla, Hiiumaa. Tel: 246-96 355, fax: 246-99 142.

SOUTHERN ESTONIA
Otepää Tourist Information, Lipuväljak 9, Otepää. Tel: 242-55 364, fax: 242-55 293.

LATVIA

RIGA: The best place for information is in the big hotels, the Latvija and the Riga. The main bookshops also sell maps and brochures on some of the regions.

LITHUANIA

VILNIUS
Norwegian Information Office, Didžioji 13. Tel: 22 41 40, fax: 22 12 55. Open: weekdays 10am–6pm. A non-profit organisation which assists visitors during their stay in Lithuania.

CONSULATES & EMBASSIES IN ESTONIA

TALLINN
Canada: Toomkooli 13, Toompea. Tel: 449 056, fax: 358 9-298 104.
Denmark: Rävala 9, 6th floor. Tel: 691 494, telex: 173 262 AMDAN SU.
Finland: Liivalaia 12. Tel. 449 522, fax: 0142-446 392.
France: Toomkuninga 20. Tel: 453 784, fax: 0142-453 688.
Germany: Rävala 9 (7th floor). Tel: 691 472.
Great Britain: Kentmanni 20. Tel: 455 328, fax: 929-8107, telex: 929-8105.
Italy: Hotel Viru. Tel: 651 435.
Latvia: Tönismägi 10. Tel: 372-681 668.
Lithuania: Vabaduse väljak 10a. Tel: 372-448 917.
Norway: Pärnu mnt. 8. Tel: 441 680.
Russia: Pikk 19. Tel: 443 014.
Sweden: Endla 4a. Tel: 450 350, fax: 450 676.
United States: Kentmanni 20. Tel: 455 005, fax: 455 157.

ESTONIAN CONSULATES & EMBASSIES ABROAD

Austria: 17 W. Hauthalerstr., A-5020 Salzburg. Tel: 662-848 4961, fax: 662-848 4964.
Belgium: Avenue de Tervuren 306-4C, 1150, Brussels. Tel/fax: 2-770 05 36.
Canada: 958 Broadview Avenue, Toronto, Ontario M4K 2R6. Tel: 416-461 0764, fax: 416-461 0448.
Denmark: Baltic Cultural and Information Centre, H.C. Andersons Boulevard 38, DK-1553 Copenhagen. Tel: 33-933462, fax: 33-913 099.
Finland: Fabianinkatu 13 A 2, Helsinki 13. Tel: 0-179 528, fax: 0-633 951.
France: 14, Boulevard Montmartre, 75009 Paris. Tel: 1-48 010 022, fax: 1-48 010 295.
Germany: Baltisches Informationsbüro, Bertha von Suttner platz 1-7, 5300 Bonn 1. Tel: 228-65 82 76, fax: 228-69 12 51.
Israel: Shoham Str 525/31, Gilo 93848, Jerusalem. Tel: 2-02 767 249, telex: 26144 BXYJM IL.
Korea, The Republic of: Cheong Ahm Building, 85–3, Seosomun-dong, Chung-gu, Seoul. Tel: 2-771 43, fax: 2-774 2216.
Latvia: L. Laicena 22, Riga 226002. Tel: 0132-611 411.
Lithuania: Turmiskiu 20, 232 016 Vilnius. Tel: 372-2-76 48 96, fax: 0122-61 45 44.
Norway: St Olavsgt. 27, 0166 Oslo. Tel: 2-11 21 48, fax: 2-11 21 45.
Russia: Sobinovski per. 5, 103 009 Moscow. Tel: (095) 290 5013, fax: 095-202 3830; also: room 245, Building 6, Smolny, St Petersburg. Saturday only 10am–2pm, 4–6pm.
Sweden: Stortgatan 38, 1tr, 11455 Stockholm. Tel: 8-665 65 50, fax: 8-662 99 80.

Switzerland: 8, Chemin des Aulx, CH-1228 Plan-les-Ouates, Geneva. Tel: 22-706 1111, fax: 22-794 9478.
United Kingdom: 18 Chepstow Villas, London W11 2RB. Tel: 071-229 6700, fax: 071-792 0218.
United States: 630 Fifth Avenue, Suite 2415, New York, NY10111. Tel: 212-247 2131, fax: 212-262 0893.

CONSULATES & EMBASSIES IN LATVIA

RIGA

Canada: Elizabetes iela 45-47. Tel: 333 355.
China: Elizabetes iela 2, room 601/2. Tel: 321 204.
Denmark: Pils iela 11. Tel: 210 433.
Finland: Teātra iela 9, 4th floor. Tel: 223 231.
France: Raiņa bulv. 9. Tel: 212 878.
Germany: Basteja bulv. 14, 4th floor. Tel: 229 488.
Great Britain: Elizabetes iela 2, 3rd floor. Tel: 320 737.
Israel: Strēlnieku 11/4. Tel: 332 778.
Italy: Teātra iela 9, 3rd floor. Tel: 216 069.
Lithuania: Elizabetes iela 2, room 340–2. Tel: 321 744.
Norway: Zirgu iela 14. Tel: 216 744.
Poland: Elizabetes iela 2 2nd floor. Tel: 321 617.
Sweden: Lāčplēša iela 13. Tel: 286 276.
Switzerland: Elizabetes iela 2. Tel: 323 188.
United States: Raiņa bulv. 7. Tel: 227 045.

LATVIAN CONSULATES & EMBASSIES ABROAD

Australia: 38 Longstaff Street, E. Ivanhoe, Vic. 3079. Fax: 34-99 7008.
Canada: 700 Bay Street, 19th fkloor, Toronto, Ontario M5G 126. Tel: 416-289 2617.
Denmark: Baltic Information Bureau, H. C. Andersens Blvd 38, 1533 Copenhagen. Tel: 33-931 867, fax: 33-913 099.
Estonia: Tonnismagi 10, Tallinn. Tel: 0142-681 668.
Finland: Boulevarde 5A, 00120 Helksonki. Tel: 0-605 640, fax: 0-605 343.
France: 14 Boulevard Montmartre, 75009 Paris. Tel: 1-34 80 90 76, fax: 1-43 26 84 74.
Germany: Annaberger Str 400, 5300 Bonn. Tel: 228-31 62 44, fax: 228-31 24 64.
Great Britain: 72 Queensborough Terrace, London WC2 3SP. Tel: 071-727 1698, fax: 071-221 9740.
Lithuania: Turniskiu 19, Vilnius. Tel: 0122-778 532.
Norway: 8 Aker Brygge, PO Box 1538 VIKA N-0188, Oslo. Tel: 2-833 670, fax: 2-836 886.
Russia: Ulitsa Chapligina 3, 103062 Moscow. Tel: 095-21 07 91.
Sweden: Stortgatan 38, Box 14085, Stockholm. Tel: 8-667 3400, fax: 8-661 9355.
Switzerland: 13 Ave de Cour, 1007 Lausanne. Tel: 21-261 720, fax: 21-617-7144.

United States of America: 4325 17th Street NW, Washington DC 20011. Tel 202-726 8213, fax: 202-762 6785.

EMBASSIES IN LITHUANIA

VILNIUS

Canada: c/o Draugystė Hotel. Tel: 66 17 31.
China: Pergalės 53. Tel: 65 11 97.
Czech and Slovak Republics: Gedimino 54-2. Tel: 62 97 13.
Denmark: Kosčiuškos 36. Tel: 62 80 28.
Estonia: Turniškių 20. Tel/fax: 76 98 48.
Finland: Klaipėdos 6. Tel: 66 16 21
France: Daukanto 3/8. Tel: 22 29 79; French Trade Mission, Šv. Jono 7. Tel: 22 38 98/22 37 86.
Germany: Sierakausko 24. Tel: 66 01 88.
Great Britain: Antakalnio 2. Tel: 22 20 70.
Italy: c/o Draugystė Hotel. Tel: 66 17 51.
Latvia: Turniškių19. Tel: 77 85 32.
Norway: Poškos 59. Tel: 22 41 40.
Poland: Aušros Vartų 7. Tel: 22 44 44.
Russia: c/o Draugystė Hotel (rooms 807, 705). Tel: 26 16 37.
Sweden: Jogailos 10. Tel: 22 64 67.
Turkey: Šv Jono 3. Tel: 22 38 80.
United States: Akmenų 6. Tel: 22 30 31.
Vatican (Apostolic Nunciature): Antakalnio 3. Tel: 74 00 66.

LITHUANIAN CONSULATES & EMBASSIES ABROAD

Argentina: Vuelta de Obligado 2702, 3B-1428 Buenos Aires. Tel: (54) 1-786-8321.
Belgium: Munthofstraat 66, 1060 Brussels. Tel: (32) 2-538 3865.
Canada: 235 Yorkland Boulevard, Willowdale, Ont. M2J 4Y6. Tel: (1) 416-494 4099.
Denmark: H.C. Andersens Boulevard 38., 1553 Copenhagen V. Tel: (45) 33-934 817.
Estonia: Vabaduse väljak 10, EE0001 Tallinn. Tel: (0142) 66 66 34.
France: 14 Bd. Montmartre, 75009 Paris. Tel: (33) 1-48 01 00 33.
Germany: Bertha-von-Suttner Platz 1-7, 5300 Bonn. Tel: (49) 228-658 276.
Great Britain: 17 Essex Villas, London W8. Tel: (44) 71-9371 588.
Norway: Stranden 3, Aker Brygge, 0250 Oslo 2. Tel: (47) 2-833 510.
Poland: al. Ujazdowskie 13-12, Warsaw. Tel: (48) 2-694 24 87.
Russia: Pisemski str. 10, 121069 Moscow. Tel: (095) 291 2643.
Sweden: Sturegatan 29, 11436 Stockholm. Tel: (46) 8-6130040.
United States: 2622 16th Street, Washington DC 20009. Tel: (1) 202-234 5860.
Venezuela: Quinta Mapi, 10 Transversal, Los Paso Grandes, Caracas 1062. Tel: (58) 2-283 8140.

GETTING ACQUAINTED

KALININGRAD GENERAL INFORMATION

The Kaliningrad region of Russia (Kaliningraskaya oblast) is the northern half of former East Prussia, a 8,100 sq. mile (21,000 sq. km) Russian enclave bordered by Poland and Lithuania. Cut off from its motherland, it is in urgent need of investment and although it was declared "Free trade zone Jantar", foreign companies are not keen on settling in the enclave. Since it opened to visitors in 1991 tens of thousands of mainly German *Heimweh* (homesick) tourists have come to visit their native land. But Kaliningrad has nothing to do with the old Prussian city of Königsburg (King's town, where Prussia's kings were crowned). In 1945, during the last assault of the Soviet troops, 80 percent of the city was destroyed, and after the war other historical sites were simply dynamited. Even the street layout has changed.

The German history of the region was systematically erased by the Soviets and in the 1970s even the castle ruins were blown up. They stood on the northwest side of the central square on the site now occupied by the drab and gloomy Kaliningrad Hotel. On the opposite corner stands the unfinished, grey Dom Sowjetow, which is to be turned into a business centre. The only monument that was not levelled is the ruined **14th-century cathedral** which stands on an island in the River Pregal. It is the city's main attraction. Imbedded in the northern side is the grave of the philosopher **Immanuel Kant**.

On the opposite side, along Lenin Avenue, stands the blue former stock exchange which was rebuilt and now houses the Seamen's Culture House. The recently restored **Town Hall** on Klinitschevskaya has an exhibition of the German history of the region. The **City Gates** are the only other building of any architectural note.

In most country villages the old farm estates are either ruined or inhabited by a number of families and churches have been used as cinemas and stores. Most of the towns in the region still bear the names of Soviet heroes: **Tcherniahovak** (Insterburg), **Gusev** (Gumbinnen), **Mamonovo** (Heiligenbeil) and **Sovietsk** (Tilsit) – notably the only town in Russia to bear that name.

Though visitors arrive with "Königsburg" on their car bumper stickers, the resurrection of the old German name has been rejected by the regional council.

The city has long been of military importance and was a German submarine base during World War II. Today numerous army convoys plough through the tree-lined country roads and the military occupies the prestigious buildings in most towns. **Baltriisk** (Pillau), Russia's most westerly town is still off-limits to visitors. Some 30,000 live in the only ice-free port left to the Rusian Baltic fleet. But the port is being opened up for a regular passenger ferry from Karlskrona, Sweden.

GETTING THERE

Russian visas need to be obtained from your local embassy before embarking on the journey, and may take some weeks. From Lithuania, the quickest (though longer in distance) way is through Kaunas and **Sovietsk** (Tilsit) across the Queen Louis bridge. The direct road from Vilnius through **Vilkaviskes** to **Nesterow** is shorter but dangerous, as constant roadworks and tree felling are in progress. In summer a direct train takes advantage of the European standard track leading to Kaliningrad and there is a regular train from Berlin.

The Polish-Russian border crossing at **Mamonova** (Heiligenbeil) has only been open to Poles and Russians.

International dialling code to Kaliningrad: 701 12.

WHERE TO STAY

The hotels are liable to be booked out in summer and it is not advisable to arrive without a reservation.
Hotel Baltika, Moskowski prospekt. Tel: 43 79 77. Outside of town on the road to Tcherniahosk.
Hotel Kaliningard, Lenininski prospekt 81. Tel: 46 94 40. Centrally located but in urgent need of repair.
Hotel Turist, Alexandra Nevskovo Street. Tel: 46 08 01. Central and reckoned to be the best at present.

WHERE TO EAT

The major hotels have Soviet-style restaurants, with loud music and unfriendly waiters.
Olsztyn, Olsztynskaya Street 1. Tel: 44 46 35. Popular with young people. Dancing in the evening.
Brigantina, Leninski prospekt 83. Tel: 44 34 43. In the cellar of the Seamen's Culture House, this is the best restaurant in Kaliningrad. Book first.

FURTHER READING

Amongst The Russians, by Colin Thubron. Penguin, 1980. Thubron describes a few days spent in Tallinn before moving on to be much less complimentary about Riga.

Baltic Countdown, by Peggie Benton. Centaur Press, 1985. An extraordinary account of the wife of a British diplomat caught up in Riga at the outbreak of World War II.

Rates Of Exchange, Malcolm Bradbury. Vintage, 1990. This sharply observed novel about a hapless visit to a mythical Eastern European state, gives a feel of life under the Soviet system.

The Baltic Experience, by Anatol Lieven. Yale, 1993. A fine background to the cultural, economic and political life in the region by a member of one of the foremost Baltic families.

The Baltic Nations and Europe, by John Hiden, Patrick Salman. Longman, 1991. A history of the 20th century in the three countries.

The Baltic States: A Reference Book, compiled and published by the encyclopaedia producers of the three countries in 1991. Lots of facts.

The Baltic States: Years of Dependence (1940–1980), by Romanuld J. Misiunas, Rein Taagepera. C. Hunt & Co, London; and University of California Press, 1983. This is a follow up to the classic *Years of Independence (1917–1940)*, by Georg von Rauch.

The Czar's Madman, by Jaan Kross. Harper Collins, 1993. Estonia's premier writer brilliantly evokes life in the times of the Russian occupation in the 17th century. Anything by Kross should be snapped up.

The Singing Revolution, by Clare Thompson, Michael Joseph, 1992. Personal account of the rebirth of the Baltics by a British journalist who was there in 1989–90.

OTHER INSIGHT GUIDES

Other *Insight Guides* which highlight destinations in this region are:

Insight Guide: Eastern Europe. The first major guide since the wall came down.

Insight Guide: Finland. Cultural cousins across the Baltic Sea.

Insight Guide: Poland. All you need to know about Lithuania's neighbour.

Insight CityGuide: St Petersburg. Russia's Baltic pride.

ART/PHOTO CREDITS

Index